Gary Skinner, Ken Crafer, Melissa Turner, Ann Skinner and John Stacey

Cambridge IGCSE® and O Level

Environmental Management

Coursebook

CAMBRIDGE
UNIVERSITY PRESS

University Printing House, Cambridge CB2 8BS, United Kingdom

One Liberty Plaza, 20th Floor, New York, NY 10006, USA

477 Williamstown Road, Port Melbourne, VIC 3207, Australia

314–321, 3rd Floor, Plot 3, Splendor Forum, Jasola District Centre, New Delhi – 110025, India

79 Anson Road, #06–04/06, Singapore 079906

Cambridge University Press is part of the University of Cambridge.

It furthers the University's mission by disseminating knowledge in the pursuit of education, learning and research at the highest international levels of excellence.

www.cambridge.org
Information on this title: www.cambridge.org/9781316634851 (paperback)

First published 2017
20 19 18 17 16 15 14 13 12 11 10 9 8 7 6

Printed in Spain by GraphyCems

A catalogue record for this publication is available from the British Library

ISBN 978-1-316-63485-1 Paperback
ISBN 978-1-316-63491-2 Cambridge Elevate enhanced edition (2 years)
ISBN 978-1-316-64602-1 Paperback + Cambridge Elevate enhanced edition (2 years)

Contents

How to use this book

Learning outcomes – These statements set the scene of each chapter, help with navigation through the book and give a reminder of what's important about each topic.

Chapter 1
Rocks and minerals and their exploitation

Learning outcomes

By the end of this chapter, you will be able to:

- describe, with examples, the characteristics of igneous, sedimentary and metamorphic rocks
- explain the formation of igneous, sedimentary and metamorphic rocks
- explain the rock cycle
- describe surface and subsurface mining
- describe the reasons for extracting rocks and minerals
- describe the impact of rock and mineral extraction on the environment and human populations
- discuss methods of landscape restoration after rock and mineral extraction
- explain the terms sustainable resource and sustainable development
- discuss how rocks and minerals can be used sustainably.

Opening discussion – An engaging discussion to bring each chapter topic to life, encouraging you to read around the topic and sparking discussion in class.

Cambridge IGCSE and O Level Environmental Management

The third rock from the Sun

The Earth is a rocky planet, compared with, for example Jupiter, which is a gas giant. This means that the Earth is made from rocks and metal ores. The Earth weighs 5 973 600 000 000 000 000 000 000 kg (5.97×10^{24} kg) and has a density of 5.2 g cm^{-3}, which makes it the densest planet in the solar system. This is mainly because the core consists of iron surrounded by a mantle of rock. However, it is only the very outside part of the Earth, above the mantle, that humans can use. The material that makes up this region is what we call **rocks** and **minerals**. Although this represents a vast amount of material, the quantity of it, like everything else, is limited. What is more, extraction and use can cause environmental and other problems. We are in danger of using up the available sources of many rocks, the most well known of which is probably coal.

Peak mineral is a concept that provides a date after which there will only be less extraction of a mineral. Peak coal, for example, is the date at which it is calculated that the most coal is being extracted, after which it will decline. Because we do not know exactly how much coal exists, estimates of peak coal vary. Some say it is 200 years away, others say it could be soon, maybe 2020. This unpredictability because of future unknowns is illustrated by the situation with oil. In 1956, the originator of the peak mineral idea, M. K. Hubbert, predicted that the peak oil date for the USA would be 1970. This did not happen, and in fact the production of oil in the USA is still rising today. However, it is true that the resources of all these commodities, such as coal, oil and phosphorus (current estimated peak date 2030), copper (current estimated peak date 2040) and uranium (current estimated peak date 2030s), are finite. It is therefore important that we limit the use of these resources, and reuse and recycle them whenever we can.

Figure 1.0 A giant bucket wheel excavator in use in an open-pit mine.

Key terms and definitions - Clear and straightforward explanations of the most important terms are provided for each topic.

KEY TERMS

Rock: a combination of one or more minerals

Mineral: a naturally occurring inorganic substance with a specific chemical composition

Igneous rock: rock made during a volcanic process

Magma: molten rock below the surface of the Earth

Solution: formed when a solid is dissolved in a liquid

Precipitates: when a substance comes out of solution

Ion: an atom in which the number of positively charged protons is not equal to the number of negatively charged electrons

Sedimentary rock: a rock formed from material derived from the weathering of other rocks or the accumulation of dead plants and animals

Self-assessment questions – Check your knowledge and understanding, and track your progress by answering questions throughout each chapter. Answers are provided at the back of the book.

SELF-ASSESSMENT QUESTIONS

1.3 What factors need to be considered before starting up a new mine?

1.4 Suggest reasons why developing surface mines is easier than developing mines underground.

Practical activity – Opportunities for developing practical skills are provided throughout the book.

PRACTICAL ACTIVITY 8.1

Seven billion and counting

The world population is assumed to have reached 7 billion in October 2011. Danica May Camacho of the Philippines was designated as the 7 billionth human.

Materials

- Access to the internet
- A3 or larger sheet of paper
- Marker pens

Method

- If you go to the BBC website (www.cambridge.org/links/scspenv4002) you can find out what number in the world's population you were when you were born.
- On a large sheet of paper (at least A3), draw the world population size from 1500 to the present day. You can get help with this on the website.
- Mark your birth number on the world population time line.
- Choose five historical world events and five events from your country's history. Mark these events on your poster.

Question

1 Estimate the world's population at the time your chosen historical events happened. For example, when the Second World War ended, the world population was about 2 300 000 000.

Case study – A variety of examples of real world scenarios are included in every chapter to illustrate relevant aspects of the syllabus, with questions to develop your higher order thinking skills. Answers are provided at the back of the book.

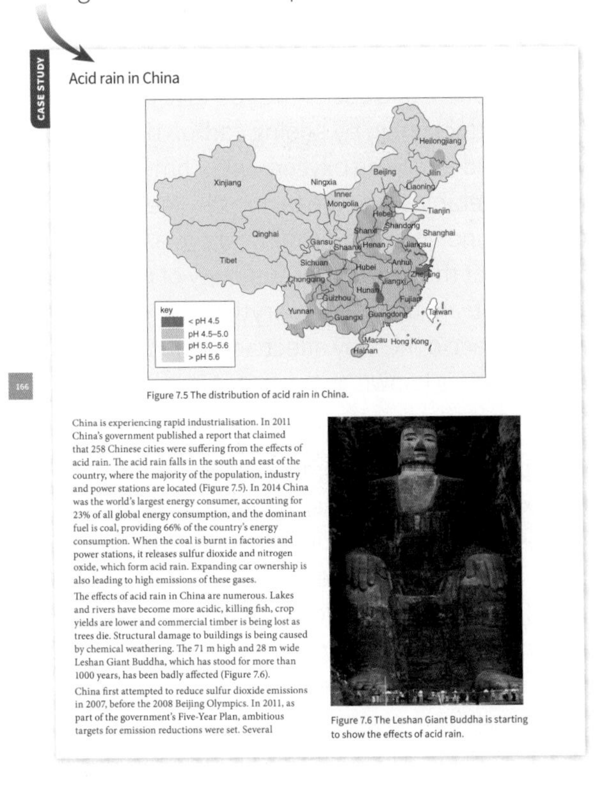

CASE STUDY

Acid rain in China

Figure 7.5 The distribution of acid rain in China.

China is experiencing rapid industrialisation. In 2011 China's government published a report that claimed that 258 Chinese cities were suffering from the effects of acid rain. The acid rain falls in the south and east of the country, where the majority of the population, industry and power stations are located (Figure 7.5). In 2014 China was the world's largest energy consumer, accounting for 23% of all global energy consumption, and the dominant fuel is coal, providing 66% of the country's energy consumption. When the coal is burnt in factories and power stations, it releases sulfur dioxide and nitrogen oxide, which form acid rain. Expanding car ownership is also leading to high emissions of these gases.

The effects of acid rain in China are numerous. Lakes and rivers have become more acidic, killing fish, crop yields are lower and commercial timber is being lost as trees die. Structural damage to buildings is being caused by chemical weathering. The 71 m high and 28 m wide Leshan Giant Buddha, which has stood for more than 1000 years, has been badly affected (Figure 7.6).

China first attempted to reduce sulfur dioxide emissions in 2007, before the 2008 Beijing Olympics. In 2011, as part of the government's Five-Year Plan, ambitious targets for emission reductions were set. Several

Figure 7.6 The Leshan Giant Buddha is starting to show the effects of acid rain.

166

End-of-chapter questions – Use the questions at the end of each chapter to check your knowledge and understanding of the whole topic and to practise answering questions in a similar style to those you might encounter in your exams. Answers are provided at the back of the book.

End-of-chapter questions

1 a Name the four components of soil. [4 marks]
  b How would a drought affect the balance of these four components? [1 mark]
2 How might changing the pH of the soil affect the growth of a crop? [1 mark]
3 Give three ways the 'Green Revolution' has helped feed a growing world population. [3 marks]
4 Explain how crop rotation can help increase the yield of a crop. [2 marks]
5 Describe three ways farmers can improve the efficiency of their water use. [3 marks]
6 Describe the impact of applying too much fertiliser to a crop. [2 marks]
7 Intercropping is identified as a useful way of helping prevent soil erosion in certain soil conditions. In addition to the prevention of erosion, what other benefits might this technique have? [3 marks]

Summary – A brief summary is included at the end of each chapter, providing a clear reminder of the key themes discussed.

Summary

After completing this chapter, you should know:

- the components of soil
- where the soil components originate
- how to evaluate the proportions of these components
- the availability of nutrients and the impact of deficiencies
- the relative merits of different soil types
- different types of agriculture
- techniques used to increase agricultural yield
- methods of controlling pests, diseases and weeds
- the techniques of selective breeding and genetic modification
- methods for controlling the growing environment
- the impacts of poor agricultural management
- different approaches to maintaining soil fertility.

Extended case study – Longer case studies related to more complex real world settings provide opportunities to practise higher order thinking skills and prepare for this element of your examinations. Answers are provided at the back of the book.

EXTENDED CASE STUDY

Controlling pests naturally: a flawed decision

Figure 3.22 The cane toad: introduced into Australia with a huge environmental impact.

Sugar cane plants were introduced into Australia as the country became populated by Europeans. Records show that there were plantations in the Brisbane area as early as 1862. Plantations were densely planted, tended to be grown as monocultures (only the one crop grown in an area) and today are highly mechanised.

As the numbers of sugar cane plantations grew, so did the incidence of pests. Two native beetle species cause major problems: the adults eat the leaves of the crop and their larvae eat the roots. These beetles have proved to be difficult to control because the adults have a tough skin that repels pesticides and the larvae are buried in the soil so are not easy to spray. When pesticides are used, not only are they not very effective on the pests but they also kill many other insects and upset the natural ecosystem. Australian scientists looked at other areas of the world and read reports of increased yields in plantations in Hawaii, the natural location of cane toads. Cane toads are relatively large in size and eat a wide range of different insects (Figure 3.22).

A small number of cane toads were imported into Australia in the 1930s, bred successfully and released into the local plantations. Unfortunately, it was then discovered that the cane toad was not particularly effective at controlling the beetles on the Australian sugar cane, but preferred to eat other insects and animals in the area. It has been estimated that there are now over 200 million cane toads in Australia. They have bred rapidly because:

- they outcompete native animals for food
- they outcompete native animals for habitat space

86

Introduction

Managing the environment might be the most important thing humanity has to do over the next century and beyond. But what is the environment and how can we manage it? In its broadest sense, the environment is everything around us. Your environment includes the room you are sitting in, the air in that room, the people in the room next door, the aeroplane flying overhead and the atmosphere it is flying through, among many other things. But how do we go about managing all of this? It is clear that we need to break things down so that the tasks become manageable. That is what the syllabus and this book attempt to do.

The environment can be split into four major categories: the lithosphere, hydrosphere, atmosphere and biosphere. Chapter 1 deals with the lithosphere: the rocks that make up our planet Earth, on which all life is found. Chapters 4 and 5 deal with the hydrosphere: the ceaseless cycle of water and what we do with it in its various forms. Chapter 7 looks at the atmosphere: the air around us, which contains vital oxygen and carbon dioxide and is the place where weather occurs. Chapters 8 and 9 look at the living world, or biosphere: the people and all the animals, plants and other organisms with which we share the Earth. Weaving through all of this is the use we make of energy, without which nothing much of what we regard as our modern world could occur. Chapter 2 considers how we acquire the energy we need and the problems we create in using it.

The environment is not necessarily well-meaning, although this might seem difficult to believe on a warm sunny day with the birds singing and soft wind blowing. Chapter 6 looks at the natural hazards that human and other life is constantly exposed to, from high winds and heavy rain that might cause problems for a few weeks, to the effects of earthquakes and volcanoes, which are the result of the incredibly slow movement of the tectonic plates on which we live.

Finally, Chapter 3 covers that most vital of human activities: farming. Recent studies have shown that nearly half of the Earth's land area is used to produce food, and this is almost certain to increase over the next few decades.

However, having said all this, it is important to realise that every aspect of the environment affects every other. This is the nature of environmental science and ecology; they are sciences that deal with interactions. You are a part of the biosphere and each time you take a breath, you affect the atmosphere by adding carbon dioxide and water vapour and removing oxygen. Every time you eat, for example vegetables, you are taking in minerals that have passed round and round a mineral cycle for millions of years. This is at the heart of the difficulty of managing the environment: anything and everything we do, either by design or by accident, may affect any aspect of the environment. This is known as the law of unintended consequences.

Food webs provide a good example of this law. In the complex interactions between species, feeding relationships make it almost impossible to predict what will happen if just one of species increases or decreases in number. Take Barro Colorado Island, formed when the Panama Canal was constructed in the early twentieth century. Some decades after this area of tropical jungle was isolated from its surroundings, it was observed that many species had been lost. These included birds such as the curassow, the wood quail and the ground cuckoo. The reason for this loss is thought to have been a medium-sized racoon, called a coati, becoming abundant. (Figure 0.1)

Figure 0.1 A coati family looking for food.

Coatis eat the eggs and young of birds like the curassow, wood quail and ground cuckoo. But why was there a big increase in coatis? In their jungle habitat, coatis are preyed upon by jaguars and pumas (Figure 0.2); the new island, with an area of under 15 km^2, was simply too small to support these large cats.

Figure 0.2 A female puma.

Figure 0.3 Two great curassows.

The cats would have died out in this isolated habitat and the coatis would escape being eaten. This would not have been predicted at the time: an unintended consequence of the construction of the Panama Canal was the extinction of the curassow in a 15 km^2 patch of tropical jungle, now an island (Figure 0.3).

An even more dramatic example comes from the story of rabbits in Australia. This European mammal was introduced into Australia in 1788 on the so-called First Fleet (the first fleet of ships that left Great Britain to found a penal colony in Australia). However, it was not until the deliberate release of just 24 individuals in October 1859 that the numbers began to soar. By 1869 hunters were killing 2 million rabbits every year with no effect on the population. The huge numbers of rabbits in Australia have caused massive species loss and even geological changes, such as extensive gully erosion.

The story of the cane toad, again from Australia (see Chapter 3's Extended case study), is another example of the important principle of unintended consequences in environmental management.

We all have an environment around us and we are all part of everybody else's environment. This simple fact makes managing the environment one of the most important challenges for humans in the future.

Key skills in Environmental Management

When thinking about an investigation in environmental management you need to find out about a problem and how it is affecting the environment. An investigation has a sequence of stages:

1. planning the investigation
2. identifying limitations of the methods that were used and suggesting possible improvements
3. presenting reasoned explanations for phenomena, patterns and relationships that you have observed in your data
4. making reasoned judgements and reaching conclusions based on qualitative and quantitative information.

All these stages involve certain skills and techniques, all of which are explained below and in the following chapters.

Planning investigations

Planning an investigation involves formulating an aim and one or more hypotheses. An **aim** identifies the purpose of your investigation and you should have a suitable aim in mind when planning. 'To investigate the effects of coal mining waste on soil pH' is an example of an aim. From the aim, the hypothesis or hypotheses arise.

A **hypothesis** is a statement on the topic that you are investigating. It is a testable prediction that proposes a relationship between two variables:

- the **independent variable**, which is not changed by other variables you are measuring e.g. the age of a person
- the **dependent variable**, which is what you are measuring.

In research, the hypothesis is written in two forms: the null hypothesis and the alternative hypothesis (called the experimental hypothesis when the method of investigation is an experiment).

The **null hypothesis** states that there is no relationship between the two variables being investigated (one variable does not affect the other). Results are due to chance and are not significant in terms of supporting the aim being investigated.

The **alternative hypothesis** states that there is a relationship between the two variables being investigated (one variable has an effect on the other). The results are not due to chance and they are significant in terms of supporting the aim being investigated.

A hypothesis can be accepted or rejected by testing. This is achieved through data collection and analysis.

A good hypothesis should:

- be a statement not a question
- be a prediction with cause and effect
- state the independent and dependent variables being tested
- be short in length.

An example of a good hypothesis is 'There will be a decrease in soil pH with increasing distance from a site of coal mining waste'.

KEY TERMS

Aim: identifies the purpose of your investigation

Hypothesis: a statement on the topic that you are investigating

Independent variable: the variable that is deliberately changed in an experiment

Dependent variable: the variable that is measured in an experiment

Null hypothesis: a hypothesis stating that there is no relationship between the two variables being investigated

Alternative hypothesis: a hypothesis stating that there is a relationship between the two variables being investigated

Collecting data

When planning an investigation, you need to plan how to collect your data. There are two types of data: qualitative and quantitative.

Qualitative data is non-numerical, descriptive data.

Quantitative data can be either discrete or continuous:

- discrete data: numerical data that have a finite number of possible values and can only take whole numbers, e.g. the number of trees or 1, 2, 3, 4
- continuous data: numerical data that have infinite possibilities and can take any value, e.g. temperature, time, speed or 1.5, 1.51, 1.512.

Both qualitative and quantitative data can be either primary or secondary:

- Primary data is data collected by you or a group doing the investigation.
- Secondary data is data that has already been collected by people unconnected with the investigation but that are relevant and useful. Examples include data from the internet, newspapers, books or past investigations.

Sampling

It is often unnecessary and sometimes impossible to carry out your investigation on the whole of the target population as it would be too expensive or time consuming. For example, it would be impossible to ask everyone in a large town for their views on the effects of air pollution or to count all the plants in a big field. For this reason a sample must be taken.

A sample should be representative of the target population. If it is, then a larger sample size tends to yield more reliable results. The target population is the subset of people or organisms to which the conclusions of the study can be applied. For example, if only women were questioned about their views on air pollution the conclusions could only be applied to women, which would be the target population.

Before deciding on the sampling method you need to think about how you are going to take the sample.

This could be by:

- point sampling: data collection is done at an exact point, e.g. a pedestrian count
- line sampling: data collection is done along a line (Figure 0.4) or transect, e.g. changes in plant height
- area or quadrat sampling: data is collected within quadrants, e.g. vegetation cover surveys.

Figure 0.4 Students carrying out a line sample across a dry river valley.

Once you have decided on the type of sampling to use, you then have to decide on a suitable sampling method. There are three types of sampling methods.

- random sampling: sample points are selected using random numbers to avoid **bias**. Tables of random numbers can be used or generated by calculators (see Chapter 9).
- systematic sampling: sample points are selected using a regular pattern or order, e.g. conducting a questionnaire on every tenth person or surveying vegetation cover every 5 metres.
- stratified sampling: when a population is divided up into groups, e.g. different ages or gender, taking a stratified sample ensures that each group is asked in the correct proportion.

KEY TERM

Bias: encouraging one outcome over another

Figure 0.5 summarises the different types of sampling methods.

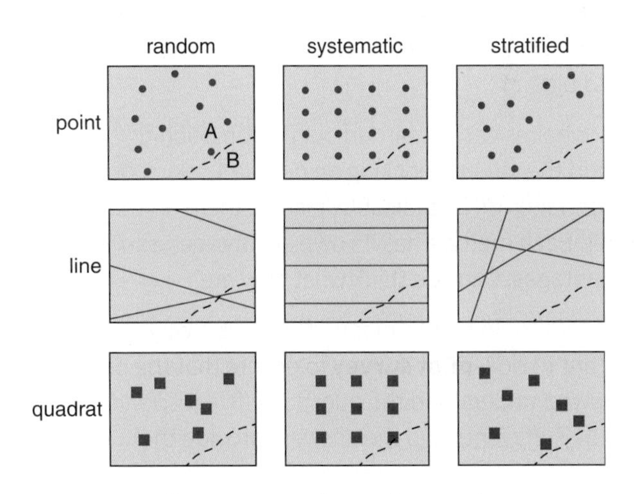

Figure 0.5 Different types of sampling methods.

For example, imagine you wanted to give a questionnaire to a sample of 50 people from a farming area. The area has three villages. How many people should be given a questionnaire from each village?

Village 1	Village 2	Village 3
356 people	233 people	426 people

Table 0.1 Population of the three villages.

a The total number of people is 356 + 233 + 426 = 1015

b To find the number of people from each village to be given the questionnaire, we multiply each village population by $\frac{\text{sample size}}{\text{total population}}$ which in this case is $\frac{50}{1015}$

	Village 1	Village 2	Village 3
Sample size	$365 \times \frac{50}{1015}$ = 17.5	$233 \times \frac{50}{1015}$ = 11.4	$426 \times \frac{50}{1015}$ = 20.9
Rounded numbers of people to be questioned	18	11	21

Table 0.2 Sample size calculations.

A further example of stratified sampling is when soil types are being investigated in an area where 70% of the area consists of rock type A and the remaining 30% consists of rock type B. 70% of the soil samples should be taken on rock type A and 30% of the soil samples on rock type B.

Questionnaires and interviews

This data collection method is used when trying to obtain people's opinions. Stratified sampling is used for questionnaires and careful consideration should be given to the day, time and location when the data are collected to avoid bias.

Questionnaires can be carried out by approaching people in the street, knocking on people's doors, posting questionnaires or, if applicable, placing them on the internet. Each method has its own advantages and disadvantages. Can you think what they are?

Questions should be pre-planned and it is always important to do a **pilot survey** to ensure that the people interviewed understand the questions (five respondents would be sufficient), and the answers provide the information you want to analyse. Always explain the aim of the questionnaire and be polite when asking people to complete them. Stress that the answers will be anonymous and although you should record the age and gender of the respondent, remember these are sensitive questions and should not be asked directly.

A good questionnaire should:

- be carefully worded so people understand the questions and questions are not ambiguous
- be quick to complete and therefore have a limited number of questions in a logical order
- have closed questions at the beginning. Closed **questions** are those which can be answered by a 'yes' or 'no', or by a definite answer to the question being asked. Open **questions** are those which require more thought and require more than a simple one-word answer. They take longer to record but are useful if more information is required. However the answers might be difficult to record and analysis.

Always thank the respondent once the questionnaire has been completed.

An interview involves talking to a small group of people or an individual. You should have pre-planned questions and the answers are usually longer than those from a questionnaire.

Risk assessment

To collect data safely, you must be aware of potential health and safety issues relating to the equipment you are using (e.g. sulfuric acid or a Bunsen burner) or to the location of the investigation. You need to decide what equipment you might use and then ensure that the equipment is tested and, if necessary, **calibrated** before the investigation starts. You should always carry out a pilot survey.

KEY TERMS

Pilot survey: a trial run of a survey, which aims to discover any problems with the survey

Calibrated: to check and make any necessary adjustments to a piece of equipment to ensure its accuracy

Recording data

It is useful to record data in a table format. The table should be created before data collection. When drawing up a table, remember the following guidelines:

- When two or more columns are used, the first column should be the independent variable (i.e. the variable chosen by you, the experimenter) and the second and other columns should contain the dependent variable(s) (i.e. the readings taken for each change in the independent variable).
- Columns should be headed with the name of the variable and the appropriate unit.
- Numerical values inserted in the table should just be numbers, without units.

Practical activity 9.1 in Chapter 9 involves estimating plant coverage using quadrats. Table 0.3 is an example of a results table for this activity.

Independent variable/ units	Dependent variable 1/units	Dependent variable 2/units	Dependent variable 3/units	Dependent variable 4/units
Distance/m	Species 1/% cover	Species 2/% cover	Species 3/% cover	Species 4/% cover
1	53	0	3	0
2	45	3	4	2
3	23	17	4	11
4	12	25	5	25
5	0	37	3	12

Table 0.3 Distribution of plant species along a transect line, following a standard layout for tables.

The first column shows the distance along the transect line (in metres), the second column shows the percentage coverage for a named species of plant, the third column shows the percentage coverage for a second species of plant, and so on.

One option in Practical activity 9.1 is to compare estimated plant coverage in two areas. Figure 0.6 shows a results table suitable for recording data for four species of plants, from two areas (A and B) using five quadrats in each area.

area A

species	quadrat number / percentage cover					
	1	2	3	4	5	average
1	19	23	18	25	14	19.8
2	0	3	4	2	1	2
3	67	75	54	49	52	59.4
4	0	0	0	0	0	0

area B

species	quadrat number / percentage cover					
	1	2	3	4	5	average
1	0	1	0	2	0	0.6
2	6	2	3	3	1	3
3	12	14	21	11	16	14.8
4	1	3	0	2	2	1.6

Figure 0.6 Data of the results of a comparison of two areas using five randomly placed quadrats.

Identifying limitations of methods and suggesting possible improvements

The chosen methods for collecting data for an investigation should be achievable and realistic, but you may still encounter limitations to your methods. The quantity and quality of data collected will be determined by available resources such as time, money, equipment, ICT, possible transport requirements and the number of people needed to collect the data.

Relying on other people to gather data can add a random element to the investigation so it is better if the same individual does the measuring. Your choice of sampling, in terms of type and size, is important and you should select a suitable sampling method at the planning stage. For example, you might think of choosing a systematic sampling method for an investigation into vegetation change along a transect but then realise that some of the sampling sites might be inaccessible.

Conditions in which data is collected, such as the weather when conducting a questionnaire, must be considered. Timing and location of data collection can also affect results, as can the sample size, so these factors should be considered too. Questionnaires should ideally be done at regular intervals as well as being timed to maximise respondents. The use of questionnaires can have other limitations, for instance some age groups can be reluctant to answer and not all age groups will be available if the questionnaire is conducted during work time.

Some data collection methods are subjective, for example visually estimating sediment shape and size. You can often use digital equipment in order to collect more objective information and limit human error. If the method involves the use of measuring equipment, ensure that it is calibrated before the investigation starts. By repeating the measurements, or using another piece of equipment, you can increase the reliability of your results.

If you use the internet for data collection, you must consider whether the websites you use are biased or if the information is inaccurate or outdated. Government websites usually provide reliable data.

Presenting explanations for phenomena, patterns and relationships

There are a wide variety of presentation techniques that can be used to display collected data. The skill is choosing the technique that is most suitable for the data. It is important that all techniques used should have a title and that axes are labelled. If you use a key, it should also be labelled. Tables of data are simple to design but when data are presented visually it is often easier to see patterns and trends, so graphs and diagrams can be a better choice.

There are many different types of graph, such as line graphs, bar graphs, histograms, pie graphs and scattergraphs. More specialised types of graph include climate graphs and population pyramids.

Line graphs

A line graph is used when there is a continuous change in the data, often over time (Figure 0.7). The points are plotted as crosses or encircled dots and are connected with a clear straight line. The axes of a line graph begin at zero and the independent variable is put on the horizontal or *x* axis (e.g. time) and the dependent variable on the vertical or *y* axis. A suitable scale is important as it will influence the appearance of the line graph.

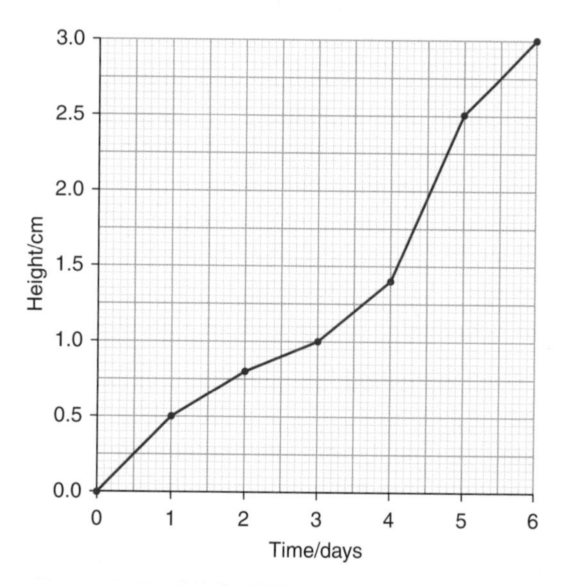

Figure 0.7 A line graph to showing the growth of a bean plant over time.

Bar graphs

Bar graphs are used to show data that fit into categories, e.g. the total number of plant species at different sites.

A bar graph has two axes. The bars should be drawn with equal width and with equal spaces between them (Figure 0.8).

A divided bar graph can be used to show a set of data that is represented by percentages and is an alternative technique to a pie graph. A single bar representing 100% is subdivided into the different data categories.

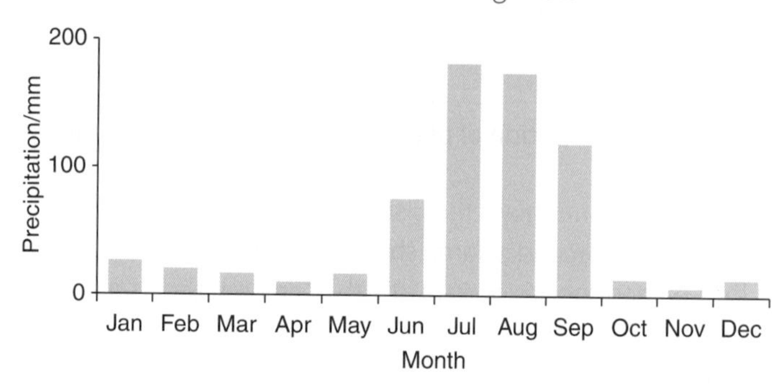

Figure 0.8 A bar graph showing the average precipitation in Agra, India.

Histograms

A histogram may look like a bar graph without the spaces between the bars, but it is different. Histograms are used to show frequencies of data in different categories (Figure 0.9) or change over a period of time. On the *x* axis the range of values is divided into intervals, e.g. 0–99, 100–199 etc. It is a continuous scale and the values do not overlap. The *y* axis shows the frequency or percentage of the collected data falling into each of the intervals. A vertical bar represents each interval and the bars are continuous with no gaps between them.

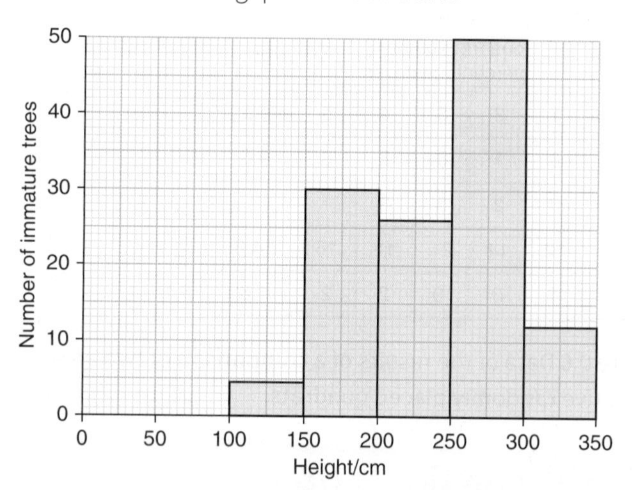

Figure 0.9 A histogram showing the height of immature trees in a plantation.

Pie graphs

Pie graphs are circular charts divided into sectors which show proportions that relate to the data in each category (Figure 0.10). There should be no more than six and no fewer than two sectors in a pie graph. The data used are often in the form of percentages and can be converted into degrees by multiplying each percentage by 3.6 to give a total of 360°. The sectors are plotted in rank order. The largest sector is plotted first starting at '12 o'clock' or 0° and drawn in a clockwise direction. The second sector is then plotted from where the first one ends.

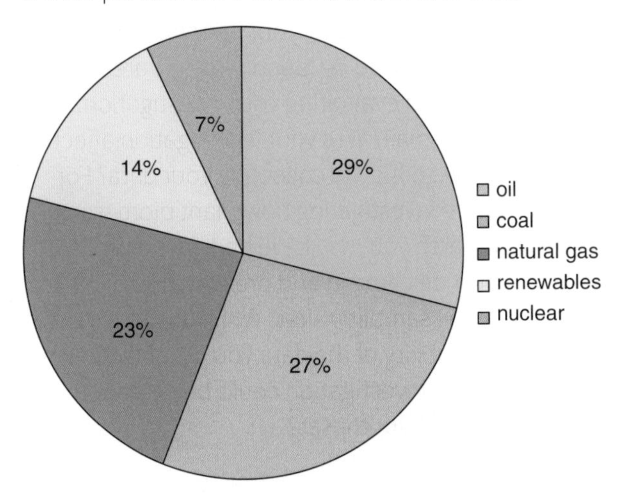

Figure 0.10 A pie graph showing the projected world energy use in 2035.

Scattergraphs

Scattergraphs are used to see if a relationship exists between two sets of data and whether that relationship is positive or negative (Figure 0.11). A scattergraph helps us to see if one set of data is likely to change in relation to a second set of data in a sytematic way. This change (called a correlation) doesn't necessarily mean that one variable *causes* the other to change.

Scattergraphs are plotted in a similar way to line graphs but the points are not joined with a line. The data set that is likely to cause the change is called the independent variable and is plotted on the *x* axis. The dependent variable is plotted on the *y* axis. If the scattergraph shows a likely linear relationship, it is then appropriate to plot the line of best fit (trend line) by eye with an equal number of points above and below the line. The best-fit line does not have to pass through the origin of the graph and should be a single, thin, smooth straight line. There is more information on scattergraphs in Chapter 6.

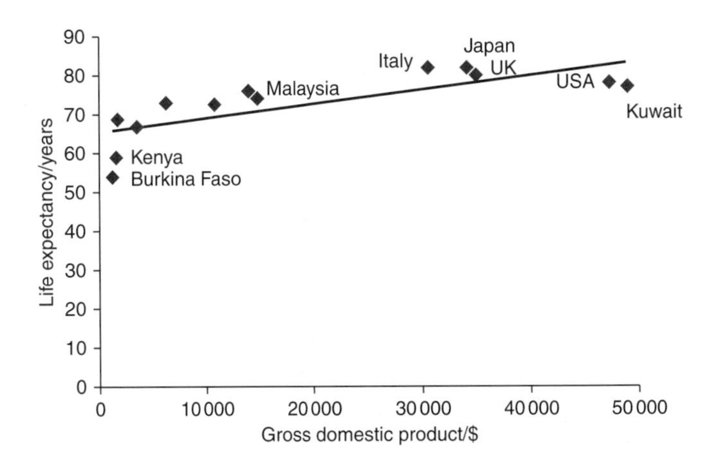

Figure 0.11 A scattergraph showing the relationship between life expectancy and GDP for selected countries.

Analysing your data

Once the data have been presented in a table, graph or diagram, it should be possible to analyse it by describing and explaining what you can see. For example, can you see any trends or associations and explain them? Simple statistical techniques can also be helpful in analysis. These include working out the range (the difference between the largest and smallest values) and the average. There are three kinds of average: mean, median and mode:

- The **mean** is the total of all values divided by the total number of values. It is used when there are no extremes of values, which would distort the mean.
- The **mode** is the value with the highest frequency.
- The **median** is the value in the middle after the data has been sorted into ascending order. It is not affected by extreme values.

KEY TERMS

Mean: the total of all values divided by the total number of values

Mode: the value with the highest frequency

Median: the value in the middle after the data has been sorted into ascending order

The median, range and interquartile range (the range of the middle 50% of the data) can be shown on a box-and-whisker plot. In Figure 0.12 the range of the data is 17–100 and the median is 68.

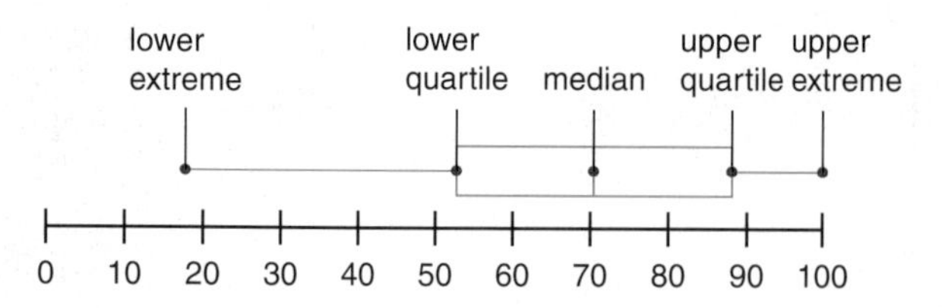

Figure 0.12 A box-and-whisker plot to show range and median values.

Making judgements and reaching conclusions

The conclusion is a summary of the investigation. Using evidence from your data analysis you should now be able to state whether you can accept or reject your hypothesis, giving reasons for your decision. For example the results for the hypothesis from the start of this chapter: 'There will be a decrease in soil pH with increasing distance from a site of coal mining waste', may show exactly that: soil pH does decrease as the distance from a coal mining waste site increases. If so, your conclusion should state this and your hypothesis can be accepted. As well as accepting or rejecting your hypothesis, the conclusion should set out the main findings and discuss if the aim has been achieved. You should also suggest reasons for your findings. For example, if you found that in some cases the soil pH remained the same at different distances, you would need to explain these findings further. Think about whether your findings relate to any previous studies you read about before you carried out the investigation or any theories you have studied.

However interesting your results, your investigation could probably be improved by identifying any areas of weakness. This is called evaluating your investigation. Was the sample, size too small? Was your investigation affected by bias? Did you have difficulty collecting your data? For example, if you were investigating how plant biomass changes in a saltmarsh you may have had an incomplete set of results if the tide came in and prevented you reaching some of the sampling sites. Which variables led to inaccuracy or unreliability of the data you collected? Also, think about how your investigation could be extended: could you test further hypotheses?

Chapter 1
Rocks and minerals and their exploitation

Learning outcomes

By the end of this chapter, you will be able to:

- describe, with examples, the characteristics of igneous, sedimentary and metamorphic rocks
- explain the formation of igneous, sedimentary and metamorphic rocks
- explain the rock cycle
- describe surface and subsurface mining
- describe the reasons for extracting rocks and minerals
- describe the impact of rock and mineral extraction on the environment and human populations
- discuss methods of landscape restoration after rock and mineral extraction
- explain the terms sustainable resource and sustainable development
- discuss how rocks and minerals can be used sustainably.

The third rock from the Sun

The Earth is a rocky planet, compared with, for example Jupiter, which is a gas giant. This means that the Earth is made from rocks and metal ores. The Earth weighs 5 973 600 000 000 000 000 000 000 kg (5.97×10^{26} kg) and has a density of 5.2 g cm^{-3}, which makes it the densest planet in the solar system. This is mainly because the core consists of iron surrounded by a mantle of rock. However, it is only the very outside part of the Earth, above the mantle, that humans can use. The material that makes up this region is what we call **rocks** and **minerals**. Although this represents a vast amount of material, the quantity of it, like everything else, is limited. What is more, extraction and use can cause environmental and other problems. We are in danger of using up the available sources of many rocks, the most well known of which is probably coal.

Peak mineral is a concept that provides a date after which there will only be less extraction of a mineral. Peak coal, for example, is the date at which it is calculated that the most coal is being extracted, after which it will decline. Because we do not know exactly how much coal exists, estimates of peak coal vary. Some say it is 200 years away, others say it could be soon, maybe 2020. This unpredictability because of future unknowns is illustrated by the situation with oil. In 1956, the originator of the peak mineral idea, M. K. Hubbert, predicted that the peak oil date for the USA would be 1970. This did not happen, and in fact the production of oil in the USA is still rising today. However, it is true that the resources of all these commodities, such as coal, oil and phosphorus (current estimated peak date 2030), copper (current estimated peak date 2040) and uranium (current estimated peak date 2030s), are finite. It is therefore important that we limit the use of these resources, and reuse and recycle them whenever we can.

Figure 1.0 A giant bucket wheel excavator in use in an open-pit mine.

1.1 Formation of rocks

The planet Earth was formed about 4.5 billion years ago. The force of gravity pulled the heavier elements together first, forming the core. The lighter elements then formed the Earth's crust about 3–4 billion years ago. The mantle developed as a layer between the dense core and the light crust. This structure still exists today (Figure 1.1).

Igneous rocks

When molten rock from the crust and upper mantle cools, **igneous rocks** are formed. The molten rock is called **magma** when it is still below the surface and lava when it reaches the surface.

Magma is found in the outer mantle; it is hot, liquid rock that is under pressure from the rocks above it. When it

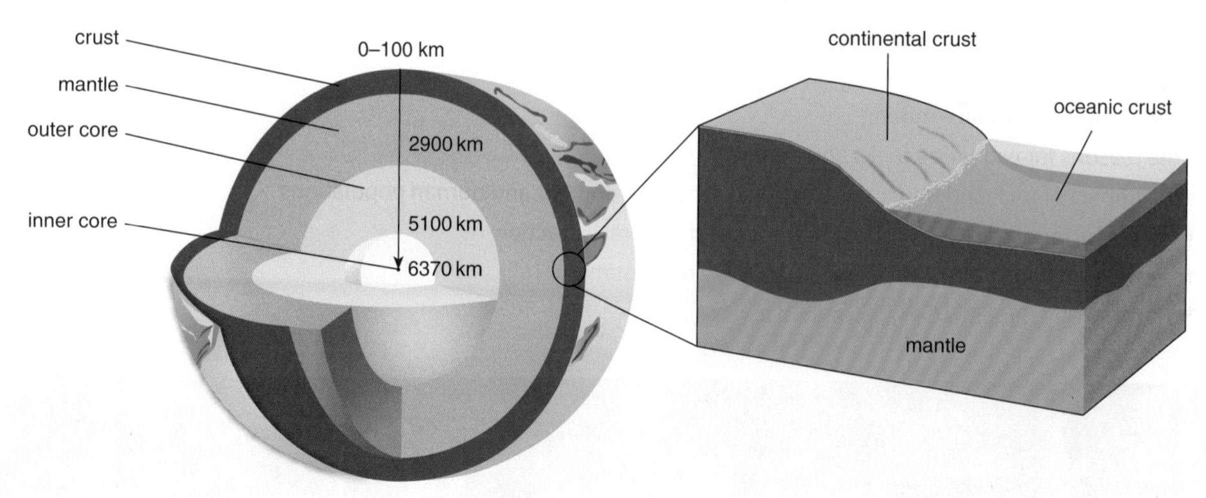

Figure 1.1 The structure of the Earth.

cools it turns to solid rock. When liquid magma rises to the surface from volcanoes the cooling occurs quickly and forms lava. Igneous rocks are made of material that was once molten; they usually contain crystals that are formed as the molten material cools.

The crystals found in rocks are formed when **solutions** of minerals cannot absorb any more dissolved minerals. Some of each mineral type **precipitates** out of solution to form the centre of a crystal. This then provides a surface for more mineral **ions** to precipitate onto. The crystal becomes larger until the solution disappears.

If the rock cools quickly, only very small crystals can form before the rock becomes solid. Rapid cooling occurs when magma is released from volcanoes onto the surface of the Earth's crust.

If magma rises from the mantle into the crust without reaching the Earth's surface, then the magma cools more slowly, allowing the formation of larger crystals. Many of these crystals contain valuable minerals that are used for a wide range of industrial processes.

Heat and pressure are the usual reason for minerals becoming dissolved; a reduction of heat and pressure usually leads to the formation of crystals.

Examples of igneous rocks are granite and basalt (Figures 1.2 and 1.3).

Figure 1.2 A piece of granite.

Figure 1.3 A piece of basalt.

Sedimentary rocks

Sedimentary rocks are formed by the weathering of existing rocks at the Earth's surface, the accumulation and fossilisation of living material, or the precipitation of dissolved materials out of solution in water. Weathering processes release small mineral particles that accumulate to form sediment. Over time, layers of sediment build up to form sedimentary rock.

The sediments include different-sized mineral particles. The smallest particles are clays, followed by silts and then sands. These particles are important in the formation of soils (see Section 3.1). Larger particles of gravels and small boulders can also be found in sediments.

KEY TERMS

Rock: a combination of one or more minerals

Mineral: a naturally occurring inorganic substance with a specific chemical composition

Igneous rock: rock made during a volcanic process

Magma: molten rock below the surface of the Earth

Solution: formed when a solid is dissolved in a liquid

Precipitates: when a substance comes out of solution

Ion: an atom in which the number of positively charged protons is not equal to the number of negatively charged electrons

Sedimentary rock: a rock formed from material derived from the weathering of other rocks or the accumulation of dead plants and animals

The particles are transported by streams and rivers and then deposited as sediment. Each layer of sediment becomes more compact and harder because of the pressure created by the newer deposits above them.

Examples of sedimentary rock are limestone, sandstone and shale (Figures 1.4, 1.5 and 1.6).

Figure 1.4 A piece of limestone.

Figure 1.5 Sandstone.

Figure 1.6 A piece of shale.

Metamorphic rocks

Metamorphic rocks are created from existing rocks when the heat (above 150 °C) or pressure (above 1.5×10^8 Pa or 1480 atm), or both heat and pressure, causes changes in the rock crystals without melting the existing rock. The existing rock therefore changes in structure, becoming a metamorphic rock. The changes in structure can be chemical or physical or both.

Sedimentary and igneous rocks can become metamorphic rocks, and a metamorphic rock can become another metamorphic rock. Metamorphic rocks are usually harder than sedimentary rocks.

Examples of metamorphic rocks are marble and slate (Figures 1.7 and 1.8).

When the Earth's crust first formed, all the rocks were igneous. These rocks were slowly eroded, releasing small particles that formed sediment, and these sediments built up over time to form sedimentary rocks. The rocks that make up the Earth's crust are always moving, which creates the heat and pressure needed to form metamorphic rock. All rock types are constantly eroded and formed in the **rock cycle** (Figure 1.9). Table 1.1 compares the characteristics of the different rock types.

KEY TERMS

Metamorphic rock: a rock formed from existing rocks by a combination of heat and pressure

Rock cycle: a representation of the changes between the three rock types and the processes causing them

Igneous	Sedimentary	Metamorphic
Made from liquid magma	Made from other rock fragments	Made from existing rock
Magma cools to form solid rock	Rock fragments become buried and increased pressure forms a rock	The original rock is changed in form by heat and pressure
Mineral crystals sometimes present; the size of the crystals depends on the speed of cooling	Crystals absent	Mineral crystals present
No fossils present	Fossils may be present	No fossils present

Table 1.1 Characteristics of the different rock types.

Figure 1.7 A piece of marble.

Figure 1.8 A piece of slate.

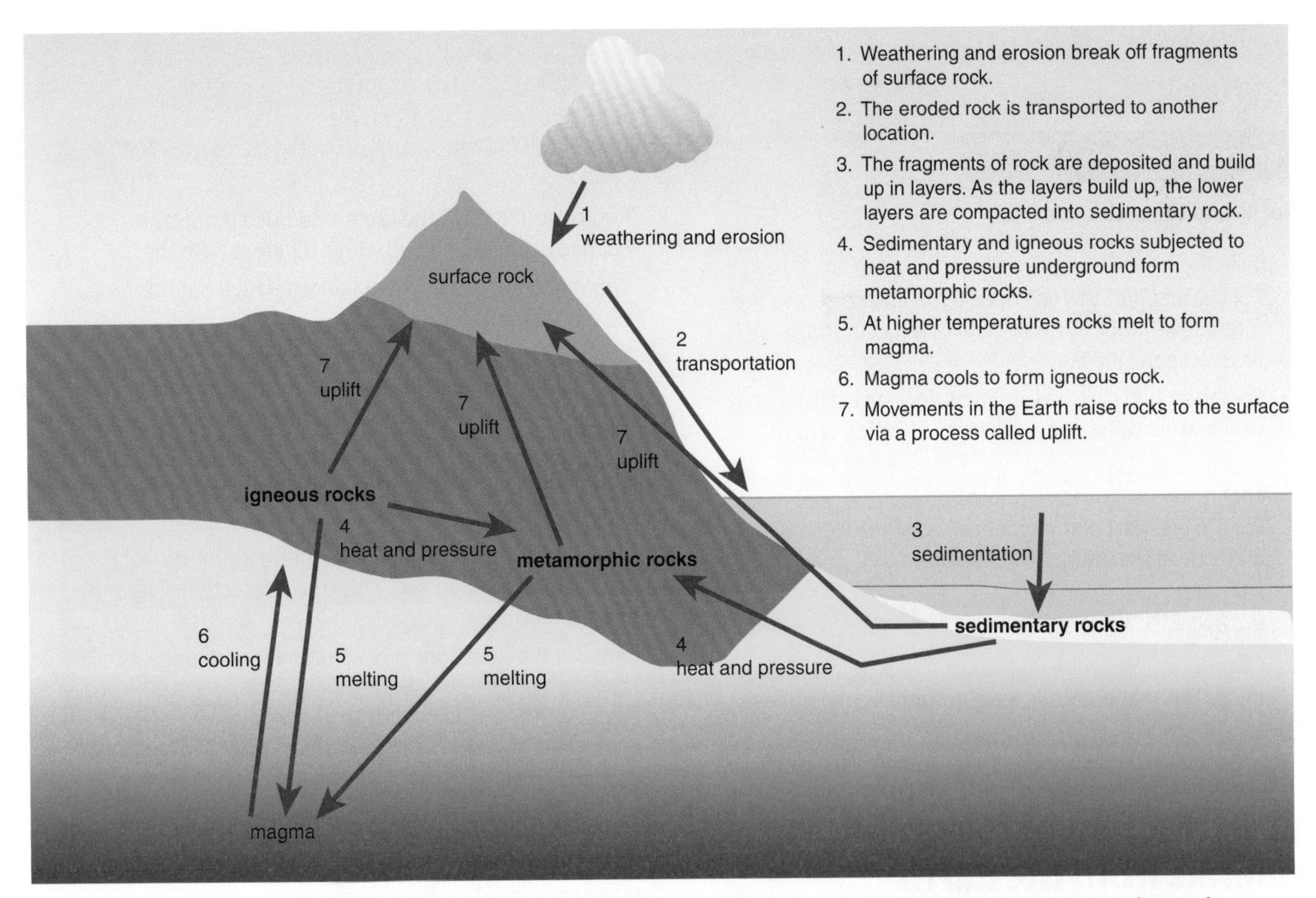

Figure 1.9 The rock cycle showing the relationship between the three rock types, sedimentary, metamorphic and igneous. The diagram also shows the interactions between these types, their origins and the processes by which they are interconverted.

SELF-ASSESSMENT QUESTIONS

1.1 Figure 1.10 shows the rock cycle.

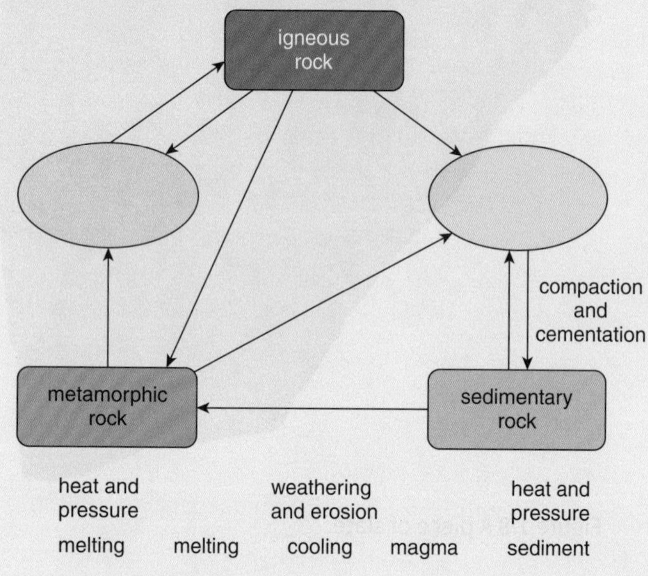

Figure 1.10 The rock cycle.

Copy and complete Figure 1.10 with processes on the arrows and intermediate stages in the ovals. The processes should be chosen from the list provided; one has been done for you.

1.2 Add the names of the correct rock type to Table 1.2.

Description	Rock Type
Rocks formed in the sea from particles of eroded rock	
Rocks changed by heat	
Rocks formed from the cooling of other molten rock	

Table 1.2 Rock types.

PRACTICAL ACTIVITY 1.1

Rocks and the rock cycle

Materials

- For the first part you will need to be able to access the Interactives Rock Cycle website (www.cambridge.org/links/scspenv4000).
- For the second part, which can be done on a different day, your teacher will provide you with a selection of rocks.

Method

- For the first part of the practical, go to the web page and look at the interactive diagram.
- For the second part of the practical, choose one of the rocks.
- Observe and describe your chosen rock, thinking about things like shape, colour, weight, softness or hardness.
- Return your rock to the table, and put a letter by it. Each rock should end up with a different letter by it.
- Working on your own, select another rock but this time do not pick it up.
- Spend about five minutes writing a description of your rock, without anyone else knowing which one it is.
- Swap your description with someone else and take it in turns to work out which rock has been described.

Questions

1. Test yourself on what you have learnt about the rock cycle using another version of the interactive diagram on the web page.
2. Answer the questions provided on the web page.

1.2 Extraction of rocks and minerals from the Earth

Minerals provide us with a wide range of materials that we use in everyday life. Coal and oil provide energy and many chemicals used in industry. Metallic **ores** provide us with the metals and alloys needed to make products such as computers, mobile phones, cars, wires and nails. The demand for minerals continues to increase, both from developed and developing countries.

Searching for minerals

People have searched for minerals for thousands of years. The simplest way to find mineral deposits is to look carefully at the surface of rocks. This process of **prospecting** has found nearly all the surface deposits of minerals worldwide.

Deposits on the Earth's surface can also be found using a range of **remote sensing** methods. For example, an area of land can be photographed from the air and the images carefully analysed for signs of minerals. Aerial photography can cover much more ground than a person walking over the surface of rocks (Figure 1.11). Images and other data from satellites can also be used to analyse very large areas.

KEY TERMS

Ore: a rock with enough of an important element to make it worth mining

Prospecting: a process of searching for minerals

Remote sensing: a process in which information is gathered about the Earth's surface from above

Geochemical: the chemical properties of rocks

Mineral deposits are weathered at the Earth's surface, producing mineral oxides. These can be detected by their unique radiation pattern, which is recorded by a satellite and downloaded to a computer for analysis.

Other satellites operate by sending signals to the surface of the Earth and then collecting reflected signals. The system works in all weathers, through complete cloud cover and at night.

Valuable mineral ores in the rocks below the surface can be located from the satellite images. Computers are used to process the data from a region of interest to see whether any minerals are present in the area. The satellite's positioning system records the exact location, and the geologists then visit the location to confirm the minerals have been identified correctly. Once in an area identified from satellite data, the geologists can check further locations to see whether the minerals of interest are present nearby as well. Using satellites means large areas can be geologically mapped quickly and at low cost.

Field surveys on the ground are used to take samples. These are sent to a laboratory for **geochemical** analysis, so that the chemicals in the samples can be identified. The samples can be taken from stream sediments, soil or rocks (using shallow drilling). The points where the samples are taken are usually selected by overlaying a grid on a map of the survey area. The location of the sample points in the field can be found accurately using the Global Positioning System (GPS).

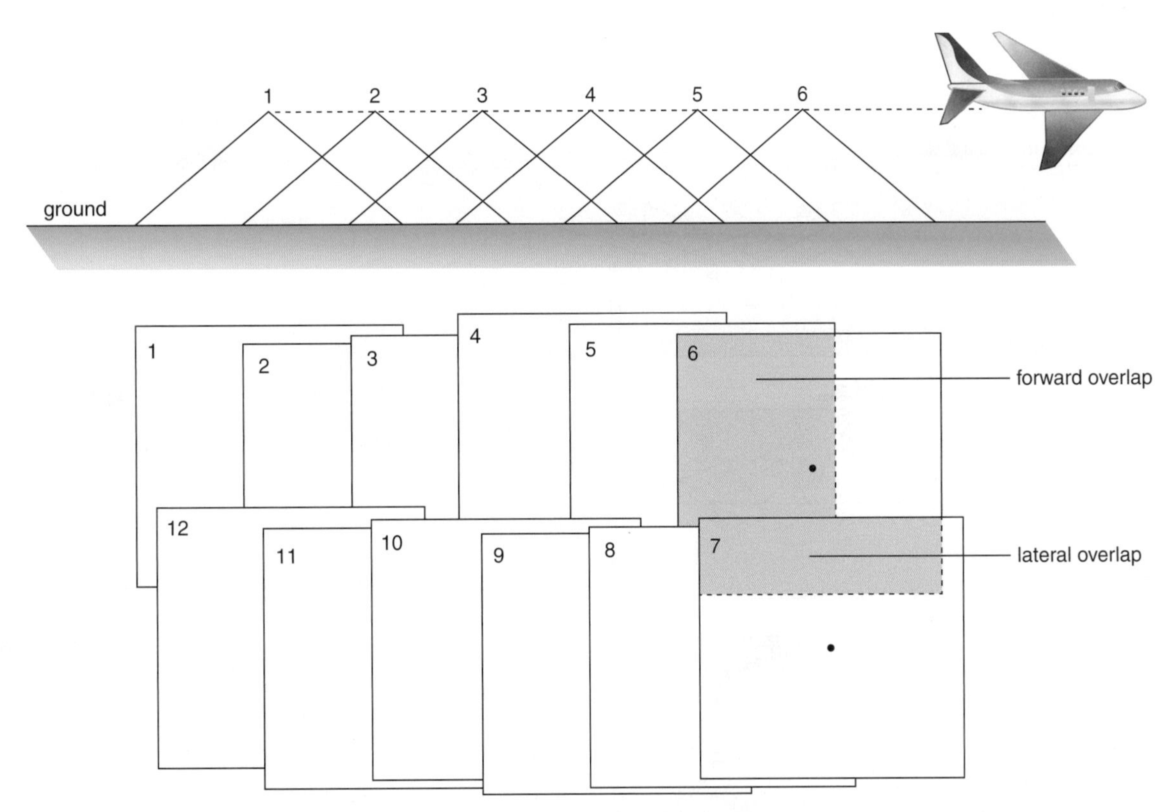

Figure 1.11 Aerial photography used for mineral prospecting. Photographs are taken with an overlap both front to back and side to side. If the overlap is sufficient, three-dimensional views can be generated, which makes the prospecting easier.

Another method used to identify the mineral ores present in rocks is **geophysics**. A series of vibrations (seismic waves) are sent through the Earth's surface. Several sensors at different distances from the source of vibrations are laid on the ground. The vibrations create shock waves that travel down into the rock layers and are reflected back to the sensors on the surface. The shock waves record different patterns depending on what minerals are present in the rock layers. Explosives can be used instead of vibrations but this is potentially more dangerous (Figure 1.12).

Mining rocks and minerals

To make sure that the deposits of mineral ores are large enough to be extracted, a resource evaluation is carried out. The aim of the evaluation is to estimate the grade and tonnage of the mineral of interest present in a deposit. Drilling to collect rock samples must be done to carry out a resource evaluation. For small deposits, only a few samples are needed. For larger deposits, more drilling is required, following a grid pattern on the ground. The aim is to identify the size of the deposit as well as the mixture of mineral ores present.

From the information collected, the deposit may be classified as a mineral ore reserve. Classifying the deposit as a reserve takes into account the amount of material that it is practical to extract. Finally, a feasibility study is carried out to evaluate all the financial and technical risks of any proposed mining project (see below). The final decision may be to develop a mine straight away or wait until conditions change in the future.

Methods of extraction

There are two main types of mining. **Surface mining** includes **open-cast**, **open-pit**, **open-cut** and **strip mining**. **Sub-surface mining** includes **deep** and **shaft mining**.

KEY TERMS

Geophysical: the physical properties of rocks

Surface mining: a type of mining used when the mineral is either exposed on the surface or overlain by only small amounts of **Overburden**

Overburden: the rock and soil overlying an economically viable mineral deposit

Open-pit mining: a type of surface mining

Strip mining: a type of surface mining

Sub-surface mining: a type of mining used when the deposit is covered by a deep layer(s) of unwanted rock

Deep mining: a type of sub-surface mining

Shaft mining: a type of sub-surface mining

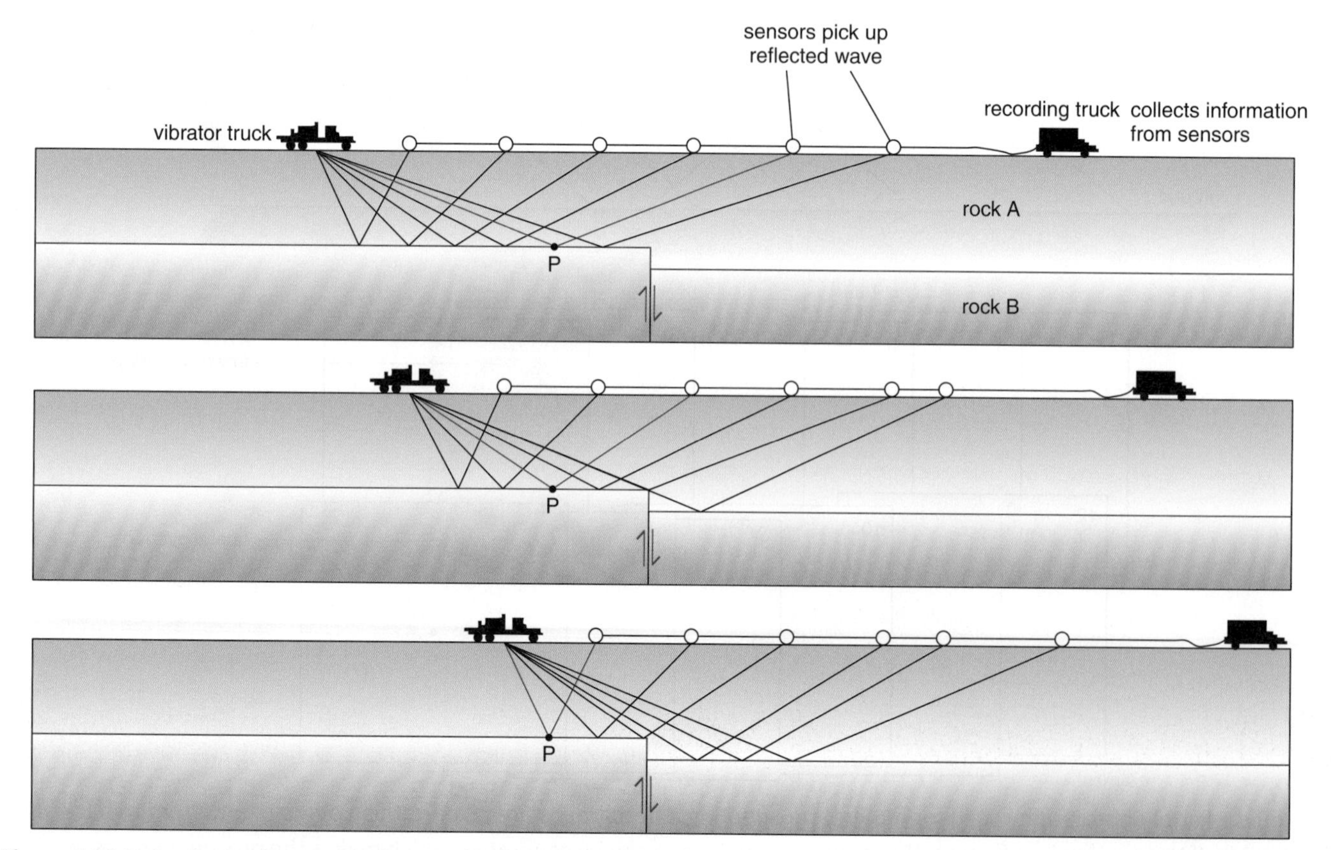

Figure 1.12 Seismic shock waves being used to locate rock or mineral deposits.

Surface mining

Open-pit mining is also called **open-cast** or **open-cut** mining. This type of mining is used when a valuable deposit is located near the surface, often buried below a thick layer of worthless material. The material above the deposit is called overburden. The overburden has to be removed first to expose the deposit, and is stored nearby to be used later for mine restoration (Figure 1.13).

Open-pit mines are carefully dug in sections called benches. The walls of the benches are kept at an angle to reduce the risk of rock falls. The safe angle of these walls depends on the type of deposit and overburden. Roads have to be made as the digging progresses to allow the removal of the mineral deposit and overburden. Building materials such as sand, gravel and stone are removed from open pits called quarries. The process of extraction from pits always uses similar methods.

There are two main reasons why open-pit mines eventually stop being worked. In some cases, as much valuable deposit as possible has been removed. In other cases, the amount of overburden that needs to be removed has increased to an extent that the mine is no longer profitable.

Strip mining is used to mine a seam of mineral. First of all the overburden, which consists of the overlying rock and soil, is removed. Strip mining is mainly used to mine coal near the surface. Figure 1.0 shows a very large bucket wheel excavator, which is often used in strip mines. These machines can move thousands of tonnes of material every hour.

Sub-surface mining

Sub-surface mining (Figure 1.14) involves digging tunnels into the ground to reach mineral deposits that are too deep to be removed by surface mining. Sometimes horizontal tunnels are dug directly into the coal seam in the side of a hill or mountain: this is a drift mine entered by an **adit**. These tunnels produce waste rock as well as the mineral ore.

A sloping tunnel is dug to reach deeper deposits. Mining machinery can be lowered down the sloping tunnels while waste rock and mineral ore are hauled up to the surface.

The deepest deposits are reached by digging a vertical shaft. Horizontal galleries are then dug into the mineral deposits. This type of mining is more expensive and technically challenging than either horizontal or slope tunnelling. Only large deposits of valuable minerals are mined in this way.

Most of the material is removed from mines by machine. The miners' job is to make sure all the machinery is working correctly and safely. Compared with open-pit mining, any form of shaft mining is more difficult because a supply of fresh air and water drainage has to be provided. There are also the dangers of collapsing tunnels as well as the risks of poisonous gas, explosion and underground fire.

KEY TERMS

Open-cast mining: a type of surface mining

Open-cut mining: a type of surface mining

Adit: the entrance to a horizontal (drift) mine

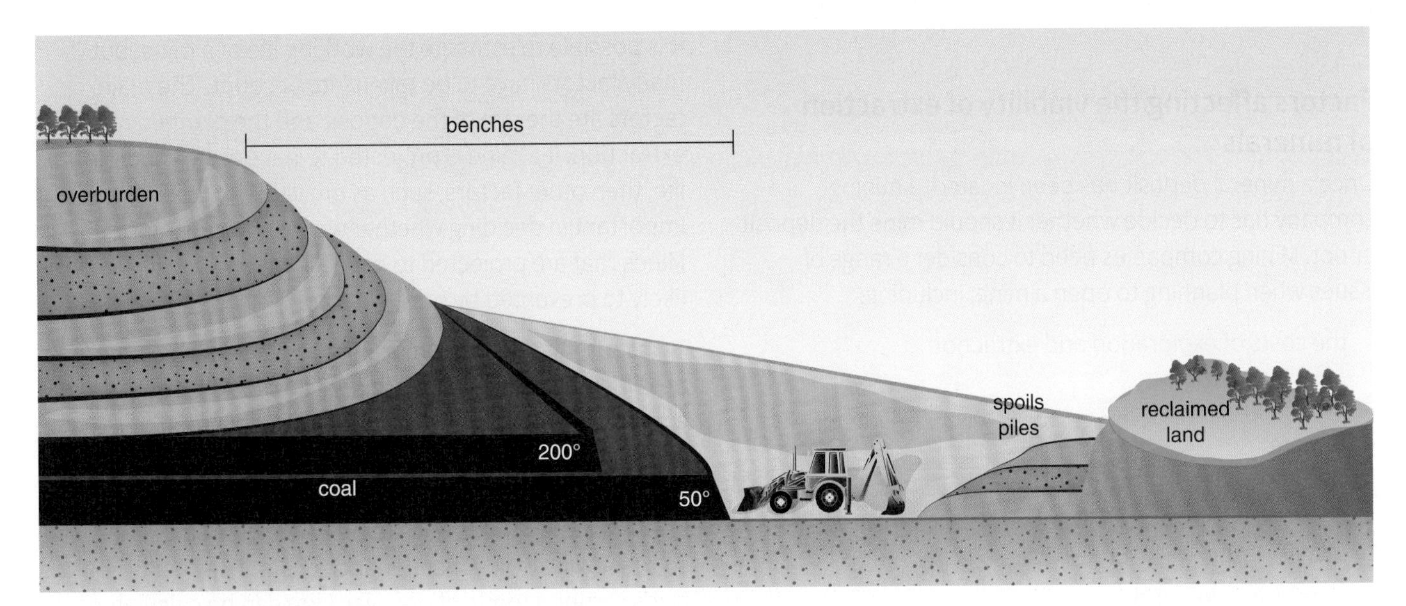

Figure 1.13 An open-pit mine.

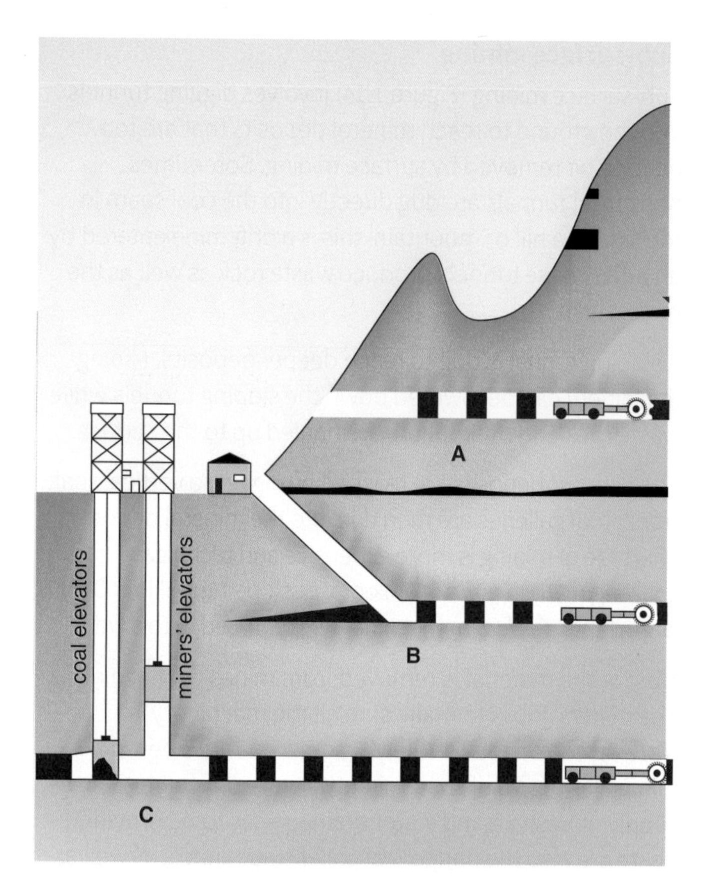

Figure 1.14 A drift mine with a horizontal entrance, called an adit. B Sloping tunnel.

SELF-ASSESSMENT QUESTIONS

1.3 What factors need to be considered before starting up a new mine?

1.4 Suggest reasons why developing surface mines is easier than developing mines underground.

Factors affecting the viability of extraction of minerals

Once a mineral deposit has been located, a mining company has to decide whether it should mine the deposit or not. Mining companies need to consider a range of issues when planning to open a mine, including:

- the costs of exploration and extraction
- geology
- climate
- accessibility
- the environmental impact
- supply and demand.

Greenfield sites are areas that have never been mined for minerals. The chances of finding a deposit there are low. For some metal ores, the **strike rate** ranges from 1:50 to 1:100. New gold deposits are very hard to find: the strike rate may be as low as 1:1000.

Brownfield sites are areas that have already been mined. They usually have a higher strike rate than greenfield sites. Even low-grade deposits that were not extracted in the past may have enough value that they can now be mined for profit.

The probable cost of extracting one tonne of ore has to be calculated. Deposits near the surface can be extracted by open-pit mining. There are usually fewer technical difficulties to mining on a large scale using this method, which leads to a low extraction cost per tonne.

Deeper deposits can only be extracted by shaft mining. This is more costly to set up and maintain, so the cost per tonne will be higher than open-pit mining. Only deposits of high value can be mined economically in this way.

The quality of the mineral deposit is another important factor in deciding to open a mine. High-grade ores will yield more of the required chemical elements than low-grade ores.

The size of deposit that can be extracted is also important. Small deposits of high-grade ore and high-value ores may be worth mining. Small deposits of low-grade ore and low-value ores that cannot be mined at a profit are left as known reserves. In the future they may be mined, either because technical advances make it less costly to do so or because of a sustained increase in world price.

It is possible to estimate the working life of a mine, but many factors have to be taken into account. The main factors are the size of the deposit and the planned rate of extraction. If a mine is projected to have a short working life, then other factors, such as ore value, will be very important in deciding whether work should be started. Mines that are projected to have a long working life are less likely to prevented by other factors.

Transporting the ore from a mine to processing plants may be difficult and expensive. This factor alone could prevent a deposit being mined. The cost of building road or rail links to the processing plants or to the nearest suitable port for export is a start-up cost that has to be considered. These transport links have to be kept in working order, so there will also be maintenance costs. The cost of transporting 1 tonne of ore over 1 km can be calculated.

For large tonnages, such as iron ore, rail transport is the only practical and cost-effective method of moving the ore. If the ore is going to be exported, large ships, called bulk carriers, can be used to keep the transport costs low.

Another way of keeping the transport costs low is to carry out some processing of the ore at the mine. The process used depends on the chemical nature and grade of the ore. The aim of processing is to concentrate the mineral ore and separate it from the waste material. The waste material is stored at the mine. This type of processing produces a higher grade of ore so it has a higher value per tonne. Some ores are high grade when they come out of the ground. For example, some iron ores are called direct shipping ores (DSO) because they have enough iron content that they do not need processing at the mine.

Mining companies can only start work after they have been given a licence to extract a deposit. The government of any country will want to earn some money from the mining activity. This means there will be a tax to be paid to the government for every tonne of mineral ore extracted. From the point of view of the mining company, it is important that a long-term agreement is reached to avoid rapid rises in tax that could make the mining operation unprofitable. From the point of view of the government, the tax needs to generate enough money to be invested in developments for the benefit of the country.

Increase in world demand for any mineral ore will drive the price up. Changes in **supply and demand** can increase or decrease profits from working mines. If the world price remains high, then deposits that could not previously be mined at a profit may become worth mining. The amount of money that needs to be invested in starting up a new mine is considerable. This means that if the world price falls because of a drop in demand, a new mine may not start working at a profit. Only when the world price rises again can a new mine become profitable. The global recession of 2008 stopped some known mineral reserves being mined because of reduced world prices. Recently, the world price of iron ore has dropped because supply is greater than demand.

An example of changes in world price are shown in Figure 1.15.

Mining companies try to predict future demand very carefully so that periods of selling ore at less than the cost of production are kept to a minimum. The profits from periods of high world prices are used to make up for periods of low profitability, as well as to pay for the development of newly discovered deposits.

KEY TERMS

Strike rate: the frequency with which attempts to find a desired mineral are successful

Supply and demand: the relationship between how much of a commodity is available and how much is needed or wanted by consumers of the product

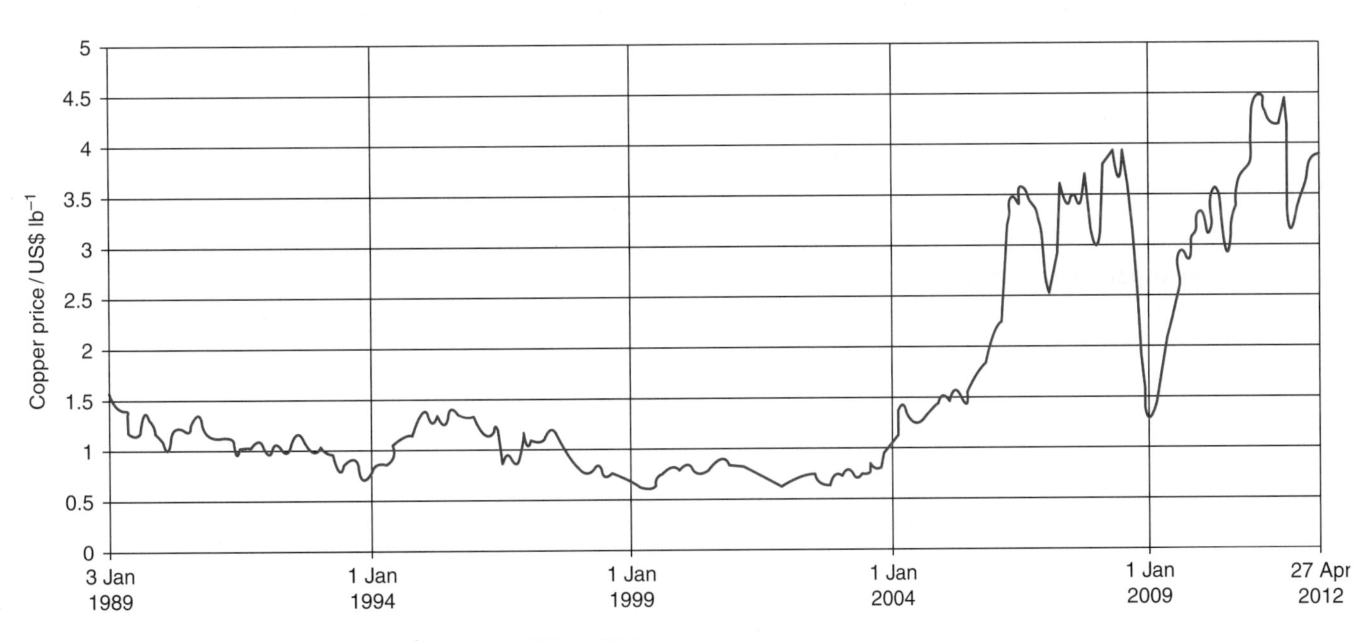

Figure 1.15 Changes in world price of copper, 1989 to 2012.

1.3 Impact of rock and mineral extraction

Environmental impacts

Impacts on the environment from the extraction of rocks and minerals range from large-scale habitat destruction to pollution of the atmosphere, land and water. Those living near the site are also affected by noise and visual pollution.

Ecological impacts

Any mining activity will involve the loss of habitat for some species of plants and animals. Even small-scale surface mineral extraction requires the vegetation to be cleared from an area of land. The plants removed have lost a place to grow, and so have the animals that depend on the plants for food and shelter.

Deep mining means that shafts have to be dug down to the seams of valuable minerals. At the beginning of deep mining operations, only a small area of land is cleared of vegetation. After this type of mine has been working for several years, more habitats will be destroyed as the amount of mine waste stored aboveground increases.

Any form of large-scale surface mining causes the greatest loss of habitat. Large areas of vegetation have to be removed and then large volumes of removed overburden have to be stored. After the seams of valuable mineral have been removed, the overburden is spread over the mined area to restore the land. The new land surface will slowly become covered in some plant species. However, this vegetation will have less biodiversity compared with the original vegetation. This means that some plant and animal habitats will still be lost from an area for many years, even though the land surface has been restored.

When a company applies for a licence to start working, an **environmental impact assessment** is carried out. The licence application is usually approved if the company has a plan to keep the loss of habitat as small as possible and then to restore the land after mining has finished. An environmental impact assessment tries to identify all the possible types of damage to the environment. To have the licence application approved, any mining company must have detailed plans to control the amount of damage to the environment.

KEY TERMS

Environmental impact assessment: a process by which the probable effects on the environment of a development are assessed and measured

Biomagnification: the process in which the concentration of a substance in living things becomes higher at progressively higher levels in a food chain or web

Pollution

The working life of any type of mine will result in some pollution of the environment (Figure 1.16).

This can take the form of noise, water, land, air and visual pollution. Noise pollution is a problem when large-scale surface mining takes place. The overburden is loosened by explosive charges and then removed by large machines. The noise can disturb the behaviour of many animal species near the mine and cause health problems for people. Deep mining usually produces less noise than surface mining. Mining licences set limits on the levels of noise and working hours of a mine.

Water pollution from any type of mine can be a major problem that can continue for many years after a mine has stopped working. The water that drains through mine waste, or comes directly from mine shafts, can cause dramatic changes to the populations of living organisms in streams and rivers. Drinking water supplies may also be polluted by drainage from mines, making it unsafe for people to drink.

This pollution is caused by chemical reactions between water and exposed rocks and mine waste. The water may become acidic and then dissolve toxic metal ions. The combination of acidic water with a high concentration of toxic metal ions kills many aquatic organisms. Some of the metal ions exist only in low concentrations in bodies of water. However, organisms absorb these ions and retain them in their body, reaching concentrations much higher than that in the water. This is called bioaccumulation. The concentrations increase further in organisms that are higher up the food chain. This process is called **biomagnification**, and can cause the death of top consumers. There are other metal ions that are toxic in high concentrations that do not bioaccumulate.

The land surrounding a mine will become polluted by mine waste. In some cases the area will be quite small but the toxic nature of the waste means that only a few plants can grow, even many years after mining has stopped.

Figure 1.16 Pollution and land degradation around a copper mine.

When mine waste is stored above natural water courses, the waste pile may collapse and cover more land. The choice of site for mine waste is an important factor to consider in plans to limit the effects of pollution.

Many mining activities release dust particles, which will settle on the vegetation near the mine. Dust reduces plant growth: the leaves of plants need to absorb light energy to perform photosynthesis. If light cannot penetrate a layer of dust on a leaf surface, then the rate of photosynthesis is reduced.

Dust from mining activities may also have toxic effects depending on the chemical components present in the dust. This can also reduce or stop plant growth, and the particles can be dangerous to human health. The biggest risk is breathing in dust that then remains in the lungs. Long-term exposure can lead to serious lung diseases that can cause death. The lungs of children are very easily damaged by breathing dust particles. Some harmful substances can also be absorbed through human skin. Mining companies provide safety clothing and breathing masks to protect the health of mine workers. However, many people make a living from small-scale mining without a licence. This is often called informal mining and it is illegal. Health problems as a result of toxic substances are common among these miners.

Evidence of mining activity can often be seen because the landscape is damaged. This is visual pollution. Large-scale surface mining will create the most obvious visual pollution during the working life of a mine. This type of pollution may only be temporary because careful restoration of the landscape is possible.

SELF-ASSESSMENT QUESTIONS

1.5 Give reasons why illegal mining without a licence is bad for people and the environment.

1.6 Explain how reduced plant growth can affect an ecosystem.

The Antamina Mine in Peru

The Antamina mine is a large open-pit mine located high in the Andes Mountains of Peru at an altitude above 4000 m (Figure 1.17). The estimated reserve is 1.5 billion tonnes of ore. Extraction of copper and zinc ores began in 2001. The mine employs more than 5000 people.

Before mining could begin, more than 100 million tonnes of surface rock had to be removed and placed in waste piles. The ores were then removed and crushed in the processing plant to produce concentrate. Wastes from this process are called tailings. These are stored in a compound to prevent water pollution. The concentrate is then mixed with water and moved in a 300 km pipeline to the coast. After the water is removed from the concentrate it is loaded into ships.

The mine was expected to stop production in 2022. However, more reserves have been found and increased investment in efficient processing machinery has extended the expected life of the mine to 2029.

Questions

1 Suggest why the mine was developed in such a remote location.

2 Water pollution is serious risk at this open-pit mine. Give three reasons why there is a high risk of water pollution.

3 a Suggest how the production from this mine been made more sustainable than originally planned.

  b Explain why it is unlikely that the land will be fully restored when this mine stops production.

Figure 1.17 The Antamina Copper mine, Peru, showing benches and the sheer size of the mine.

Economic impacts

Extracting valuable minerals provides employment for people and provides taxes for the government. Modern mining is carried out using machines so only a small number of people will be directly employed to extract minerals. However, if the mineral is then refined and processed in the same country, further jobs are created. In many cases minerals are exported from one country to be used in manufacturing processes in another country. This can create jobs in the country importing the mineral. Overall, mineral extraction does provide employment, even if modern methods mean that the total number of mining jobs may only be a few hundred.

Mineral extraction usually benefits both local and national economies. Jobs are created directly to extract minerals and further jobs to supply transport and mining equipment. More jobs are created when the mineral is refined to make products. If all these activities occur in the same country, this will generate the most income for buying goods and services as well as investing in infrastructure projects.

Some improvements to transport and services, such as healthcare and education, will be required to supply any mining industry as well as support the mineworkers and their families. Some improvements will be paid for by the mining companies as a condition of their mining licence. Taxes paid by mining companies and individual workers can provide a country with enough revenue to invest in infrastructure projects to benefit the whole population of the country.

1.4 Managing the impact of rock and mineral extraction

Management of a mining operation should start with plans for safe waste disposal and end with plans to return the land to its original state when mining is over.

Safe disposal of mining waste

In the past, mining waste was usually been put in piles near the point of extraction. In some cases, stable waste piles were placed on top of water courses, which then become polluted with toxic chemicals. In other cases, waste piles were unstable and collapsed. Apart from the possible loss of life caused by a collapse, collapsed waste piles increase land and water pollution.

Today, safe storage and disposal of mine waste is one of the most important aspects of any mining licence application.

In a well-regulated system, applications must provide a detailed plan to show how mine waste will be stored to prevent collapse. The site of the mine waste must also prevent the possibility of water pollution. The plan must include details of how the waste will be monitored to detect any movement or water pollution.

Land restoration and bioremediation

When mining has finished, the land needs to be restored. Sometimes mine waste can be reshaped to blend in with the surrounding landforms. The waste can then be covered by a layer of soil, which may be enriched with fertiliser. Such an area can then be planted with trees. This will help other plants and animals to colonise the area. As time passes, the soil will be improved by the addition of organic matter from plant and animal wastes. This method of land restoration is often used to manage the waste from coal mining. Planting trees creates habitats fairly quickly even though the trees are only able to grow slowly.

Some mine waste does not allow the growth of tree roots, so other methods of restoration have to be used. Contaminated waste can be treated where it was left (in situ treatment) by **bioremediation**. Alternatively, waste can be removed from a site to a treatment plant (ex situ treatment).

KEY TERM

Bioremediation: a process in which living things are used to remove toxic chemicals from a natural site

Bioremediation is the process of removing pollutants from waste using living organisms. Many organisms are able to break down toxic substances into less hazardous substances. This often happens slowly in natural environments. Some microorganisms, such as bacteria found in soils, are able to absorb pollutants and process them via metabolic pathways into less harmful substances. When bacteria take in pollutants they usually gain either energy or nutrients.

Microorganisms can remove and process pollutants at a faster rate if their environment provides a source of oxygen and nitrogen. Some plants are also naturally able to bioaccumulate toxic metals, and this process can be speeded up with the addition of fertilisers. These plants are grown on contaminated waste. The plants absorb toxic metals, and later the parts of the plant aboveground are removed so the waste left in the ground becomes less toxic.

Figure 1.18 Former granite quarry on Bornholm, Denmark, the steep sides now a paradise for sea gulls.

After this treatment, the land is often turned into a nature reserve as, even though the ground surface is less toxic, it may still not be possible to use it for farming or to build houses on. Several tree and herb species are introduced, and as the plant populations grow they create habitats for many animal species. These nature reserves become valuable green spaces for human recreation, as well as helping to maintain biodiversity (Figure 1.18).

Mineral extraction often creates large holes in the landscape. If the rock lining the hole is impervious to water and non-toxic then it can be allowed to fill with water to form a reservoir. This water could be used for irrigating farmland or processed to provide clean, safe drinking water for humans. Sometimes, these holes are filled with household waste until they are full. The waste is then covered with soil and planted with trees. This is referred to as landfill.

How successful are these strategies? The Society for Ecological Restoration International (SERI) proposed a number of ecosystem-related variables to measure the success of a land restoration programme. In summary, a successful scheme will return the site to as close as possible to the native ecosystem that existed before the mining began. In this respect, although all strategies have a value, some scientists believe that allowing a site to undergo a natural process of recolonisation and slow change to the environment (a process called succession) may actually be the most beneficial method. Active reclamation is important to reduce the incidence of such events as landslides and erosion. However, once this has been done, the natural process of succession can probably be relied on to achieved the ecosystem recovery SERI and others think we should aim for.

1.5 Sustainable use of rocks and minerals

The supply of rocks and minerals that are used as building materials and for industrial production is finite. It is hard to see, therefore, how the use of these materials can meet the definition of sustainability. Sustainable use means use that meets the needs of the present without affecting the ability of future generations to meet their needs. A fully sustainable resource will never run out, and this can be achieved in fisheries, agriculture and forestry where the resource is biological and can be regrown. Unlike these biological systems, such things as rocks and minerals will not last indefinitely.

Human societies need to use any resource with care so that its use is at least more sustainable than it has been in the past. The sustainable development of the reserves of any rock or mineral must take into account environmental, economic and social factors. The aim is a planned and controlled use of any reserve to provide the most benefit to people, maintain economic growth and stability and prevent widespread environmental damage. National laws and international agreements encourage sustainable development of resources.

The term sustainability is now widely used. However, as the world population continues to increase, it is difficult to see how the challenge of complete sustainability can be met. Perhaps the best that can be achieved is the prolonged use of resources with limited environmental damage and the most benefit for human societies.

On the other hand, it may be possible to find substitutes for the use of relatively scarce materials. For example, copper is quite rare and is used for, among other things, the conduction of electricity. When the purpose is to transmit information, copper wire can be replaced by fibre optic cables, which are made from the much more common element silica.

Several strategies can be used to make the exploitation of rocks and minerals more sustainable.

Efficiency of extraction

Increasing the efficiency of extraction seems an obvious starting point. For example, underground coalmines only remove between 55 and 70% of the coal present in the reserve. This is because of the technical difficulties of extracting the remaining coal in a safe and cost effective manner. Open-pit mining is more efficient at extraction than underground mining but some wastage still occurs.

To improve the efficiency of extraction, many mine wastes are now being processed for a second time. This allows valuable materials to be recovered and reduces the risk of pollution from stored mine waste. New extraction methods include chemical treatment of the waste, which extracts much of the valuable mineral still within it. Biological treatment with microorganisms can also be used to extract more product from the waste.

Improvements in the performance of the machines used in mining and processing also increase the efficiency of extraction. Greater use of data analysis by computers is likely to lead to improvements as well. However, surface mining has more potential for an increase in efficiency of extraction than underground mining. This is because it is more difficult to predict geological conditions underground.

Efficiency of use and recycling

Recycling materials makes an important contribution to the sustainable use of rocks and minerals. Many manufactured goods, from cars to steel cans, are recycled in most countries. Most metals can be recovered and refined back to clean metals to be used by industries again. This uses less energy than processing the ores or concentrates to make metals. Many countries still have the potential to recycle far more materials in the future (Figure 1.19).

Attempts to use minerals such as metals more efficiently include engineering solutions. For example, it is possible

Figure 1.19 Scrap metal in a scrapyard.

to design steel beams used in buildings to have the same strength but use less steel. In the 1980s titanium became very expensive and there was an incentive to design products that used less of this metal. Many countries may in the future require car manufacturers by law to take back their products when they are finished with. It is hoped this will encourage them to make more durable products that use less minerals and last longer.

The major way in which governments are trying to encourage a more sustainable use of minerals and rocks is to pass laws that requires manufacturers to become responsible for recycling and reuse. For example, the Waste Electrical and Electronic Equipment (WEEE) Directive of the European Union, was passed in 2002. Although some of the items covered are not mineral rich (for example televisions are only 6% metal) others are: a typical cooker is 89% metal.

SELF-ASSESSMENT QUESTIONS

1.7 Suggest one advantage of *in situ* waste treatment and one advantage of *ex situ* waste treatment.

1.8 Describe three ways in which recycling materials is important for the sustainable use of resources.

Summary

After completing this chapter, you should know:

- the characteristics of named igneous, sedimentary and metamorphic rocks
- how these rocks are formed in the rock cycle
- the features of surface and subsurface mining
- how we decide to extract rocks and minerals
- the environmental, economic and social impacts of rock and mineral extraction
- how landscapes damaged by rock and mineral extraction can be restored and how successful these strategies can be
- the meaning of sustainable resource and sustainable development
- how rocks and minerals can be used sustainably.

End-of-chapter questions

1 An important local fishery exists in Lake Titicaca, Peru. The lake is 100 km from a mercury mine. A study was carried out on the levels of mercury in fish caught in the lake. Some of the data are shown in Table 1.3.

Length of fish / mm	Mercury concentration / ppm
104	0.20
124	0.32
125	0.30
128	0.20
136	0.30
140	0.32
146	0.35
159	0.45
160	0.35
178	0.55
196	0.85

Table 1.3 Fish and mercury levels

The same data are plotted in Figure 1.20.

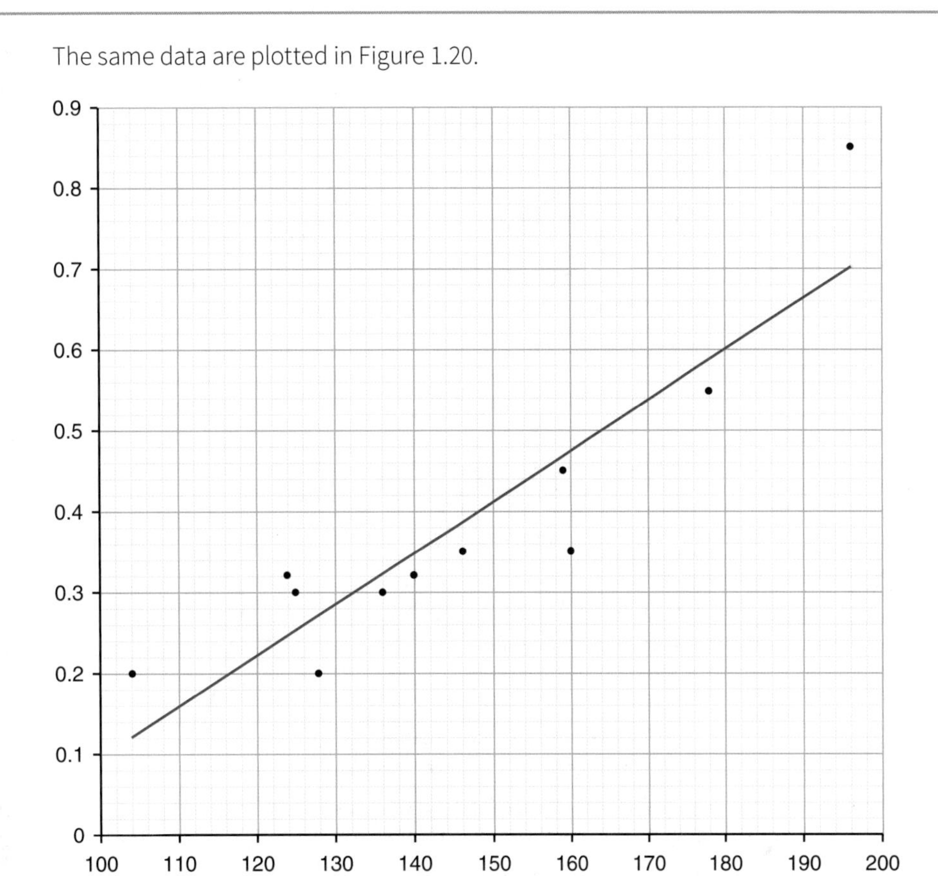

Figure 1.20 Fish and mercury levels.

a Copy and complete the graph by labelling the axes. **[2 marks]**

b Describe and suggest an explanation for the relationship shown by the data in Figure 1.20 and Table 1.3. **[5 marks]**

c The recommended maximum level of mercury in food is 0.30 ppm. Suggest the maximum length of fish that people in this area should consider eating on a regular basis. **[1 mark]**

d It was suggested that the source of the mercury in the fish in the lake was a mercury mine 100 km upstream. To test this, water samples were taken from a river as shown in Figure 1.21. They were analysed to discover the concentration of mercury.

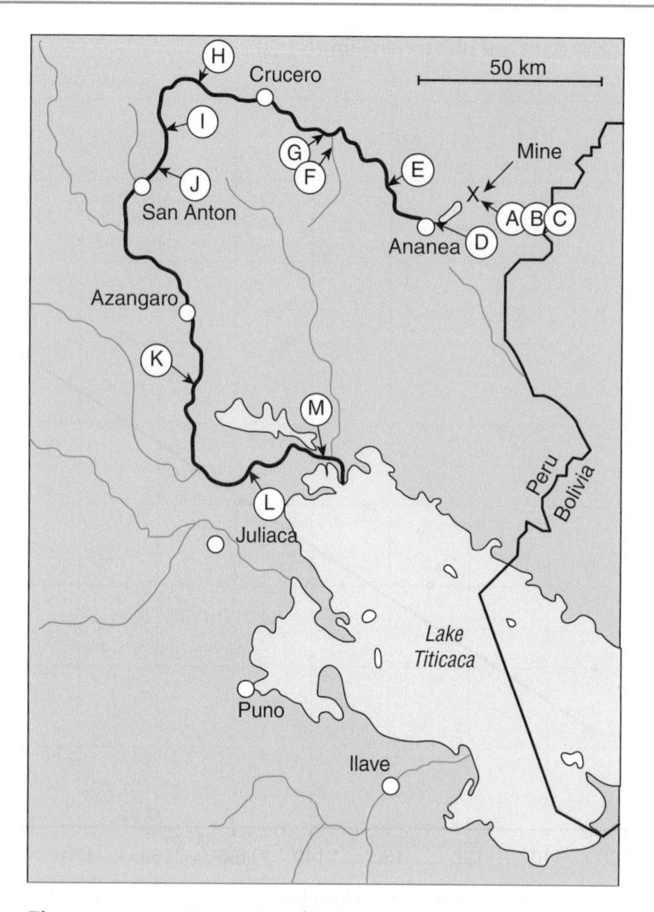

Figure 1.21 Mercury sampling

The data from some of the sites are shown in Table 1.4.

Sampling site	Mercury concentration / microgram per litre of river water
A	0.12
B	0.26
C	0.10
F	0.38
G	0.06
H	undetectable
J	undetectable
K	undetectable
M	undetectable

Table 1.4 Mercury sampling.

State and explain the conclusion you would reach from these data about the source of the mercury in the fish. **[3 marks]**

2 Aluminium is produced from bauxite. Five tonnes of bright red bauxite are made into 2 tonnes of a white powder called alumina (aluminium oxide) in an alumina plant. The bauxite is usually obtained from open-pit mines. Hot caustic soda solution is added to the crushed rock to get rid of impurities. The alumina is then converted into 1 tonne of aluminium in a smelter. An electric current is passed through the alumina and molten aluminium is siphoned off.

- **a** State the name given to any rock that contains a valuable metal. **[1 mark]**
- **b** Calculate the mass of solid waste that would be produced from the processing of 25 tonnes of bauxite. **[3 marks]**
- **c** Calculate the mass of bauxite that would be needed to produce 25 tonnes of aluminium. **[1 mark]**
- **d** Suggest two environmental consequences of aluminium production after the bauxite has been mined. **[3 marks]**
- **e** Explain how the landscape may be restored after bauxite mining is finished. **[3 marks]**

3 Figure 1.22 shows a deep coal mine and the area around it.

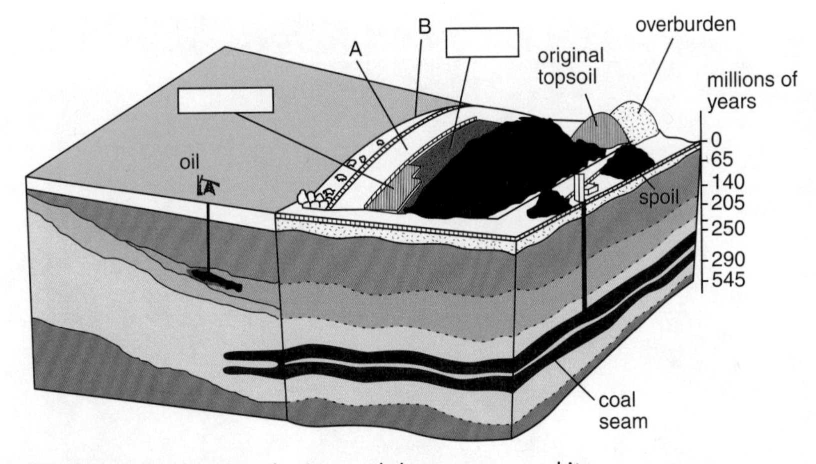

Figure 1.22 A deep coal mine and the area around it.

- **a** State the rock type to which coal belongs. **[1 mark]**
- **b** Explain how the coal is extracted from the location shown in Figure 1.22. **[3 marks]**
- **c** State the age of the coal and oil deposits shown in Figure 1.22. **[2 marks]**
- **d** Copy and complete the labelling of the diagram by adding the correct names to the boxes. **[2 marks]**
- **e** Explain, using the names and letters, how the spoil heap has been reclaimed. **[5 marks]**

4 Figure 1.23 shows how the production of a mineral changed over time.

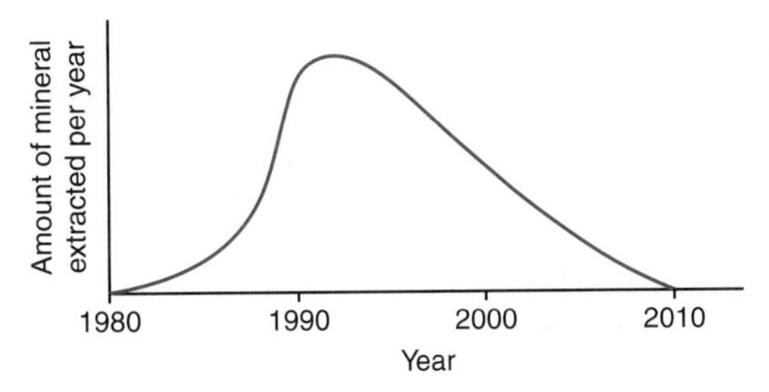

Figure 1.23 The production of a mineral over time.

- **a** Choose a word from the list to describe the situation for this mineral in 1980, 1993 and 2010. **[2 marks]**

  exhaustion   peak production   discovery
- **b** Suggest what might have happened between 1993 and 2010. **[3 marks]**
- **c** Suggest how the mineral could have still been extracted after 2010. **[2 marks]**

The Island Copper Mine, Vancouver Island, British Colombia, Canada

The Island Copper Mine started production in 1971. It was finally closed in 1995 because there was insufficient ore left to make further extraction economically feasible. It was an open-pit mine and employed 900 people at its peak. During its lifetime 363 million tonnes of ore were extracted. The ore contained an average of 0.41% copper and 0.017% molybdenum. Extraction involved the removal of a billion tons of material in all, at a maximum rate of 170 800 tonnes per day. The pit produced by the mine was 2400 m long, 1070 m wide and had a depth of 400 m. The waste from the mine, which is called tailings, was disposed of in the sea. Seepage from the mine was restricted by a 33 m deep, 1 219 m long seepage barrier. The final production figures for the mine were 1 299 978 tonnes of copper, 31 000 tonnes of molybdenum, 31 700 000 g (31.7 tonnes) of gold, 335 994 324 g (336 tonnes) of silver and 27 tonnes of rhenium. These materials were exported to many countries around the world (Figure 1.24).

Figure 1.24 Open Pit Copper Mine, Vancouver Island, British Columbia, Canada

During its lifetime the environmental impact of the mine was carefully managed and monitored. All water run-off from dumps was controlled by a system of water management.

The impacts of the mine can be summarised under four headings.

- Physical: 400 million tonnes of tailings deposited into Rupert Inlet reduced its depth by 40 m. These materials, leading to a reduction in its biodiversity, regularly smothered the bottom fauna. A small rocky beach was formed where once it was sand, and copper-tainted sediment was found many kilometres away.
- Chemical: Over 25 years of monitoring, no trends were seen in any of the variables measured (pH, oxygen and dissolved heavy metals including copper, manganese and zinc).
- Biological: Although there was evidence that the water became more turbid, there was no measurable effect on productivity of the biological systems. The reduction in species diversity on the seabed was the biggest effect. A site near the mine had 15 species in 1995, whereas one unaffected site had 41. Despite early fears, no dead zone, an area with no life, was created.
- Tissue metal: There was very little evidence of an increase in the levels of any metals in the tissues of animals. This suggest that neither bioaccumulation nor biomagnification was occurring.

Port Hardy, a small town near the mine, originally had a population of 700 that grew after the opening of the mine to have a population of over 5000. The company spent over 2.9 billion US dollars (USD) in its 25 years of life. From early on during the life of the mine, tax was paid at a rate of about 3 million USD year^{-1}. The mining company provided 400 houses for its employees, with another 600 being constructed by other developers. All the necessary services, including sewage, roads and water, were paid for and provided by the mining company. The mine's opening also led to the provision of a hospital, a swimming pool, a theatre and some parks.

The plans for the eventual mine closure were in place even when its opening was being prepared in 1969. Nearly 5 million tonnes of overburden were kept and used for land reclamation during the 25 years of the mine and after its closure. The features of the mine covered by the closure plan were the open pit, the waste rock piles, the sea and the buildings.

The open pit was flooded with seawater after closure, creating a 300 m deep lake with an area of 215 hectares. The possibility of using this lake for aquaculture was considered.

A further 200 hectare area was recontoured and over 600 000 alder and lodge pole pine seedlings were planted during the life of the mine. The hope is that a cedar–hemlock forest will eventually result from this, as a result of succession.

Questions

1 Explain why the mine was closed in 1995.

2 Calculate the percentage of the total material extracted that was waste. Quote your answer to two decimal places.

3 One of the biggest concerns about the operation of the Island Copper Mine was the possible effect of disposing the tailings at sea. Various studies were started as soon as the mine opened to monitor this. In one study, a commercially important top predator, the Dungeness crab (*Metacarcinus magister*) was checked for the levels of copper and other metals in its tissues yearly over the life of the mine.

The data from this study are given in Table 1.4

Year	Copper / mg kg^{-1} wet mass
1971	7
1972	6
1973	5.7
1974	8.1
1975	7.7
1976	9.7
1977	11.8
1978	11.6
1979	9.9
1980	8.5
1981	8.5
1982	10
1983	7.7
1984	9.1

Year	Copper / mg kg^{-1} wet mass
1985	6.5
1986	6.6
1987	6.4
1988	8.1
1989	9.9
1990	10.4
1991	9
1992	9
1993	10
1994	11
1995	9
1996	10.3
1997	12.3
1998	9.3

Table 1.4 Copper levels.

a Copy and complete Figure 1.25 using the data in Table 1.4.

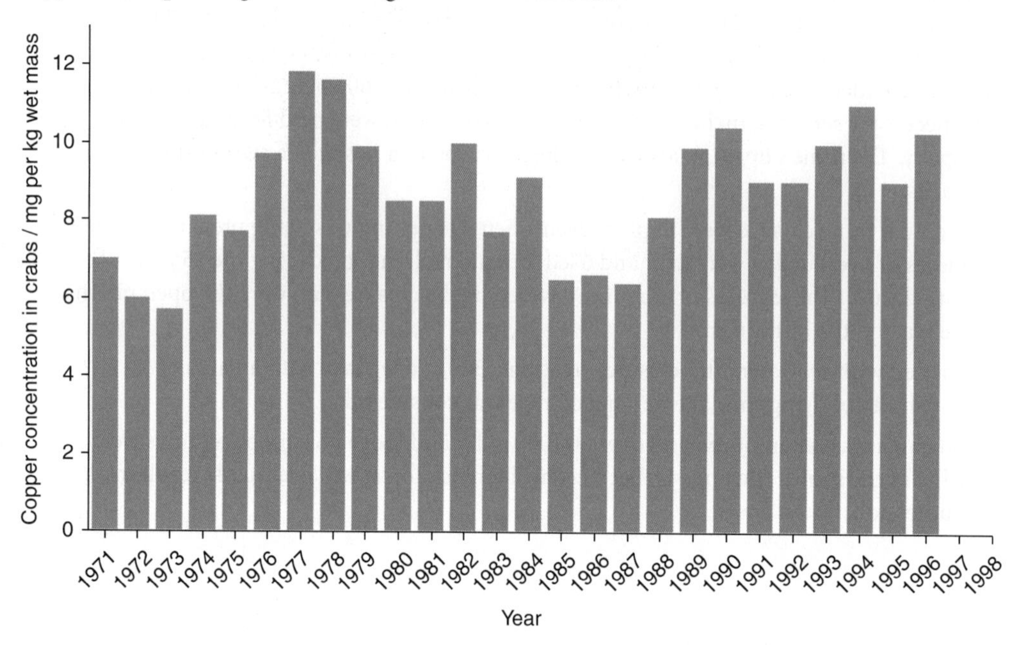

Figure 1.25 Copper levels in crab tissue.

b i Describe the trend in copper in crab tissue from the opening of the mine until 1977.

ii In the late 1960s the Society for Pollution and Environmental Control (SPEC) was formed in British Columbia where Island Copper is situated. This organisation was involved in actively campaigning against industrial pollution. Write a brief assessment of the situation with regard to copper in the Dungeness crab as it might appear in a report to SPEC in 1978.

iii Write a new report updating SPEC on the situation for a new report in 1996.

c Suggest why *Metacarcinus magister* was chosen to monitor copper levels in the tissues of living things in this study.

Chapter 2
Energy and the environment

Learning outcomes

By the end of this chapter, you will be able to:

- name fossil fuels and describe how they are formed
- classify energy sources into renewable and non-renewable types
- describe how different energy sources are used to make electricity
- explain the environmental, economic and social consequences of different energy sources
- discuss different demands for energy
- explain how energy sources can be managed efficiently
- discuss the current research into possible new energy sources
- describe the impact of oil pollution
- describe how the impacts of oil spills can be minimised.

The need for power

Many scientists agree there is a link between the burning of oil, coal and gas and climate change. While there are still reserves of these fuels, the decision facing governments around the world is whether we should be using them.

Fuel is enormously useful, very valuable and very important politically, but tackling global warming might mean choosing to leave the untapped reserves in the ground.

While not all scientists will agree on all facts of climate change, the consensus is that human activity is a significant cause. It is also recognised by governments that the rise in global temperature should be halted at 2 °C. While this is not a 'safe' level, it is thought to be enough to prevent the worst impacts of the temperature changes. There also seems to be a link between the amount of carbon products emitted into the air as gases through burning and climate change.

So what are the options? Could the world ignore all the oil, coal and gas that has not been extracted to prevent emission of more carbon? How would vehicles operate without these sources? Could the world cope with using other forms of energy production? Would all governments work together in this way? At the moment, these are questions without answers. As you work through this chapter you will see that many of the potential answers are not straightforward.

Figure 2.0 The human population is using greater amounts of energy; this has impacts on the world around us.

2.1 Fossil fuels

The world population uses energy in a variety of ways, much of it by direct combustion (burning) to produce heat and light. Combustion requires a suitable fuel source, typically something with large amounts of carbon.

While items such as wood contain carbon and are used for burning, there are other sources that are far more 'energy dense', producing a greater amount of heat from a unit of fuel. These sources, natural gas, coal and oil, are often known as **fossil fuels.**

How fossil fuels are made

Despite the name, fossil fuels are not made from fossils, but is it a useful term to reflect upon the amount of time it takes to produce them. Fossil fuels are produced from the decay of plants and animals. These remains formed organic matter that became covered in layers of sediment.

Over millions of years, and buried deep in the ground by the addition of further layers of sediment, the organic material was subjected to great pressure and heat.

KEY TERM

Fossil fuel: a carbon-based fuel, formed over many millions of years from the decay of living matter

The precise conditions, and the type of animal and plant material available, determined whether coal, oil or natural gas is produced.

Figure 2.1 shows how coal is formed. The processes for oil and gas are similar and are shown in Figure 2.2.

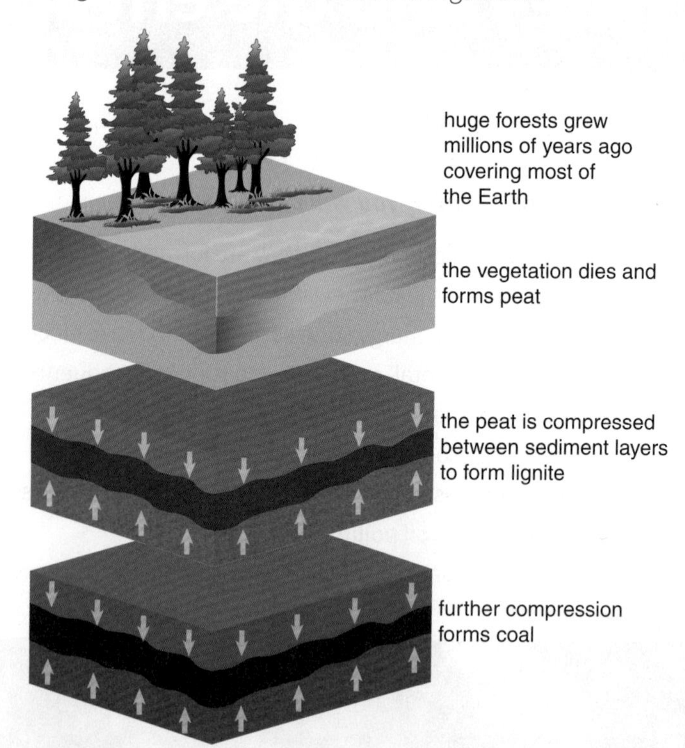

Figure 2.1 The process by which coal is made.

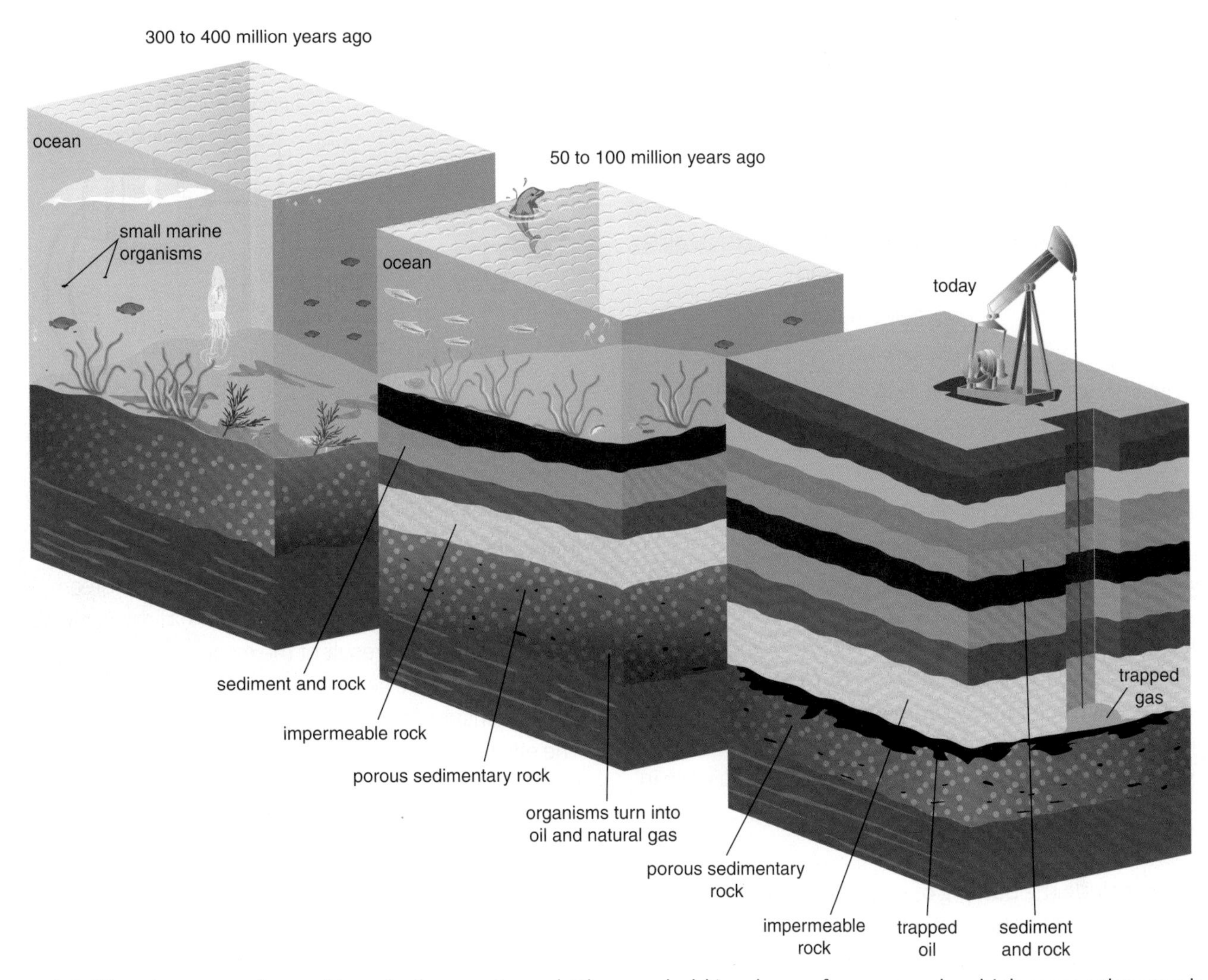

Figure 2.2 Oil and gas were formed in a similar way to coal. They are held in a layer of porous rock, which means they can be accessed by drilling.

In both cases the dead remains from animals and plants are buried under many layers of sediment, so extracting them involves digging or drilling deep underground. The length of time needed to create fossil fuels means that there is only a limited supply.

2.2 Energy resources

The demand for energy is increasing worldwide. There are a number of reasons for this:

- increasing population size
- increasing industrialisation and urbanisation
- improvements in standards of living and expectations.

In order to meet the demand for energy, existing sources need to be used more efficiently and methods that until now have been too difficult or too expensive to use need to be explored further. Improvements in engineering and advances in technology may well reveal new opportunities.

Types of energy sources

Different types of energy sources can be described by whether they are limited resources or available in unlimited supplies.

Limited sources of energy are often described as being **non-renewable**: as they are used they cannot be replaced.

Renewable sources of energy are those than can be replenished and therefore can be used over and over again.

KEY TERMS

Non-renewable: an item or resource that exists in a finite amount that cannot be replaced

Renewable: an item or resource that will not be used up or can be replaced

Table 2.1 provides a list of the most common examples of renewable and non-renewable types of energy. More detailed descriptions and explanations of the different types will follow later in the chapter.

Non- renewable energy sources	Renewable energy sources
Oil	Geothermal power
Coal	Hydroelectric power
Natural gas	Tidal power
Nuclear power	Wave power
	Wind power
	Solar power
	Biofuels, e.g. bioethanol, biogas and wood

Table 2.1 Classification of energy sources.

While some of the energy sources in Table 2.1 are easy to classify, others are more complex. Nuclear fuels, for example, will last for many centuries and are seen by many scientists as a more suitable replacement for fossil fuels. However, the source material (uranium) is only available in limited supply so, although will last a long time, it cannot be replaced.

Biofuels include the burning of wood, of which there is only a limited amounts at any one point in time, but it is possible to replace felled trees with new ones, therefore it is classified as being renewable.

How energy sources are used

While many energy sources can be burnt (combusted) to produce heat or light, the main use for many of them is the manufacture of electricity.

Most electricity is generated by **electromagnetic induction**. This process was discovered in the 1820s by Michael Faraday, and it transforms kinetic energy (the energy from movement) into electrical energy using loops of a conducting material such as copper and a magnet. As the coils are rotated close the magnet, electricity is generated. Over many years the process within this **generator** has been made more and more efficient.

Clearly a power source is needed to rotate the coils. This comes from a **turbine** connected to the generator.

Turbines are designed to provide the rotary motion needed in the generator. This is typically done by passing a stream of gas or liquid over the turbine blades, causing a shaft to move.

Figure 2.3 shows a simple electricity generation system using a turbine.

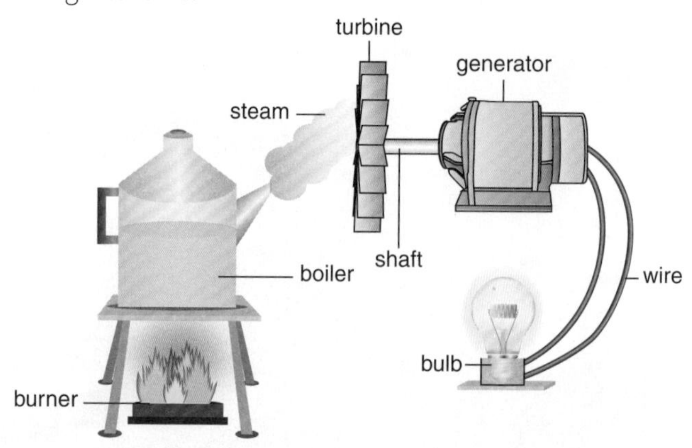

Figure 2.3 A simple electricity generation system.

In this simple system, a heat source (in the **burner**) heats up water (in the **boiler**), which is converted to steam. The steam passes through the blades of the turbine, causing them to move. As a result of the rotation on the shaft, the copper coils in the generator move, producing electricity that is transferred by conductive wires to the light bulb. The efficiency of the turbine can be increased by fitting more blades, or increasing the flow of gas or liquid that causes it to move by pressurising them.

Figure 2.4 shows a simplified diagram for the production of electricity from a geothermal source. In this case, cold water is pumped under pressure into a layer of hot rocks. The rocks heat the water and the hot water then returns to the surface under pressure. The hot water heats up a second supply of water using a heat exchanger. The steam produced in the second supply moves the turbine, which generates electricity in the generator. Water can then be re-used in the system to continue the process.

Energy sources such as fossil fuels, biofuels and nuclear and geothermal power are usually used to heat up water to produce steam. Other energy sources, such as wind, wave, tidal and hydroelectric power, are used to turn a turbine directly without the need to produce steam first.

KEY TERMS

Electromagnetic induction: a process used for generating electricity that uses the movement of a metal coil and a magnet

Generator: a machine that converts mechanical energy (such as movement) into electrical energy

Turbine: a machine, often containing fins, that is made to revolve by the use of gas, steam or air

Burner: a receptacle used to hold fuel as it is burned

Boiler: a vessel used to heat water to convert it into steam

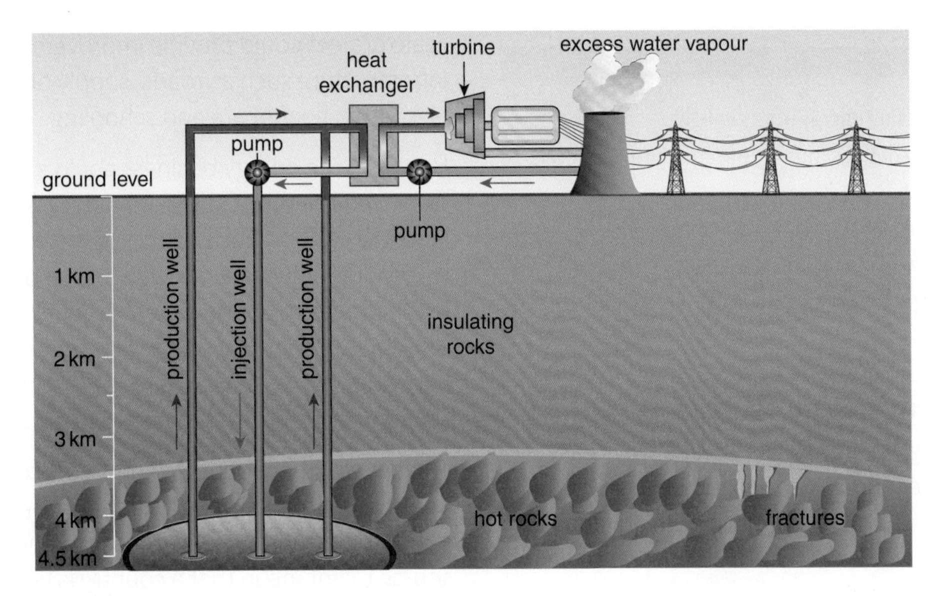

Figure 2.4 Production of electricity from a geothermal source.

Figure 2.5 shows a wind turbine. Note the addition of a gearbox to maximise the rotation of the shaft as it enters the generator. The brake will slow down or stop the rotor blade in very windy conditions to prevent the blade being damaged.

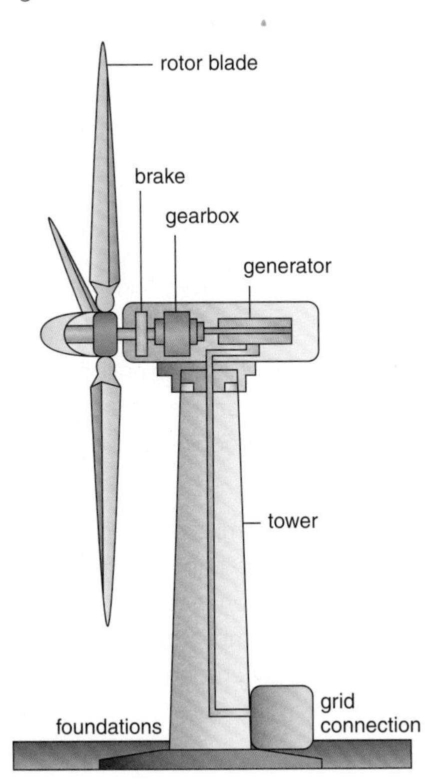

Figure 2.5 A wind turbine.

Solar power is the one main exception in the way that electricity is produced. Most electricity produced by this method uses photovoltaic cells. While the chemistry and construction of photovoltaic cells is quite complex, they all work on the principle that certain materials produce a small electric charge when exposed to light. Even though the electricity produced by one cell is small, a bank of cells organised into solar panels, and a group of panels organised into a solar array, can produce a significant amount of electricity.

Technological advances in the design and manufacture of photovoltaic cells are making them far more efficient, but many of the metals used within them are relatively rare and expensive to obtain.

Wave and tidal power systems both use the sea or large rivers to generate electricity, but the technology and availability of power can be very different.

Tidal power uses the natural rise and fall in the level of water in an area during a day. As the levels drop, water is held back by a tidal barrage – a small dam that releases water back through a turbine. This, in turn, generates the electricity using a generator. The amount of power that is generated is dependent on the change in tide level throughout the day.

Wave power also uses a turbine and generator to generate electricity, but these use the smaller differences in water levels that are caused by wind action. Power is therefore produced by channelling the energy of waves at sea, rather than by tides. Unlike tidal power, wave power is not limited to the regular pattern of the tides; however, electricity generation may stop when calm weather conditions mean that there is little or no wave production in an area.

KEY TERMS

Solar power: harnessing energy from sunlight

Tidal power: the use of tides (the natural change in sea levels) to generate electricity

Tidal barrage: a small dam used to hold back a tide

Wave power: the use of changes in the height of a body of water to generate electricity

Using the different energy sources

Deciding which energy source to use is not always easy because of different economic, social and environmental impacts. One source of power may have both advantages and disadvantages.

Economic factors

The supply of energy is expensive, particularly in a world where the demand is ever increasing and the supply from many sources is limited. If a fuel is in high demand and in short supply, then the price for that item rises. Clearly if a country has its own fuel supply then it can often use this more cheaply than importing other sources from other countries.

It is therefore logical for a country to rely on its local fuel supply, for example the Middle East relies on its own oil, Russia relies on its natural gas and the USA relies on its coal. Some countries have other naturally occurring sources they can take advantage of, such as high (and consistent) amounts of sunlight near the equator or geothermal energy (heat from underground rocks) in areas such as Iceland.

While plentiful supply and ease of access might be good economic arguments for using certain types of fuel, some countries face an economic barrier that prevents them from using certain energy sources. The cost of investing in technology, for example, might prevent a country or region developing solar power even though it has a plentiful supply of sunlight.

Social factors

The impact of different fuel sources will depend on the local area and the industry that it supports: the mining of an area for coal or drilling for oil might mean that the land is no longer available for agricultural use, but the new industries might mean greater local employment. The increase in industry locally might also mean that other businesses are needed to supply the needs of the energy business and its workers. The development of a large-scale project could provide improvements to the local infrastructure such as roads, supply of mains water and electricity, healthcare and schooling.

However, the energy business could also cause the displacement of a whole community, for example if the land in a valley is flooded during the construction of a dam to develop hydro-electric power. The development of new technologies might be a great asset to a community if it brings new manufacturing opportunities to the area, but might be seen as a disadvantage for those working in a sector that then starts to decline.

The development of new energy sources can change the political relationships and trading patterns between two nations. For example, developing a renewable energy source might mean that a country is less dependent on oil from one of its neighbours, reducing the trade in oil.

The investment in certain energy sources might also have health effects for the local population, for example dust from extraction, noxious fumes from combustion, or the risk of radiation from nuclear power.

Environmental factors

Impacts on the environment will vary from region to region. Many renewable sources (such as wind, solar and wave power) do not produce carbon dioxide emissions, which are linked to climate change. Biofuels will produce carbon dioxide when combusted, but the growth of the plants will also use carbon dioxide during photosynthesis. Fossil fuels are a major contributor to carbon dioxide in the atmosphere.

Other environmental impacts may be less obvious, but no less important.

- Pollution: spillage of fuel into the environment, such as oil spills in the ocean, can cause damage to wildlife. Burning fuels can also produce toxic gases and waste products.
- Changes to the ecosystem: extraction of fuels from underground can destroy habitats for a range of animals or their food sources. Even renewable sources can cause problems, for example the damming of a river for hydroelectric power generation can affect the ability of fish to breed.
- Visual impact: the nature of the landscape can be changed, for example large areas of solar panels or wind turbines impact on an area's natural beauty as well as changing the local ecosystem.

Table 2.2 summarises the advantages and disadvantages of different fuel types.

Fuel type	Advantages	Disadvantages
Fossil fuels (oil, coal, natural gas)	Plentiful supply in some locations. Extraction provides jobs Existing technology: the fuel is available for most countries to use	Carbon dioxide and toxic gases when burnt (impacting on climate change) Extraction causes damage to local area Limited supply: prices will rise as the supplies get smaller
Nuclear power (using uranium)	Does not produce carbon dioxide (impact on climate change) Small amount of fuel produces large amounts of energy Power plants employ lots of people	Risk of radiation leakage (impact on human health and environment) Waste products cannot be recycled as radiation active for centuries Limited supply
Biofuels (bioethanol, biogas, wood)	A renewable source: bioethanol and wood are both obtained from growing plants, biogas from the recycling of waste products Growing more plants uses carbon dioxide Potentially a plentiful supply	Carbon dioxide and other toxic gases produced when burnt A lot of land is needed to grow crops for fuel Potential removal of natural ecosystems to grow fuel crops
Geothermal power	Does not produce carbon dioxide Unlimited supply as uses the heat from the Earth as the power source	Can be expensive to install Only certain areas have suitable conditions
Hydroelectric power	Does not produce carbon dioxide Water can be reused for other purposes	Building of dams impacts the natural flow of water Villages and ecosystems may be destroyed when dams and reservoirs are built
Tidal power	Does not produce carbon dioxide Tidal movements not dependent on weather conditions	Limited to specific coastal areas Impacts on the tourist industry and local fishers
Wave power	Does not produce carbon dioxide A renewable source of power	Limited to specific areas Currently not very efficient, so large amounts of resources needed
Solar power	Does not produce carbon dioxide Sunlight is not a limited resource	Only efficient under certain weather conditions Generation only occurs in daylight hours Visual impact and potential damage to local ecosystems
Wind power	Does not produce carbon dioxide Uses a renewable resource	Not all locations are suitable Generation only occurs in certain conditions (at certain wind speeds) Visual impact Uses a large area

Table 2.2 Advantages and disadvantages of different fuel types.

CASE STUDY

Biofuels: the future of fuels or a misguided technology?

Figure 2.6 Aerial view of ploughed land on sugar cane plantation near Ribeirao Preto, Brazil. The crops from this plantation is used for biofuels.

Fuels that are extracted from crop plants are known as biofuels. The three most common types are **bioethanol**, **biogas** and wood: the growing and burning of timber to produce heat.

Bioethanol is a renewable energy that is mainly produced by fermentation of the sugar found in some crops. Crops that can provide this sugar include maize, wheat, corn, willow, Miscanthus and similar tall grasses, sorghum and Jerusalem artichoke. These crops are often grown especially for biofuel production. Bioethanol can be used as a substitute for petroleum (gasoline).

Biogas is the common name for a mixture of gases formed by the decomposition of organic matter in the absence of oxygen (anaerobic decomposition). Biogas's main component, methane, is highly flammable and is therefore suitable as a fuel source. Biogas can be produced from a range of organic wastes such as animal manure, food waste and household waste.

Bioethanol is believed to have great potential as a fuel for cars and trucks; it is already commonly mixed with petroleum or diesel oil to make these finite resources last longer.

Supporters of bioethanol production state a range of benefits.

- Easy to source: crude oil is a non-renewable resource whereas crops can be grown around the world for years to come.
- Reduces greenhouse gases: the burning of fossil fuels causes increased levels of carbon dioxide production. While the same is true of bioethanol, the plants grown to provide the fuel use carbon dioxide to produce sugars via the process of photosynthesis.
- Economic security: not all countries have a supply of oil, but many can grow suitable crops to produce bioethanol. There is less risk of a lack of supply if a country can produce its own fuel.

Those against increasing the use of bioethanol state a range of disadvantages.

- Food shortages: bioethanol is produced from crops with high quantities of sugar that also tend to be food crops. When there are people short of food across the world, it does not seem right to use potential food as fuel rather than feeding the hungry.
- Water usage: the crops need a lot of water, which can lead to a shortage of water in some areas for humans and their livestock.
- Industrial pollution: while the amount of carbon dioxide produced by bioethanol may be less than by fossil fuels, the factories that produce bioethanol do emit pollutants, which can affect the local population.
- Monoculture: the energy crops used to make bioethanol are grown in the same large fields year after year. This means the soil becomes short of nutrients, adding fertilisers can cause water pollution and the crop will also need the application of pesticides, which will affect the local ecosystem.

Questions

1 Why might the production of bioethanol be more attractive to a country with few oil supplies rather than one with large oil reserves?

2 Why, on a worldwide scale, is the growing of biofuels seen to be important, even though there are some clear disadvantages?

3 Why might a farmer choose to grow crops for bioethanol production rather than crops for food production?

KEY TERMS

Bioethanol: the creation of ethanol from fermentation

Biogas: the creation of methane from the breakdown of organic materials in an anaerobic digester

2.3 The demand for energy

All experts predict that human use of energy will continue to increase over the next 40 years, with the challenge of a limited supply of non-renewable resources. Nobody knows exactly how long the supplies with last. Predictions from many years ago have proved to be inaccurate as new deposits have been found and, as the price of the materials has increased, it has made mining or drilling in new areas economic.

What is certain is that the world price of non-renewable energy sources will continue to rise with the increase in demand and there is only a finite amount of these resources.

The demand for energy

A review of the energy use within different countries shows that there is a significant difference in the amount of energy used per person of different populations. There are a number of contributing factors.

Industrial demand

The use of energy per head of population is far lower in a traditional farming community that it is in a community that has become industrialised. Manufacturing requires the use of large quantities of energy in all stages of production.

Iron and steel production, for example, has an extremely large energy demand, using fuel to melt iron ore and refine it (Figure 2.7). Additional heat is also needed to shape the resulting product.

The advance in manufacturing techniques has resulted in technological advances in the products and also made them more affordable. This means that many items are no longer considered as luxuries but instead as necessities: more people want to buy them, and the

Figure 2.7 The production of iron and steel requires the use of very high temperatures, needing large quantities of energy.

increase in demand leads to increasing energy needs for increased production.

Domestic demand

The impact of more efficient manufacturing processes has meant that many goods have become more affordable. Televisions, for example, were once only seen in the homes of high earners in the developed world because they were so expensive to produce. They are now widely available, many households having more than one. The same trend can be seen with cars, computers and mobile phones, to name just a few.

Domestic demand is created by affordability and availability but is also driven by the need to keep up with the neighbours. Items that a decade ago would be seen as a luxury are now considered to be a necessity in many cultures. Most of these purchases increase the demand for energy supplies, most notably the need for a reliable electricity source.

Domestic demand and changing purchasing patterns have resulted in consumers in some countries wanting and expecting to be able to get fruit and vegetables that are not naturally in season locally. This demand can be met by either producing them in controlled conditions such as a glasshouse (see Section 3.4) or growing them in a more favourable climate and transporting them via air freight. In either scenario, the energy cost is significant.

Transport demand

The drive to develop efficient systems of production has meant that in many locations manufacturers are supplying customers across the globe. While this may decrease production costs it has significantly increased the costs of transportation. Some estimates suggest that there has been a fourfold increase in the number of shipping journeys in the past 20 years. There has also been a significant increase in the amount of air transport.

Both modes of transport require large amounts of fossil fuels to operate. Although the cost of transporting goods across oceans is significant, the cost savings in manufacturing still make them attractive to the end customer, albeit the amount of energy used in the process is greater than if produced locally.

Economic factors

Domestic demand for energy (and the purchase of manufactured goods) will be dependent upon the relative affluence of the people within a country. If economic conditions are good, there will be higher employment and more money to spend on luxury items. If economic conditions are poor, families will have less available money and will need to make savings, which could include reducing the use of fuel and the purchase and use of electrical items (which also use energy).

What is seen at a small scale (within a family) can also occur at a national level within the economy of a country. If a country has less income because of a reduction in manufacturing, it will have less ability to import foreign goods.

A poor economy will mean:

- less manufacturing (less energy used)
- fewer goods to transport (less energy used)
- an inability to purchase foreign energy supplies.

Sometimes the impact of a reduction of manufacturing in one country can have an impact on the global economy. A reduction in the economy of China in the mid-2010s meant a worldwide:

- reduction in demand for steel
- a decrease in the amount of manufactured goods transported by ships
- a decrease in the price of oil (because worldwide demand had decreased as a result of the two factors above).

Climate

Comparing the energy usage in one country with another is also complicated by the prevailing weather conditions.

People living in a temperate climate are likely to experience colder winters than those living in a more equatorial climate. The energy demand for heating in colder climates is likely to be far higher. In the winter months, the population also experiences fewer hours of daylight, with a corresponding increase in use electric lighting.

Climate change has resulted in extremes of weather that have not been experienced in over a generation, for example excessive cold and heat to name but two. These have resulted in increased energy consumption, particularly from those living in urban areas, either through the need for additional heating or the installation and operation of air-conditioning units.

SELF-ASSESSMENT QUESTIONS

2.1 Table 2.3 shows the approximate amount of energy used per head of population in a year

Country	Energy used per head of population / watts year^{-1}
Eritrea	188
Iceland	22 560
Sri Lanka	636
USA	9538

Table 2.3 The approximate amount of energy used per head of population in a year (expressed as watts year^{-1}).

a What percentage of the annual energy use of a person from Iceland is used by an equivalent person from Eritrea?

b Explain the reasons for the differences in the energy use between the two higher countries and the two lower use countries.

2.2 Iceland relies mainly on geothermal energy as its power source. Describe how this could be used to generate electricity.

2.3 It has been stated that a healthy or strong world economy is poor news for energy use. Describe why this might be thought to be the case.

2.4 Conservation and management of energy resources

As identified above, the world is faced with an increased need for energy because of an increasing population, a greater demand by industrialisation and improved living standards. It is not known how long supplies of non-renewable fossil fuels will last, and there is currently insufficient generation from renewable sources to meet all of the world's needs.

What are the options for resolving this situation? Would governments agree to all countries taking a share of the available energy resources? If so, what about countries that are colder and need energy to keep warm and use lights in the winter months? Should industrialised countries cut back on their use of energy while others catch up?

It is unlikely that any of these situations would be agreed upon by all countries. However, there could be agreement on careful management of the resources that are used.

Strategies for effective energy use

Reduce consumption

Energy use has increased rapidly within the last decade, and there is the prospect of an energy gap: a difference between the potential demand and the available supply. When this occurs, it means power cuts and, in the case of fuels such a petroleum, the risk of fuel rationing.

It may be possible to use more equipment and less energy if the equipment uses energy more efficiently, i.e. there is less waste. One example would be to reduce the amount of energy used to heat a building. In colder climates, a large proportion of energy is used to heat buildings so that they are at a suitable temperature for people to live comfortably.

A standard house loses heat through a variety of routes. Figure 2.8 shows the proportions lost.

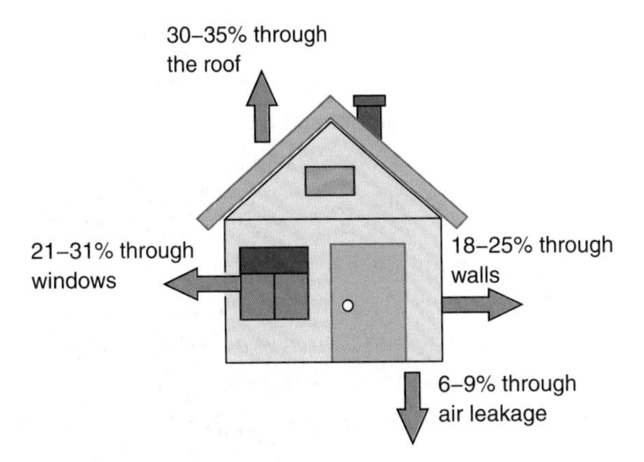

Figure 2.8 The percentage of heat lost from an insulated house in a temperate climate.

How can this heat loss be reduced? There are a number of different technologies that can be used, one of them being insulation. Using a construction material with good insulation properties will prevent loss of heat to the air in the same way a blanket keeps a person warm. Less heat lost will mean less energy is used in replacing it. In our example house in Figure 2.8, it would be possible to add an insulation layer into the roof space (sometimes called loft insulation). This is where most heat is lost, so an investment in this area is likely to have the largest impact. Similarly, a lot of heat can be lost through the walls so including an insulation layer here will also reduce energy use. Some homes are built with a cavity between the inside and outside walls. If this gap is filled with an insulating material, heat will pass through far more slowly than if this space was filled with air. Figure 2.9 shows the construction system for cavity insulation.

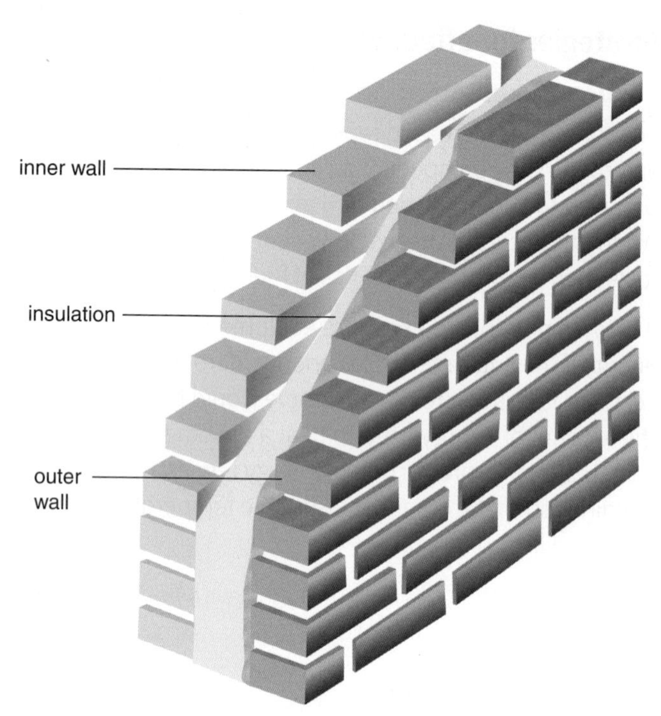

Figure 2.9 Heat from within the house is prevented from escaping by an insulation layer inserted between the two walls. This cavity wall insulation can be made from a variety of insulating materials.

In our typical house in Figure 2.8, a lot of energy is lost through the windows. A reduction in window size would reduce this energy loss, but is likely to increase the amount of energy used from artificial light. Instead, energy use can be reduced by double glazing the window. This technique uses two panes of glass with a gap in the middle to act as an insulator. The gap needs to be filled with a clear material (unlike cavity wall insulation). This sealed gap is sometime filled with an inert gas such as argon, or might simply be filled with air. The fact that the gap is sealed will improve the insulation properties of the window.

Further savings could be made using triple glazing (three panes of glass), but many householders consider this to be too expensive for the amount of energy they are saving.

Other ways of reducing consumption

While house design and the use of insulation may be major ways of reducing consumption, there are other practical things that can be done.

Electrical devices should be turned off when not in use. Many devices, such as televisions and computers have a so called 'standby' mode that enables them to be accessed rapidly. It has been calculated that the average device uses around 15 watts of power even when it is in this mode. Four or five devices left on standby in a household is the equivalent of leaving an electric light on permanently.

More energy-efficient devices should be bought. Appliances and machines use energy, either directly as fuel, in the case of vehicles, or indirectly by using electricity to operate. In either case, if newer more efficient versions are used there can be a significant saving in the amount of energy used.

While vehicle models have changed, which makes a direct comparison difficult, it is estimated that in the USA cars averaged less than 15 miles gallon^{-1} in 1975 (6 km litre^{-1}) whereas in 2010 this figure has reached 33 miles gallon^{-1} (14 km litre^{-1}). The fuel used now is able to transport a vehicle more than twice as far as it could in the 1970s! However, developments in alternative fuels for vehicles and further developments in engine technology are still needed to meet rising demand.

Some countries have offered 'scrappage' schemes to remove inefficient machines from use, whether that be electrical appliances or vehicles. In these types of schemes, the consumer is paid a sum of money to trade-in their old machine, which is then recycled. The purchase of a new version improves energy efficiency and, in the case of vehicles, has a great impact on air quality as well.

Energy from waste

The consumption of finite resources such as fossil fuels can be reduced by reusing existing materials to extract the energy from them before they are thrown away.

There are a number of schemes, currently all on a fairly small scale globally, that could become important in some countries.

Anaerobic digestion is the breaking down of organic waste (such as waste food and vegetation) using bacteria. This process takes place in a sealed container and produces methane, a flammable gas that can be used for a variety of heating purposes. The composted waste can be used on land to improve soil structure.

Household rubbish can be incinerated (burnt) to produce heat, which again can be used to generate electricity. While this process is disliked by many because it may produce poisonous gases during combustion, the waste from burning (ash) is small in volume and does not take up lots of space when disposed of.

The food-processing industries use large quantities of cooking oils in the preparation and manufacture of foods. These vegetable oils, once used, need to be disposed of. Schemes in many countries exist to collect these oils and recycle them into biofuels suitable for running vehicles. In some cases, it is an additive to fuels such as diesel, in others, the vehicles may run exclusively on this biodiesel.

Education

While new technologies and innovative designs can be developed, they will have little impact unless the benefits of the technology is communicated to others. Many countries have set up special energy conservation departments to help promote new ways of thinking and the purchase of more energy-efficient systems. This education process is not always easy; investment in new equipment for the home or factory might be expensive, and more expensive than a traditional method. Research has shown that while individuals are concerned about the environment and the use of natural resources, they are not often prepared to pay extra to care for it.

The educational message must be that significant savings in energy bills can be made over the longer term by reducing energy use, even if there is an initial cost. This education should be re-enforced by governments insisting that energy-efficiency ratings are provided for

CASE STUDY

A house that needs no energy: is it possible?

The challenge for many designers is to develop a house that requires as little energy input to run it as possible (Figure 2.10). This is particularly difficult in countries where winter temperatures drop below 0 °C.

The Passivhaus Institute in Germany has pioneered the development of building design technology that reduces the use of energy used to operate a house. In a comparable temperate climate, a Passivhaus (or passive house) can reduce the amount of energy used by up to 90% compared to a 'standard' house.

Figure 2.10 The use of different materials and technology can significantly reduce the energy use of a house.

Design features often include:

- high levels of insulation
- airtight construction
- high insulation windows (using special reflective glass and triple glazing)
- use of a heat exchanger to capture excessive heat produced by the occupants
- a ground heat exchanger to capture heat from lower levels in the ground
- solar panels to produce electricity and to heat water pipes.

To date it has been estimated around 20–25 000 structures have been built on this principle worldwide, the majority in Germany and Austria.

Questions

1 It has been calculated that the energy used within a Passivhaus is approximately equal to 1.5 dm^3 of heating oil per square metre of living space. How much oil would be used in a 'standard' house?

2 The energy savings from this building design are huge. Suggest reasons why so few houses have been built so far, even though so much energy can be saved.

3 Why might the aim of a house with no energy input not be possible?

new products to they can be compared with other models when making a purchasing choice (Figure 2.12).

In some countries, where the use of education to get the desired response is too slow, governments have passed laws to make changes happen more rapidly. Examples include:

- stricter building regulations requiring new constructions to be more energy efficient
- preventing the sale of inefficient types of light bulbs to force the use of other types.

PRACTICAL ACTIVITY 2.1

How well do materials reduce heat loss?

One way to reduce the amount of energy used is to make sure it is not wasted. In temperate climates a lot of energy is used to heat a building. This simple investigation will help to evaluate how much heat insulation will retain, reducing the amount of energy used.

Materials

- Three identical glass jars with lids, each lid with a hole for a thermometer or temperature probe
- Three temperature probes, for the top of each jar
- Boiling water
- A towel or sock
- A piece of paper

Method

- Set up the three jars in a row, each with a thermometer (or probe) through the lid (Figure 2.11).
- Label the jars A, B and C.
- Jar A: do not add any covering.
- Jar B: add a covering of paper.
- Jar C: wrap in the towel or put inside the sock.
- Add the same volume of boiling water to each jar and put on the lid on firmly.
- Record the temperature in each jar over the space of 1 h at 5 min intervals.
- Present your results in a table and in a line graph.

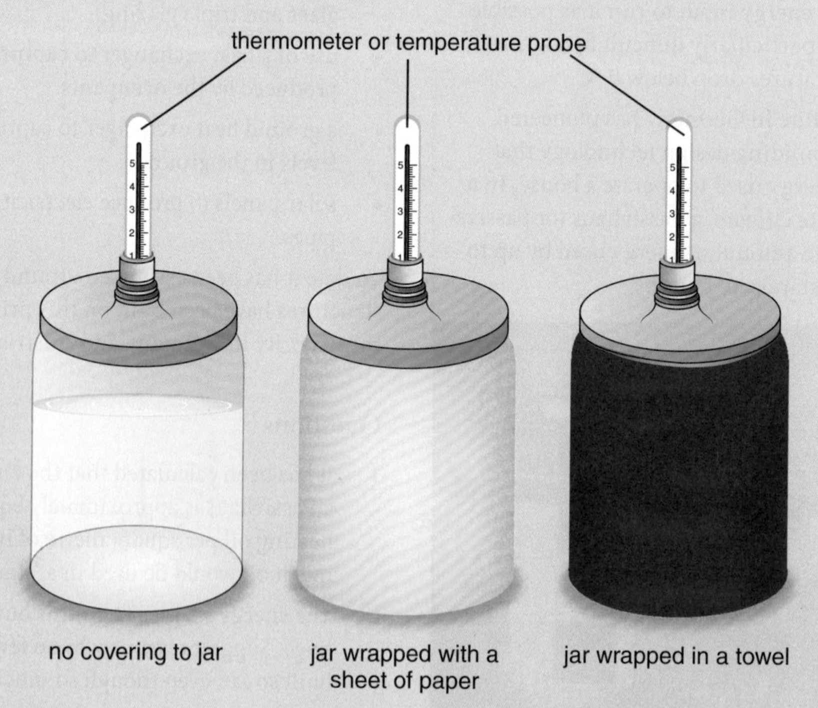

Figure 2.11 The experimental set-up.

Questions

1. What does the temperature changes in jars A and C tell you about the heat loss through glass and through an insulator?
2. Why was jar B included in the experiment?
3. What could be done to make the water stay hotter for longer?

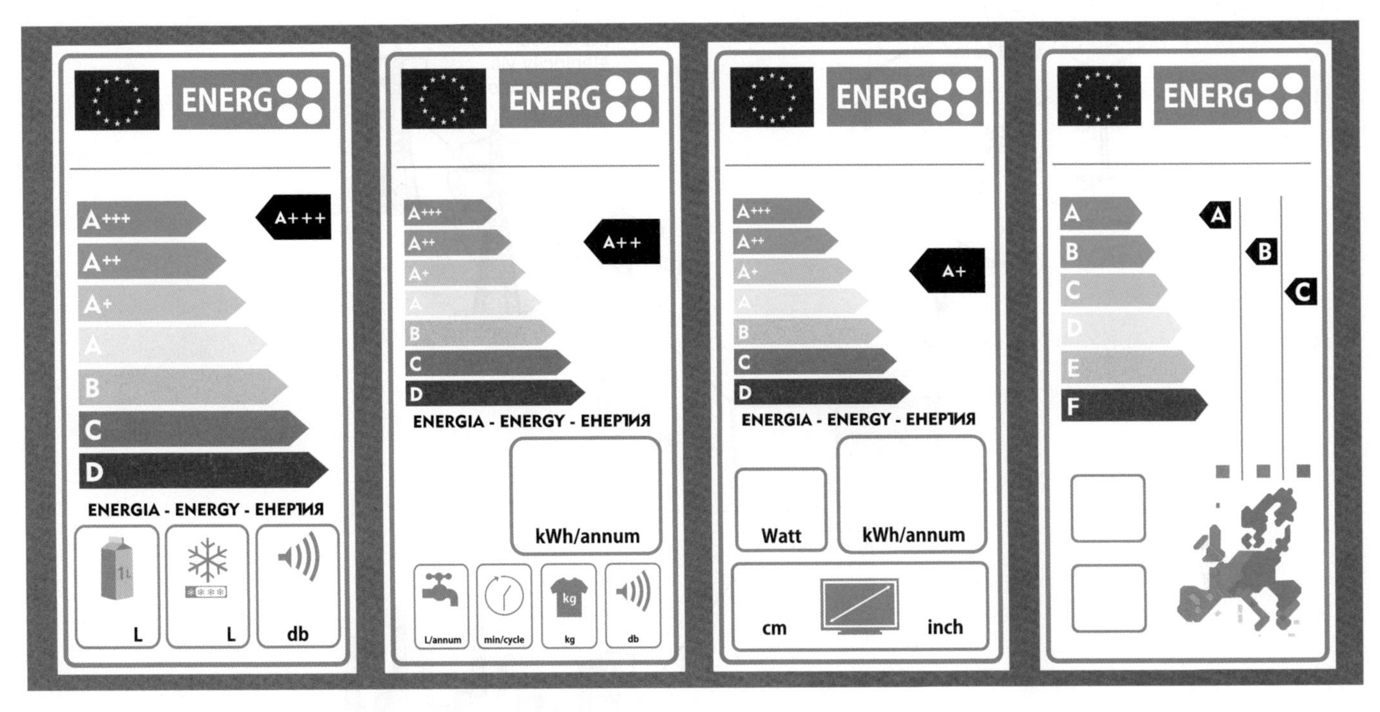

Figure 2.12 Examples of customer information labels for new products. If they all have the same type of information label, it is possible to compare the energy efficiency between models before deciding which one to buy.

Alternatively, some governments have provided grants to encourage the purchase of more efficient technologies. Examples of the use of these grants include:

- insulating older houses that are energy inefficient
- replacing older, inefficient heating boilers
- scrapping older, inefficient cars, which also emit more pollutants into the air.

While one method is not likely to have a major effect on its own, the use of education, legislation and grants together often have a significant effect.

Exploiting existing energy sources

The choice of which energy sources to use is often a complex decision. As identified earlier, there may be social and environmental factors to consider, but in many situations the economic cost has considerable influence. Some countries, for example, have large coal reserves but are not exploiting them because the cost of extraction is too high and it is perhaps cheaper to import fuel from elsewhere to provide the energy needed. As world resources become scarcer, the price for the fuel will rise, making coal extraction a suitable option in the future.

Inhabitants in most countries expect an uninterrupted supply of energy from their suppliers. Electricity shortages (power cuts), for example, disrupt everyday life and cause dissatisfaction within a population. The responsibility of the power generation companies is therefore to provide an uninterrupted supply, and the end-consumer may not be aware what power source has been used to generate the energy.

However, this is a problem for electricity suppliers, because the sources of energy with an available supply and that can be stored tend to be the fossil fuels, which are the types of energy source that are most polluting to the environment and non-renewable.

Renewable sources are not always consistently available, presenting problems for maintaining a consistent supply. The current solution is to use a renewable source, for example wind turbines on a wind farm, when possible and have a fossil fuel-powered power station available to supply energy when conditions are not right for wind generation (Figure 2.13).

This approach to energy supply means that there is a reliable source for industry and households and a reduction in the amount of fossil fuels used. It may be a more expensive option for electricity generators, but international agreements on emissions and use of fossil fuels can mean that the electricity generators are forced to use this type of system.

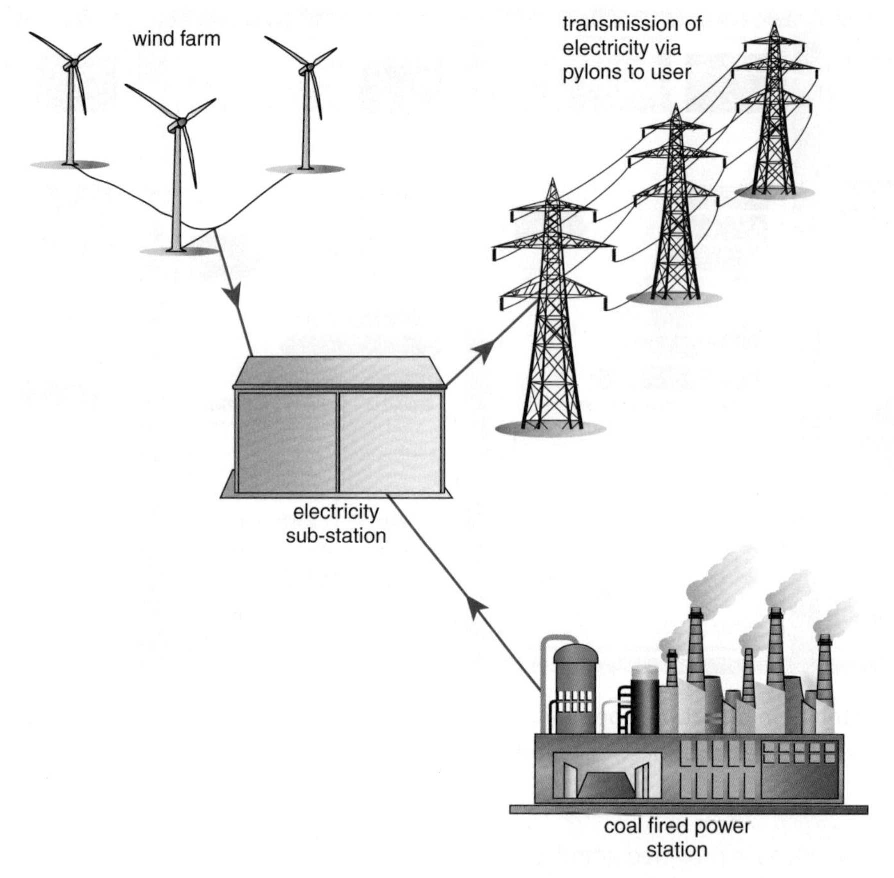

Figure 2.13 A mixed generation system. Electricity is supplied by the renewable source. When conditions are not optimum, additional supplies are provided by the power station.

Development of other renewable technologies, such as biofuels, could reduce the amount of fossil fuels that need to be burnt, but currently there are insufficient supplies of renewable sources worldwide.

Transport policies

While the manufacture of goods is a major use of the world's energy, the transportation of these items across the world and the use of vehicles for personal transportation are also significant users of energy. Governments have a large part to play in regulating the use of transport and encouraging more efficient use, which will mean less impact on the world oil reserves and improve air quality.

Current government initiatives include:

- regulations regarding the quality of exhaust gases from vehicles, and fuel efficiency
- restrictions on where vehicles may go
- taxation on fuels
- surcharges for travelling to certain places, such as cities, at peak times
- improving public transport so it is easier and cheaper to use than cars
- improving routes for cyclists and pedestrians
- encouraging car-sharing
- restricting when cars can be used, for example in New Delhi and Paris, regulations have been imposed that only allow cars with odd-number license plates to operate on odd-number dates and vice versa
- providing grants to buy more fuel-efficient vehicles
- providing grants for vehicles using cleaner technology, such as electric-powered vehicles.

Development of new resources

There are considerable concerns that the worldwide increase in demand for energy will not be met by the current development of renewable technologies, putting greater pressure on the finite supplies of fossil fuels. International agreements have also prevented the exploitation of potentially large supplies of oil, gas and coal in Antarctica, because the environmental impact would be too great and the damage to the ecosystem irreparable.

Research has identified potential sources of fuels that so far have not been utilised. The most prominent and controversial of these uses a technique known as **fracking**.

Hydraulic fracturing (fracking) involves blasting large amounts of water, sand and chemicals deep underground to extract oil and natural gas. In order to obtain these resources, a vertical hole, often 2–3 km deep, is drilled to reach the fuel-rich rocks (shale rocks).

Water, chemicals and sand are pumped down into the shale rock layer under pressure. This causes the rocks to fracture (split open), releasing the oil and natural gas, which are forced back to the surface and collected. Figure 2.14 shows the process.

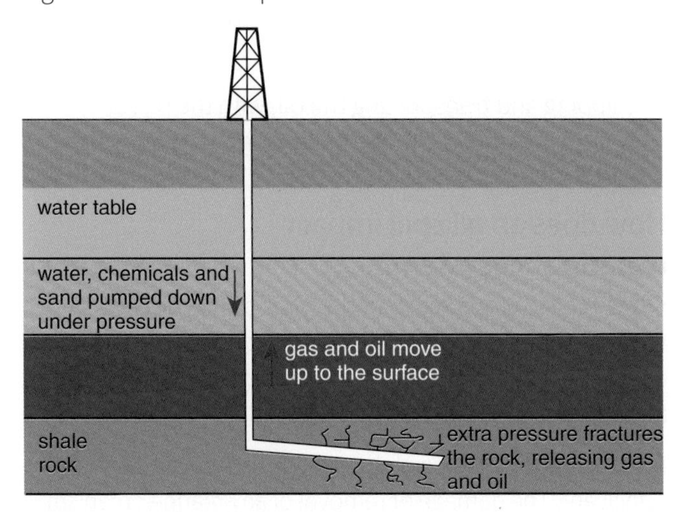

Figure 2.14 The fracking process: splitting open oil-containing (shale) rocks deep underground.

The three components each serve a different purpose:

- water is plentiful, easy to handle and can be pumped under pressure
- chemicals are added to assist the process and to stop the blockage of pipes, but many of them toxic
- sand is used to keep the cracks in the rock open as they occur, allowing the oil and gas to escape, it is sometimes referred to as the **proppant**.

KEY TERMS

Fracking: the common term for hydraulic fracking, the process of obtaining oil or gas from shale rock by the breaking open to rocks using water, sand and chemicals

Proppant: a material, such as sand, used to keep cracks in the shale rocks open to allow gas or oil extraction

Why the controversy? There are two main viewpoints concerning the use of fracking to obtain oil and gas (Table 2.4).

The arguments presented in Table 2.4 are based mainly on economic reasons in the first column and environmental reasons in the second column, but both sides have valid cases. The decision about whether fracking should be allowed in a country or not will ultimately be made by the government.

Fracking is safe and should be encouraged because:	Fracking is unsafe and should be banned because:
It allows access to more gas and oil, which are in limited supply	There is a risk of toxins from fracking entering the water table
Using gas and oil produces less pollution than burning coal, so it is better to extract extra supplies than rely on coal	The mixture of chemicals used is toxic and may affect local residents
It reduces the need to import oil or gas from other countries	Fracking uses a lot of water, which may reduce availability for other purposes
Shale rock is a long way underground, far below the water table, so poses little threat.	Noise pollution: fracking in an area will affect the local community
Oil and gas have been drilled for many years and this is just another deep method	Natural areas will be destroyed when new drills are developed
Fracking will supply many jobs locally	Fracturing lower levels of rock may cause additional earth tremors
	The longer term impact of the technology is not known and any damage done may be irreparable

Table 2.4 The views of those in favour and against the use of fracking.

SELF-ASSESSMENT QUESTIONS

2.4 Governments need to encourage businesses and individuals to become more energy efficient. They can do this in a number of ways, by legislation (to force a change) or by policies that encourage change. Copy and complete Table 2.5 with examples of programmes that have been introduced by governments. One has been filled in for you.

Government forces a change	Government encourages change
Restrictions on when cars may be driven	

Table 2.5 Methods used by governments to encourage energy efficiency.

2.5 It has been suggested that in a world with limited energy supplies governments should reach an agreement to share energy resources equally based on the number of people in their populations. Explain why this might be unfair.

2.5 Impact of oil pollution

Despite the research into other forms of energy, the world is still very reliant on oil. There are a number of reasons for this:

- it is relatively easy to store and transport
- it is easier to extract from the ground than solid materials such as coal
- it can be made into a number of different products
- it usually produces less pollution when burnt compared with coal.

The challenge for the world economy is that oil is not present in every location, so the supplies have to be transported great distances to reach the customers. The scarcity of supplies also means that those who have oil reserves have great economic power because the demand is so great.

Oil is a toxic material and spillages can cause great damage. Crude oil (the unprocessed form of oil, extracted straight from the ground) is thick, dark and sticky. It is also flammable. The impact of an oil spill can be devastating. Table 2.6 lists of some of the largest oil spills recorded and their causes.

Table 2.6 does not tell the whole story, however, because the amount of oil spilt does not necessarily indicate the level of environmental impact. The oil tanker Amoco Cadiz released a far smaller volume of oil than many of the other spillages listed but had a far greater impact because of the spread of the oil and the difficulty in cleaning it up. Oil spills at sea generally have a far greater impact than those on the land.

The three main causes for marine oil spills are:

- offshore oil extraction, with leakage from the rigs
- oil pipelines, with leaks in the pipework moving the oil to storage
- shipping and transporting the oil, with the risk of collision or damage to the oil tankers.

How does an oil spill impact a marine ecosystem?

While Table 2.6 lists many of the high-profile oil spills, environmental damage also occurs around the world as a result of small spills, the washing and cleaning of boats and through seepage from the seabed.

Regardless of the cause of the oil spill, the impact can be very significant. The damage or removal of any marine organism will have an impact on the food web for the area, potentially resulting in food shortages for animals that use the initially affected organism as a food source, or a population explosion of organisms if their predator has been removed.

Oil spills can cause the extinction of a species within a locality; if that species is already critically endangered, the loss of one more population may mean the loss of the entire species.

The long-term impact of an oil spill is not fully known; clearly some organisms are killed outright, but the long-term effects on the health of organisms consuming quantities of oil during the first generation and future generations is uncertain. Some of the known effects of an oil spill on particular organisms are listed in Table 2.7.

Oil slicks will also have an impact on the local economy of affected coastal areas. There may be a reduction in fish population, which will affect the livelihoods of fishers as well as affect the availability of food for locals. Many coastal areas rely on the tourist industry, and oil on beaches can have an impact on tourism by reducing an area's attractiveness as a holiday destination.

Oil spill	Location	Cause of spill	Approximate amount of crude oil spilt (thousand tonnes)
Kuwait Oil Lakes 1991	Kuwait	War	5000
The Lakeview Gusher 1910	USA	Onshore oil extraction	1200
Deepwater Horizon 2010	USA coast / Gulf of Mexico	Offshore oil extraction	575
Ixtoc 1 1979	Mexico / Gulf of Mexico	Offshore oil extraction	475
Atlantic Express 1 1979	Trinidad and Tobago	Oil tanker collision	287
Fergana Valley 1992	Uzbekistan	Onshore oil extraction	285
ABT Summer 1991	Angola	Oil tanker	260
Amoco Cadiz 1978	France	Oil tanker crash	223

Table 2.6 Location of large oil spills and their causes.

Organism or habitat	Description	Impact of oil
Phytoplankton	Microscopic organisms living in the seawater with the ability to photosynthesise. They provide food for many larger organisms	Oil floats on the surface of the water and prevents light from entering. This prevents the phytoplankton from photosynthesising, so they die
Fish	Different species are present throughout the oceans, some feed on phytoplankton and some prey on other fish. They are food for mammals and birds	Shortage of food due to reduction in phytoplankton. Oil floating on water surface prevents gas exchange. Fish become short of oxygen and die. Fish are also affected by the oil through direct contact, which affects their gills
Birds	Mobile over large distances, feeding on fish, often diving into the water to catch them. Others wade at the coastal edge feeding on fish and shellfish	Shortage of food as fish and other creatures die. May consume oil when eating fish (which can be toxic); when hunting for food, feathers become coated in oil, affecting their ability to fly and buoyancy
Mammals	Marine-based mammals, for example dolphins and whales, will often travel great distances chasing prey	Food sources are depleted by the impact of the oil. The mammals may also swallow oil while feeding, which will be toxic to them. A coating of oil will affect their skin, etc.
Reefs	A complex ecosystem, the habitat for a wide community of organisms	An oil slick will prevent sunlight from reaching plants and phytoplankton, preventing photosynthesis occurring. Lack of oxygen will cause other species to die. The impact on the balance of the whole reef might cause complete devastation. Areas of reef may become covered in oil
Beaches	A distinct ecosystem supporting a range of land-based and aquatic organisms	Oil is often washed in by tides, coating rocks. Organisms living in shallow water and rock pools may be killed by the toxic effects of the oil. Animal food sources will be affected

Table 2.7 The effects of an oil spill on different organisms and habitats.

SELF-ASSESSMENT QUESTIONS

2.6 Referring to Table 2.6, explain why the amount of oil spilt does not have a direct correlation with the amount of environmental damage that results.

2.7 Why does preventing light from reaching the surface of the sea have such a big effect on the marine ecosystem?

2.6 Management of oil pollution

As long as oil is being used and transported there will continue to be oil pollution incidents. Worldwide cooperation is allowing the development of strategies to reduce the number of marine oil spills, and avoid spillage of other substances that may affect the environment.

Reducing oil spills in marine environments

MARPOL

After many years and intense diplomatic negotiation, the International Maritime Organization, a United Nations (UN) group that supervises the safety and security of shipping, obtained agreement for the MARPOL treaty. MARPOL (which stands for Marine Pollution) is the International Convention for the Prevention of Pollution from Ships and sets out a number of regulations covering pollution by oil, sewage, rubbish and toxic liquids, among others. The initial agreement was signed in 1973, updated in 1978 and came into force in 1983. Prior to MARPOL it was common for ships to dispose of waste, or clean their storage tanks, in the middle of an ocean, with unknown environmental effects.

Under the MARPOL regulations, rules have been introduced to cover the process of transferring crude oil from one vessel to another while at sea, a common cause of smaller oil spills. All tankers must be certificated to show they have appropriate systems in place, and records to show that they are being used. Failure to comply with these regulations can result in a heavy fine or the ship not being given permission to leave port until suitable systems are in place and verified as working.

Tanker design

As well as regulations to ensure best practice by those transporting potentially damaging substances, attention has also been focused on the design of ships themselves. As highlighted above, while there may be larger oil spills on land, the ability of oil to spread on water makes the impact at sea far greater.

The most likely reason for a significant oil spill from a tanker is some form of damage to the hull. Clearly a hole in the hull of the boat will allow its contents to escape.

Two design features have been added to modern tankers. The first is an increase in the number of compartments contained within the hull of the ship; if there is damage in one section the contents of the whole hull are not lost. The second and more important development has been the introduction of **double-hulled** tankers. A double-hulled ship is one that has been built with two hulls, so that if there is damage to the outer layer (or plate) the contents are still held securely by the inner plate. Figure 2.15 illustrates this.

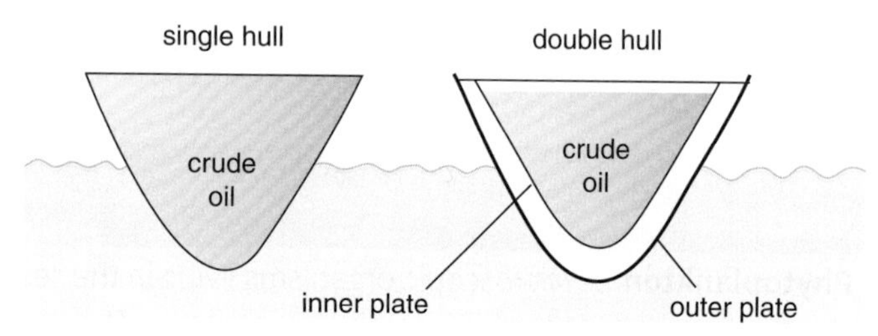

Figure 2.15 A cross-section through a single-hulled and a double-hulled tanker. The inclusion of another layer (plate) provides protection for the cargo if the hull is punctured.

The cost of building double-hulled tankers is significantly more than the cost of a single-hulled ship but the risks of oil spillage are far less. The cost of buying these new oil tankers has meant that phasing out single-hulled tankers has taken 25 years. While the use of double-hulled tankers has not prevented all spills, there is evidence of a significant reduction.

KEY TERM

Double-hulled: a ship design that uses a second layer, allowing the cargo to remain safe if the external layer is damaged

Minimising the impact of oil spills

Even with good planning and design oil can still be spilt. The main focus in such a situation is to reduce the impact of the spillage. The technique used will depend very much on local weather conditions, the proximity to land and calmness of the sea. There are various common strategies.

- Use of floating booms: a boom is a floating barrier that can be used to surround the oil slick and prevent it spreading to other areas. This process works well when the spill is covers a relatively small area and the sea is calm. It can also be used as a barrier to protect environmentally sensitive areas (such as a river estuary) while a spill is dealt with. Booms do not work very well when the sea is rough and stormy, conditions that sometimes were the cause of the damage to the ship.

- Detergent sprays: detergents help break down the oil slick into smaller droplets and disperse it. The smaller droplets of oil will float away and degrade over time. Detergents are most effective on smaller spills but recent research has suggested they can cause more environmental damage than the crude oil itself. Coral reefs appear to have a low tolerance to detergents.
- Skimmers: these clean the water without changing the chemical or physical properties of the oil. Using a material that oil easily attaches to, the skimmer drags oil off the seawater surface, which is then mechanically scraped off into a container. This system is often used once an oil slick has been contained within a boom. It is a very useful technique, but skimmers will not work effectively in rough or stormy sea conditions.

When oil reaches beaches, the only effective way to clean the beach it is to physically remove the oil by hand: a difficult and time-consuming operation.

Whichever method is used for collecting spilt oil, the authorities are then faced with the challenging job of disposing of it safely and in an environmentally sensitive way.

Summary

After completing this chapter, you should know:

- the names and formation of fossil fuels
- the classification of energy sources
- how energy is used to generate electricity
- the advantages and disadvantages of different energy sources
- the factors affecting energy demand
- strategies for management of energy resources
- the impact of oil pollution on marine and coastal ecosystems
- strategies for managing marine oil spills.

End-of-chapter questions

1. Some people argue that while it is a non-renewable resource, using a nuclear fuel such as uranium is a suitable replacement for fossil fuels. Give three pieces of evidence that might support this view. **[3 marks]**
2. Obtaining energy from the burning of household waste is one solution to meeting energy needs. Give one environmental advantage of using waste in this way and one disadvantage. **[2 marks]**
3. A company has produced a planning application to start fracking in your local area. Outline a case to present to the local planning board to object to this application. **[4 marks]**
4. Suggest reasons why the MARPOL agreement might not be as effective as it was intended to be. **[3 marks]**
5. Describe how an oil spill and the clean-up operations may have damaging effects on a coral reef. **[3 marks]**

6 Different fossil fuels produce different amounts of carbon dioxide and sulfur dioxide when burned. The table below shows the amount of carbon dioxide produced when you burn each fossil fuel to transfer the same amount of energy.

Fossil fuel	Units of carbon dioxide produced (based on oil = 100)
oil	100
gas	75
coal	150

a What is the most appropriate type of graph or chart to display this data? **[1 mark]**

b Draw your chart or graph to display the data in the table. **[2 marks]**

c From the table, gas appears to be the least environmentally damaging fossil fuel. However, what other factors do you need to consider before drawing this conclusion? **[3 marks]**

EXTENDED CASE STUDY

Exxon Valdez: an environmental disaster

The *Exxon Valdez* may not be listed among the largest oil spills in Table 2.6 but it has certainly proved to be one of the most environmentally destructive (Figure 2.16).

On 24 March 1989 the tanker had just left the port of Valdez in Alaska fully loaded with oil. An inexperienced junior officer in charge of the ship steered the tanker wide to avoid ice in the shipping lane and collided with the nearby Bligh reef. The tanker, the *Exxon Valdez*, was of single-hull construction, and the jagged rocks of the reef created a large hole in its side, allowing around 36 000 tonnes of oil to escape into the sea.

The local area, the bay of Prince William Sound, was soon covered in oil. The slick spread far and wide: oil was reported to have reached beaches over 1000 km away from the incident (Figure 2.17).

Figure 2.16 A spill of crude oil causes significant environmental damage and is costly to put right.

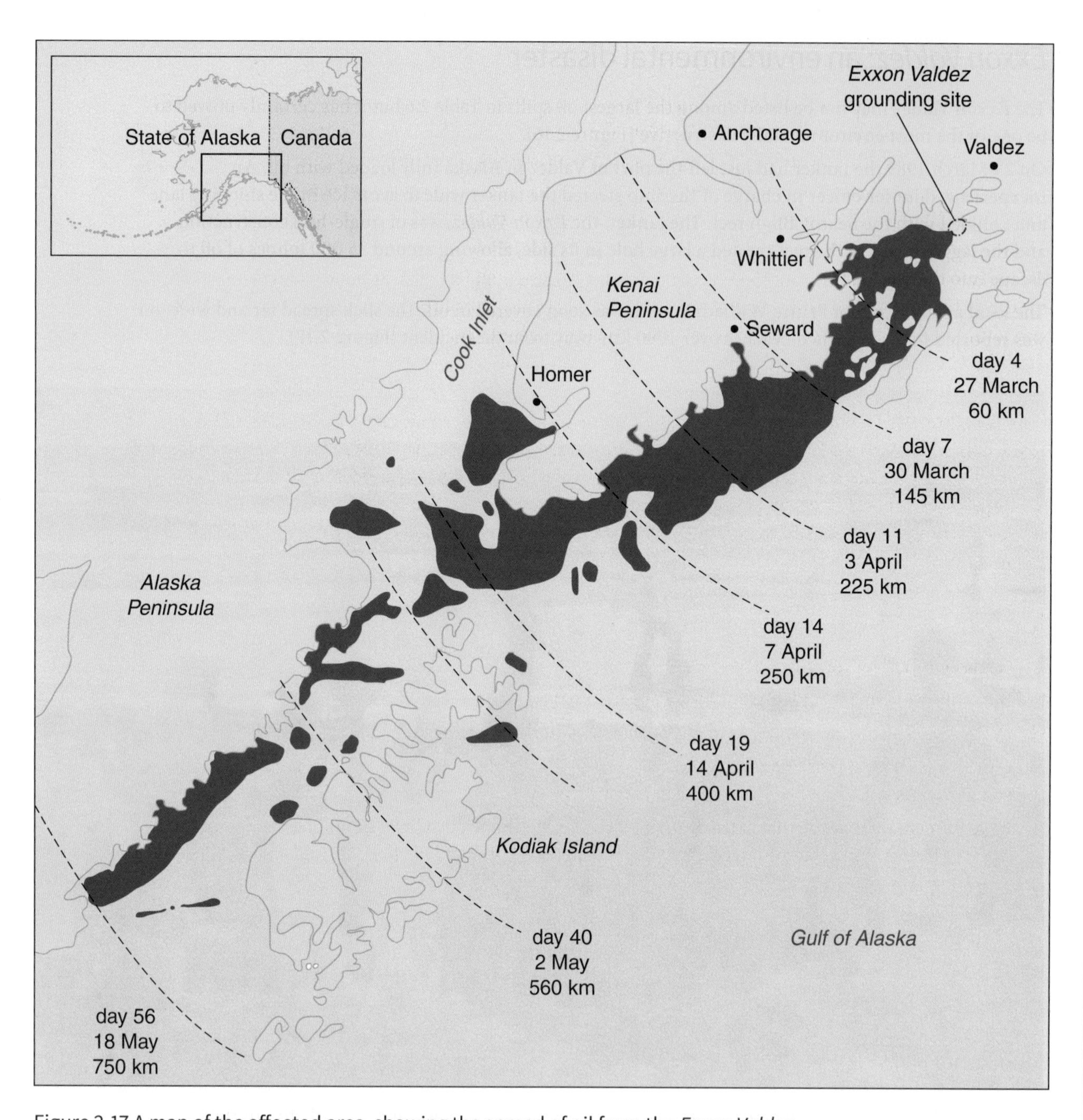

Figure 2.17 A map of the affected area, showing the spread of oil from the *Exxon Valdez*.

Alaska is a unique area for wildlife, with harsh weather conditions. It is sparsely populated but has large reserves of crude oil. Part of Alaska is within the Arctic Circle, and the seas often freeze, with areas of ice and snow present for much of the year. As a result, the local ecosystem is fragile, and animals are well adapted to the local weather conditions and food sources.

The *Exxon Valdez* accident had a major impact on local wildlife: large numbers of killer whales (orca), eagles, otters, seals and thousands of sea birds were killed in the first few weeks. Many of these organisms had either come into direct contact with the oil or ingested it while hunting for food. The toxic effect of the oil caused slow, painful deaths. The crude oil also impacted the local stocks of herring and salmon, both important items for the local fishing industry.

The clean-up

Even though people were on the scene rapidly, the oil had already spilt across the sea's surface. Detergents were used to try to break up the slick, but there was insufficient wave action for this to work efficiently. A second attempt to apply detergent (this time by aircraft) missed the target area.

An alternative method was tried: to ignite an explosion in the oil slick to get the oil to burn. The trial explosion did cause the oil to burn but lead to health problems for local villagers, so no more attempts were made.

The remoteness of the site meant there was a delay in getting equipment such as booms and skimmers to the site. While some areas of the slick were successfully held back by the booms, the skimmers could not cope with the quantity of oil clinging to seaweed and soon clogged up. It has been calculated that only around 10% of the ship's cargo was recovered because so much oil was swept into remote rocky coves that were difficult to reach.

More than 25 years later, it is still possible to find oil on local beaches: a potential toxin to all wildlife. Items such as shellfish, which filter feed from the local water, are polluted with oil and unfit for humans to eat, although birds and otters still do. The impact on local wildlife is immense; researchers have looked at 32 animal types and habitats and have found that only 13 have fully recovered. They have concluded that the ecosystem will never be entirely restored. Since the *Exxon Valdez* disaster changes have been made to try and prevent such an accident happening again.

Questions

1 Outline the causes for the accident.

2 Explain why so many large mammals have been affected by the oil spill.

3 Other than the environmental damage, how have locals been impacted by the oil spill?

4 Changes have been made as a result of the *Exxon Valdez* incident. Suggest three recommendations you would make to prevent a similar accident from occurring.

5 Environmentalists argue that extraction of oil so close to the Arctic Circle should be banned because the area is so environmentally sensitive. Give an opposite argument in support of oil extraction.

Chapter 3
Agriculture and the environment

Learning outcomes

By the end of this chapter, you will be able to:

- describe what soil is made of
- describe the components of soil that make it good for plant growth
- explain how sandy and clay soils are different
- discuss the different types of agriculture
- discuss how agricultural yields can be improved
- discuss the impact agriculture has on people and the environment
- explain the causes and effects of soil erosion and how it may be reduced
- discuss different ways in which agriculture can work sustainably.

Food for thought

Whether measured by the area of land used or the numbers of people involved, agriculture, the provision of food, is the largest industry on the planet. It is not surprising, therefore, that it can potentially have a major environmental impact. Knowing about all the potential effects and how they can be managed is of great importance to the health of the planet. The challenges are large and the solutions are complex: the human population is growing rapidly and needs to be fed, and existing farmland is often overused, depleted of mineral nutrients and suffering from soil erosion.

What are possible answers? Cutting down more forest to turn into farmland will mean a reduction on natural habitat for other animals and plants. Increased use of artificial fertilisers and pesticides will increase the amount of food but can also damage the ecosystem. More irrigation will help crops grow better but can also mean less drinking water for the increasing human population. Some parts of the world are already short of water.

Should we be banned from eating 'luxury foods' so that the resources can be used to produce larger quantities of staple foods that will feed a larger population? Would such an idea cause riots and wars? What about freedom of choice?

There are no easy answers, but some creative solutions to the problems are presented in this chapter. This chapter will help you understand the fundamentals of the precious resource soil, how it can be used and misused. This understanding will help you identify strategies that are needed for feeding the world population now and in the future.

Figure 3.0 Agriculture: a large worldwide industry with big responsibilities.

3.1 The soil

Soil is fundamental to the growth of plants, and ultimately the success of all other living creatures. It can be argued that a person's standard of living is determined by the quality of the soil where he or she lives, and the types of plants and animals that are farmed there as a result. Soil is a natural resource and needs careful management to keep it in good condition.

What is soil?

Soil is a habitat for plants and other organisms that grow within it. It is made up of a number of components. There are four main groups:

- mineral particles, which are a combination of rock fragments and other smaller inorganic (non-living) items
- organic content, which is a mixture of living plants and animals and their dead remains
- air, which is held within the spaces (pores) between the particles and organic content of the soil
- water, which is also held within the soil pores and is the water that is available for plants to grow.

The proportion of each of these four components will vary depending on the type of soil and the way it has been managed, the local climatic conditions and the size of the mineral particles.

Figure 3.1 shows the composition of a typical cultivated soil. In most soils the volume of solid material (organic content and mineral particles) will be in excess of 50–60%. The pore spaces will contain a mixture of water and air, and the proportions of these will vary constantly depending on rainfall and the uptake of water by the plants' roots. The amount of air in the soil will also be reduced by soil compaction and increased with cultivation.

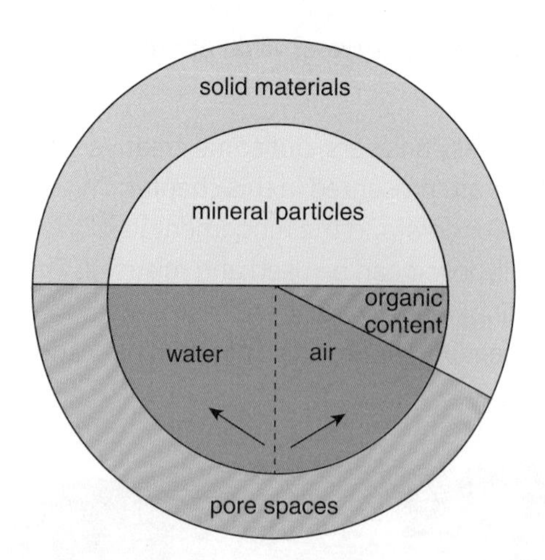

Figure 3.1 The proportions of components in a typical cultivated soil. Note that the proportions of air and water will vary depending on plant water use and rainfall.

Where do the soil components come from?

The mineral particles occupy the largest volume within soil. The particles are formed from the weathering and erosion of the parent rock (the rock underlying the soil). Over time these rocks are broken down into smaller and smaller particles. This process is known as **weathering**. The movement of these fragments (and other soil components) is known as **erosion**. The weathering of rock can take a number of forms.

Physical weathering is often caused by frost, heat, water and ice or wind. The rock can be broken down in a number of ways, such as water expanding as it freezes within cracks in a rock, rocks heating up, causing them to expand and crack, or wind blowing fragments of rock that collide with other rocks, wearing them away. Glaciers also cause weathering as they move through a valley: the large volume of ice causes friction against the rocks, wearing them away.

Chemical weathering can be caused by carbon dioxide (in the air) combining with water to form a weak acid, carbonic acid. This acid can react with alkaline minerals in the rock, causing the rest of the rock to crumble. The increase in air pollution has also increased the amount of other acids within precipitation, often described as acid rain. These acids also attack the surface of the rock, causing it to break down.

Biological weathering is caused by processes such as the growth of plant roots into the cracks in rocks, causing the rock to split open and small fragments to break off. Rocks can also be broken by the movement of animals across them. Organisms in the soil can also produce carbon dioxide, which, when combined with soil water, will form carbonic acid, adding to the chemical weathering effect.

The word **organic** means derived from living things. The organic component of the soil is a mixture of living plants, animals and microorganisms along with their dead remains. Many of the organisms present in soil have a role in the decomposition of these remains, releasing nutrients that are then available for use by plants. These processes and the movement of soil animals (such as earthworms) make channels within the soil that allow air and water to be held in the soil pores (spaces). Air enters the soil by diffusion; water enters the soil when there is precipitation or when the soil is irrigated.

KEY TERMS

Weathering: the processes that cause rock to be broken down into smaller particles

Erosion: the movement of rock and soil fragments to different locations

Organic: derived from living organisms

Particle size

The size of the soil particles has a major effect on the properties of the soil: how well it holds or drains water, its capacity to hold mineral nutrients and the ease with which plants can grow in it and be cultivated. Soil mineral particles can be classified according to their size into three groups:

- sand
- silt
- clay.

Sand is the largest mineral component of soil. The International Society of Soil Science (ISSS) describes sand as having particles between 2.0 mm and 0.02 mm in size. It is easy to see the individual grains with the naked eye, and sand feels gritty to the touch. The large size and irregular shape of the particles mean that they do not pack together easily, so there are large pores between the grains of sand; this allows water, air and soil organisms to move through sand easily.

Silt particles are smaller than those of sand, being between 0.02 mm and 0.002 mm in size. Silt feels silky or soapy to the touch and when rubbed between the fingers the particles slip over each other easily, unlike sand particles.

Clay particles are the smallest mineral component, being smaller than 0.002 mm in diameter. Their small size means that they pack closely together, which reduces the ability of water to drain through the soil. When damp, clay particles feel very sticky and are easily moulded; when dry they stick together solidly. This is why clay is used to make pottery: imagine trying to make pots out of sand! Clay particles have surface electrical charges that affect the way they behave and the way they link with and release nutrients. Table 3.1 compares the characteristics of sand, silt and clay.

Particle type	Size of particle	Texture	Characteristics
Sand	2.0–0.02 mm	Feels gritty	Large pore sizes Drains well Contains large air spaces
Silt	0.02–0.002 mm	Feels silky or soapy	Less friction than sand Particles slippery
Clay	<0.002 mm	Sticky when wet	Particles held together tightly Poor air spaces or drainage Forms a hard mass when dried

Table 3.1 The classification of soil particle types and their characteristics.

PRACTICAL ACTIVITY 3.1

Classifying soil

Materials

- Soil samples
- Water
- Jar

Method

Part 1: The feel test

- Take a small amount of the soil sample (ideally removing any large roots and stones).
- Add a small amount of water to make it into a ball.
- Rub the ball between your thumb and fingers. How does it feel? Mainly gritty means there is a high proportion of sand; silky or soapy means there is a large amount of silt; sticky means there is a high proportion of clay.

Part 2: The moulding test

- Take a ball of moist soil (not too wet).
- Follow the flow chart in Figure 3.2.

Part 3: The jar test

- Fill a jar (or other clear container) a third full with soil.
- Add enough water to almost fill the jar.
- Shake vigorously for 2 min.
- Allow the contents of the jar to settle.
- Look at the different soil components (Figure 3.3 shows an example of what it could look like).

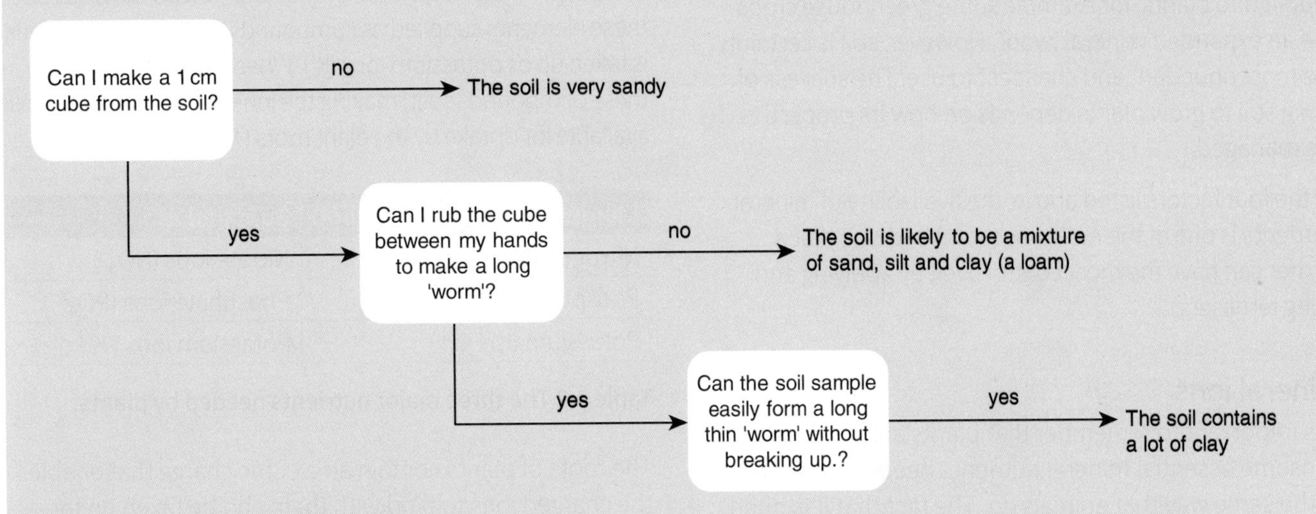

Figure 3.2 Flow chart for classifying soil.

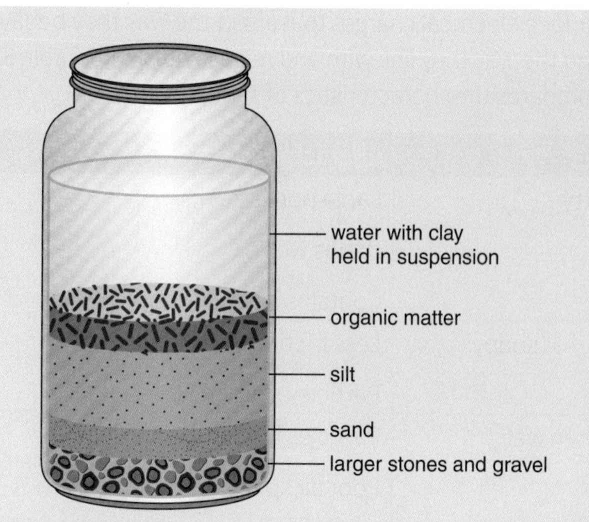

Figure 3.3 Components of soil separated out by shaking a sample of soil in a jar of water. The heaviest items fall to the bottom first. Clay particles are so small that they can remain floating in the water for a long time, but they will settle out over a few days.

Questions

1 Draw up a table of your results and compare the different parts of the test for different soil samples.

2 Could the results of just completing the 'jar test' predict the results that would be obtained from the 'feel test' and the 'moulding tests'?

3.2 Soils for plant growth

Most plants require a combination of factors to grow successfully. These include:

- the availability of important mineral nutrients to support plant growth
- anchorage to hold the roots securely in one place
- a supply of water
- oxygen around the roots to enable the root cells to respire.

Soil is not the only medium in which these factors can be supplied to plants, for example some greenhouse crops use an expanded mineral 'wool'. However, soil is certainly the most abundant and cheapest to use. The success of using soil to grow plants depends on how its properties are managed.

Of the four factors listed above, the availability of mineral nutrients is one of the most important and one that a farmer can have the most control over, by applying and using fertilisers.

Mineral ions

It is important to remember that plants are not able to consume essential mineral nutrients needed for growth in the same way that animals do. The fact that it is often stated that plants are able to manufacture their own food (glucose) through photosynthesis is also confusing: if this is the case, why do farmers give fertilisers (plant food) to their crops?

In addition to carbon dioxide and water for the production of sugars, which are primarily used as an energy source, plants also require a supply of nitrogen, phosphorus, potassium and a range of other essential elements to construct proteins, and other chemicals to carry out plant processes. These mineral nutrients are typically obtained through the roots of the plant. In element form, nitrogen and phosphorus are not accessible to a plant, therefore when scientists talk about the application of nitrogen and phosphorus they actually mean the oxides of these elements supplied as compounds. Potassium, however, is taken up as potassium ions (K^+). When dissolved in water, these compounds split, making the ions of the minerals available for uptake by the plant roots (Table 3.2).

Element name (and symbol)	Supplied as
Nitrogen (N)	Nitrate ions (NO_3^-)
Phosphorus (P)	Phosphate ions (PO_4^{3-})
Potassium (K)	Potassium ions (K^+)

Table 3.2 The three major nutrients needed by plants.

The roots of plants contain an electric charge that enables the charged ions to bind with them and be taken up for use within the plant.

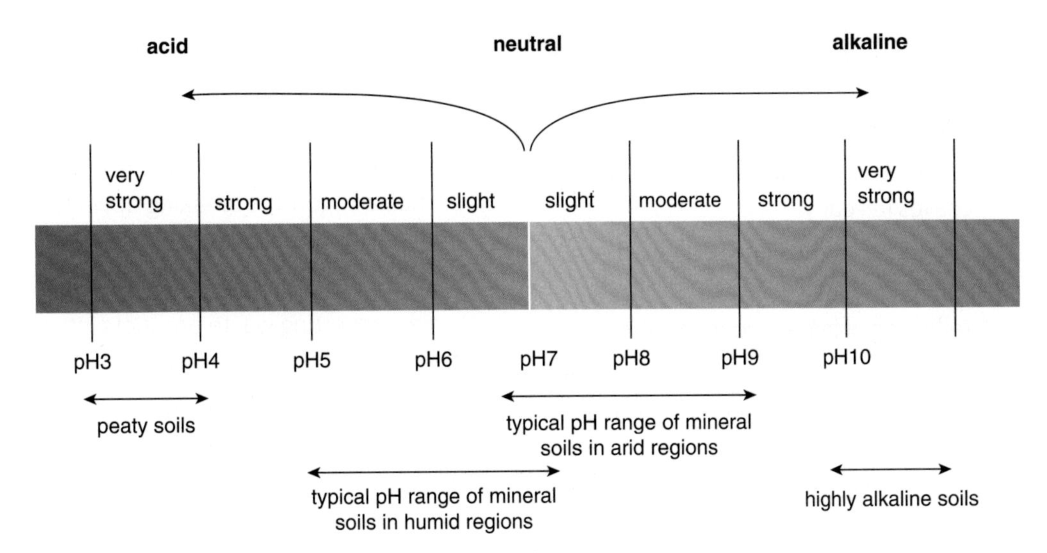

Figure 3.4 Scale showing the range of soil pH normally recorded.

Soil pH

The uptake of nutrients by plant roots is affected by the pH of the soil, a measure of the acidity or alkalinity. In absolute terms the pH scale runs from pH 1 (acid) to pH 14 (alkaline). It is very rare for a soil to be at the very extremes of this scale, except after major chemical spills or pollution incidents.

The pH of a soil may be dependent on a number of factors, but in most cases the biggest influence tends to the type of parent rock the mineral components are formed from or the pH of the water that flows into the area via rivers or lakes. The range of typical pH values found in soil is shown in Figure 3.4.

Why is soil pH important?

Plant growers and farmers have known for a long time that some plants fail to grow well in certain soils even if supplied with additional fertiliser. Sweet potatoes, for example, grow better at a pH of 5.0–5.5 rather than a more alkaline soil of pH 8.0. If grown at a pH of 8.0, sweet potato plants show signs of nutrient deficiency (such as yellow leaves), even though the farmer may have provided enough nutrients. Clearly the pH must have an impact on the uptake of nutrients.

Research has shown that while every plant has its own preferred soil pH, not all mineral nutrients are taken up equally. The pH of the soil will also impact on the availability of these mineral nutrients within the soil. Some ions (the form the plant uses) are less available at certain soil pH levels. Figure 3.5 shows this effect. If the pH of a soil is 6.0, a grower would need to be aware that while there is likely to be plenty of nitrogen, potassium, phosphorus and sulfur available (where the bars in Figure 3.5 are wide) there is a risk the crop will be short of magnesium, molybdenum and calcium, which are less readily available at that pH.

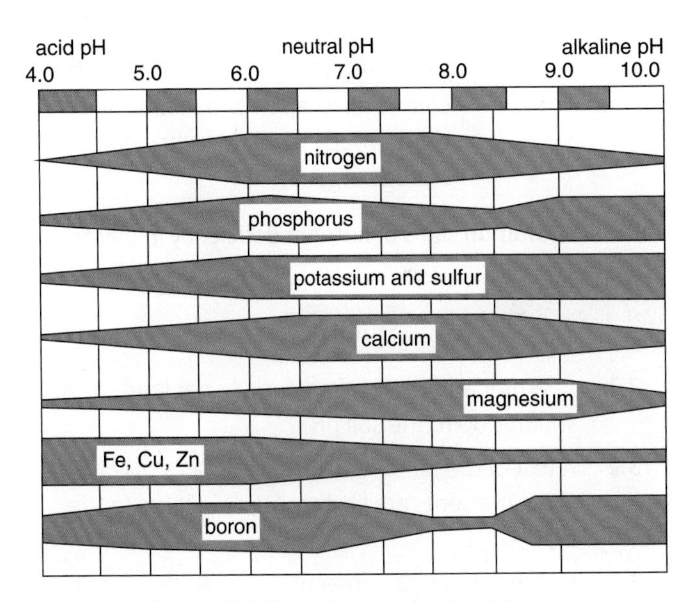

Figure 3.5 The availability of some plant nutrients at different soil pH levels.

This information gives the farmer or grower two choices to maximise their yield (and use of fertilisers). Either they need to check the crop and look for deficiencies on a regular basis and apply the relevant mineral nutrient as it is needed, or they could try to change the pH of the soil to either acidify it, which is often achieved using specific fertilisers that have an acidifying effect, or make it more alkaline using a substance such as ground limestone, a naturally occurring rock.

Signs of mineral nutrient deficiencies in plants

The symptoms of mineral nutrient deficiencies vary from plant to plant but there are some common signs (Table 3.3).

Plant nutrient	Symptoms of deficiency include
Nitrogen (N)	Slow growth, yellowing leaves (oldest first)
Phosphorus (P)	Leaves dull with blue-green colour. Leaves fall early
Potassium (K)	Poor-quality fruits and seeds, leaves with brown edges
Sulfur (S)	Yellowing of leaves (youngest first)
Calcium (Ca)	Death of plant tissues. Poor fruit storage
Magnesium (Mg)	Yellowing of leaves between the leaf veins. Early leaf fall
Iron (Fe)	Yellowing of leaves between the veins (youngest leaves first). Failure to flower
Copper (Cu)	Dark green leaves become twisted and withered (young leaves first)
Zinc (Zn)	Leaves show poor development, might only grow to a very small size
Boron (B)	Leaves misshapen and malformed. Hard 'woody' areas in fruits and other storage organs

Table 3.3 Common signs of nutrient deficiency in plants.

SELF-ASSESSMENT QUESTIONS

3.1 A farmer adds some limestone to her land. What will this do to the soil pH?

3.2 A test of the famer's soil shows it has a pH of 8.0. What nutrients are likely to less available to the plants?

3.3 List three ways a farmer might know his plants are short of mineral nutrients.

Soil organic content

The organic content of the soil is a combination of living organisms and their dead remains. As with other plants and animals, the organisms that live within soil form part of the complex interactions within food webs and the recycling of materials for future use. A range of decomposers (organisms that break down organic matter) take part in complex interactions that eventually return the nutrients contained within dead matter back into a form that is readily available to plants to use as nutrients.

Many different types of organisms are involved in the breakdown of organic matter, including:

- earthworms, which help break down vegetation by digesting it as it passes through their bodies and excreting the remains
- fungi, which feed directly on dead matter and are particularly good at breaking down tough materials such as woody items
- bacteria, which work on organic material at a smaller scale, converting waste products into simple chemicals that can be used by plants.

In addition to providing a store for plant mineral nutrients, organic matter has a number of other effects on soil characteristics. High levels of organic matter have the following positive effects.

- Increase the water-holding capacity of a well-drained soil. The organic matter acts like a sponge and absorbs additional water when it is available and releases it when it is required by plants. This means less **irrigation** is required.
- Increase the air spaces in the soil. The open, sponge-like structure of organic matter allows air to penetrate, which is very useful for soils that naturally have few air spaces. Plant roots need oxygen for respiration, and insufficient oxygen results in root death.
- Increase the number of decomposer organisms. Extra organic matter means a more abundant food source. An increase in worms, for example, increases the number of tunnels or burrows in the soil, providing additional drainage in poorly drained soils and less compaction, increasing the amount of oxygen available to plant roots.
- Prevent the loss of mineral nutrients. Some mineral nutrients are washed away (leached) in excess water. Humus, the material left after organic matter has been partially decomposed, has the ability to hold onto mineral nutrients until they are needed by plants.

As with the availability of mineral nutrients to plants, the pH of the soil has an impact on the well-being of decomposers in the soil. Different organisms thrive in different conditions. Changing the soil pH can affect the ability of these organisms to break down organic matter effectively.

Sandy soils verses clay soils

The ideal soil is a mixture of sand, silt and clay (a **loam** soil) with a high quantity of organic matter and a neutral pH. However, it is very rare for soils to have all these characteristics. In some places, for example, soils have a high proportion of sand particles, and in other places a high level of clay. So what are the advantages and disadvantages of each?

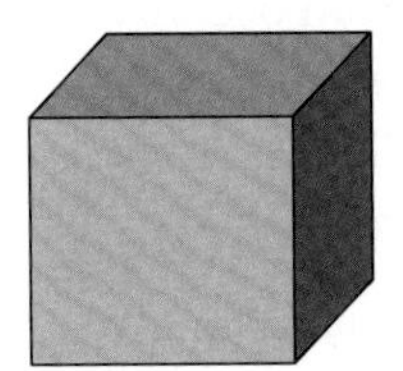

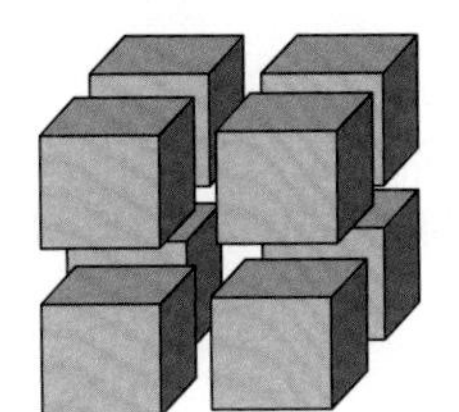

Figure 3.6 The impact of particle size on surface area by volume.

KEY TERMS

Irrigation: the supply of water to a crop by the grower

Loam: a soil that is mixture of sand, silt and clay, combining the best properties of each

- Air content: clay soils have small air spaces that can limit the amount of oxygen reaching plant roots. This in turn can limit respiration and the amount of possible root growth. In contrast, sandy soils have large air gaps allowing good transmission with high levels of oxygen and therefore a healthy root system.
- Water content: water tends to cling to the surface of particles. A clay soil has far more particles, and therefore a far larger surface area, compared with a sandy soil. Clay soils therefore hold significantly more water.

The concept of a larger surface area is explained in Figure 3.6. In this calculation, the smaller cubes are only half the size of the larger ones; clay particles are in fact 1000th of the size of a sand grain. Reducing the average size of a cube by half, doubles the surface area for the same volume.

There is no one ideal soil for all crops in all situations, so the composition of a soil affects the way soils are managed and used.

The characteristics of sandy soils include:

- free draining (because of the large air spaces between particles)
- low water-holding capacity
- quick to warm up (because the spaces between particles hold less water)
- easier to cultivate (because the particles do not stick together easily)
- poor retention of nutrients (because there is less opportunity for the particles to bind mineral ions and more opportunity for leaching)
- a greater risk of erosion (because the particles do not stick together tightly).

The characteristics of clay soils include:

- high water-holding capacity
- slow to warm up (because of the large amount of water held in the spaces between the particles)
- small air spaces, which are harder for roots or organisms to penetrate and contain less oxygen
- water does not drain away easily
- hard to cultivate (because it is sticky and wet after heavy rain, dries hard and cracks after prolonged exposure to sunlight, and is heavy because of its high water-holding capacity)
- retains nutrients well (clay particles have an electric charge that binds to mineral ions).

The properties of organic matter mean that when it is added to either of the two types soils it helps reduce their negative impacts, for example it provides additional water-holding capacity to sandy soils and increases the size of air spaces in clay soils.

3.3 Agriculture

While there is no one definition, agriculture is typically defined as 'the cultivation of animals, plants and fungi for food and other products used to sustain human life'. It is relatively easy to identify the food items, but the 'other products' can include growing timber in a plantation for house building or fuel, growing plants to produce medicines, breeding fish for fish oils or growing roses to produce table decorations in up-market restaurants.

Agriculture therefore has a much wider meaning than you might realise, and it does not even need to use soil. The type of agriculture used in different parts of the world depends on a number of factors, including:

- climate
- culture
- technology
- economics.

Types of agriculture

With such a range of different products, grown in different ways, it is useful to group types of agriculture together using various classifications.

Subsistence versus commercial

Subsistence farming is the cultivation and production of food to meet the needs of the farmers and their families. There is very little surplus food; if there is any surplus it is often exchanged (bartered) for other things the family needs, and perhaps a small amount of cash. Subsistence farmers aim to grow almost everything they need.

Commercial farming is the cultivation of products with the main focus of selling them for cash. While some of the food may be used by the farmers (and their families), this is only a very small proportion compared with the amount that is sold. Commercial farms often use technology to increase yields and reduce the costs of production. Commercial farmers aim to grow crops to obtain money to buy the things they need.

While it is possible for both farming systems to provide a farmer with money, it is the proportion of food that is used for each purpose that is important.

Arable versus pastoral

Another way of describing the type of farming is by the type of product.

Arable farming is the production of plants for consumption by humans. Examples include growing rice, maize, wheat and soybeans. The scale of production (size and number of fields) can vary greatly and there are examples of subsistence arable farmers and commercial arable farmers.

Pastoral farming is the production of animals or animal-related products. This may also be known as livestock farming or grazing. Plants such as grass or grain may be grown on the farm but they will be used to feed the animals. Pastoral farms can produce meat or other animal byproducts, such as milk, wool or eggs.

A third type of farming exists: farms that grow crops for food and rear animals. This is commonly referred to as **mixed farming**.

Extensive versus intensive

Farm production can also be described by evaluating the relative yield compared with the size of space used.

Extensive production occurs when there is a relatively small amount of production (either crops or animals) from a large area of land.

Intensive production occurs where large amounts are produced from small areas of land. This style of production tends to have high 'inputs', such as a lot of labour, fertilisers or machinery.

Intensive production is often considered to be very efficient, so why do we not see it used more widely? The answer to this question is quite complex. While yields are high, so are the costs involved, which can be a barrier for many farmers. Similarly, some people choose to ignore intensive production on ethical or environmental grounds: it can have an increased impact on the local ecosystem and, in the case of livestock, there are welfare issues associated with keeping animals in small confined spaces.

These descriptions can be combined, for example you can have an intensive, commercial, arable farm, or an extensive, subsistence, pastoral farm.

KEY TERMS

Arable farming: the production of crops from land

Pastoral farming: farming that focuses on breeding and rearing livestock

Mixed farming: farming that practises both rearing livestock and growing crops

Extensive production: farming that is spread over a wide area and uses less resources per metre of land

Intensive production: farming that aims to maximise the yield from an area using a large amount of resources

SELF-ASSESSMENT QUESTIONS

3.4 Place the letter for each of the following farms/production types into a copy of Table 3.4:

- **a** An intensive banana plantation in the Caribbean
- **b** Battery (caged) hens used to produce eggs
- **c** Rice production by a farmer on a small scale in Asia using hillside terraces
- **d** Tree plantations grown for the timber industry
- **e** Nomadic farmers keeping sheep or goats
- **f** A small family farm in North America growing a range of vegetables and keeping chickens, trying to be self-sufficient

	Subsistence	Commercial
Arable		
Pastoral		
Mixed		

Table 3.4 Examples of different types of farming.

3.4 Increasing agricultural yields

The demands for food keep on increasing as the global population increases. The world population is predicted to increase to 9 billion people by 2050, an increase in 20% from 2015.

Increasing populations also increase pressures in other ways: the demand for places to live has seen the expansion of cities and towns, and the deforestation of large areas for building materials and fuel. Often the expansion of built-up areas has been at the expense of local farmland. Therefore, there is pressure on food production in a number of ways, including:

- an increasing world population needing more resources
- climate change affecting the availability of fertile land
- increasing settlement sizes reducing available farmland
- increases in the standard of living creating a demand for more food variety
- larger populations impacting on the availability of water for irrigation.

Solutions to world hunger

The problems the world is encountering now is not a surprise to some: scientists, economists and politicians have been debating this issue for years. Here are some suggestions to solve the problem.

- Reducing the population increase, as this will decrease the predicted demand for food. Initiatives such as China's one child policy are an attempt to reduce population numbers in a managed way (Figure 3.7).

Figure 3.7 In 1979 China introduced a one child policy to reduce the rate of population growth.

- Growing more staple crops that are high yielding, and fewer luxury items that are not so productive. Current resources could be used to grow a greater mass of food if humans ate more staple foods (such as rice, wheat, maize and soy) and fewer luxury items. However, as countries become more developed, their populations want to try a wider range of items.
- Ensuring greater food equality. While some people do not have enough to eat, others have more than they need. Should there be laws (rationing) to ensure that everyone has similar access to foods?
- Eating less meat. Eating meat wastes a lot of resources. The study of food webs and pyramids of energy (see Section 9.1) shows us that a lot of energy is wasted when an animal converts plant material into meat for us to eat. If we ate the plant material (became vegetarians), we need less land to produce the food.

These are all interesting ideas, but in most countries they would be very unpopular because they require legislation restricting what people can eat or do. It is very unlikely that there would be international agreements to promote these ideas.

Scientists have therefore been working hard to develop techniques that will increase production from the land that is currently available and still allow the world's population the freedom of choice. There are already some successful techniques that help farmers meet the need for increased food production to feed a growing population.

Often referred to as the Green Revolution, since the mid-20th century a number of techniques and improved varieties have been developed to increase, for example, the production of wheat in Mexico, and the production of rice in Asia, most notably with the introduction of a high-yielding rice called IR8. This has seen a large increase in yield from these staple crops, preventing significant food shortages in rapidly increasing populations. The Green Revolution is not one activity but a range of improvements to many aspects of agricultural production that, combined, means there is an increase in crop yield.

Techniques for improving crop yield

Crop rotation

Crop rotation is the principle of growing different types of plants in different plots each year. Related groups of plants are grown together during a season, then at the start of the next season moved to a different plot of land that has just been used for a different plant group. There is a planned sequence to the rotation. Research over many years has shown that many plants grow using this system than if continually grown on the same plot.

Farmers observed that growing the same type of plant in the same plot year after year often resulted in a decrease in yield over time. Further investigation has shown that continually growing the same plants in the same place causes:

- a build-up of diseases in the soil that affect plant growth
- an increase in the pests that attack the plants
- a depletion in soil nutrients, because the same crop uses the same ratio of nutrients each year.

Moving a crop to a different piece of land each year means that:

- diseases in the soil affecting that plant are left behind and have nothing to infect
- pests need to find the new site and so their numbers are reduced
- the soil in the new plot is more likely to have the nutrients the crop needs.

It has also been known for a long time that certain plants are able to produce their own fertiliser (nitrates). These plants, known as **legumes,** have nitrogen-fixing bacteria in their root nodules, which take nitrogen from the air and convert it into a form that the plant can use. At the end of a growing season, when the crop is removed, any nitrogen not used by the legumes is left in the ground and can be accessed by the next plants in the rotation.

KEY TERM

Legumes: plants that contain nitrogen-fixing bacteria in their roots to produce a source of nitrates

Figure 3.8 shows an example of a simple crop rotation and how each crop benefits another. In this example, a large plot of land has been divided into four smaller areas, each to contain a particular type of plant.

- Legumes: plants in the pea and bean family, which are able to fix nitrogen from the air using bacteria in nodules on their roots.
- Leafy crops: a range of vegetables grown for their leaves, which require a lot of nitrogen fertiliser (left in the soil by the legume roots). These plants are grown in a plot the season after legumes.
- Root crops: plants that have deep root systems, which help to break up the soil. A lot of soil cultivation is needed to harvest the roots. Legumes like well-cultivated soils and so benefit from being grown in a plot the season after root crops.
- Fallow: the land is left to rest, so no crops are grown.

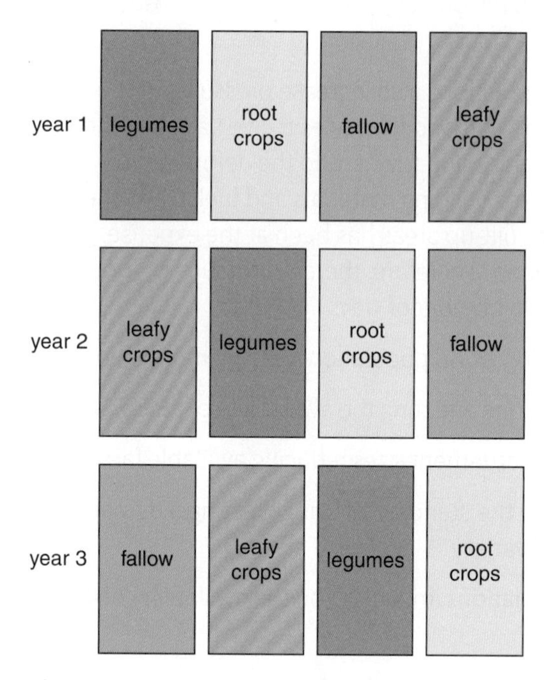

Figure 3.8 An example of a four-part crop rotation.

While the original planned rotation consisted of four plots, depending on the amount of land available to a farmer it is quite common to see a three-part rotation, without the fallow plot (when the ground is given a chance to replenish its resources naturally).

In different climates, this process will look slightly different depending on the types of crops grown and the local seasons. Nevertheless, some form of rotation is usually very beneficial to plant yield and has been adapted to a number of situations. Some mixed farms, for example, will include grazing in their rotation rather than the fallow plot, and the animals naturally fertilise the plot as they feed.

The use of crop rotation helps reduce the numbers of pests and diseases and needs less fertiliser (if legumes are included), but it is less useful if one of the crops to be grown has little commercial value (in the case of commercial production) or little nutritional value (in the case of subsistence farming), as this would have a serious impact on the effectiveness of the land under cultivation.

Another less obvious advantage to this system is the fact that crops can be ready to harvest at different times, which means overall that the farmer needs less labour and less machinery and has less potential waste at harvest time because there is more time for the process.

Fertilisers

Fertilisers contain minerals such as nitrogen, potassium and phosphorus, which are essential for healthy plant growth. When used correctly, fertilisers increase crop yield because they add to the amount of mineral nutrients already present in the soil. When used incorrectly, they can cause environmental damage because they are washed into rivers and lakes by rainfall.

Not all plants use the same ratio of mineral nutrients, which is one of the reasons why the crop rotation technique is popular: the next crop can use some of the excess mineral nutrients left behind by the previous crop. The fact that different plants require different mineral nutrients means that manufacturers use different mixes (formulations) of ingredients to make the fertilisers better suited for particular crops, and so prevent mineral nutrients being wasted.

Organic versus inorganic

The wide range of fertilisers available is often classified into two groups: organic and inorganic fertilisers.

Organic fertilisers are substances that have been derived from natural sources (typically living sources). Most commonly this includes animal manures, but also includes composted plant materials. Other examples of organic fertilisers are bone meal (ground-up animal bones), hoof and horn (these parts of the animal ground up) or dried blood. Manure and compost are quite bulky because they contain a large amount of organic matter, which means they are also good soil improvers, increasing water-holding capacity of sandy soils and increasing air spaces in compacted, clay soils.

Inorganic fertilisers are manufactured within a factory. They are typically more uniform from batch to batch, and can be formulated to provide a precise amount of each nutrient. They are often cleaner and less unpleasant to handle than composts and manures, and are less bulky so can be stored and transported more easily.

If a farmer has a mixed farm then he or she may have a plentiful supply of organic fertiliser (in the form of manure). Many intensive commercial farms use inorganic fertilisers because they are more cost effective, being easier to obtain and easier to apply to the crops using machinery.

Plant roots absorb the ions of the chemicals in the fertiliser and are unable to distinguish which source they have come from.

The effect of fertilisers

Plants need a range of essential nutrients to grow effectively. The three major nutrients (nitrogen, phosphorus and potassium) are needed in relatively large quantities, a range of minor nutrients (including magnesium, sulfur and calcium) are needed in smaller quantities, and a larger selection of nutrients (including zinc, iron and boron), called trace elements, are needed in relatively tiny amounts. Shortage of any one of these nutrients will mean the plant does not grow at its optimum rate; a significant shortage in any one can result in a deficiency disease, impacting on the yield and appearance of the crop.

Fertilisers provide an additional supply of essential nutrients that help the plants build protein (in the case of nitrogen) and help the effective development of cells (in the case of the trace elements).

Applying fertilisers safely

Fertilisers should be used to boost the natural availability of essential mineral nutrients in the soil. If they are applied at a time or a quantity not suitable for the plants, they will be wasted and washed away in rainwater, potentially causing environmental damage.

Best practice for a farmer is to identify the crop that needs additional fertiliser, either through visual inspection of plants and looking for signs of deficiency, or by testing the soil to find out the naturally occurring nutrient levels. Fertilisers will be wasted unless the plant is able to absorb the nutrients through their roots, which requires moisture. If there is a drought, adding fertilisers will have little effect unless the farmer can also supply water for irrigation.

Fertilisers will also be wasted if there is too much rain: if a fertiliser can dissolve easily it should not be applied until heavy rains have ceased, otherwise the mineral nutrients will be leached (washed) away. If fertiliser has to be added during a rainy season, the farmer should choose a slow-release fertiliser (one that dissolves slowly over time) so that the roots are able to absorb small amounts over a longer period. However, this approach means there is little instant impact. Table 3.5 compares the different types of fertiliser.

Irrigation

In many locations the availability of water within the soil is a major limitation to the growth of a crop. Water is also in demand for human consumption, industry and livestock, and the use of water for crops may fall below these priorities. In such situations it is important to ensure that water is used efficiently. It has been calculated that farming accounts for almost 70% of the water used in the world today.

Why is irrigation important?

A large percentage of a plant is made up of water. Water is essential for cell activity and used in photosynthesis. Mineral nutrient uptake by the roots requires water in the soil.

Fertiliser type	Advantages	Disadvantages
Organic	Uses natural resources Bulky types also supply organic matter to improve the soil	Can be unpleasant to handle Bulky types are harder to transport May be variable in composition
Inorganic	Can be manufactured to meet a particular need Can be easier to store	Cost of manufacture Transportation costs
Quick acting	Fast acting: deficiency problems are dealt with swiftly	Can easily leach out in heavy rain
Slow acting	Long lasting: no need to reapply	Little immediate impact if plants may already have a deficiency problem

Table 3.5 Advantages and disadvantages of different types of fertiliser.

Symptoms of a plant lacking water include wilting of leaves. When this occurs, photosynthesis ceases, so plant growth processes slow down. If the lack of available water continues, this could ultimately lead to the death of the plant.

Using water wisely

In many locations water is in short supply. While it might be possible to use water that is not suitable for drinking purposes, the water must still be free from pollution and sufficiently low in salt that it does not damage the crop plants. Many farmers look for opportunities to extract or store water when it is abundant for use later when it is in short supply. Rainwater can be collected from field **run-off** or from the roofs of buildings.

Reservoirs do not need to be sophisticated, but in hot climates large expanses of water provide a large surface area for evaporation. Underground or covered sources are more expensive to develop but suffer from less water loss.

Some farmers may have access to underground supplies such as bore holes, or have the facilities to extract water from rivers or lakes. However, use of these sources of water is coming under increasing pressure as drinkable sources of water for human use become more scarce.

The process of supplying water to plants can be divided into three stages: storage of the water, transportation to the required site and application to the plants. Strategies for water conservation can be applied to each of these stages.

KEY TERM

Run-off: the process by which water runs over the ground into rivers

While the cheapest option, transportation of water to the crop though channels in the soil (rills) is extremely wasteful because the dry soil will absorb much of the water before it reaches the plants. However, this method is easy to construct and new channels can be cut very flexibly, so it is attractive to many farmers.

Solid pipes are far more expensive, harder to construct, but less prone to water loss. This distribution system also requires additional skills and construction knowledge.

Once the water has reached the crop field, there can be a significant difference in the efficiency of using the water depending on how it is applied.

Common water application methods

Overhead sprinkler systems use a special sprinkler nozzle with a small aperture that forces the water out under pressure. This pressure causes the jet of water to turn into droplets, which will fall on top of the crop rather like rainfall. The average size of the droplets can be adjusted; large droplets will cover a larger area, small droplets are finer on plant leaves and cause less damage (Table 3.6).

Advantages	Disadvantages
Relatively easy to set up Can cover a large area from one sprinkler No need to attach pipes or equipment to each individual plant	Large droplets may 'cap' the soil (damages the structure to form a hard crust), reducing the ability of rain to enter Small droplets easily blown by wind so not all plants may be irrigated Water lands on leaves and surface of soil, which may evaporate before roots can use the water Not very precise

Table 3.6 Advantages and disadvantages of overhead irrigation.

Clay pot systems use porous clay pots that are buried in the soil next to the roots of the plants. Each pot is filled with water, which gradually seeps into the soil around the roots (Figure 3.9). Table 3.7 compares the advantages and disadvantages of this system.

Figure 3.9 Example of a clay pot irrigation system. As water seeps out the pot, it can be taken up by the plant's roots.

Advantages	Disadvantages
Simple technology: little can go wrong	Only suitable for larger (more permanent) plants
Easy to check the amount of water provided to the soil	Large labour cost (burying pots, checking on water levels, topping up manually)
Little surface evaporation because the water released into the soil	

Table 3.7 Advantages and disadvantages of clay pot irrigation.

Trickle drip systems, sometimes referred to as 'leaky pipes', use a series of flat polythene hoses laid on the surface of the soil between the rows of crops. When additional irrigation is needed, water is transported to these hoses through pipes and released slowly at the soil surface via tiny holes in the hoses. Some systems have microtubes (emitters) allowing water to drip directly onto the plant concerned. An example layout is shown in Figure 3.10. Table 3.8 compares the advantages and disadvantages of this system.

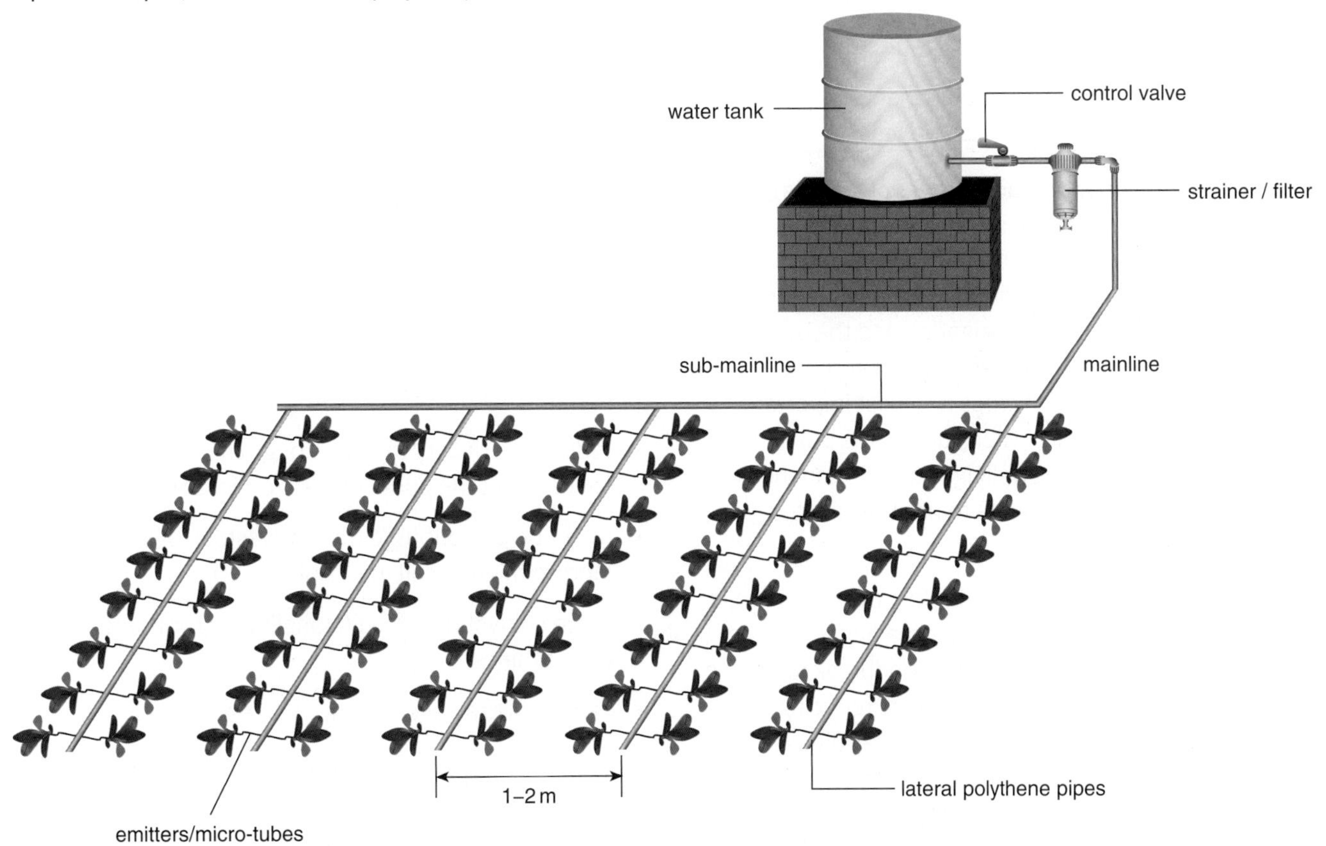

Figure 3.10 An example of trickle drip irrigation system. Plants are watered directly through either microtubes (emitters) or a porous hose.

Advantages	Disadvantages
Water placed directly at the base of the plant The system can be automated and controlled via computer Water is used very efficiently	Expensive to install and complex to maintain Small particles such as grit can block tubes Inflexible: cannot easily be moved

Table 3.8 Advantages and disadvantages of drip irrigation systems.

Flood irrigation is probably the most ancient method of irrigating crops. Water is delivered to the field by a soil channel or pipe and allowed to flow freely over the ground throughout the crop. To be effective, the fields have to be reasonably level and barriers need to be in place to prevent water simply running away at the edges of the fields. Table 3.9 compares the advantages and disadvantages of this system.

Advantages	Disadvantages
Inexpensive Can cover large areas quickly	Very inefficient use of water (run-off, evaporation, etc.) Damages soil structure Non-targeted plants (such as weeds) also benefit

Table 3.9 Advantages and disadvantages of flood irrigation.

Newer techniques in water conservation use data such as the current water content of the soil and weather forecasts to identify when best to apply irrigation and the quantities needed. Research is being carried out to determine at what stages in the growth of crops it is most important to ensure there is sufficient water (such as the point of flowering or when fruit are swelling). Farmers can then decide when is most appropriate to use their limited water resources.

Farmers can reduce the rate of water loss from their crops by providing them with shelter, either shading them from the intense heat of the Sun or using a windbreak to reduce wind speed across the crop, and therefore reducing the rate of **transpiration** from the leaves. Additional measures, such as covering the ground with a polythene sheet or natural compost layer, will **mulch** the base of the plant, reducing water loss by evaporation from the soil and cooling down the root zone.

KEY TERMS

Transpiration: the movement of water up plants and its subsequent loss as water vapour from their leaves

Mulch: a natural or artificial layer on the soil surface used to reduce water evaporation and weed growth

Weed: a plant growing in an inappropriate place

Control of competing organisms

While it is possible to provide a crop with adequate irrigation and nutrients to grow at an optimum rate, not all of the nutrients and water may be taken up by the crops. The growth of a crop plant can also be reduced by attacks from other organisms that can feed on it, weaken it and in extreme cases kill it.

For centuries farmers have lost a large proportion of their potential crops because of weeds, pests and diseases. Prior to the introduction of chemical controls, it is estimated that the level of loss may have been as high as 70%.

A **weed** is a plant that is growing in an inappropriate place. Examples include 'jungle rice' (*Echinchloa colona*), a plant that competes with rice crops. This grassy plant is common throughout Asia and likes similar conditions to cultivated rice. As a result, it uses space and nutrients that could be used by the food crop.

A previous food crop growing among the next crop in a crop rotation is also a weed. If some were missed during harvesting, potato tubers can survive in the soil and grow and shade the next crop (such as peas or beans), reducing that crop's yield.

Weeds need to be controlled because they:

- compete with crops for water, light and nutrients
- reduce the quality of a seed or grain crop (the weed seeds affect the purity of the crop for sale)
- might be poisonous, either to livestock or to humans (and so might result in a tainted crop)
- make cultivation difficult, tangling up tools and clogging up machines
- can block drainage systems with excessive growth
- can be a source of pests and diseases that also attack the crop
- can look untidy, which might have an impact in tourism areas.

Chemical control of weeds is probably the most efficient system for a large area. Weed-killing chemicals are known as **herbicides**. They can be used to completely clear uncultivated areas of all previous vegetation before sowing or planting a crop, or to selectively kill weeds growing among a crop.

The definition of a weed is a plant growing in an inappropriate place, so the success of a herbicide is linked to the accuracy of the farmer in applying it. Applying herbicide carelessly can damage the crop or other important vegetation in an area, impacting on the local ecosystem.

Most herbicides are applied in a liquid format via a sprayer that splits the liquid into very fine droplets. These form a fine covering on the weeds, allowing the chemical to act. In windy conditions fine droplets are likely to spread over a wide distance.

An alternative method is to use herbicide granules, which are heavy enough to fall to the ground when applied and do not stick to the leaves of most plants. The herbicide starts to act as the granules dissolve in the water within the soil.

The impact of weather

Before using herbicides, a farmer needs to be aware of the current weather conditions and the forecast. Wind affects the spray pattern from the sprayer, which can mean other plants can be affected. Heavy rain soon after application will wash the herbicide off the leaves of the weeds or cause the chemicals within granules to leach into the surrounding area. Extreme sunlight can scorch foliage through herbicide droplets acting as lenses. Some herbicides work more efficiently on plants that are actively growing, so in temperate climates these can only be applied during the growing season.

Controlling pests and diseases

Weeds, pests and diseases can be controlled with the use of chemicals. A **pest** is an animal that attacks or feeds upon the crop plant. A chemical used to control a pest is known as a **pesticide.** The most common pests of plants are insects. A chemical used to control insects is called an **insecticide.**

A crop **disease** is caused by fungi, bacteria or viruses. These are collectively known as **pathogens.** Of these three groups fungal diseases of crops are most common. Fungal diseases are controlled by chemicals known as **fungicides.**

Unfortunately, there is not a collective term to describe pest and disease control chemicals so the term pesticide is sometimes used to describe all control chemicals. Make sure you know which meaning is being used when you are reading about pesticides.

As with herbicides, insecticides and fungicides can be applied in a number of ways, the choice will often depend on which part of the plant is affected. Again, there is an environmental risk if they are applied incorrectly because they will affect other organisms in the area, potentially affecting food webs. The chemicals can also be poisonous to humans: farmers may need to wear personal protective equipment (PPE) while using them. If chemical residues remain in the crops they can pose safety concerns if the concentrations get too high.

KEY TERMS

Herbicide: a chemical used to control weeds

Pest: an animal that attacks or feeds on a plant

Pesticide: a chemical used to control pests, but also, less accurately, used as a collective term to describe pest- and disease-killing chemicals

Insecticide: a chemical that kills insects

Disease: a pathogen (fungus, bacterium or virus) that attacks a plant

Pathogen: a collective name to describe disease-causing organisms (bacteria, fungi and viruses)

Fungicide: a chemical used to control fungal diseases

Alternatives to chemical control

There is no doubt that the use of synthetic chemicals to control pests, diseases and weeds has resulted in huge increases in yield for farmers, which means the use of chemicals is very popular. However, some people, including some scientists, are concerned about their widespread use. As early as the 1960s, biologists highlighted the impact that pesticides were having on food webs. A reduction in insects, for example, means there is less food for their predators (small birds and reptiles). This is turn means there is less food for the top consumers such as birds of prey.

It was also discovered that while the pesticides may not directly kill predators feeding on treated insects, the chemicals do not break down in their bodies. When organisms are eaten by top predators, the amount of toxic chemical builds up in larger quantities (biomagnification). For the top predators the higher concentrations can be toxic. In many areas this has been seen most clearly by a large reduction in numbers of birds of prey after pesticides were introduced. As a result of these observations, many people would like to see the use of chemical controls reduced and alternative methods used instead to solve pest, disease and weed problems.

Biological control

One alternative way to control pests and diseases is to find natural predators that can solve the problem. If the natural predators can be bred in large enough quantities and introduced to a crop, they can feed off the pest and therefore control the infestation.

The advantages of biological control methods are:

- no chemical residues are left in the crop
- there is no impact of sprays on the surrounding ecosystem
- once introduced, the population of the control agent should increase and breed, so there is no need for reapplication
- when the pest has been controlled, the lack of food will mean the predator will naturally reduce in numbers
- there is no need to wear protective clothing when applying the predator.

Disadvantages of using biological control are:

- the control is not as instant as chemical control
- climatic conditions might mean the pest breeds faster than the predator, so the problem is not controlled
- the predator might not stay on the crop and move elsewhere, instead of feeding on the intended pest
- the predator might escape into the local countryside and impact the natural ecosystem and food web.

Why not leave it all to nature?

While an ecological balance is achieved naturally in a natural environment, growing crops creates an unnatural environment: it is rare to find large numbers of the same plant naturally growing together in one place with few other species present. Crop plants are also grown in areas where they do not grow naturally in the wild, away from their natural predators. In a natural environment, crop plants may yield less or suffer high levels of damage, which farmers do not want.

Alternatives to herbicides

As with pesticides, some people, including some scientists, have issues with the use of herbicides and are concerned about the impact they may have on the soil ecosystem. There are alternative methods for controlling weeds.

- Cultural controls: hand weeding and hoeing are useful methods for removing individual weeds but require a lot of labour.
- Weed barriers: using black plastic sheeting over the ground or a deep layer of composted organic matter (mulches) helps smother weeds. Mulches help to stop the growth of weeds by stopping light reaching germinated weed seeds, as well as preventing evaporation of water from soils, which leads to waterlogged soils.
- Flame guns: paraffin (kerosene) is a highly flammable liquid that can be used in a flame gun to scorch off the tops of weeds and kill weed seeds at the soil surface. This process has risks and is only really suitable for use in areas before crops are planted.

Farmers may prefer to use herbicides rather than a non-chemical control because:

- herbicides are easier to manage and the weed control can be applied over a longer season
- alternatives may be less effective and more variable
- the use of herbicides can be cheaper
- the results are more predictable, with less risk of failure
- less labour is needed compared with cultural controls
- the effect of herbicides can be more rapid.

Efficiency gains through mechanisation

There is no doubt that across much of the world there have been major changes in farming techniques. Many crops were traditionally labour intensive to produce, and the availability of the workforce limited the amount of land that could be cultivated. Using machines such as tractors means that larger areas can be cultivated easily by one person. This reduces the labour costs for the farmer and also means they are cropping from a larger area. The power of the machine's engine means work like ploughing can take place when there is more water in the soil (when it is heavier), extending the season when soils can be cultivated.

As well as basic cultivation tasks, additional attachments can be added to a tractor to allow efficient application of fertilisers or pesticides. Tractors also have the capacity to transport large loads, which is useful at harvest time.

With some crops modern farming techniques have changed the landscape: large machines work best in large fields because time is lost when they need to change direction. This has led to the removal of natural vegetation to remove obstructions to the smooth operation of the machines.

Selective breeding

Selective breeding is the traditional method used for improving the performance of crops and livestock, and has been carried out across the world by farmers for generations.

The process of selective breeding is as follows:

- identify which characteristics of the species are important
- choose parents that exhibit these characteristics
- raise the offspring from these parents
- select the best offspring that show the desired characteristics
- repeat the process.

This can be applied to both plants and animals. Examples of desirable characteristics in certain organisms include:

- dairy cattle, an increase in milk yield
- beef cattle, an increase in muscle size
- wheat, increased disease-resistance and higher yields
- rice, an increase in yield, for example IR8.

How big an impact has selective breeding had?

Selective breeding of dairy cattle in the USA has led to double the milk yield per cow compared with 40 years ago. Selective breeding of beef cattle has developed a breed called the Belgian Blue that has exceptional muscle growth, resulting in a greater amount of meat from an animal. Improvements to wheat varieties have helped double the production of wheat in India since it was introduced in the mid-1960s; similar results have been seen in Pakistan, where production has doubled in 5 years. Selective breeding of rice has resulted in the production of a strain called IR8, which has had a huge impact on rice production in many areas of the world. For example, the use of IR8 (and other new cultural techniques) has increased annual rice production in the Philippines from 3.7 tonnes to 7.7 tonnes in 20 years.

It should be remembered that selective breeding is continuous: combining the existing characteristics of parents and selecting the best offspring for future crosses. It is a relatively slow process and has a low success rate. It is estimated that only 1 in 20 000 new plant seedlings will become a successful commercial variety. Testing and evaluation can take 20 years, and the timescale is likely to be longer for many animals than selective breeding because it will be a few years before the offspring are mature enough to breed.

Genetic modification

Genetic modification can produce faster results. Technology has enabled scientists to map the genetic material (DNA) of different plant and animal species to understand their genetic code. This genetic mapping has brought about a greater knowledge of how short sections of DNA called **genes** relate to the characteristics of a living organism.

Understanding this code has enabled scientists to insert a piece of DNA from one organism into the genetic code of another. The result is called a **genetically modified organism** (GMO). The process is controversial, with supporters both for and against the technology.

KEY TERMS

Gene: a sequence of DNA that is responsible for a characteristic of a living organism

Genetically modified organism (GMO): an organism whose genetic material has been altered by genetic engineering

There are many different reasons for genetically modifying plant species.

- Disease and pest resistance: genes can be cut from a resistant plant and added to a crop plant.
- Nutritional value: plants can be developed that are more nourishing.
- Growth of plants in inhospitable areas.
- Higher yields.
- Herbicide resistance, which would allow farmers to spray the whole crop and its weeds and only affect the weeds.
- Less use of pesticides, if the GMO plant is pest resistant.
- Crops with longer storage lives, leading to less food wastage.

Concerns about the development of GMOs include:

- the unknown impact of the new characteristics on human health
- the products are not natural
- the genes might get into wild plants if they interbreed with GMOs
- issues for other insects caused by insect-resistant varieties.

It is possible to transfer genetic material between species of plant or even between animals, not just between breeds of the same species. The resulting organisms are called transgenic. This process provides even more possibilities for scientists to manipulate the way in which a plant or animal grows. Scientists are using this technology in some unexpected ways, such as using genetically modified carrots to make a drug within the carrot cells that can be used to treat humans. If successful, the growth of these GMO carrots could provide another commercial crop for farmers.

Controlling the crop environment

One of the largest variable factors that has an impact on the yield of a crop is the growing environment, for rearing livestock as well as growing crops. Over very large areas it can be difficult or expensive to try and control the environment, although there are some important techniques such as:

- providing shade for cattle so that they do not get too hot
- using windbreaks at the edges of crops to reduce wind speed and prevent damage to the crops
- removing trees that shade a crop in order to maximise the light the plants receive.

While these techniques can change the environment and prevent extreme conditions, they are not easily reversible or adaptable if the local weather conditions change.

Over smaller areas, it is possible to invest more money in controlling the environment, resulting in an end product that can be sold for a high price and so make a profit. One example of this is the use of greenhouses.

The term **greenhouse** is a collective term for structures that support the controlled growth of plants. It is a more accurate term than glasshouse because not all structures are made of glass. Many greenhouses use transparent plastic sheets made from, for example, a polycarbonate, which is far stronger than glass and often sold as a double-walled material, providing good insulation against colder external air temperatures and so reducing the cost of the internal heating (Figure 3.11).

Figure 3.11 A modern greenhouse. Built on an aluminium frame, the sides are constructed of glass and the roof of double-walled polycarbonate (which is stronger and a better insulator than glass). The mixture of glass and polycarbonate mean this cannot be described as a 'glasshouse'.

The term greenhouse also includes structures such as polythene tunnels (or polytunnels), where plastic film is stretched over large metal hoops (Figure 3.12). This is far cheaper to install than a more robust greenhouse but is not as effective in controlling the environment and does not last as long.

Figure 3.12 A polythene tunnel (polytunnel) is a relatively cheap structure that is commonly used for growing food crops.

Growing plants within an enclosed space means that the grower has a better opportunity to manage the space. A greenhouse allows many different environmental factors to be managed (Table 3.10).

Investment in additional equipment for a greenhouse system is expensive and only cost effective for an expensive crop. Operating all the additional systems can require a lot of labour. However, most modern greenhouses use a range of sensors to monitor the environmental conditions. These sensors, linked to a computer, can operate the equipment automatically so a worker does not need to be present all the time.

KEY TERM

Greenhouse: a building made of glass or similar transparent material that is used manage the environment for plant growth

Growth factor	How it might be increased	How it might be decreased
Temperature	Operate greenhouse heating system	Open roof ventilators
Light level	Use supplementary lighting	Use shading material in the roof
Humidity	Use misting units to add moisture to the air	Open roof ventilators or use extractor fans
Day length	Use supplementary lighting at the end of the day	Use shading material in the roof and curtains at the side
Water	Use a sprinkler or irrigation system	Install drainage material underneath the pots or beds

Table 3.10 Managing factors that affect plant growth.

Research into many greenhouse crops has identified a **growing blueprint**: the ideal environmental conditions needed by a plant for maximum growth. If this is programmed into a computer, the greenhouse can be managed remotely. The computer system is also linked to sensors outside the greenhouse and to accurate weather forecasts, so that it can predict future environmental conditions and adjust the greenhouse's environment accordingly. For example, approaching clouds will mean there will be less sunlight, so more heating will be needed. The computer will predict this and turn up the greenhouse heating system so that it can compensate when the temperature starts to drop.

The greenhouse effect

Greenhouses heat up using the Sun's rays. This effect been noticed for centuries and gives the name to the global warming effect we see happening to the Earth (see Section 7.1). In the case of a greenhouse, sunlight passes through the glass (or other transparent material). Moving through the glass causes the wavelength of the energy to change, converting a proportion of the energy into heat. Once inside the greenhouse, the heat is trapped and so the temperature inside the greenhouse becomes warmer than outside. Of all the different materials used to glaze a greenhouse, glass is the most effective in converting the Sun's light energy into heat.

Controlling the whole environment

The greenhouse environment allows farmers to control most environmental conditions and increase crop yields. Advances in selective breeding or genetic modification can also greatly increase potential crop yields. Another factor a grower can try to optimise is the material the plants are actually growing in.

As discussed earlier, soil is very variable, which means that farmers may need to make large modifications to make it an ideal growing environment. At a large scale this is not cost effective, but it can be worthwhile within a greenhouse. Scientists have developed a range of different composts and growing media that can remove the need for soil. The plants are grown in a material that is uniform for each crop and provides the ideal structure. This is a very successful technique, but the concept has been taken even further: growing plants using just water and dissolved nutrients. This is called **hydroponics**.

KEY TERMS

Growing blueprint: the growing requirements of a crop throughout its life, which a grower can use to maximise the yield

Hydroponics: growing plants without soil, with the nutrients the plant needs dissolved in water; this technique is often used in conjunction with a growing blueprint

There is a number of hydroponic techniques, but a common method is to float plants on polystyrene rafts on a reservoir of moving water (Figure 3.13). Water flows through the roots of the plants and is recycled. Sensors measure the amount of key mineral nutrients in the water and add more as they are needed. Air is bubbled into the mineral nutrient solution to ensure the plant roots have enough oxygen to respire.

Advantages of hydroponics include:

- no need for soil
- can be used anywhere (there are experiments being carried out in space)
- an intensive system that can provide high yields
- easy to harvest
- plants are given exactly the nutrients they need in the irrigation water
- water is recycled, so used efficiently

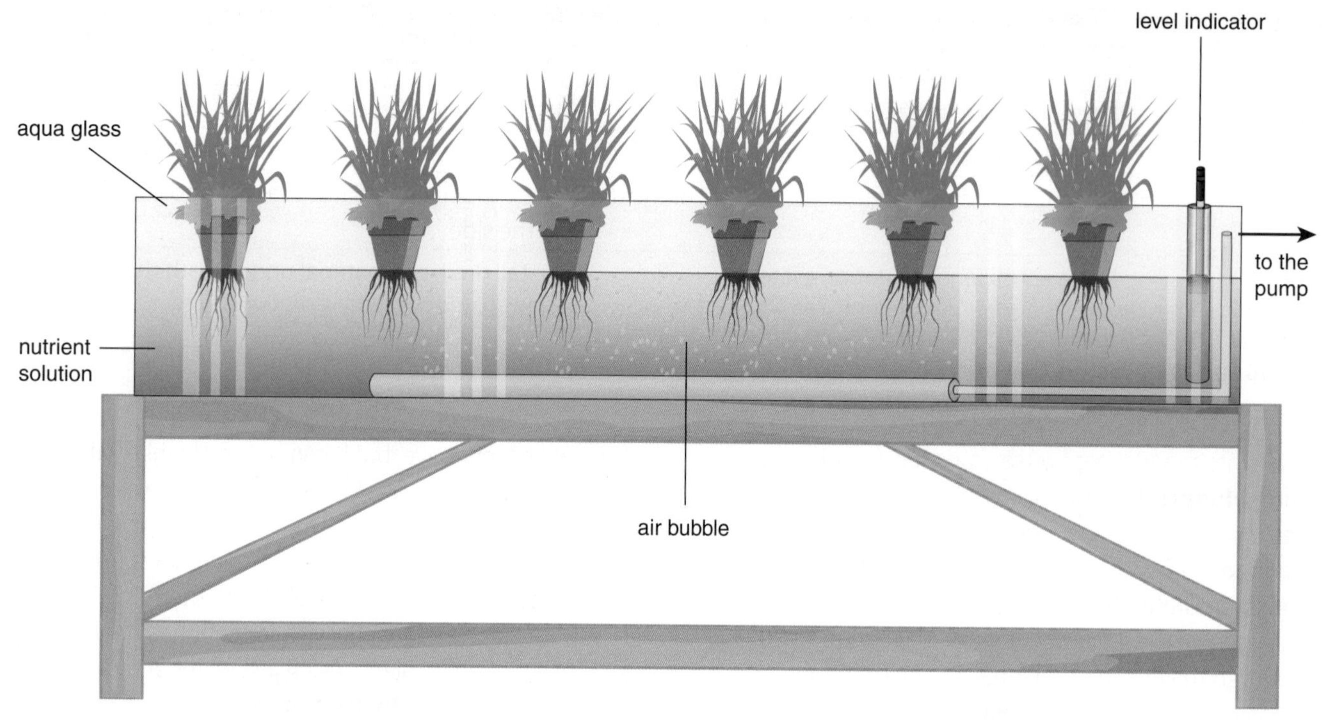

Figure 3.13 An example of a hydroponic growing system. Sensors within the system allow the process to be automated once it is set up.

- no weeds or pests and diseases in the 'soil'
- pollutants are not released into the environment.

Disadvantages of hydroponics include:

- it is expensive to set up
- only suitable for small production areas
- requires a lot of technical knowledge
- disease, if present, is rapidly spread through the water supply to all plants
- plants can die quickly if conditions are not maintained at optimum levels.

SELF-ASSESSMENT QUESTIONS

3.5 Using a growing blueprint requires close control of the growing environment. This will be an expensive investment for the grower. Give three reasons why the grower may still consider the investment worthwhile.

3.6 Give two advantages the use of genetic modification has over the use of selective breeding when developing a new breed or type of animal or plant.

3.5 The impact of agriculture on people and the environment

The agriculture industry has a major impact worldwide: it is the largest user of land, the largest user of water and the largest employer. Therefore, the sector has a great responsibility for the planet as well as the responsibility of feeding the ever-expanding world population. The pressures to maximise production efficiency and resource use can have other consequences. How does mismanagement of farming systems impact the planet?

Overuse of insecticides and herbicides

The use of chemical sprays to control populations of insects and weeds has increased yield and also prevented the loss of food in storage. However, overuse can cause problems that have implications for future production.

KEY TERM

Resistance: the ability of a living organism to survive when exposed to a toxic chemical (such as a pesticide or herbicide)

Regular use of one insecticide chemical can cause **resistance** within the pest population. This means that the toxic chemical no longer kills all the target pest individuals. The same principal results in herbicide resistance.

Figure 3.14 shows how resistance develops. It takes a number of generations before a pest becomes fully resistant. However, many pests, such as insects, have very short life cycles, which means a number of generations can occur in just a few weeks.

Once an insect is no longer being controlled effectively by an insecticide, farmers tend to apply an increased dose to improve the effect. While this may work in the short term, it can help pesticide resistance build up even more rapidly. The best practice for farmers is to use a range of different pesticides so that if resistance starts to build up to one product another product is still likely be toxic to the pest.

Insecticides and herbicides can also cause unintended environmental damage. In the case of insecticides, their application can kill beneficial insects such as bees, which will then affect the pollination of plants. A change in the availability of insects can also impact on the wider food web, because many animals feed on insects.

In the case of both insecticides and herbicides, there can be issues of spray drift: the chemical may reach an unintended target and so cause environmental damage. Herbicides can remain within the soil long enough to disrupt the growth of other plants. Heavy rainfall can cause leaching of insecticides and herbicides into rivers and lakes, causing damage to other organisms. There is some evidence that herbicides can have an impact on soil organisms such as microscopic animals and fungi, which has an effect on the food web.

These problems are not just confined to plants. In many countries livestock are given routine medication, not because they are sick but to prevent infection from occurring. This is good practice if used well, but if overused problems can occur. Many animals are given antibiotics as part of their medication. The same or very similar products are given to humans. As with insecticides, there is a risk of

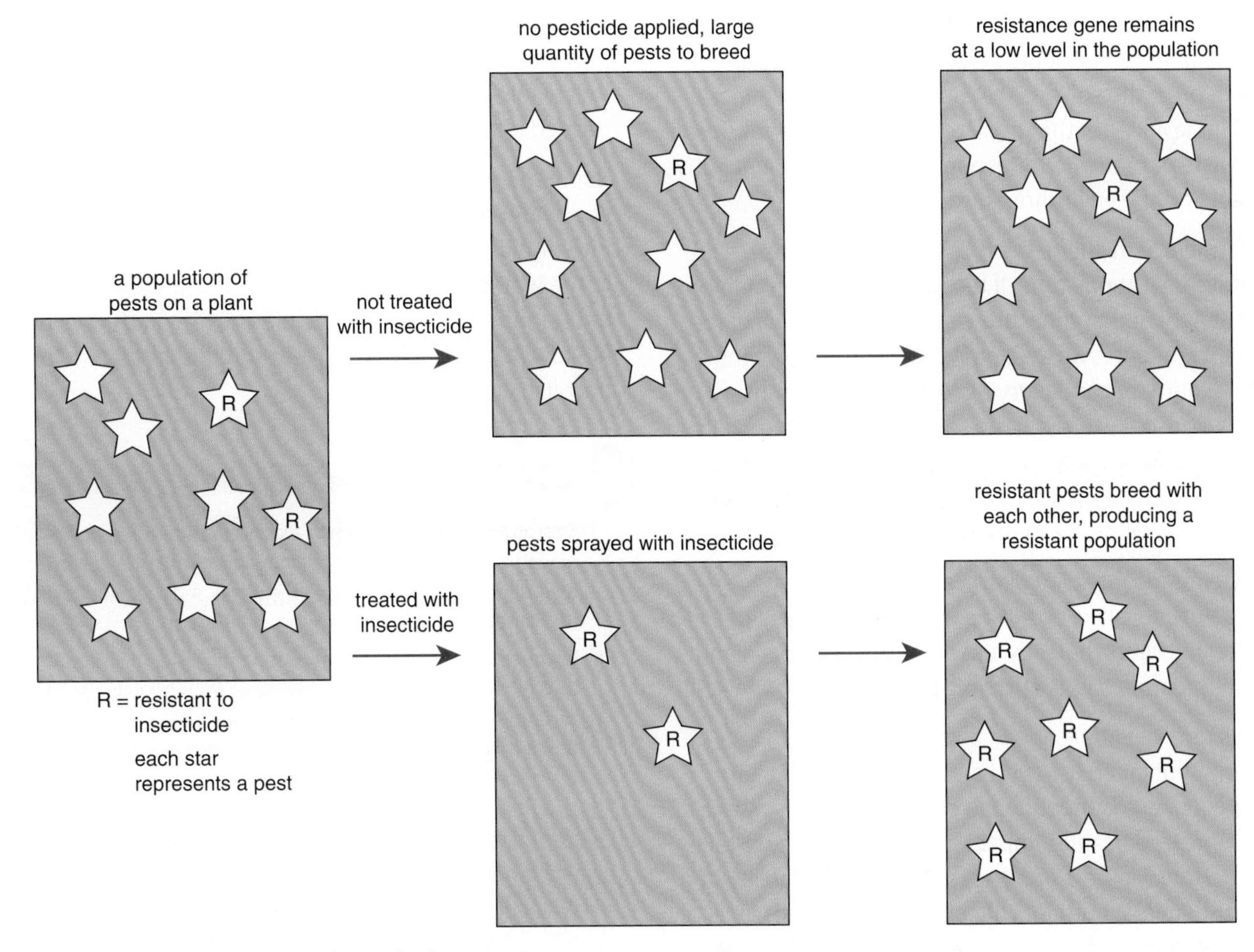

Figure 3.14 How resistance to an insecticide occurs.

resistance building up to these antibiotics, so the products may be ineffective in controlling diseases, leaving the human population, as well as the livestock, at greater risk of illness or death.

SELF-ASSESSMENT QUESTIONS

3.7 It has been discovered that an insect pest is no longer being controlled by an insecticide that has been used on a farm for years. Suggest two things the farmer could do to control the problem.

3.8 What should be done to prevent a similar problem happening again?

Misuse of fertilisers

It is well known that adding fertilisers to soils that are short of mineral nutrients will increase the growth of plants. It is therefore easy to assume that adding fertilisers to any soil will increase the growth of plants and therefore increase their yield. However, the addition of extra mineral nutrients stops having a beneficial impact once the soil has reached its maximum mineral nutrient level. After that point, any additional application is a waste of money and resources. There will be negative impacts on the environment too.

For farmers, it might be most cost effective to apply a lot of fertiliser all at one time. If the weather or soil conditions are not right at that time, this can mean that much of the nutrient content is wasted: heavy rain can dissolve the mineral nutrients and carrying them away as it runs-off the land or soaks through the soil (leaching). If the weather conditions do not support rapid plant growth, the roots will take up fewer mineral nutrients and again there is a chance they will be washed away before they are needed.

Excess water containing dissolved fertilisers drains into rivers and lakes, upsetting the natural balance of mineral nutrients there. Excess amounts of nitrogen and phosphorus can cause **eutrophication** (see Section 4.8).

Excess fertiliser application can also impact the environment in other ways. Large quantities can alter the pH of the soil, affecting the organisms that live there and, more importantly, impact on a plant's ability to take up nutrients. Figure 3.5 shows the way the availability of different mineral nutrients affected by pH. It is possible for the addition of fertiliser to reduce the availability of nutrients by changing the pH of the soil.

Some mineral nutrients are only needed by plants in small quantities (often referred to as trace elements). Too much of these within a soil can be toxic to plants, again having the opposite effect to the one intended.

Overapplication of fertilisers can affect a plant's ability to take up water. Roots use a process called **osmosis** (where minerals flow from an area of lower concentration to an area of higher concentration through a membrane) to take up water. Normally the solution inside the plant's cells is more concentrated than the soil solution. Too much fertiliser can increase the concentration of solutes in the soil solution, causing water to flow out of the plant. This dehydrates the plant (often called scorching). This is a risk when a fertiliser is misapplied over a field, but can be also seen around manure (dung) heaps, where plants fail to grow and there is also a greater risk of nutrients leaching into the surrounding soil.

Excess nutrients can also affect the growth of plants directly. Too much fertiliser can cause excessively lush growth: the plant grows too rapidly and is unable to support itself. Lush growth is more susceptible to pest and disease attack. An imbalance of nutrients (such as a high nitrogen to potassium ratio) can cause a plant to produce lots of foliage and be less likely to flower, which is not the desired effect if the crop is the fruit.

Using too much fertiliser can have an impact on humans too: water quality can be affected by nutrients leaching into drinking supplies. A high concentration of fertiliser in the water supply can cause the development of blue baby syndrome: newborn babies have skin tissues that are low in oxygen, which gives them a slightly blue or purplish colour.

KEY TERMS

Eutrophication: a sequence events starting with enrichment of water by mineral nutrients or organic matter that leads to a reduction in oxygen levels in the water and the death of fish and other animals

Osmosis: the process by which mineral molecules pass through a semi-permeable membrane from a weaker solution to a more concentrated solution to make the concentration of the mineral the same on both sides of the membrane

Overapplication of fertilisers is a risk for users of both organic and inorganic fertilisers. Inorganic fertilisers are a risk because they tend to be more soluble in water; a benefit to farmers as they will be quickly available to the crop, but also more prone to leaching if there is heavy rain or irrigation. Bulky organic fertilisers release their nutrients over a longer period of time, but it is harder to determine the precise nutrient content, so there is a risk of overapplication.

Some developed countries have laws in place to reduce the potential impact of overapplication of fertilisers. In the UK, the government has designated nitrate vulnerable zones (NVZs): areas where levels of nitrogen are already high. In these places there are strict limits on when fertilisers can be applied (to reduce the risk of leaching), and detailed records have to be kept by the farmer to show how much fertiliser has been applied. Failure to keep the records can result in large fines.

Misuse of irrigation

Water is needed by all living organisms. The demand for water means that many countries are facing water shortages. Agriculture is under pressure to use water wisely and to recycle wherever possible. Wasting water can result in a shortage of water for human or livestock use. Too much irrigation can have various negative effects.

- Damage to the soil structure: when wet, air pockets are lost and the soil is compacted.
- Death of plant roots: waterlogged soils prevent plant roots getting sufficient oxygen to respire and cells start to die.
- Loss of nutrients: nutrients dissolve in the water in soil, and as water drains away nutrients are taken away with it.
- Soil erosion: large amounts of water run-off will take some of the soil particles with it.
- Soil capping: the surface of the soil can become hard and compact, which makes it harder for plants to grow through the soil.
- Salinisation: the salt content of the soil can increase. Scientists have estimated that around 20% of irrigated land has become saline in the last 20 years. Salts dissolve into the water within the soil but are normally at their highest concentrations deeper in the soil. Over-irrigated soils become waterlogged and therefore the salts are able to move throughout the soil. When the Sun causes evaporation of water from the soil, the salts are left behind. If the salt levels become too high, plants will have difficulty taking up water (by osmosis) and water supplies may also become unsuitable for drinking.
- Preventing soil cultivation: if the water content is too high, the soil can be too heavy to cultivate. Machines can get stuck because the soil structure cannot support their weight.

The application of too many pesticides, fertilisers or water can all cause problems for people and the environment. The challenge is that simply using them less also causes problems: reduced yield and even fewer resources for future crops. It is not a good decision to apply none of these items. Failing to add extra mineral nutrients to a soil slows down plant growth because there are insufficient nutrients for the construction of plant proteins, for example, or the development of supporting fibres. Plants will grow less quickly, have a smaller yield and perhaps produce a crop of poor quality, either in nutrient content or its ability to be stored for a long period. A mineral nutrient deficiency within a plant can make it less able to withstand a pest or disease attack.

If soils yield less, there is less grazing available for livestock, and less food for farmers and their families. Famers may need to relocate if the land cannot provide them with sufficient food to survive.

Poor management of the soil can lead to **desertification**: the process of fertile land being transformed into desert. Desertification of previously fertile land can be a result of soil erosion, and agricultural methods can greatly influence the risk of erosion. This issue will be discussed further later in the chapter.

KEY TERM

Desertification: the process by which fertile land becomes desert

Choice of crops

Most farmers have some level of choice over the types of crops they grow. For many subsistence farmers, the choice is likely to be the type of plants that will feed their families most effectively (either directly from the plant harvest or by feeding livestock).

Farmers who earn a profit by growing crops (commercial production) may make different decisions about which plants to grow. However, the most profitable product to grow in terms of generating cash may not be the best choice for the wider community. One example of this conflict is where the most fertile land, in countries such as Afghanistan, is used to grow poppies for opium production, either for the legal production of drugs or the illegal drug trade. Another example is the use of the most fertile land in countries such as Kenya to produce cut flowers for rich countries such as in Europe or North America.

While it could benefit the population as a whole if the fertile land was used to produce food to feed local people, this does not necessarily provide the local farmers with a large income. There can be benefits for the country has a whole if it has commercial crops it can trade with other countries. International trade allows a country access to (and the cash to purchase) other resources and technologies not available to them internally.

This raises more ethical and moral dilemmas about whether governments should dictate what their countries' populations can and cannot eat. Should a government tell farmers what they can or cannot grow? Should a government control the actions of its citizens, or should the population be given a free choice? Over the centuries different countries (and political parties) have taken different views on these questions. Indeed, there is probably not a correct answer. However, poor decisions made by governments can result in a change in government at the next election or, in extreme cases, violent revolution to affect change.

Overproduction and waste

Allowing farmers the opportunity to choose which crops to grow (to maximise their profits) might also mean that too much of a particular crop is grown. When there is a greater demand for a product than there is supply, a farmer can charge more when selling a crop. The opposite also happens, when a product is widely available and there is more than people wish to buy, farmers will get less money for their crop and potentially some of the crop is wasted. If a farmer has failed to make a profit in a particular year he or she may start to grow a crop that others have made a profit from that year, causing oversupply and undersupply of different crops the following year. Thus allowing farmers the freedom to choose and manage their own land can lead to a waste of resources in a number of ways.

- Waste from over-production: too much of a crop might mean that some will not be sold.
- Waste of storage space: it may take longer to sell a crop, so buildings are needed to store the spare harvest. Some crops need special conditions so they do not spoil.
- Waste of transportation: to sell all the crop, a farmer may need to travel larger distances, using more fuel, etc.
- Waste of quality produce: if a crop starts to decrease in quality because it has not been sold quickly enough, it will be worth less money.
- Waste of labour: the farmer may have to staff to help grow and care for the crop, which is not an efficient use of time and labour if too much crop is produced.

Even when a farmer or grower does sell their crop, if there is overproduction the price will be low. After bills have been paid, does the farmer have enough money to buy seed to plant a new crop for the next season?

Mechanisation

While the use of machinery has helped the large increase in yields that have been achieved over the last few decades, it does have a number of impacts on the environment and the local population.

For machines to work efficiently, fields have been made larger, removing natural vegetation that may provide habitats for other organisms. This may also have an impact directly on the crop by removing natural predators of pests.

Machines such as tractors use fossil fuels, which are a non-renewable resource. Their exhaust gases also contribute to air pollution. Large machines (and their fuel) can be expensive for a farmer. While the use of mechanisation can increase yield, the extra costs can mean the farmer makes little profit and is unable to pay the bank loans, for example, to cover the cost of a new machine.

SELF-ASSESSMENT QUESTIONS

3.9 It has been said that too much irrigation might be as much of a problem for plants as too little water. Use Table 3.11 to describe how the amount of water can affect certain growth factors.

	Too little irrigation	Too much irrigation
Nutrient availability		
Root growth		

Table 3.11 Problems caused by irrigation.

3.10 Adding more fertiliser does not necessarily mean an increase in crop growth. Give three reasons why this might be the case.

Large machines exert a high pressure on the soil through their tyres. The areas where these tyres move can become very compacted as the soil is squashed together, and air spaces are removed. This can reduce the area where plant roots can grow and also reduce the natural drainage of the soil.

Use of machinery can have an impact on jobs and employment. A large tractor with a range of cultivation attachments can do the job of many people in less time. This means there are fewer opportunities for local people to work on the land. Without jobs and income to feed their families, some people might be forced to relocate. Often people will migrate from rural areas to cities in the hope of getting work, which can cause additional problems if there is inadequate housing and competition for jobs.

3.6 Causes and impacts of soil erosion

Soil erosion is a naturally occurring process that affects all types of land and plays an important role in shaping the landscape around us. Apart from natural disasters, soil erosion is usually fairly slow. Human activity, such as agriculture, can result in large, rapid changes to the landscape, affecting the natural equilibrium. Figure 3.15 shows a simplistic diagram of the different layers within the soil.

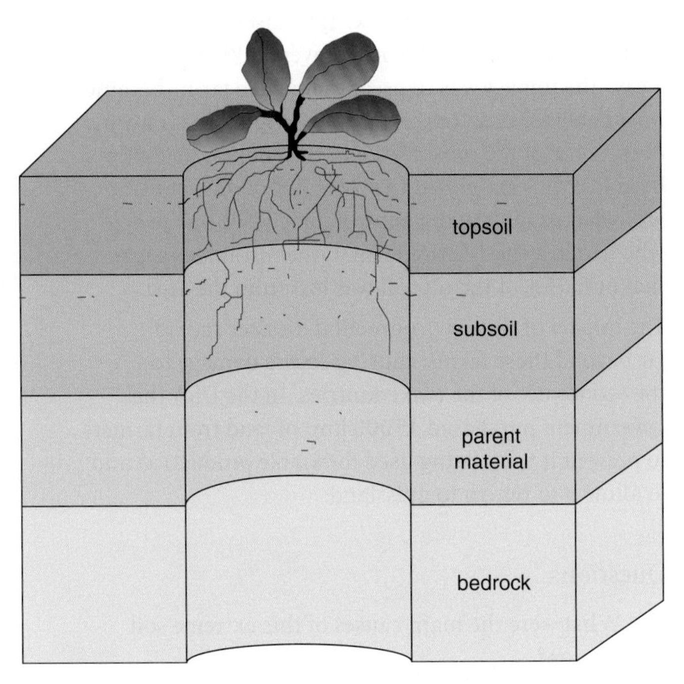

Figure 3.15 The horizons (layers) of soil. Most plant roots are found in the topsoil.

While there are a number of distinct layers (horizons) to soil, the topsoil, located just below dead leaves and plants, is the most fertile. The structure of topsoil allows the most root growth, because it holds water but also supports air spaces. Topsoil is often a dark layer, because it contains organic matter and potentially a large quantity of nutrients. Loss of this layer can seriously affect the fertility of the soil. There are a number of ways in which topsoil can be eroded.

- Removal of natural vegetation. The demand for land for grazing, crop growing or timber has had a catastrophic effect on natural habitats. The roots of existing plants help bind the soil together. Once these are removed, the soil structure is not strong enough to withstand intense rainfall. Flash flooding and other rainwater run-off picks up topsoil in its path and moves it away from its original location. Tree roots are useful in slowing down the speed of flowing torrents of water and providing places for any soil that is carried along to get trapped and deposited. When vegetation is removed there may be nothing left to prevent run-off and soil erosion. Areas of rainforest that are cleared for cultivation often suffer severe erosion because the original vegetation was the only factor binding the soil together. Growers often need to relocate frequently because the erosion prevents them planting subsequent crops.
- Overcultivation. Soils that are cultivated regularly start to lose soil structure: ploughing or digging breaks up large clumps into smaller amounts. While this may be good in the short term for even sowing and the development of seedlings, the mechanical breakdown of soil means that the smaller particles are easier to move and more vulnerable to erosion.
- Overgrazing. Pressure on grazing land means that the number of livestock present can reduce the vegetation to nearly ground level. Constant hard grazing weakens the plants because they do not have sufficient foliage to photosynthesise, and therefore they gradually die out. Lack of vegetation cover means that there are no longer plant roots to hold the soil together and so the soil becomes vulnerable to erosion. Large numbers of animals within an area will also trample down the plants, damaging them in the process. Animal hoofs compact the ground, and compaction reduces the number of air spaces in the soil, reducing root growth and further weakening the plants.
- Wind erosion. Removal of vegetation makes the soil far more prone to being blown around by the wind. The vegetation might be cleared for a number of reasons: the need for more space, excessive grazing by animals, an increase in the development of arable crops, or the

need to remove hedges and boundaries to allow large machines to operate effectively.

- Water erosion. Water is probably one of the more common causes of large-scale erosion and a contributory factor to some of the other types of erosion. Water can erode soils in a number of ways.
  - Heavy rainfall: heavy rain (with large droplets) dislodges soil particles with their force and they are then loose enough to be eroded in other ways.
  - Rainwater run-off: excess water that cannot be absorbed by the soil will transport soil away from the area. Water infiltration may also be reduced if the soil surface has been capped (by large water droplets) or compacted by feet or machines.
  - Gulley erosion: gullies and streams contain a volume of water moving at speed that erodes the local soil even further, forming deeper and deeper crevices. Gullies are initially formed as rainwater run-off flows across the land. Problems can be made worse where there is a natural slope in the soil, causing the rainwater to move faster, which then has a far stronger scouring effect.

The impacts of soil erosion

While the loss of topsoil from an area is one clear sign of extensive soil erosion, other direct and indirect impacts are far more complex. Loss of the topsoil means that the most productive layer of the soil has been removed. The subsoil is not capable of maintaining plant growth in the same way as topsoil, because of a lack of nutrients, typically insufficient air spaces and challenging water availability. The structure of the subsoil will not allow plant roots to penetrate easily, hence the reason there were very few shown in Figure 3.15. This inability to support vegetation leads to the desertification of the area: the lack of fertility means few plants survive, and few plants surviving means that little organic matter is re-entering the soil and improving its fertility.

CASE STUDY

The impact of wind erosion

Figure 3.16 Soil drifting over a farm in the 1930s as a result of severe erosion.

One major example of wind erosion was seen in the prairies of USA and Canada in the 1930s. Farmers had converted grassland into arable cropland, cultivating large areas using tractor-drawn ploughs. The area experienced extreme drought and the soil, no longer held together by the deep-rooted grasses, was blown around in the wind in huge dust clouds. These dust clouds, known as "black blizzards" were so dense they choked humans and livestock. They also impacted cities and shipping in the ocean over 3000 kilometres away. The impact was so great that whole farms became unsuitable for use; topsoil that was originally up to 2m deep, some of the most fertile in the country, had now been lost. It is estimated that over 400 000 km^2 of land was affected, displacing approximately 500 000 people who had lost their entire farm. Other estimates suggest that over 75% of the topsoil was lost from the area.

The impact of this environmental disaster spread far beyond these farms, causing severe damage to the economies of the two countries. In the USA the government purchased 45 000 km^2 of land from farmers to prevent it from being used for arable production and to allow it to return to grassland.

Questions

1. What were the main causes of this extreme soil erosion?
2. Why were farmers allowed to work in this way?
3. State two major impacts of this extreme soil erosion.
4. How did the purchase of land by the US government help to address the problem?

As a result of the loss of topsoil, there is a loss of habitats for many organisms in the area. Organisms living or feeding within the topsoil will lose their habitat. Animals supported by local vegetation have fewer sources of shelter and food. Thus soil erosion has an impact on the whole ecosystem. Interference with the local ecosystem can also cause unforeseen problems, such as an increase in pest problems if sufficient levels of their natural predators cannot be sustained in the new landscape.

Soil erosion can have an effect well beyond the initial area. Flowing water eventually enters rivers and lakes. As the flow of the water slows down, the soil being carried along starts to settle, silting up water courses, rivers and lakes. This can alter the capacity of the water bodies to hold water and cause flooding in new areas after heavy rainfall, because the volume of silt deposited means there is nowhere to hold the water. In other cases rivers are no longer navigable by boats because the waterways have become too shallow, affecting the livelihood of those who rely on the rivers for employment or as a supply route.

Silt deposits can form small lagoons, providing new breeding opportunities for insects such as mosquitoes, a vector of malaria (see Section 4.7). Silt can also affect the quality and availability of water for drinking. Silty water may affect the health and viability of aquatic organisms, burying them at the bottom of the silty layer or preventing light reaching the leaves of aquatic plants, which ultimately affects the oxygen content of the water and its ability to provide a healthy living environment. Fish numbers, for example, may be badly affected because soil in the water can reduce the effectiveness of their gills in extracting oxygen from the water.

The process of desertification means that the soil can no longer adequately support the growth of plants. This will have an impact on both the raising of crops and the rearing of livestock (which feed on plant material). With a fall in productivity from the land, locals may be forced to relocate to make a living. In the case of severe drought, this can result in the migration of a whole community. As with the impact of mechanisation, there can be an increase in the number of people moving into cities, but for many farming communities the displacement might include their livestock, which are valuable possessions. The movement of a whole community causes problems for the wider region, with potential conflict (even war) between displaced farmers and the original farming communities.

Once a family or community has been displaced, even if they are able to find land to cultivate, there will be a significant delay before any planted crops will yield any food. Without a reliable source of food, people and populations are at risk of **famine** and **malnutrition**. Foraging for food and fuel can have a negative impact on the natural vegetation in the new area as well. The need for food and a clean water supply becomes a priority when populations are displaced, and the focus of foreign aid agencies is to supply basic food and medical needs in order to prevent people dying and avoid a crisis developing.

Often the migration of communities means relocating to a neighbouring country, causing the additional complication of countries working together. Sometimes the location of temporary encampments for populations and the need for agreement between different countries results in a delay in getting the right resources to those who need it.

KEY TERMS

Famine: a lack of access to food, often over a large area

Malnutrition: not having enough of the correct nutrients to eat, causing ill health

Terracing: the artificial development of flat areas (for growing crops) in a sloping terrain

3.7 Methods to reduce soil erosion

Farmers need to cultivate land efficiently if they are to maximise its yield. If the techniques used result in the loss of the topsoil, fertility is lost. Keeping soil healthy, and in the correct place, is essential for the future production of good crops and the health of the local ecosystem. There is no one technique that can be applied in all situations: it is the responsibility of those cultivating the land to identify the risks within their own landscape and farm in a responsible way. The list below highlights some of the most common methods and the ways in which they help prevent the erosion of soil:

Terracing

Terracing is a common technique used in a lot of areas of the world. It helps to prevent the erosion of soil by rainwater on steep slopes. Figure 3.17 shows how terracing changes the shape of a hillside. When rainfall falls on a natural slope, it runs down the hillside due to gravity. As it does so, the volume of water increases and so does the speed (because of the gradient of the slope). Both of these factors dislodge soil, which is then carried within the surface run-off. When the speed of the water decreases (typically in a valley or at the mouth of a river), the soils

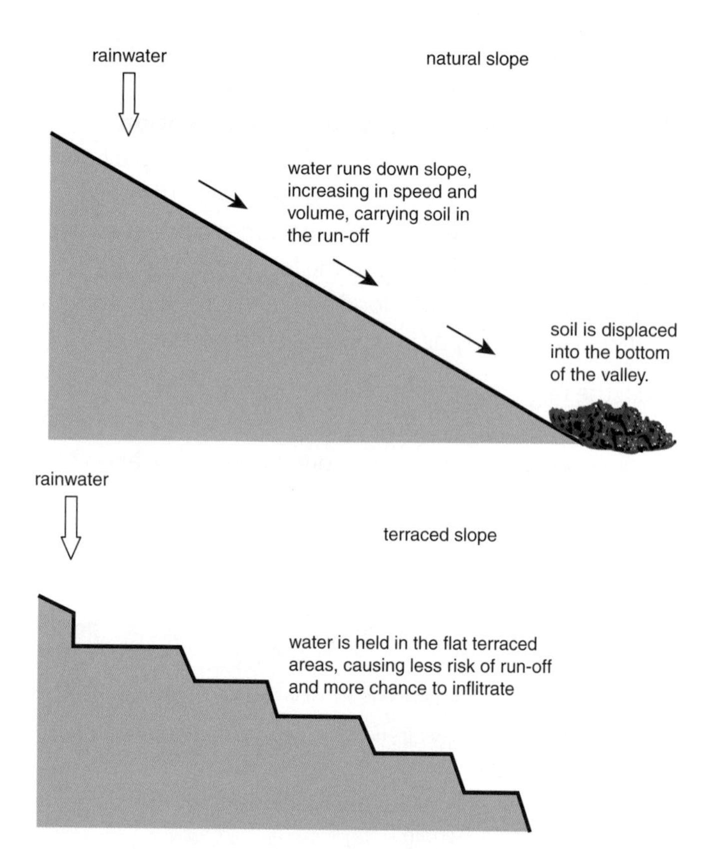

Figure 3.17 The impact on terracing on soil erosion. Flat areas tend to have a reduced water flow, decreasing the risk of topsoil being carried in run-off.

particles will be deposited. If there are no natural barriers left because of bad cultivation, the hillside is left without any useable topsoil, crops are washed away and areas where the soil has been deposited are covered in thick silty mud. In some cases whole villages can be submerged by mudslides, causing loss of life and loss of property. When washed further down into rivers or lakes, the silt can cause transport issues as well as damage to the ecosystem.

While very labour intensive, the re-modelling of a hillside into a series of terraces (or steps) means that when heavy rain does occur it is less likely to run down a slope. The water sits within each of the level, terraced areas longer than run-off, and the majority will infiltrate (soak) into the soil, where it can be used as needed.

Some crops benefit from the presence of standing water: terracing is often used for the cultivation of rice, using the pools of water formed to grow the plants in.

Contour ploughing

Based on a similar principle to terracing, when an area of land is ploughed there are benefits to ploughing so that the ridges and troughs run along the contours (rather than up and down) the land. While at a far smaller scale than that used with terracing, each plough furrow holds water back and prevents large torrents of water running down the slope, so preventing the formation of larger gullies and the run-off of topsoil.

Contour ploughing is suitable in a number of situations and useful on all gradients of slope. When land is cultivated and left without vegetation for a period of time, while the seeds start to germinate and emerge, the root system will be insufficient to bind the soil. If contour ploughing is used, the furrows help prevent erosion until the plants are established.

Bunds

Often linked to terracing, **bunds** are artificial banks at the edges of growing spaces designed to hold back water. This technique is especially useful for crops (such as rice) that need to be submerged at some stage or require very moist soils. Figure 3.18 shows how water is retained. The lack of the water flow also means that any soil that has been eroded from higher up the slope will be deposited in that terrace, increasing the quantity of soil available to the crop and potentially increasing its fertility.

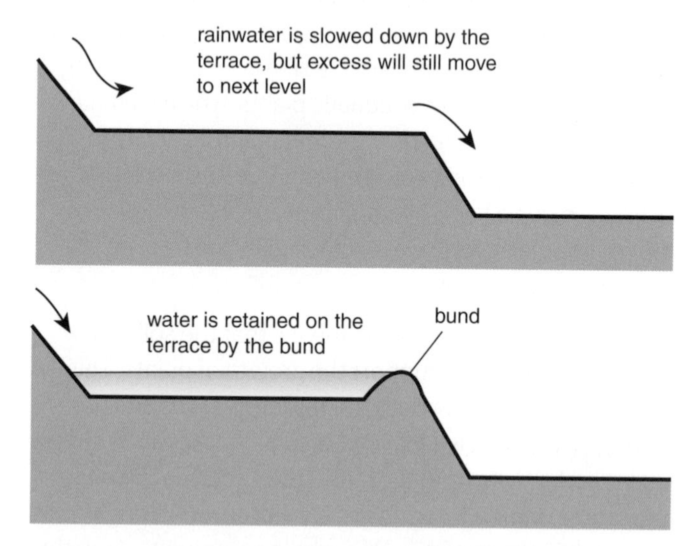

Figure 3.18 Bunds (banks of soil) are useful for holding back water and preventing soil erosion from run-off. The bund also helps to protect the soil from wind erosion, depending on its height and the direction of the prevailing wind.

KEY TERMS

Contour ploughing: a technique where the furrows caused by ploughing follow the contours of the land

Bund: an embankment constructed around the edge of an area to reduce the loss of a liquid (such as water)

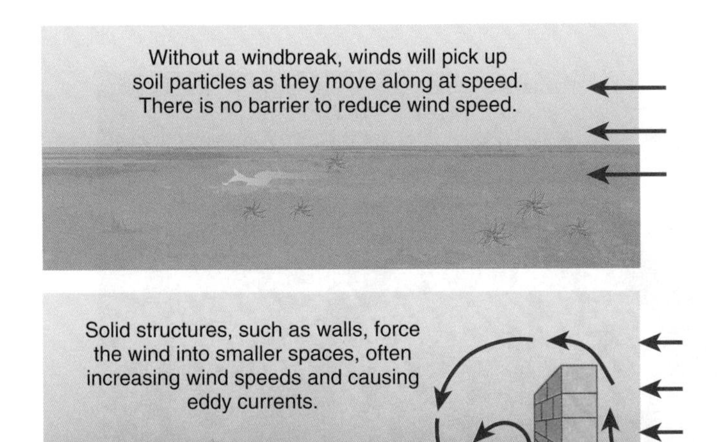

Figure 3.19 Natural windbreaks are more effective than solid structures because they reduce the speed of the wind as it flows through the foliage.

Windbreaks

Widely used in many parts of the world, **windbreaks** (as the name implies) are a useful tool for reducing wind erosion. While many different materials can be used, natural vegetation is one of the best materials. Many artificial windbreaks aim to reproduce the same effect as natural windbreaks. Figure 3.19 shows how wind speed is reduced. Natural windbreaks can have other benefits:

- they can provide additional habitats for beneficial insects (or other animals) that help control crop pests
- the roots of the windbreak will help hold back soil if the area is prone to erosion by run-off.

SELF-ASSESSMENT QUESTIONS

3.11 A farmer wishes to cultivate a steeply sloping field. Suggest two techniques she could use to prevent excessive soil erosion.

3.12 Give two advantages and two disadvantages of planting a windbreak at the edge of a field.

3.13 Suggest one other (non-natural) way a windbreak could be made.

KEY TERM

Windbreak: a permeable barrier, made of either living vegetation or artificial material, used to reduce the impact of the wind on an area

CASE STUDY

Flower power

The Netherlands has a long agricultural history. Its temperate climate and fertile soils are ideal for growing a wide range of crops and pasture.

The Netherlands' location within Europe has meant that it has been a strong trading nation for hundreds of years. Good transport links have helped the Netherlands develop the largest wholesale flower markets in the world, importing flowers from across the globe and selling them on to customers across Europe and beyond. In addition to trading in cut flowers from across the world, the fertile land within the Netherlands is used for growing flower bulbs, the most famous being the tulip. This is done on a large scale and, to increase the productive space, low-lying lands have been drained and large embankments (dams) built to hold back the water. The soil is peaty (contains a high level of organic matter) and is managed using drainage systems to take away extra water, which is then pumped outside the dams. Draining the low-lying land has allowed the growers to produce large fields on reclaimed ground without the need to remove natural vegetation. This process has also meant that the fields can be given straight edges, so using the large cultivation machines is very efficient.

Figure 3.20 shows an area of flower bulb production. The production of bulbs is mechanised: tractors do most of the work, with special attachments for planting the bulbs and harvesting the bulbs and additional equipment for applying fertiliser and pesticides. Large areas of land can be cultivated, and the crops cared for by a small number of workers, so the costs of producing

Figure 3.20 An area used for cultivation of flower bulbs.

flower bulbs can be lower and more competitive than those grown in other countries.

Tulips bulbs are planted very close together to maximise the use of the land. This means that a lot of nutrients are needed from the soil, and so the growers use large quantities of chemical (inorganic) fertilisers. The bulbs are a high-value crop so the growers also work hard to prevent the spread of any pests or diseases and typically control these problems with chemical sprays.

Tulip growers can get two 'harvests' from the same crop. Bulbs are lifted from the crop in late summer and sold around the world. In addition, the tulip flowers are picked and sold through the Netherlands' wholesale cut-flower markets, again being transported around the world. The flowers are cut in the spring, which is useful for the flower growers because there is employment for workers over a longer season.

Questions

1 **a** Describe the type of agriculture used by the flower growers in the Netherlands.

b Wind erosion is a major problem. Give three reasons why this might be the case.

2 What will be the biggest risk of applying pesticides and fertilisers by tractor? Outline the potential risks to the ecosystem.

3 This land is some of the most fertile in the Netherlands, yet the farmers are growing flowers rather than food. Give arguments for and against allowing farmers to choose their own crops to grow.

Maintaining crop cover

Cultivated soil is most vulnerable to erosion when there is little to hold it together. Erosion in natural ecosystems is normally limited by the vegetation growing within it: the roots of the plants bind the soil together as they anchor themselves into the ground. When an area is ploughed and cultivated, many of the natural safeguards against soil erosion are removed: the soil is broken up into smaller, more uniform pieces, any plant growth on the surface of the soil is removed, and this is usually done at a time in the year when the soil is relatively lightweight (if the soil were heavy with water, it would be too difficult to cultivate).

There are many examples of major ecological disasters in different parts of the world where farmers have cultivated large areas of land and it has become vulnerable to erosion. Even on a small scale, it can be a serious problem for a farmer. However, it is relatively easy to reduce the risk by maintaining a vegetative cover on the land for as long as possible. In some cases this might mean planting of an additional cover crop to help maintain the health of the soil. Some farmers, for example, will sow a legume such as clover immediately after a crop has been harvested. While not producing a saleable product itself, the clover helps to prevent erosion and (as a legume) means there will be more nitrogen in the soil for the next major crop. When the farmer is ready to cultivate the land for a crop, the clover can simply be ploughed into the soil immediately prior to sowing.

Other methods using the same principle include a 'no dig' method: existing vegetation is left until the moment a new crop is ready to be sown, but rather than cultivate the soil the farmer applies a herbicide to kill off existing weeds. The ground has not been disturbed and the roots of the original vegetation still bind the soil together until the new crop has started to establish itself. There are still risks with this method: herbicide residues can build up in the soil and affect the crop, and if control of the cover vegetation is ineffective it will compete with the new crop as a weed.

Adding organic matter

A soil is more at risk if it is has been left uncovered, if it has been broken down into small particles and if it is lightweight (and so has a low water content). This last issue can be addressed by adding more organic matter, such as animal manure or composted plant material, to the soil. Additional organic matter has a number of effects: it provides additional air gaps in heavy soils, increases the number of soil organisms in the soil (because they are feeding on the organic matter), adds nutrients to the soil and, regarding soil erosion, improves the general soil structure. Acting rather like a sponge, organic matter holds extra water, preventing the soil from drying out (when it is more prone to blowing away). Having larger, more irregularly sized particles, it helps form a base for other soil particles to bind to, again reducing the chances of small particles being blown away. An increase in organic matter, as well as increasing the general fertility of the soil (and therefore more vegetation on the soil surface) allows plants to develop stronger and more widespread roots, which help hold the soil together even when the tops of the plants are removed during cultivation.

A multi-layered approach to cropping

Most of the techniques discussed so far have focused on the planting of just one crop in an area (monocropping), but this has not been the traditional approach in many countries. With the risk of soil erosion becoming greater as resources are exploited further, many researchers are now revisiting older, established processes to see if they can be applied within a modern setting. Tree planting, for example, has many advantages:

- a row of trees can form a windbreak to protect other crops
- the tree canopy can provide shade for smaller crops that do not naturally thrive in direct sunlight, for example commercial coffee plants are derived from species that occupy the understorey of a woodland or forest where they would be shaded by taller trees
- the trees can also provide a natural habitat for animals that feed on the crop pests, reducing loss of the crop and the costs of buying expensive insecticides
- tree leaves fall to the ground and will add to the organic matter content of the soil

Other cropping systems have many benefits as well. Mixed cropping, growing more than one type of plant in the same area, means the resources in the soil, such as nutrients, are used more efficiently. If the plants grow at different heights, for example, they can use the same space without too much competition. If one plant has a deeper root system, it can be grown in the same area as a plant with a shallower root system. A smaller, sturdier plant can act as a support for a taller, more unstable crop.

A specific type of mixed cropping is **intercropping**: rows of a different crop are grown in between the established rows of the main crop. Typically of shorter duration than other types of mixed cropping, intercropping is used to maximise the use of space and other resources in a field. It is often used in new plantations, when the main tree crop will take a while to mature. Other plants can be grown at ground level and provide a profit for the farmer while the main plantation matures.

Crop rotation can also be used to use resources efficiently. Planting different crops over successive years in the same plot of land helps reduce the incidence of pests, improve the quality of the soil and utilise nutrients more effectively.

KEY TERM

Intercropping: the technique of growing other crops between the rows of a main crop, maximising the use of nutrients and water

3.8 An integrated approach for sustainable agriculture

While many of the techniques discussed so far can be used isolation, the most benefit can be derived by using a combination of techniques and adapting them for the local soil and climatic conditions. Historically, there are many examples of techniques that been researched and used successfully in a certain climate, and then used elsewhere on the assumption it will just as successful. However, this is often not the case, resulting in ecological damage and little understanding of the long-term effects, even with the original research.

Well-known examples include the use of some of the early chemical insecticides. Chemical compounds like DDT were seen as major breakthroughs in pesticide research, killing almost all insects. It was realised that beneficial insects were also killed, but this considered to be an insignificant side-effect of successful pest control. What was poorly understood was the long-term effects and impacts on the wider food web. There was initially little understanding or concern for the long-term impact or the sustainability of the technique.

More recently there has been increasing interest in the concept of sustainable agriculture, to maximise yields in a way that does not damage the wider environment unduly and maintains resources for future generations. The aims of sustainable agriculture include the following:

- meeting the needs of the population for agricultural produce
- making efficient use of non-renewable resources
- supporting the natural ecosystem and mimicking natural processes with farming techniques
- sustaining the economic independence of farmers.

Sustainable agriculture can use a number of 'organic' techniques, that is using materials derived from natural, living sources, but it does not prevent the use of artificial, manufactured materials if they have an overall beneficial impact on the farming ecosystem. It might still be appropriate to use some insecticides or herbicides, but their use might be limited to specific seasons (for example when pollinating insects will not be affected), the use of non-persistent chemicals (so that residues are not be left that could affect other organisms) or when there is no better cost-effective alternative. How such decisions are made can be the subject of much debate. What one person may consider to be sustainable may not acceptable to another. Regarding some of the more common systems and techniques used in agriculture today, an evaluation of the most appropriate, sustainable approach could include the following.

Fertilisers: the application of too much fertiliser at any particular time can cause serious environmental damage, in particular water contamination and subsequent eutrophication (Figure 3.21). Artificial fertilisers use a

Figure 3.21 Eutrophication of a drainage ditch.

lot of energy in their production, and many are fast acting, releasing nutrients quickly into the soil, which is a risk when there are high volumes of rain. A sustainable alternative is the use of natural, bulky organic fertilisers such as animal manures and composted crop remains. Such organic fertilisers:

- tend to release their nutrients slowly, reducing the risk of eutrophication
- in many areas are a waste product, so using them for agriculture saves on disposal costs
- are already present on many farms, so there are minimal transport costs associated with using them
- do not require energy for their manufacture
- also improve the soil structure.

Grazing: most livestock feeds on the vegetation grown within the farm. While this can occur randomly, a sustainable, managed approach has a number of benefits. A managed approach looks at the stocking density in an area and evaluates an appropriate timescale for allowing the animals to graze before moving them on to another area. The benefits of managing the grazing of livestock include:

- the prevention of overgrazing (when too much foliage is removed) and reducing the ability of grazed plants to regrow
- ensuring sufficient grazing by preventing scrubland plants from establishing because they are eaten as young seedlings
- maintaining appropriate soil fertility, by moving livestock between different fields they are all fertilised by the animal waste and no area receives too many nutrients
- maintaining good drainage, as appropriate grazing by livestock helps prevent unnecessary compaction of the soil by the animals' hooves (compacted soil does not drain as easily, which affects the growth and cover of grazing plants).

Crop rotation: a planned rotation (movement) of crop plants between different fields or plots has a number of beneficial effects for sustainable agriculture:

- less risk of pests and diseases because the crop is not grown in the same plot as the previous year
- efficient use of cultivation techniques, for example with plants that need deep cultivation being sown after the harvesting of root crops
- efficient use of available fertilisers, for example by utilising the nitrogen fixed in the roots of legumes
- growing a range of crops which means there is less likely to be an over-supply in the marketplace
- increasing the likelihood of at least one good crop in any one year, as crop success can vary each growing season and a range of crops spreads the risk of complete failure
- a wider diet for the farmer, if a range of crops is available rather than one monoculture
- natural fertiliser for the soil if animals are included in the rotation, and old crop residues can be eaten by the livestock.

Choice of varieties: plant breeding has led to a huge advancement in the quality of crops available, not just in terms of their yield but in their reliability. Some newer varieties are able to cope with situations in which their predecessors would certainly have failed. This is a more contentious aspect for some sustainable farmers, as the techniques that have resulted in some (but only a small minority) of the new species are the result of genetic modification. The question posed by some scientists is whether this technology is safe because the long-term effects on both humans and the ecosystem are not known or understood as yet. However, even conventional plant breeding has resulted in a number of important improvements. The choice of crop varieties now available offers farmers:

- reduced pesticide use, because of pest-resistance
- the ability to combat certain plant diseases (such as viruses) where no other form exists
- a reduced need for irrigation throughout the plant's life, because of drought resistance
- shorter cropping cycles, allowing two or more crops a year
- reduced herbicide use, because of herbicide resistance, although so far this has only been achieved through genetic modification, for example resistance to the herbicide glyphosate means a growing crop can be sprayed and only the weeds affected
- an extended harvesting season, providing a range of food for longer than possible with traditional varieties.

Irrigation

Efficiency in the use of water has become a priority in many countries where the water resources available are incapable of meeting the full demands of agriculture as well as the needs of a growing population and increasing use by industry. Sustainable agriculture has focused on the targeted use of water. Trickle-drip irrigation (delivering water to the base of plants using small pipes) provides the following sustainable benefits:

- minimising the amount of water used
- targeted delivery of water to the plants
- the ability to only use the system when the plants need water
- automation of the process to reduce the amount of labour needed to operate it
- a reduced risk of salinisation of the water in the soil, because less water evaporates from the soil surface and therefore salts are not drawn up from deeper in the soil.

A sustainable approach to water use includes reviewing the methods of extraction and the natural availability of water. Water for agriculture has to be of a suitable quality for irrigation (low in dissolved salts and levels of pollution) but does not have to be as clean as required for potable (drinking) water and water supplied to livestock. Sustainable agriculture uses alternative water supplies, reserving water from bore holes and other clean sources for other uses. For example, the collection of water from the roofs of buildings is ideal for irrigation. This is known as **rainwater harvesting**: collecting rainwater from buildings and hard-standing areas means it can be stored in tanks or reservoirs until needed. The water is then pumped through an irrigation system from the storage container to where it is needed, when it is needed.

In systems where a large amount of water is being used, the irrigation run-off can be collected and returned to the storage point for re-use later. This is a riskier method because salts may be leached out into the water and build up over time. Silt can also be carried in the run-off and potentially block the irrigation system.

KEY TERM

Rainwater harvesting: the collection of rainwater, for example from the roofs of buildings, and storage in a tank or reservoir for later use

Towards a sustainable future?

As a major employer and the largest land user of any industry in the world, agriculture has a major part to play in the maintenance of a healthy and viable ecosystem. The pressures on agriculture to supply an increasing population but in a sustainable way is one the biggest challenges the world currently faces. To rise to this challenge, environmentalists need to understand and manage a number of competing factors.

- The need to understand the nature and composition of soils: how the individual components have an impact on how the soil reacts to changing circumstances.
- Why soil is important for plant growth: the need for sufficient nutrients and how to manage the soil to maximise the nutrient availability (and the consequences of getting it wrong).
- How to manage soils with different characteristics to maximise their performance.
- The role of different types of agricultural systems: how to address the different aims of different farmers.
- Ways in which yields can be improved and how the choice of different practices has an impact on the local ecosystem and local people.
- The impact different practices have on soil erosion and what can be done to reduce it.
- How agriculture can produce the yields needed in a way that is sustainable for the planet.

These are issues as much for the future as they are for today, because the challenges will not diminish. Other questions will come to the fore, such as the role of genetic modification and its potential to feed the hungry of the world, or whether global food problems can be solved by dictating what people are allowed to eat, using land for a larger quantity of crops rather than the luxuries of fine foods and flowers that are available now.

Summary

After completing this chapter, you should know:

- the components of soil
- where the soil components originate
- how to evaluate the proportions of these components
- the availability of nutrients and the impact of deficiencies
- the relative merits of different soil types
- different types of agriculture
- techniques used to increase agricultural yield
- methods of controlling pests, diseases and weeds
- the techniques of selective breeding and genetic modification
- methods for controlling the growing environment
- the impacts of poor agricultural management
- different approaches to maintaining soil fertility.

End-of-chapter questions

1 a Name the four components of soil. **[4 marks]**

b How would a drought affect the balance of these four components? **[1 mark]**

2 How might changing the pH of the soil affect the growth of a crop? **[1 mark]**

3 Give three ways the 'Green Revolution' has helped feed a growing world population. **[3 marks]**

4 Explain how crop rotation can help increase the yield of a crop. **[2 marks]**

5 Describe three ways farmers can improve the efficiency of their water use. **[3 marks]**

6 Describe the impact of applying too much fertiliser to a crop. **[2 marks]**

7 Intercropping is identified as a useful way of helping prevent soil erosion in certain soil conditions. In addition to the prevention of erosion, what other benefits might this technique have? **[3 marks]**

Controlling pests naturally: a flawed decision

Figure 3.22 The cane toad: introduced into Australia with a huge environmental impact.

Sugar cane plants were introduced into Australia as the country became populated by Europeans. Records show that there were plantations in the Brisbane area as early as 1862. Plantations were densely planted, tended to be grown as monocultures (only the one crop grown in an area) and today are highly mechanised.

As the numbers of sugar cane plantations grew, so did the incidence of pests. Two native beetle species cause major problems: the adults eat the leaves of the crop and their larvae eat the roots. These beetles have proved to be difficult to control because the adults have a tough skin that repels pesticides and the larvae are buried in the soil so are not easy to spray. When pesticides are used, not only are they not very effective on the pests but they also kill many other insects and upset the natural ecosystem. Australian scientists looked at other areas of the world and read reports of increased yields in plantations in Hawaii, the natural location of cane toads. Cane toads are relatively large in size and eat a wide range of different insects (Figure 3.22).

A small number of cane toads were imported into Australia in the 1930s, bred successfully and released into the local plantations. Unfortunately, it was then discovered that the cane toad was not particularly effective at controlling the beetles on the Australian sugar cane, but preferred to eat other insects and animals in the area. It has been estimated that there are now over 200 million cane toads in Australia. They have bred rapidly because:

- they outcompete native animals for food
- they outcompete native animals for habitat space

- they have no natural predators in Australia
- if attacked, they produce a toxic liquid on their skin
- they are mobile, and the population area increases by approximately 40 km $year^{-1}$.

Cane toads reduce the number of natural organisms within an area. The local population of the Argos monitor, a large lizard, can be reduced by as much as 90% once the cane toad arrives in its community. The lizards eat the toads but die from the toxin on the skin, and the death of the lizards and increase in toads affects the whole food web. Figure 3.23 shows the spread of the cane toad population and what scientists believe to be the potential range of the toad.

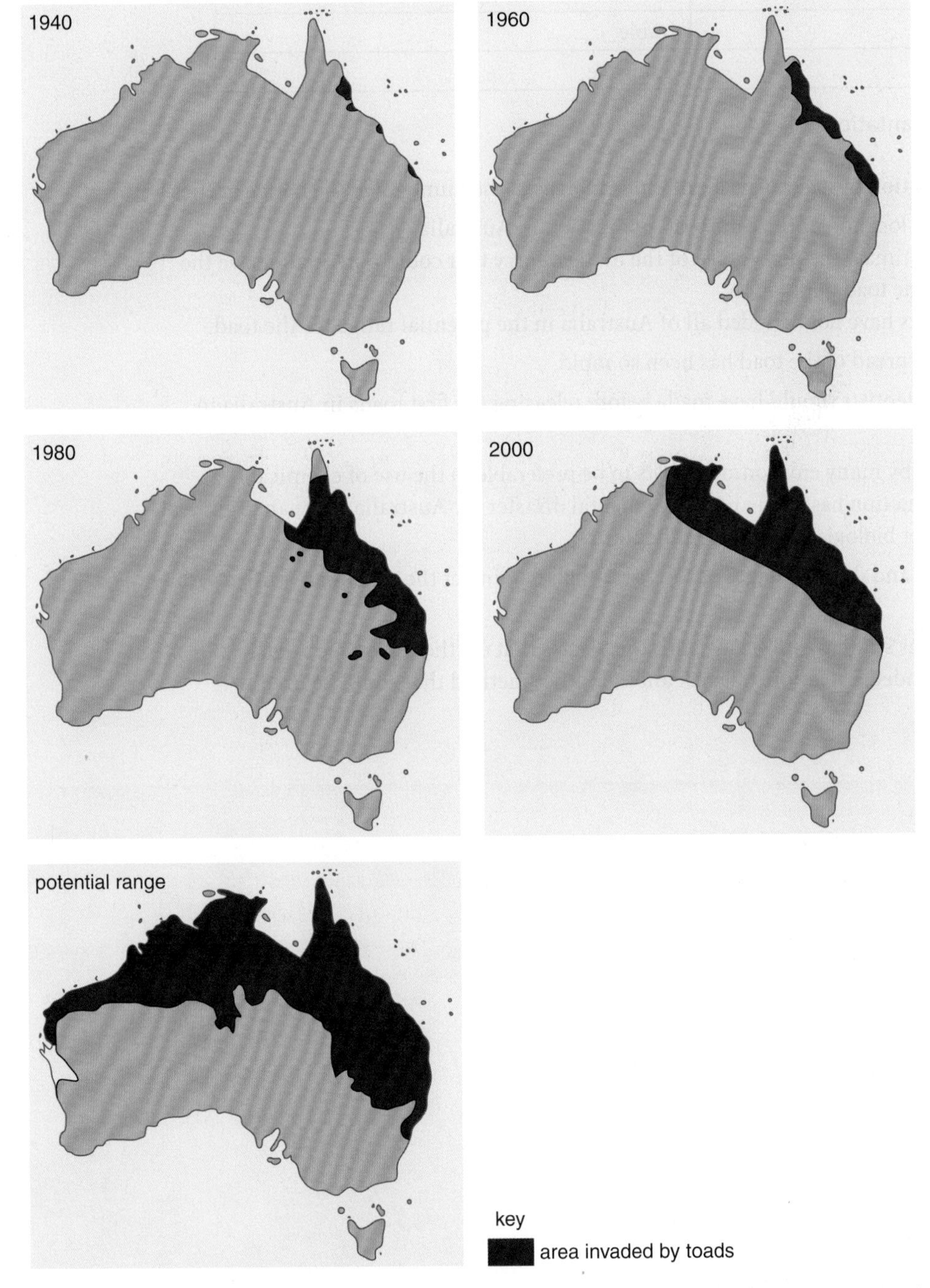

Figure 3.23 Maps of Australia showing the spread of the cane toad and the area scientists think might be at risk from invasion.

Scientists are now looking for ways to control the spread of the cane toad. One suggestion is to infect the cane toad population with a viral disease that will spread among the population when the adults mate. The population is too widely spread and numerous to simply collect or trap.

Questions

1 Copy Table 3.12 then circle the words that best describe the type of agriculture used to farm sugar cane plantations (choose one from each pair).

subsistence farming	commercial farming
pastoral	arable
intensive	extensive

Table 3.12 Sugar cane plantations.

2 Suggest how the introduction of sugar cane plantations increased the numbers of the native beetles.

3 a Describe the current location of the cane toad population in Australia.

b Using Figure 3.22, estimate the percentage of the total country that could potentially have the right habitat for a cane toad population.

c Suggest why scientists have not included all of Australia in the potential range for the toad.

4 Suggest reasons why the spread of the toad has been so rapid.

5 Outline the checks the scientists should have made before releasing the first toads in Australia in 1936.

6 Biological control is seen by many environmentalists to be preferable to the use of chemical pesticides, yet this introduction has been an environmental disaster for Australia. Give an argument to support the use of other biological controls in the future.

7 Suggest some advantages and disadvantages of the current plan to infect the cane toads with a virus that will kill them.

8 The sugar cane plantations still have problems with the beetles that eat the leaves and roots. Cane toads have not provided a solution. Suggest another other method that could be used to control this pest.

Chapter 4
Water and its management

Learning outcomes

By the end of this chapter, you will be able to:

- discuss how water is distributed over the Earth
- discuss the water cycle
- explain how people can obtain fresh water, and what they use the fresh water for
- discuss the availability of water that is safe for drinking across the world
- discuss the use of dams
- discuss different causes of water pollution
- discuss the effects of water pollution on human populations and the environment
- discuss methods for improving access to good quality and reliable quantities of water
- explain the methods used to control and eradicate malaria and cholera.

Amazing water

Water (H_2O) is a remarkable substance. It is a liquid at room temperature, which is unusual enough compared with closely related compounds, such as hydrogen sulfide (H_2S), which are gases at room temperature. Add to this the fact that the solid form (ice) is less dense than the liquid and many substances can dissolve in the liquid it is not hard to see why people are fascinated by it. More than this though, water is vital for life as we know it. Astronomers searching for evidence of life outside Earth often look for water as a sign that such a thing may be possible. Recent evidence that water exists on Mars has fuelled speculation that life may exist there as well or at least may have done so in the past.

Crucially, water is also transparent. We think life on Earth arose in the sea about 3000 million years ago and did not emerge on land until about 600 million years ago. A vital process for life is photosynthesis by green plants, which requires light to occur. The ability of water to let at least some light penetrate it would have allowed photosynthetic organisms to develop in the sea thousands of millions of years ago. Its ability to dissolve many substances makes water a very good source of small molecules, such as the minerals and sugars that life requires.

However, the World Health Organization (WHO) is concerned that not enough people have a basic level of access to clean drinking water and sanitation. Dr Maria Neira, the WHO's Director for Public Health, commented in May 2014 that too many people lack a basic level of drinking water and **sanitation**. Water is vital for life, and it is required not only in quantity but, importantly, in good quality. Even though we rely on water so much, both at a personal and at a national level, we also abuse and pollute it.

Figure 4.0. Some people have to travel a long way each day to collect water.

4.1 The distribution of water on Earth

Although more than 75% of the Earth's surface is covered in water, only 3% of this water is fresh (non-salty) and potentially usable by humans. This is about 42 million km^3 of fresh water. However, much of this water is locked up in the polar ice caps or glaciers. In fact, less than 1% of the Earth's fresh water is readily available for people to use (Figure 4.1).

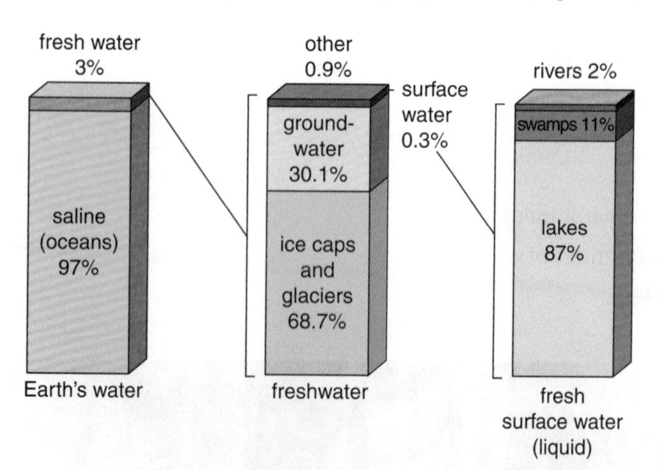

Figure 4.1 The distribution of the Earth's water.

KEY TERM

Sanitation: the conditions necessary for health, such as providing clean drinking water and the safe disposal of sewage

This amounts to 420 000 km^3, which is about 60 million litres of water for every person on Earth. On average, one person uses about 1.5 million litres a year. This is both directly, for drinking and washing, for example, and indirectly, in the manufacture of products that a person uses. Although it seems that there is plenty of water for everyone, the situation is not that simple. Half of the available fresh water is found in just six countries: Brazil, Russia, Canada, Indonesia, China and Colombia. In addition, much of it is not suitable for drinking. So, there are many challenges to providing people with enough clean, safe water.

Worldwide, women suffer the burden of collecting water, which can take them up to 6 hours a day. Women walk an average of 6 km in Africa and Asia to collect water. A study in Tanzania showed that reducing the time for collecting water by 15 min increased girls' school attendance by 12%. Collecting water can deny women time for a significant education from an early age.

4.2 The water cycle

The 1 386 000 000 km^3 of water on Earth is a fixed amount that neither increases nor decreases. However, water exists in different forms and is found in many places. At one time a particular water molecule may be within ice in a glacier, at another in a drop of rain. It may be in the ocean or in a fast-flowing river in the far north. The change in the state of water will often lead to a change in where it is. The ice in a glacier may melt and become liquid water. It may then enter a river that flows into a lake. With the warmth of the Sun on the lake, water may **evaporate** and become vapour. This vapour can then rise into the sky, **condense** and form clouds. Under certain circumstances, the water in these clouds will fall as rain or snow, called **precipitation**. It may then enter the soil and be taken up by the roots of plant, to be transported up the plant in the transpiration stream. This movement is driven by the loss of water from the plant in the process of **transpiration.** Other possibilities are that that it will flow along the ground in a process called **surface run-off**, be trapped by the leaves of plants, a process called **interception**, or enter the ground by **infiltration** and then become part of **groundwater flow** (if it flows through rocks) or **through flow** (if it flows through soil).

All these changes in the state of water and its place on the Earth are summarised in the water cycle (Figure 4.2).

KEY TERMS

Evaporation: the process in which liquid water turns into vapour, the opposite of condensation

Condensation: the process in which water vapour turns in to liquid water, the opposite of evaporation

Precipitation: the process in which liquid water (as rain) or ice particles (as snow or hail) fall to Earth due to gravity

Transpiration: the movement of water up plants and its subsequent loss as water vapour from their leaves

Surface run-off: the process by which water runs over the ground into rivers

Interception: the process by which precipitation is stopped from reaching the ground surface by the presence of trees and other plants

Infiltration: the process by which water seeps into the ground

Groundwater flow: the process by which infiltrated water flows through rocks

Through flow: the process by which infiltrated water flows through the soil

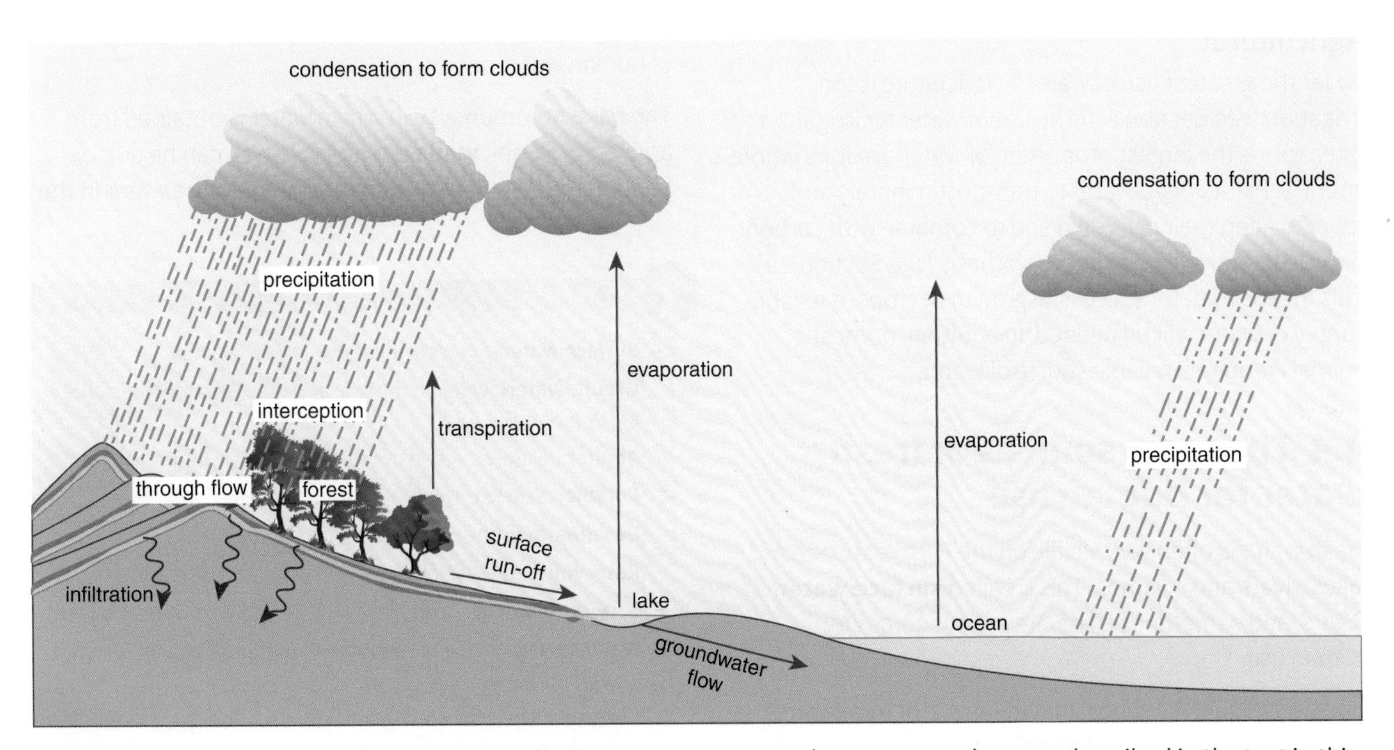

Figure 4.2 The main processes in the water cycle. The arrows represent the processes, these are described in the text in this section.

4.3 Why humans need water

Humans need water for domestic, industrial and agricultural purposes.

Domestic

In the home water is, of course, used for drinking and cooking, but this only accounts for about 3% of domestic use. In more economically developed countries (MEDCs) about 50% of domestic water is used for washing and flushing the toilet and a further 20% for washing clothes. Much less domestic water is used for washing, flushing the toilet and laundry in less economically developed countries (LEDCs), although the actual proportions vary. In some situations quite a lot of water is used for watering the garden and a substantial amount is often lost in leaks. The proportions of these uses and losses varies. Water for domestic use needs to be especially safe.

Industrial

Water is used in a vast range of industrial processes. One of the largest uses is for cooling in the production of electricity. Another use of water relies on the fact that a very wide range of substances is soluble in it. Water is often described as the universal solvent.

Agricultural

By far the greatest use of water in agriculture is for irrigation (see Section 3.4).The use of water for irrigation often forms the largest proportion of water use for a whole country. Plants need water to transport minerals and food, to keep their cells rigid and to combine with carbon dioxide to make food in photosynthesis (see Section 9.1). This means that, for successful growth of crops, a reliable supply of water will be needed. In addition, domestic animals require a reliable source of water.

4.4 The main sources of fresh water for human use

Fresh water is often very visible on the Earth's surface as lakes, rivers and swamps. This is called **surface water**. Rivers, and sometimes lakes, are major sources for human use.

However, Figure 4.1 shows that there is a lot more water in the ground, known as **groundwater**. Vast quantities of water are stored in the spaces of porous rock (limestone or sandstone). Such a store is referred to as an **aquifer**.

In regions of the world where insufficient water is present from both surface water and groundwater sources, other solutions to water supply have to be found. One of the most common of these is to use salt water from the sea. This water is made safe for human use (**potable**) by removing the salt. This carried out in a **desalination** plant.

Water from rivers

Water can be taken from rivers by simply dipping a bucket into it. This is still the only way to get water in many parts of the world. At the other extreme are huge national projects, often involving the construction of a **reservoir**. A reservoir may be created behind a dam or by the side of the river (a bank-side reservoir). In both of these cases the reservoir forms a large store of water. Usually, this water is not safe but can be treated to make it potable.

Another type of reservoir is the **service reservoir**, in which treated, and therefore potable, water is stored for use. **Water towers** and underground **cisterns** are examples of service reservoirs.

Water from the ground

Water that infiltrates the ground may accumulate in porous rocks such as sandstone and limestone. These stores of water are called aquifers. The global quantity of water in aquifers is relatively large, about 30% of all fresh water (see Figure 4.1). Aquifers fulfil a very significant proportion of human water needs.

The most common way in which water is obtained from aquifers is to sink **wells** into them. A well can be dug by hand or bored into rock with machinery. If the water in the

KEY TERMS

Surface water: water in lakes, rivers and swamps

Groundwater: water in the soil, and in rocks under the surface of the ground

Aquifer: water stored in porous rocks under the ground

Potable: safe to drink

Desalination: the removal of salt from water

Reservoir: an artificial lake where water can be stored

Service reservoir: a reservoir in which potable water is stored

Water tower: a type of reservoir where potable water is stored for immediate use

Cistern: a vessel in which water, usually potable, is stored, forming a type of covered reservoir

Well: a hole bored or dug into rock to reach the water stored there

aquifer is not under pressure, it has to be raised to the top of the well. This can be done by simply lowering a bucket on a rope or with a hand-operated pump. This would usually be the method used in LEDCs. In MEDCs, some form of motor-driven pump is more likely to be used.

If the water is stored under pressure, the aquifer is referred to as an **artesian aquifer**.

Water from a well sunk into an artesian aquifer (an artesian well) will rise to the surface without the need for a pump.

Water from the sea

In principle, to make salt water suitable for human consumption, the salt simply has to be removed in a process called desalination. Over 97% of all the world's water is in the ocean and salty. Salt water cannot be drunk, as it would cause health problems and, eventually, death. Two processes can be used to make salt water potable.

The first method of desalination is **distillation**, in which the water is boiled and released as vapour, leaving the salt behind. The vapour is condensed as liquid water and can then be used. Desalination by distillation is about 10–30% efficient. The process produces large quantities of waste, salt water (brine), which needs to be disposed of. This can be a source of pollution. Energy is needed for the distillation, and the provision of this energy may itself cause pollution. However, the transport of fresh water from more remote sources also requires energy. Distillation may be no more costly than other methods of providing fresh water unless there are alternative local sources. Desalination plants using this method are mainly found in energy-rich countries, such as those of the Middle East.

The second desalination process is called **reverse osmosis**, in which salt water is pumped at high pressure through very fine membranes (Figure 4.3). Desalination by reverse osmosis is about 30–50% efficient. As with distillation, brine is a byproduct of reverse osmosis and requires disposal. This process also requires energy, but less than distillation. Most new desalination plants use the technique of reverse osmosis.

KEY TERMS

Artesian aquifer: an aquifer in which the water is under pressure

Distillation: the purification of a liquid by boiling a solution so that the liquid evaporates and can be collected when it condenses at a lower temperature

Reverse osmosis: the purification of water by pumping it at high pressure through a fine membrane

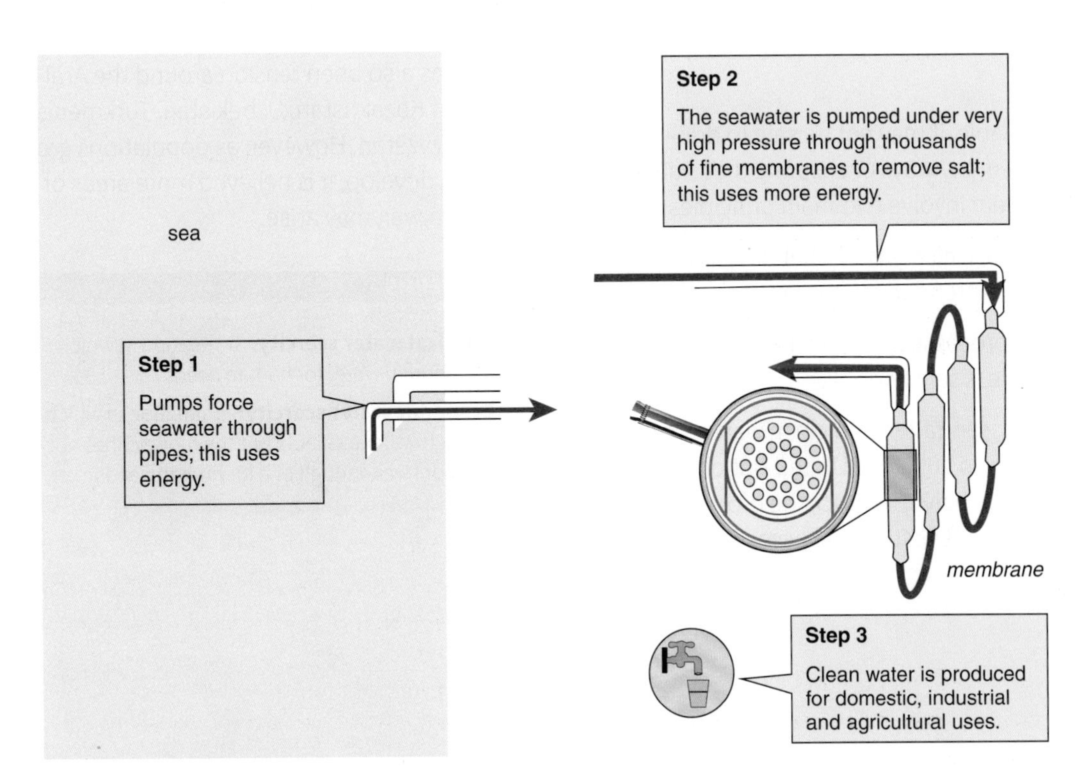

Figure 4.3 Desalination by reverse osmosis.

4.5 Availability of safe drinking water around the world

The most important factor when considering a country's water wealth is the amount of rain it receives. Using this measure, for example, Brazil and Russia are two of the most water wealthy nations, and the United Arab Emirates and Kuwait are two of the most water poor.

However, having plenty of water does not mean that there is plenty of safe water for everyone. The number of people needing water has to be considered. In China, which has the largest population in the world at over 1.3 billion, the water availability is about 2800 km^3. This works about at about 2300 m^3 $person^{-1}$ $year^{-1}$. In Singapore, which has only 0.60 km^3 of water available, the supply is only about 110 m^3 $person^{-1}$ $year^{-1}$. In these two examples, a water-rich country seems to have enough water for its people, and vice versa.

However, another very water-poor country, Mauritius, has a water availability of only about 2 km^3, but this supplies its 1.3 million population with 1700 m^3 person $year^{-1}$.

The lack of water may be because of low rainfall and / or high levels of evaporation; this is referred to as **physical water scarcity**. A second reason for a lack of water is economic. A country may have a lot of water but cannot afford to extract it, purify it and make it available for the population. Such as country is suffering from **economic water scarcity**.

Even if water is available, it may not be safe to drink (potable). There are many ways of ensuring that water is potable but all of them involve two main principles:

- sanitation systems, which ensure that dirty water does not mix with water intended for human use
- water-treatment processes, which ensure that the water supplied to people is safe to drink.

Worldwide, however, sanitation and clean water are not available to everyone. In 2000, the United Nations (UN) said that its aim was to halve, by 2015, the proportion of the population without sustainable access to safe drinking water and basic sanitation. Since then 2.1 billion people have gained access to improved sanitation. But, despite this progress, 2.4 billion are still using unimproved sanitation facilities; 946 million of these still practice open defecation. A child dies every 2.5 min from diseases linked to open defecation.

In some LEDCs, less than a quarter of the population has access to safe water. In Europe and North America, it is taken for granted that 100% have such access.

Just as access to safe water varies from country to country around the world, it also varies within countries. One striking contrast is between rural and urban areas.

In many cities and towns, more people have access to both clean water and improved sanitation than in rural areas in the same country. The main reasons for this difference are that:

- there is more wealth and more wealthy people in cities
- large numbers of people can act together to pressurise authorities to provide safe water
- it is cheaper to install piped water when many people live close together than in a scattered rural community.

At a larger scale, differences in the availability of water can also lead to actual conflict: water wars. Currently such conflicts are quite restricted in range. There is some tension over the use of the River Jordan in the Middle East. There has also been tension around the Aral Sea in Asia, between Kazakhstan, Uzbekistan, Turkmenistan, Tajikistan and Kyrgyzstan. However, as populations grow and cultures develop, it is believed more areas of such tension, and even war, may arise.

KEY TERMS

Physical water scarcity: a situation in which there is simply not enough water for human needs

Economic water scarcity: a situation in which there is enough water available but the money does not exist to extract and / or treat enough of it for human needs

SELF-ASSESSMENT QUESTIONS

4.1 Copy and complete the following paragraph about the water cycle.

Liquid water is found on the surface of the Earth in ...., ... and ....
It is also found inside plants. Water turns from a liquid to a gas, water vapour, in a process called ....
The water vapour then .... to form clouds. Liquid water falls from clouds to the Earth in the process of .... Some of the water is prevented from reaching the ground by plants in the process of ....
Water that reaches the ground may enter it in a process called .... The rest enters rivers by ....

4.2 Explain why nearly 70% of fresh water on Earth is very difficult for humans to use.

4.3 Using Figure 4.1, calculate the percentage of the Earth's water that is in lakes. Show your working,

4.4 Explain why desalination plants are common only in oil-rich countries.

4.5 Suggest and explain which of groundwater, surface water or ice caps and glaciers is likely to be the main source of fresh water for humans.

4.6 Multipurpose dam projects

The construction of a dam (see Figure 4.4) across a river can be a very expensive and controversial project, but the benefits are usually great. In many cases dams are constructed with a number of aims in mind. A dam may help with:

- the generation of electricity in hydroelectric power plants
- flood control
- irrigation
- tourism and leisure
- the provision of water
- creation of habitat for wetland species
- access by boat to otherwise inaccessible areas.

The disadvantages of dam projects include:

- relocating people
- flooding land
- disrupting the life cycles of fish and other aquatic organisms

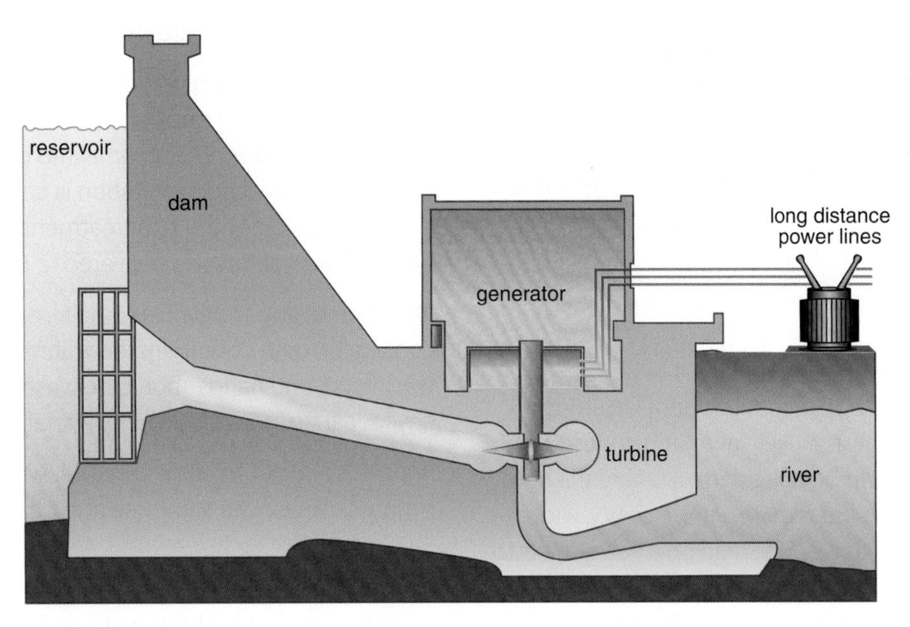

Figure 4.4 The structure of a dam.

- altering the water supply for people downstream of the dam
- reducing the enrichment of soil downstream of the dam (which natural flooding of the original river course would have contributed to)
- the dam may become redundant as sediment in the river sinks to the bottom of the reservoir (siltation).

Figure 4.5 A dam and reservoir. The dam is in the foreground of the photo and the reservoir is behind.

SELF-ASSESSMENT QUESTIONS

4.6 Look at the lists of the advantages and disadvantages of dam projects given above. Copy and complete Table 4.1 by adding each advantage or disadvantage to the correct cell.

	Advantages	Disadvantages
Environmental		
Economic		
Social		

Table 4.1 Advantages and disadvantages of dam projects.

4.7 Explain how it could be argued that a multipurpose dam project is unsustainable.

Where to build a dam

Deciding where to build a dam requires detailed study of many factors. It has to be in a river valley and, for economic reasons, the valley should be quite narrow where the dam is built. A wider valley would require a more costly, wider dam. A dam also needs to be quite high up a valley if it is to be successful at producing hydroelectric power (HEP). The higher it is, the greater the pressure of water, which means it will have more potential energy. Dams should be sited away from developed areas if possible, to reduce the risk of pollution in the reservoir.

Are dams sustainable?

Dams are often thought of as a permanent solution to electricity generation. However, there are sometimes problems with their operation in the long term. The reservoir can become silted due to the material carried into it by rivers. The dam structure, which is under a lot of pressure, can deteriorate and eventually fail. Dams can also have negative effects on the surrounding environment, including fish populations. These problems suggest that dams are not necessarily sustainable solutions.

The opposite view is that dams are a far superior alternative to the burning of fossil fuels because they produce electricity without producing greenhouse gases and pollutants. In this sense, sustainability can be thought of as a continuum with dams towards one end and fossil fuels at the other.

4.7 Water-related diseases

Cholera and typhoid

Water provides a very good habitat for many living things. Because of the presence of plants in water and their ability to photosynthesise (see Section 9.1), there is plenty of food in water. Water provides a nutrient-rich environment for bacteria. Bacteria may enter drinking water from **sewage** if sanitation is poor. If these bacteria are **pathogens**, and the water in which they live is drunk untreated, diseases can be spread.

Two major diseases caused by water contaminated with human faeces are cholera and typhoid. The main features of these two diseases are shown in Table 4.2.

The crucial element in preventing these diseases being transmitted within a population is to ensure that sewage and drinking water do not come into contact with each other. Therefore, good sanitation is crucial, with sewage being removed directly to a treatment works and water being treated before it is delivered to people to drink.

Attention to good hygiene is crucial, as is the thorough cooking of food. Contaminated water should not be used to wash food, and hands should be washed after contact with any faecal material. Use of efficient latrines is essential.

If there is any doubt about whether water is safe to drink, simply boiling it can eliminate most harmful organisms.

Malaria

Like cholera and typhoid, malaria is a water-related disease, but the similarity ends there. Bacterial diseases, such as cholera and typhoid, are carried in water and referred to as water-borne diseases.

CASE STUDY

A multipurpose dam on the Ramganga River at Kalagarh, India

In 1961, the construction of a large multipurpose dam was started at Kalagarh across the Ramganga River, which is a tributary of the Ganges in India. It was completed in 1974 (Figure 4.6).

The dam:

- is 127.5 m high
- generates 451 million units of power annually from three 66 mW power houses
- has a reservoir area of 80 km^2
- stores 2447.6 m^3 of water
- has a catchment area made up of 57% forests, 8% grassland and 30% agricultural lands.

Figure 4.6 A satellite image of the Ramganga Dam, Uttarakhand, India.

In its construction:

- no crop lands were submerged and there was no flooding of railways or roads
- there was no need to relocate any people
- 4220 hectares of forest and 2500 hectares of plantations were submerged
- the owners of the forests were paid compensation and there was afforestation of the plantations in an adjoining area
- a 7.5 ha area was landscaped and tourist facilities were installed.

The dam is in a highly seismic area and a seismological observatory with the latest equipment was installed.

Since construction:

- flooding of a large area around the dam can now be controlled
- wildlife has increased and many species of migratory birds have been attracted to the reservoir
- the reservoir water quality is suitable for aquatic life and for use in irrigation
- thousands of hectares of land in the Ramganga flood plains are now being used successfully for agriculture
- little treatment is needed to make the water safe to drink
- Delhi receives 5.67 m^3 of water per second (cumec) through concrete pipes.

Over 10 000 jobs were created by the building of the dam, and 3000 officials and workers are employed in maintenance of the dam project. The transport infrastructure has been improved: Kalagarh is now very well connected with important cities such as Delhi.

In a report in 2014 some local farmers claimed that the dam was affecting their crops and their fish catches. They said that the dam gates are opened and closed to suit the water level in the dam. Their land therefore receives a variable amount of water from extreme flooding to near drought. This pattern means they lose crops.

In addition, the annual floods of the Ramganga River used to bring in fine silt and replenish the fertility of the soil, but now the dam has altered the sediment characteristics bringing in coarse sand.

Fish have become isolated above the dam and only get released to the lower river below the dam when the dam gates are opened. This disruption to their breeding cycles has led to a decrease in fish size, number and diversity.

Questions

1 Suggest reasons why the dam took 13 years to be completed.

2 Explain why:
  - a a seismological observatory was built
  - b the authorities are monitoring sedimentation behind the dam.

3 To what extent do you agree that the dam is beneficial to:
  - a local people
  - b India?

Malaria is caused by a microscopic organism called *Plasmodium*. Malaria is water-related because the organism that passes the disease to humans requires water to breed. This organism is an insect called a mosquito, which lays its eggs in still water, where the larvae develop. Mosquitoes can pass malaria on to humans, acting as a **vector**. The relationship between mosquitoes, *Plasmodium* and human beings is best understood with a life cycle diagram (Figure 4.7).

Malaria occurs in 97 (out of 193) countries around the world, mainly in Africa, Asia and the Americas (Figure 4.8). These countries are home to 3.2 billion people, nearly half the world's population. In 2015 there were 214 million cases of malaria, with about 438 000 deaths. Sub-Saharan Africa suffered 89% of the malaria cases, with 91% of the deaths.

The symptoms of malaria are flu-like and include fever and chills at first. The disease can be fatal. Malaria can be treated but a much better option is prevention.

KEY TERMS

Sewage: waste matter that is carried away in sewers or drains from domestic (or industrial) establishments

Pathogen: an organism, including bacteria and viruses, that can cause disease

Vector: an organism that carries a disease-producing organism, such as the mosquito which carries the malarial parasite

Prevention and control is best achieved by avoiding bites from the mosquito.

Individuals can prevent being bitten by mosquitoes by:

- avoiding being outside between dusk and dawn in countries where malaria mosquitoes are active, the species of the *Anopheles* mosquito that transmits malaria only flies at night
- wearing clothing that covers most of the body and treat exposed parts of the body with mosquito-repellent products
- sleeping under a mosquito net treated with an **insecticide**
- spraying the inside of accommodation with insecticide.

For governments, strategies for malaria control are focused on controlling the vector. This can be achieved by:

- spraying insecticide inside buildings, including houses
- draining wetland areas to remove mosquito-breeding sites
- introducing fish, which eat the larvae and pupae of the mosquito, into ponds and other bodies of water
- pouring oil onto the surface of the water where mosquitoes breed, which stops the larvae from breathing and stops the adults from laying eggs.

Eradicating malaria means completely removing the malarial **parasite** from the population. Controlling the vector is not enough, so methods must be sought to actually destroy the parasite.

	Cholera	Typhoid
Infective bacterium (pathogen)	*Vibrio cholerae*	*Salmonella typhi* or *Salmonella paratyphi*, which causes a less severe illness
Time before onset of symptoms after infection	A few hours up to 5 days	6–30 days
Symptoms	Diarrhoea and vomiting	Fever, abdominal pain with a skin rash Diarrhoea and vomiting are not uncommon
Consequence	Can be mild but can lead to dehydration and death	3–5% of infected people remain as carriers with no symptoms If untreated, fatal complications can arise
Treatment	Rehydration A vaccine exists	Antibiotics A vaccine exists
Occurrence in 2015	172 454 cases were notified to WHO from 42 countries, including 1304 deaths	Around 21 million a year with about 161 000 deaths worldwide

Table 4.2 A comparison of typhoid and cholera.

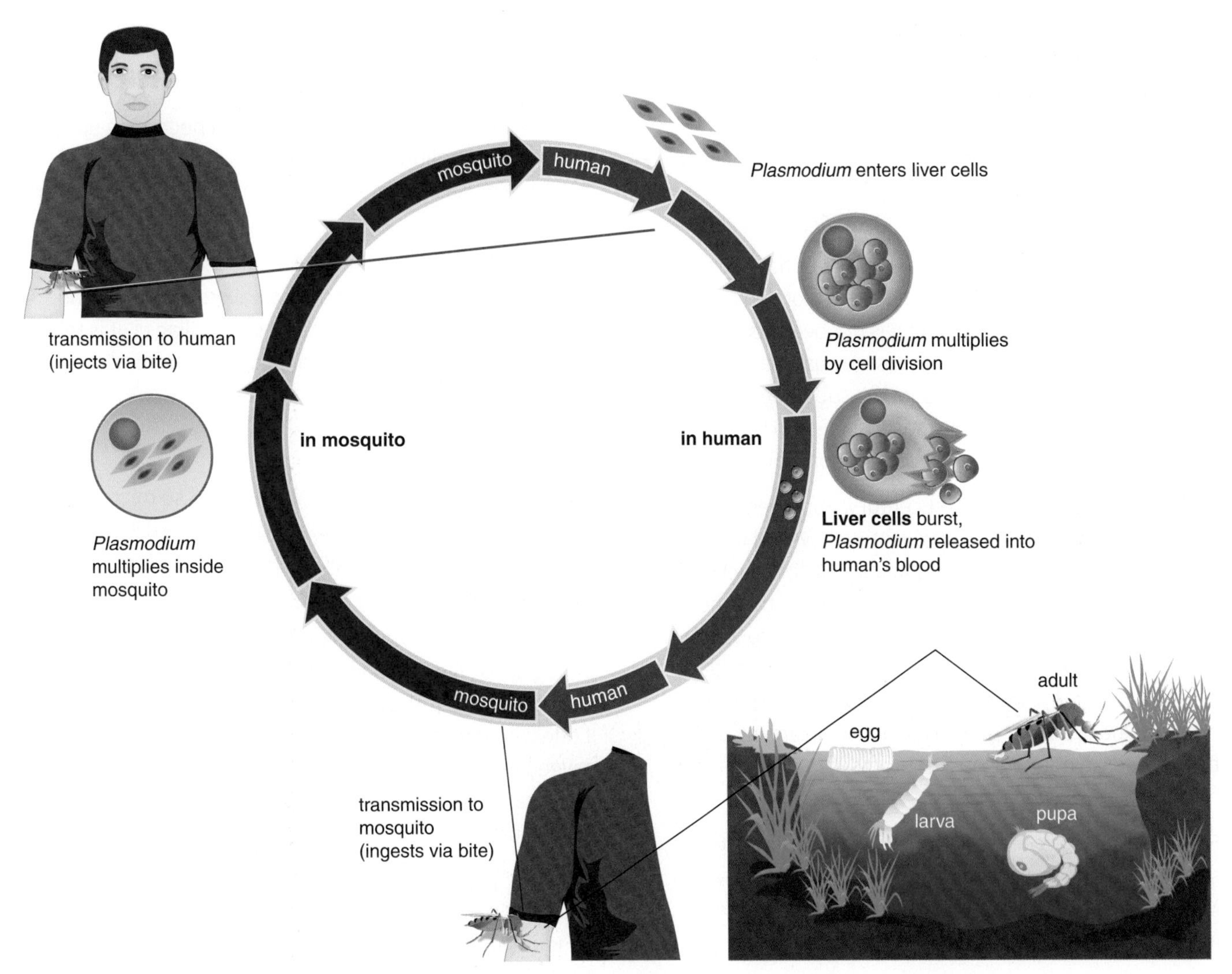

Figure 4.7 The life cycle of malaria.

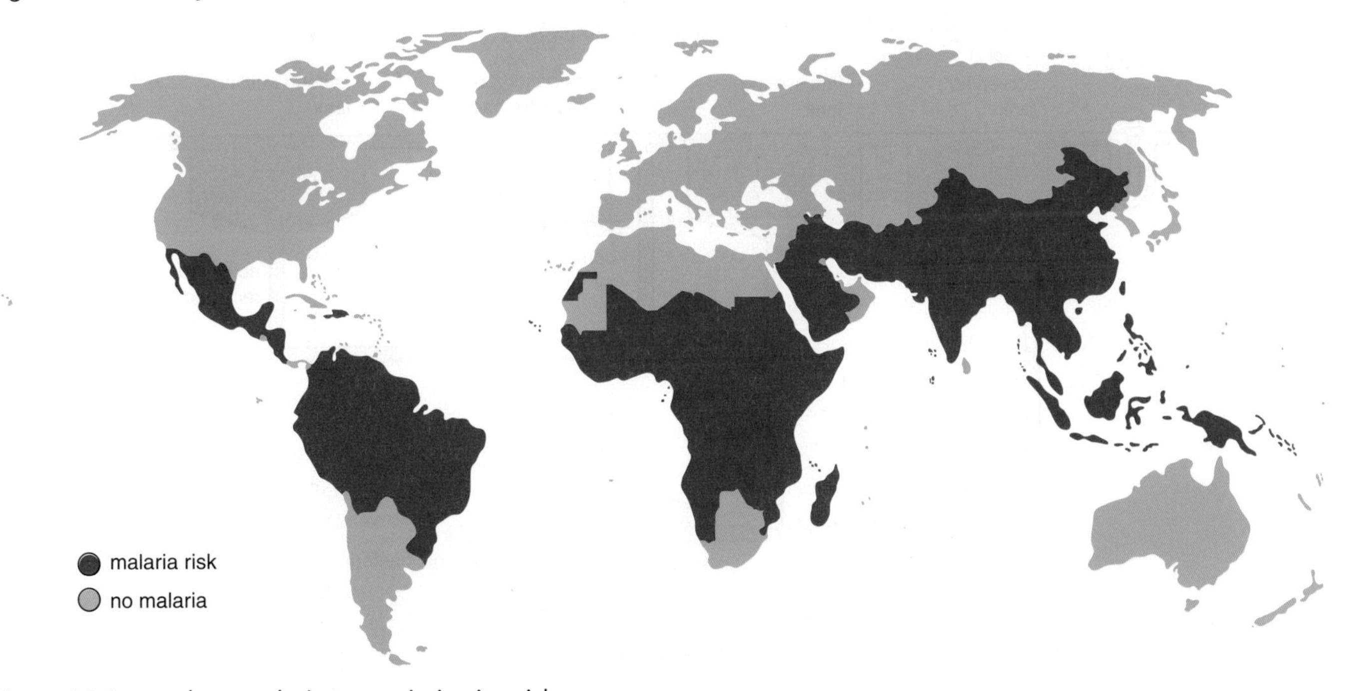

Figure 4.8 Areas where malaria transmission is a risk.

WHO now encourages a programme of eradication of malaria from all countries of the world. In the first half of the 20th century, malaria was eradicated from western Europe and the USA. The main challenge for the 21st century is to achieve eradication in sub-Saharan Africa, where nearly 90% of all cases occur.

Unfortunately, there is the possibility that malaria is favoured by global warming. Recent studies have shown that it is now occurring in highland regions of Kenya, Colombia and Ethiopia, where it has not been seen for over 50 years. However, another recent study using a predictive approach and taking into account the subtleties of climate change, which involves more than just a rise in temperature, concluded that few changes in distribution would occur.

In the first 12 years of the 21st century, improvements in diagnosis, treatment and prevention have led to a 25% decline in incidence in malaria and a 42% decline in deaths from malaria. However, it is unlikely that these methods will result in elimination. The mosquito vector is evolving resistance to insecticides and the parasite is also becoming resistant to available drugs. Much more attention needs to be given to people who are infected by the disease but have no symptoms. It is clear that new methods for controlling malaria are needed.

Be careful not to confuse malaria with bacterial diseases, such as cholera and typhoid. Bacteria breed in the water. Malaria is a caused by a parasite, which breeds in an insect, which breeds in water.

4.8 Sources, impact and management of water pollution

Using water very often results in it then becoming unusable as a result of pollution. Not surprisingly, therefore, the three main uses of water are also the three main polluters.

Domestic waste

Sewage is waste matter carried away from houses and other buildings in both cities and small villages. It is taken away in drains called sewers and is then dumped or converted into a form that is less harmful.

Sewage treatment

Sewage is very rich in organic matter and so microbial organisms can thrive in it. Sewage has to be disposed of, and this is usually into bodies of water, so it must be treated beforehand.

The main aim of sewage treatment is to reduce the biological oxygen demand (BOD) of the sewage. The BOD of sewage is the amount of oxygen it would use up if released directly into a river or lake. The removal of this oxygen from the river or lake would cause problems for the organisms, such as fish and insect larvae, living in the water. Further details about these problems are given below in the section on eutrophication.

The main parts of a sewage treatment works can be seen in Figure 4.9.

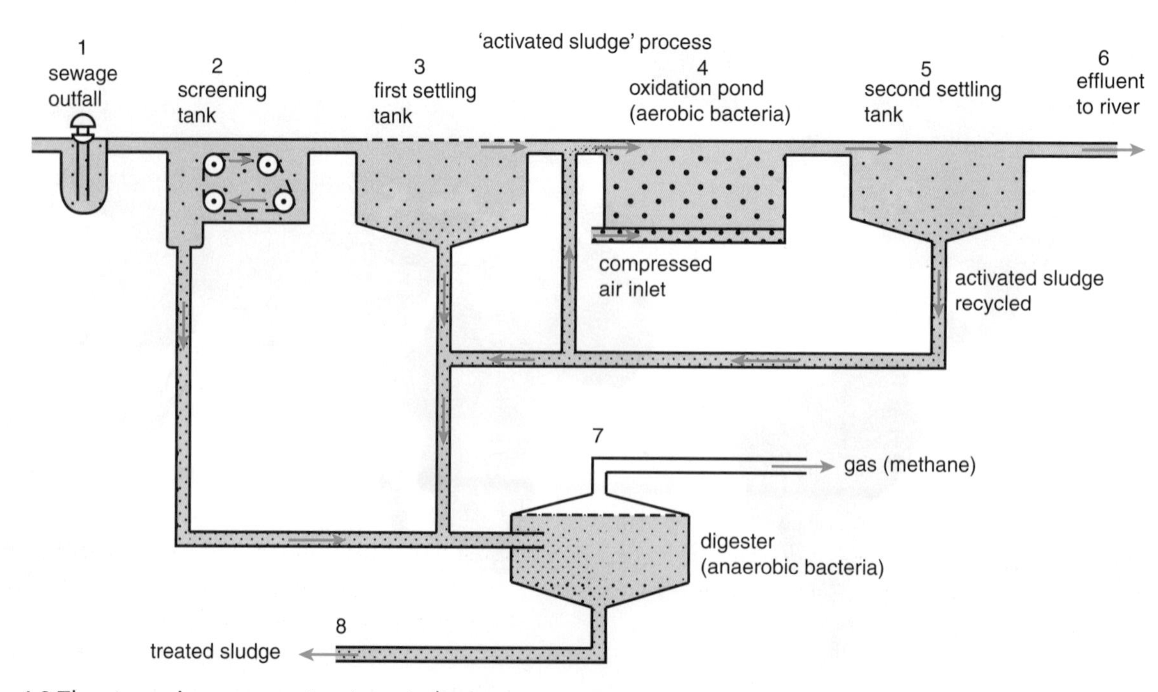

Figure 4.9 The stages in a sewage treatment plant.

1 Sewage outfall: waste water from homes, and sometimes industry, is taken to a sewage treatment works in pipes called sewers.
2 Screening tank: large objects are removed from the waste water using a coarse grid.
3 Primary treatment, first settling tank: the solid organic matter, mainly human waste, is allowed to settle to the bottom of the tank. This settled material is called sludge, which is treated in the sludge-digester (see step 7). The cleaned water overflows the sides of the tank and is taken to the next stage.
4 Secondary treatment, oxidation: the water is now pumped into a tank where oxygen is bubbled through it. This encourages the growth of bacteria and other microbes, which break down dissolved organic matter, which causes the BOD.
5 Secondary treatment, second settling tank: the water now enters the second settling tank, where the bacteria settle to the bottom, forming more sludge. This cleaner water overflows the sides of the tank as **effluent.**
6 The effluent is discharged into the environment, usually a river.
7 Sludge digester: in the sludge digester, oxygen-free conditions are created that encourage the growth of bacteria which can break down the sludge, releasing methane, which can be burnt.
8 The treated sludge can be dried in sludge lagoons and used as organic fertiliser on farmland.

In some sewage works, tertiary treatment is carried out. This may involve further filtering of the effluent or its chlorination (see below). This produces even cleaner effluent, which may be needed to protect the habitat into which the effluent is released.

KEY TERM

Effluent: a discharge of liquid waste

Improved sanitation

An improved sanitation facility is defined as one that separates human excreta from contact with humans. This can be achieved using a variety of toilets and latrines.

- A flush toilet uses a holding tank for flushing water, and a water seal that prevents smells. A pour flush toilet has a water seal but uses water poured by hand for flushing. In either case the waste needs to be removed by:
  - either connection to a system of sewer pipes, also called sewerage, that collects human faeces, urine and waste water, which is then removed from the house
  - or connection to a septic system, which consists of an underground, sealed settling tank.
- A pit latrine with a platform is a dry pit fully covered by a platform that is fitted with a seat over a hole, or just has a hole, in the platform. The platform covers the pit without exposing the contents, other than through the hole. Sometimes these latrines are ventilated to take away smells.
- A composting toilet is a dry toilet into which vegetable waste, straw, grass, sawdust and ash are added to the human waste to produce compost.

Water treatment

Water that is fit for domestic use such as drinking, washing and cooking is called potable water. To make water potable it undergoes coagulation treatment, and is filtered and disinfected.

Coagulants make particles in the water stick together and settle to the bottom of the container. The water is then filtered through sand. To kill any disease-causing organisms (pathogens) that may remain, chlorine is added to the filtered water as a disinfectant; this process is called **chlorination** (Figure 4.10)

SELF-ASSESSMENT QUESTIONS

4.8 Typhoid, cholera and malaria are water-related diseases. Which of these could be transmitted by drinking contaminated water? Explain your answer.

4.9 A school party was told that a man had drunk a glass of water from a tap that drew water from treated sewage. They were told that this water was potable. To what extent do you think they were being told the truth?

KEY TERM

Chlorination: adding chlorine-based substances to water

Industrial processes

Industry produces and uses a wide range of chemicals that can be harmful to both humans and the environment. Because of its excellent solvent properties, many of these chemicals end up in water bodies and cause pollution. Outfalls from industry often discharge into rivers and lakes.

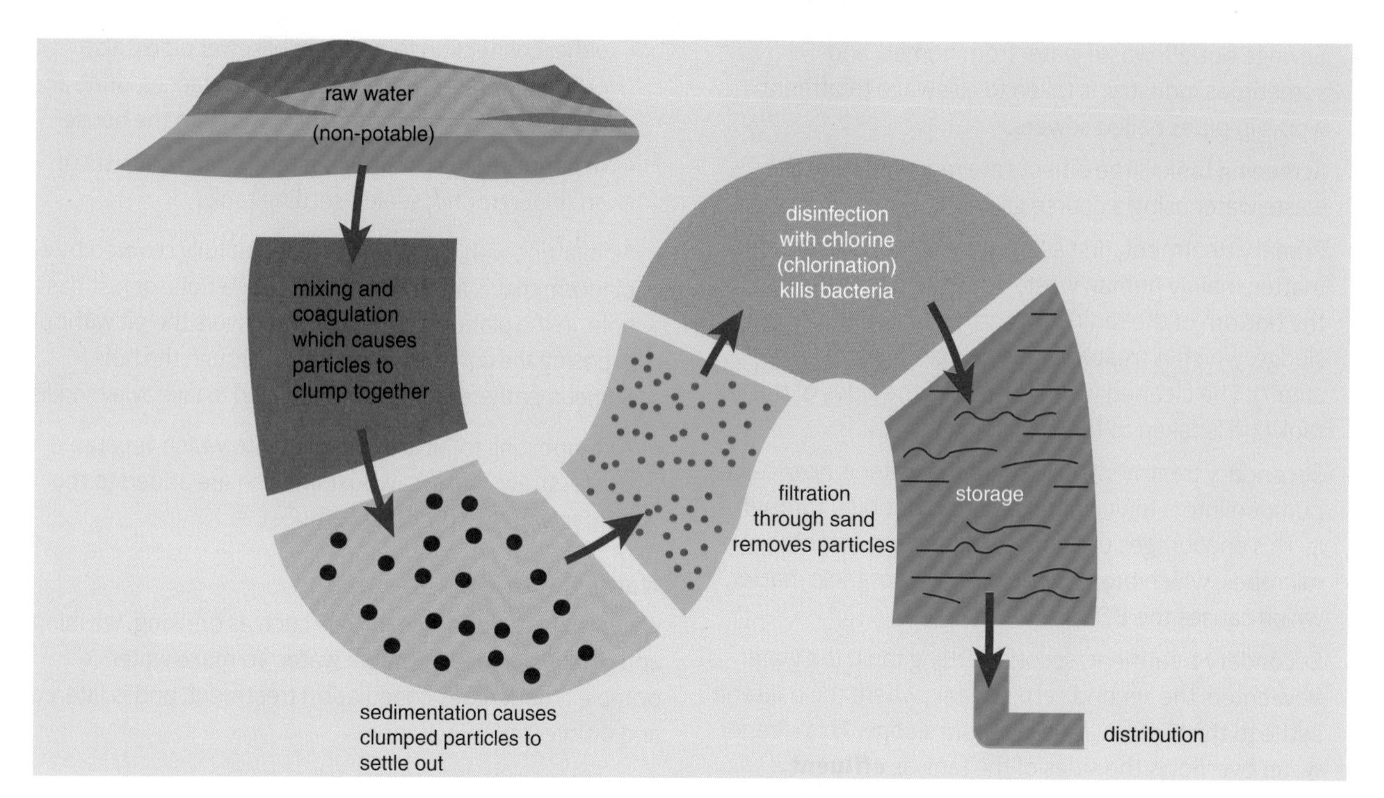

Figure 4.10 The stages in the treatment of water to produce potable water.

Gases from industrial chimneys enter the atmosphere, where they dissolve in water and form acid rain. The bodies of living things are at least 75% water and so these water-soluble pollutants can easily enter organisms and cause problems.

Toxic compounds from industry

Many industrial processes use and produce a variety of poisonous (toxic) substances. Some of these may enter bodies of water and cause immediate harm and even death to the organisms living there. In other cases, a less dramatic effect is seen. This may be because, although the substance is toxic, it only enters the water in very small amounts. However, because of a process called **biomagnification**, such substances may achieve levels where they become toxic.

The most well-known examples of biomagnification are heavy metals and some pesticides.

Many industrial processes involve the use of heavy metals such as lead, mercury and cadmium. These metals are toxic and can be stored in the bodies of plants and animals, including humans. This means they may build up to high levels, which can cause illness.

Acid rain

In the mid-19th century it was noticed that, in some industrial countries, forests downwind of industrial sites showed signs of damage. In 1872, Robert Smith showed that acid water could damage plants and various materials. By the 1970s, acid rain was recognised as a serious problem. The water in lakes and rivers was more acidic than previously. Fish in the lakes and rivers were dying. The leaves and small branches of trees in many forests of the world were dead (**dieback**) (Figure 4.11).

Figure 4.11 Dieback in coniferous trees.

KEY TERMS

Biomagnification: the process in which the concentration of a substance in living things becomes higher at progressively higher levels in a food chain or web

Bioaccumulation: the build-up of a substance in the body of a living thing

Dieback: the death of a tree or shrub that starts at the tip of its leaves or roots and spreads towards the centre of the plant, caused by unfavourable environmental conditions or disease

What causes acid rain?

The pH of water is a measure of how acid or alkaline it is (Figure 4.12). A pH of less than 7 is acid, 7 is neutral, and above 7 is alkaline. The pH range is from very acid (0) to very alkaline (14). Rain usually has a pH of between 5 and 6, so is always slightly acidic. Acid rain has a pH lower than this: values as low as 2 have been recorded, which is about the same as battery acid.

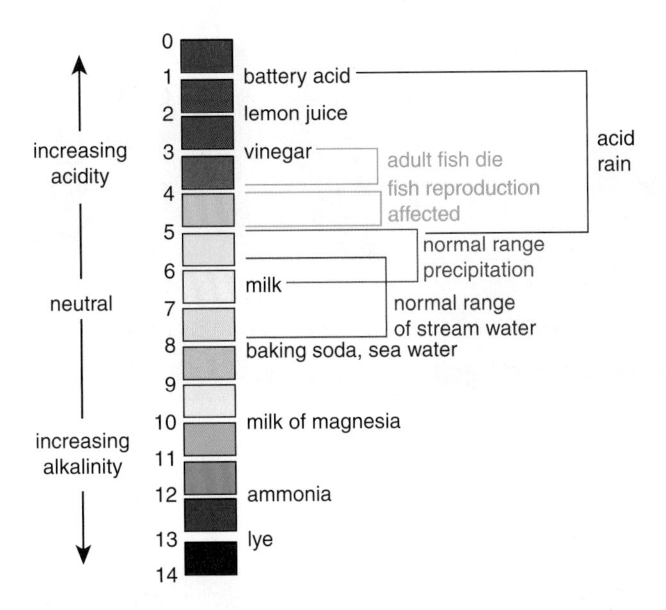

Figure 4.12 The pH scale, with some everyday examples.

When fossil fuels, such as coal and oil, are burned, the gases sulfur dioxide (SO_2) and oxides of nitrogen (NO_x) are produced. They enter the atmosphere and can be blown long distances. These gases react with water in the atmosphere to form acids.

SO_2 dissolves in water in clouds, producing sulfuric acid, and NO_x produces nitric acid (Figure 4.13). When it rains, these acids fall to the ground (see Section 7.2).

The gases can be blown from one country to another, for example many coniferous forests in Scandinavia are thought to have been damaged by acid rain gases from northern Europe in the 1960s and 1970s.

The impact of acid rain on aquatic ecosystems

When water in a river or lake is acidified, the lower pH makes it intolerable to organisms. Fish egg-laying is often reduced and young fish are malformed. Acid rain can also lead to **leaching** of heavy metals, such as aluminium, lead and mercury, from the soil into the water. This leads to further harmful effects. Aluminium, for example, clogs fish gills and can cause suffocation. Another effect is that some minerals essential for life, notably calcium and potassium, are washed out of the lake or river. This reduces algal growth, leaving less food for fish and other animals. The direct and indirect effects of acid rain and run-off of heavy metals from surrounding soils affect the whole ecosystem.

KEY TERM

Leaching: the movement of a soluble chemical or mineral away from soil, usually caused by the action of rainwater

Reducing acid rain

A reduction in the production of acid rain-causing gases is achieved when substitutes for fossil fuels are found to produce energy.

To reduce SO_2 emissions, low-sulfur varieties of fossil fuel should be used. Any sulfur still in the emissions can be removed by scrubbers. There are various forms of scrubber but for all of them, once the sulfur has been removed, the waste then has to be disposed of safely. NO_x emissions can be reduced by burning with a cooler flame or adjusting the air to fuel ratio.

Clean air acts have been passed to encourage power plants and others to employ some or all of these methods so that they stay within permitted emission levels.

Agriculture

Modern agriculture makes use of many chemicals called agrochemicals (see Section 3.4). These include pesticides, herbicides and fertilisers. All of these are water-soluble and can cause pollution in water bodies, with a variety of consequences for humans and the environment.

Eutrophication

Nutrients such as nitrate and phosphate can enter water from many sources, including farmland, industry

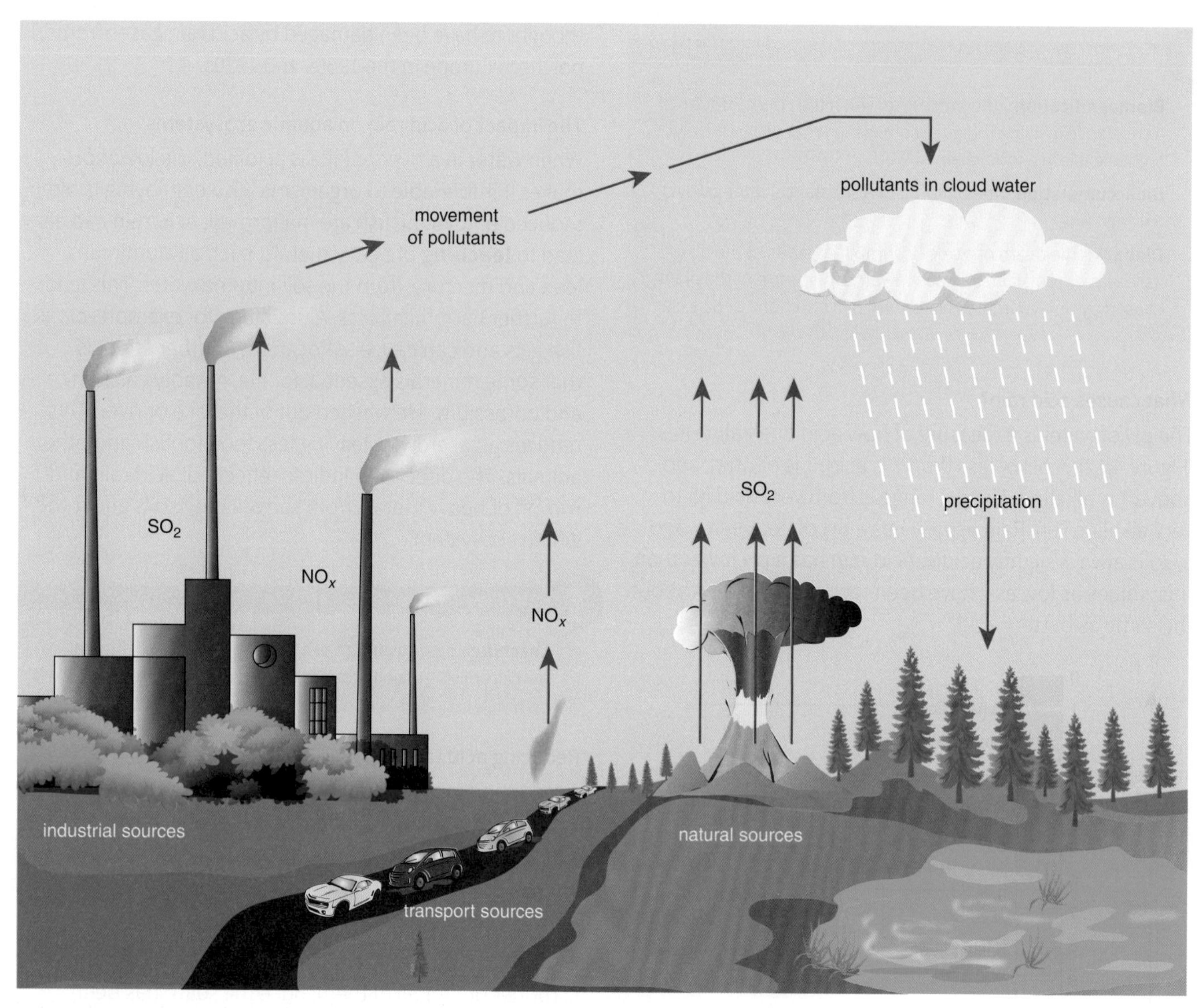

Figure 4.13 How acid rain is formed.

and domestic outputs. In addition, organic matter can enter water directly as sewage and from other sources (Figure 4.14).

Any increase in nutrients, such as nitrates and phosphates, in a river or lake will cause a rapid growth of **algae**. This is called an **algal bloom**. When the algae die there is an increase in **organic** matter in the water. This acts as food for bacteria as they decompose the dead algae. These bacteria use up oxygen, lowering its level in the water. Most living things rely on oxygen, so this can lead to the death of other organisms in the water. See Figure 4.15 for a summary of this process, which is called **eutrophication**.

KEY TERMS

Algae: plant-like, photosynthetic organisms that lack true stems, roots and leaves

Algal bloom: the rapid growth of algae in water, caused particularly by a surge of nutrients

Organic: derived from living organisms

Eutrophication: a sequence events starting with enrichment of water by mineral nutrients or organic matter that leads to a reduction in oxygen levels in the water and the death of fish and other animals

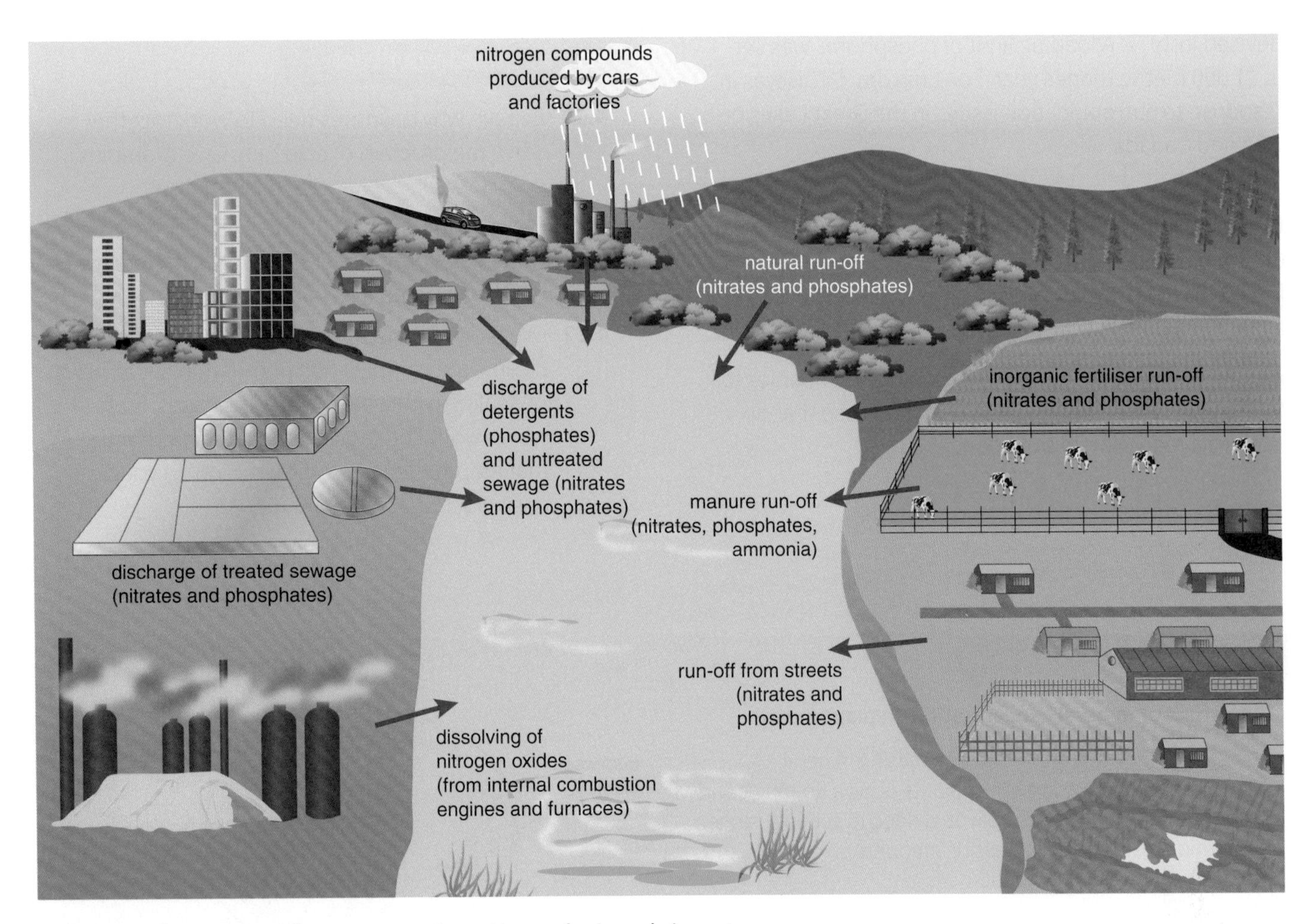

Figure 4.14 The sources of excess organic matter and minerals in water.

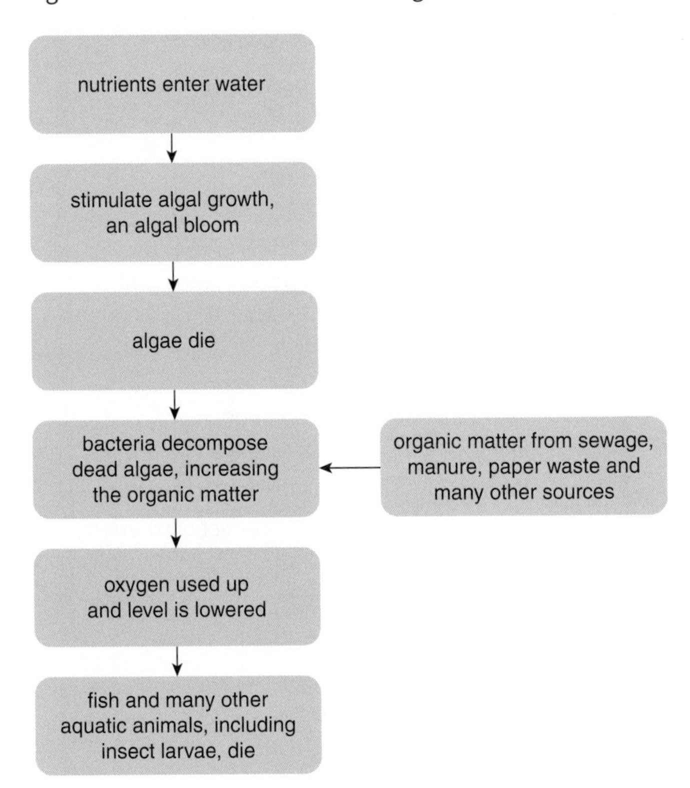

Figure 4.15 A flowchart showing how eutrophication occurs.

Pesticide and herbicide pollution

Pesticides are designed to kill living things, but not humans. However, because human physiology has much in common with other living organisms, it is not surprising that pesticides can have negative effects on humans. Insecticides, a class of pesticide produced to kill insects, will kill both the target species (the pest) and non-target species, which worryingly can include the natural enemies of the pests. Pesticides are generally water-soluble, so water pollution by these agrochemicals is a major concern. The impact of agrochemicals is covered in more detail in Section 3.4.

Pollution control and legislation

Governments around the world have been tackling pollution by legislation. Industries in participating countries are required to monitor the pollution they cause and keep it within set levels. The legislation puts pressure on the polluters to find ways to reduce the pollutants.

An example of this approach is the bi-national Great Lakes water quality agreement (GLWQA) which was devised in 1972. A loading limit of phosphorus was set at 11 000 metric tonnes $year^{-1}$ or 1 mg dm^{-3}. This was in response to eutrophication issues in the Great Lakes of USA and Canada.

Such legislation uses various tools to make sure companies follow the rules. There can be fines for exceeding set limits. Companies may be prosecuted and, in extreme cases, forced to close down. Companies might need government agreement on strategic plans to reduce pollutions levels.

Incentives can also be used to encourage companies to take part, such as grants or tax relief for those that do achieve a reduction in pollution.

SELF-ASSESSMENT QUESTIONS

4.10 Explain why countries need to work together to solve the problem of acid rain. Give examples in your answer.

4.11 Explain why it would not be a good idea to use water from ponds or small lakes in preference to water harvested from a roof.

4.12 Drugs, vector eradication, improved sanitation, clean water supply and chlorination are all ways of dealing with water-related diseases. State which would be most suitable for controlling malaria, cholera and typhoid. Explain your answers.

PRACTICAL ACTIVITY 4.1

The effect of mineral concentration on plant growth

It is easy to look at the effects of increasing mineral concentration on the growth of plants using a floating pond weed such as duckweed. You would need to set up a range of solutions containing increasing amounts of minerals and follow the growth of the plants.

Materials

- Pond weed, such as duckweed
- Houseplant food
- Petri dishes or glass bowls
- Beakers
- Forceps or brush to handle duckweed

Method

- Make a range of solutions, each with a different concentration, of houseplant food from dilute to strong. You could use 100%, 75%, 50% and 25% of plant food.
- Pour each of your solutions into a Petri dish or glass bowl.
- Place the same number of duckweed plants onto the surface of each solution and count them (Figure 4.16).
- Place the dish with plants in a well lit place
- Count the number of plants at regular intervals over a few days

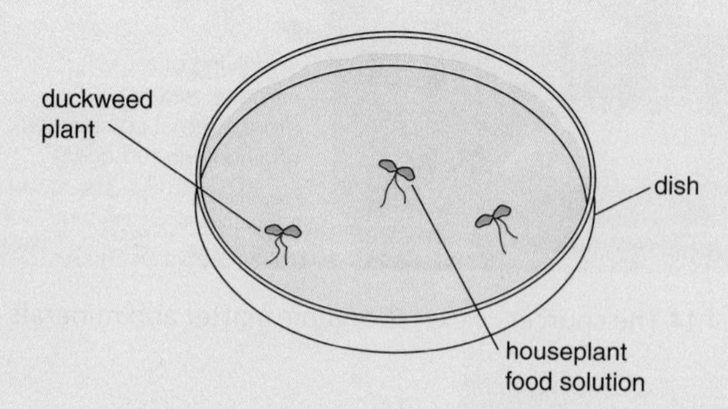

Figure 4.16 Duckweed plants in a Petri dish.

Questions

1. Plot graphs to show your data, including graphs of the number of plants plotted against time in days for each concentration of solution and a graph of the number of plants at the end of the experiment plotted against the concentration of the solution.
2. Calculate the doubling time of the number of duckweed plants at each concentration of solution.
3. Write a conclusion about the effect of the strength of houseplant food solution on the duckweed growth.
4. Suggest what the implication of this effect of solution concentration might be on a pond.

Summary

After completing this chapter, you should know:

- how to describe the water cycle
- the distribution of water around the world
- the different uses of water
- sources of water
- the impact of multipurpose dam projects
- the causes of water pollution
- the impact of water pollution on people and the environment
- strategies for improving water quantity and quality
- strategies for the control and eradication of malaria and cholera
- about water pollution in Haiti.

End-of-chapter questions

1 Copy and complete the passage.

The Earth has about 1.4 billion .... of water. The majority of this (about 97%) is in the .... The rest is called .... and is found in rocks, where it is called .... , frozen in .... and .... and as .... in rivers, lakes and swamps. **[7 marks]**

2 List four purposes of a multipurpose dam project. **[4 marks]**

3 Copy and complete the passage.

Both typhoid and cholera are water-related diseases and both are caused by .... Malaria, however, although water-related is caused by .... Both cholera and typhoid have symptoms of .... and .... but .... also causes a skin rash and ....

Some diseases can be prevented by vaccination but of malaria, cholera and typhoid only .... and .... have vaccines available. Of the three water-related diseases, ... causes the most deaths worldwide. **[8 marks]**

4 Explain the difference between primary and secondary treatment in a sewage works. **[3 marks]**

5 State precisely what causes the reduction in oxygen levels in the water of a eutrophic lake. **[4 marks]**

6 Figure 4.17 shows several sources of water pollution.

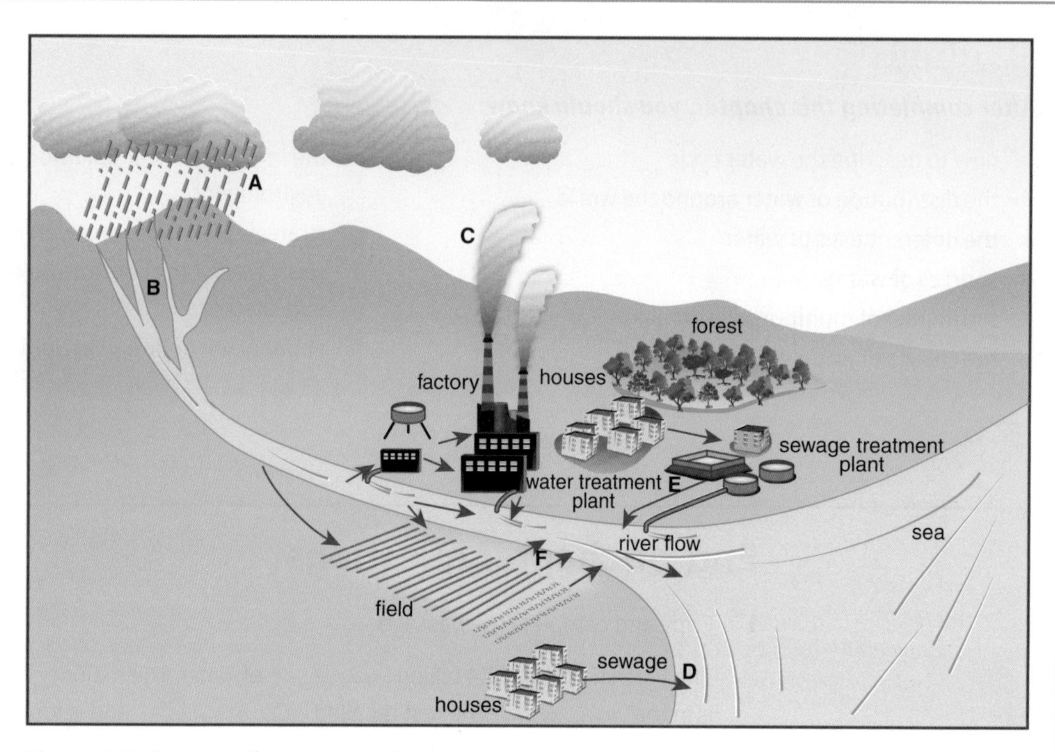

Figure 4.17 Sources of water pollution.

Using Figure 4.17 and your own knowledge answer the following questions.

a Describe how the effluent at D differs from that at E. **[2 marks]**

b Describe how the sewage treatment plant achieves this difference. **[5 marks]**

c State the name of two gases, produced by the factory, which may lead to die-back damage of trees. **[2 marks]**

d Explain why the trees in the forest close to the factory may be less affected by die-back than trees in a distant forest. **[2 marks]**

e Suggest the effects that the run-off from the field may have on the ecosystem of the river estuary. **[7 marks]**

EXTENDED CASE STUDY

The cholera outbreak in Haiti, October 2010

Haiti was hit by a devastating earthquake of magnitude 7.0 at 16:53 local time, on 12 January 2010. The epicentre was 25 km west of the capital, Port-au-Prince. The number killed is estimated to have been between 100 000 and 160 000 (government figures state even more but there are concerns that these figures are inflated).

At the time of the earthquake, the sanitation in Haiti was very poor. Only 71% of the population had access to improved water and 24% to improved sanitation.

Despite this, there had not been a case of cholera in Haiti for nearly a century prior to the earthquake. Within 10 months of the earthquake, however, a cholera outbreak had begun. This spread quickly to the whole country over only 4 weeks.

By August 2015, over 700 000 cases, and about 9000 deaths, had been reported.

Several suggestions were made about the origins of the bacteria that had caused the outbreak.

Help was provided by many nations. This included a group of UN aid workers flown in from Nepal. Their military base in Haiti was on a tributary of the Artibonite River (Figure 4.18).

It was discovered that sewage had leaked from the military base camp into the Artibonite River. Most of the affected people in the original outbreak had drunk from the river. The bacterial strain responsible for the outbreak was identified as one closely related to a Nepalese strain.

Several strategies were used to try and control the cholera. These included:

- installation of latrines
- thorough cooking of food
- education about hand washing.

By 2014 the number of cases had been significantly reduced to only about 10% of the peak in 2011. However, every rainy season leads to an increase in the number of cases. Disappointingly, the number of cases also rose dramatically in the last few months of 2014 (Figure 4.19).

→

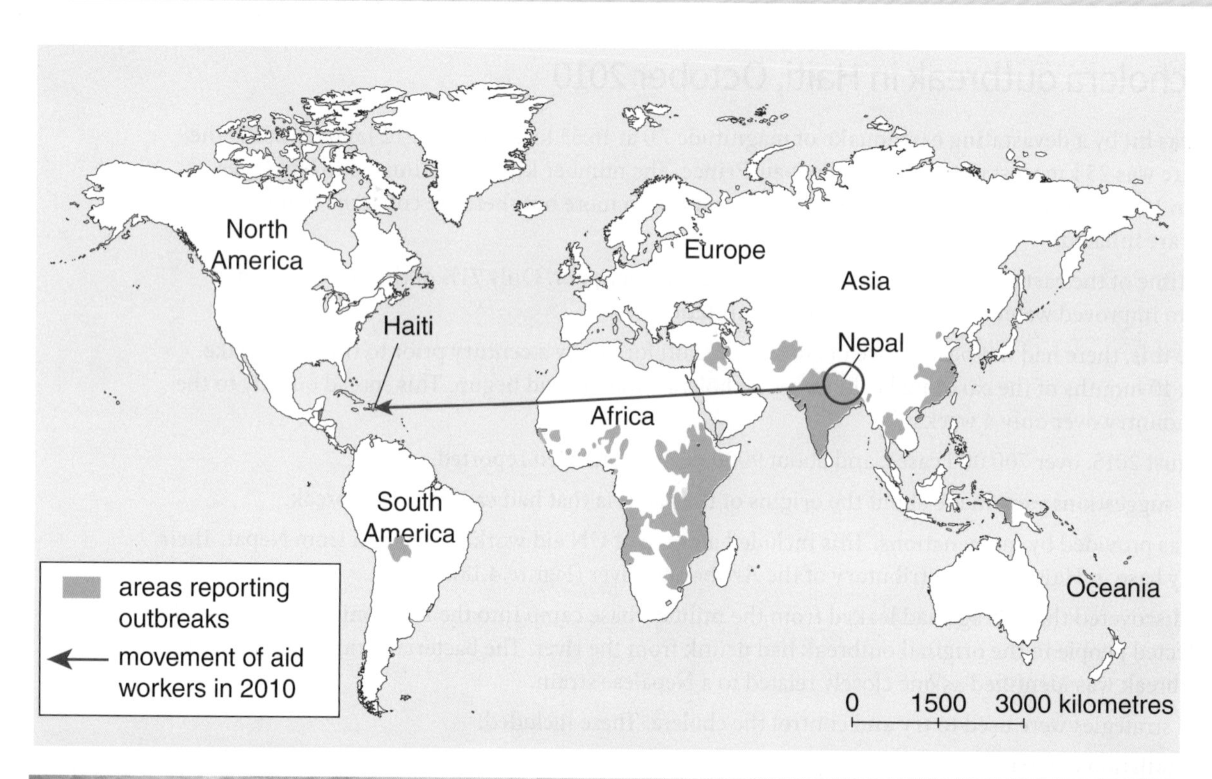

Figure 4.18 A world map showing where cholera has occurred in the recent past. Also shown is where some aid workers travelled from to help in the cholera outbreak of 2010 in Haiti. The picture shows the Artibonite River, the source of the Haitian outbreak.

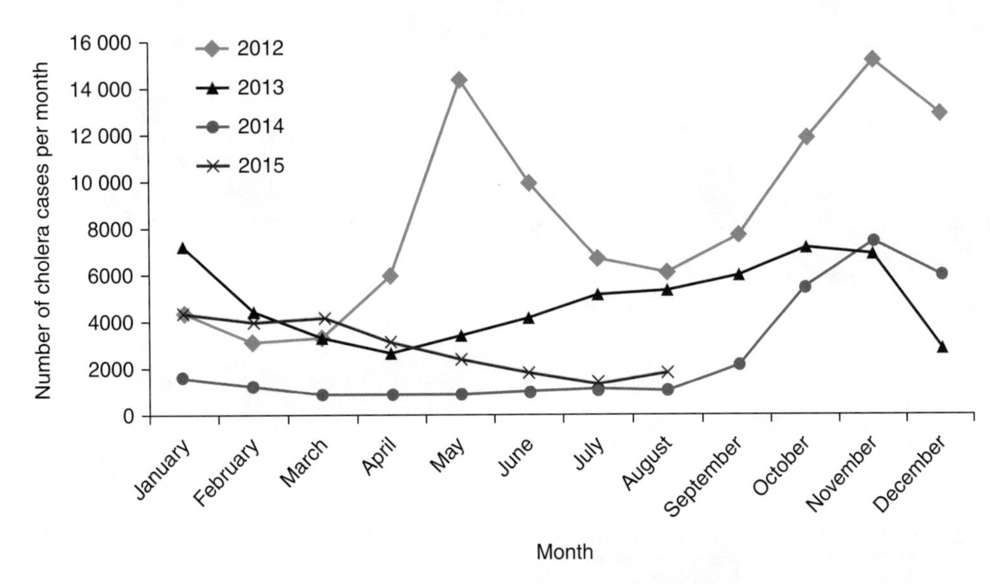

Figure 4.19 New cholera cases in Haiti every month from January 2012 to August 2015.

This is thought to have been caused by:

- heavy, late rainfall
- continued inadequate sanitation
- an assumption that the disease was now under control.

Questions

1 a It has been suggested that some aid workers, carrying the infection, caused the cholera outbreak. Explain why this suggestion has been made.

b It was also suggested that the cholera bacteria might have come from a source in South America. Using Figure 4.18 suggest how the cholera bacteria might have reached Haiti from a source in South America.

2 Describe how strategies used to control the outbreak could reduce the numbers of people infected.

3 a From Figure 4.19 state the month and maximum number of cases in 2012.

b From Figure 4.19 state the month and maximum number of cases in 2014.

4 Calculate the percentage reduction in cholera cases from the peak in 2012 to the lowest number in 2014.

5 Describe the pattern of cholera cases recorded in 2015.

6 In 2012 rainfall peaked in May and in November. How does this explain the pattern of cholera cases in that year?

7 To what extent do you agree with the statement that 'Haiti has managed to control the cholera outbreak which began in 2010'?

Chapter 5
Oceans and fisheries

Learning outcomes

By the end of this chapter, you will be able to:

- describe the resources we obtain from the oceans
- describe the distribution of marine fisheries
- describe the ocean currents of the world
- explain the effects of the El Niño Southern Oscillation
- describe how fishing has affected fish populations and fisheries
- explain the relationship between farming marine species and the fishing industry
- consider the ways in which fisheries can be managed successfully.

The bountiful oceans

Only 29% of the surface of the Earth is actually land, leaving the oceans covering 71%. The vast majority of this area, however, remains relatively unknown. Only about 10% of the ocean is over the continental shelf, where the water is relatively shallow. The remaining 90% of the ocean is over an abyss. Not only are these deep regions almost impossible to access, they are also very unproductive. Over 50% of the biological productivity of the oceans occurs in the 10% that is over the continental shelves, and 95% of all commercially caught fish are found here too. So, despite its vast size, its depth and low productivity mean the ocean is a relatively minor source of food for humans. Land-based agricultural production stands at over 6 billion tonnes whereas the total food obtained from the ocean is only about 90 million tonnes. However, most of the food harvested from the ocean is animal-based and so rich in proteins, fats and oils, which are much needed by those living at subsistence level.

The ocean has appeared so vast to humans in the past that we have tended to assume we can have no effect on either it or its ecosystems. However, it is now becoming clear that fish stocks are declining because of over-fishing, and pollution, by such things as oil, mercury and rubbish, is becoming a huge problem, even in the open ocean. For example, over 250 000 tonnes of waste plastic are currently circulating in five huge ocean regions known as gyres. It is estimated that an ambitious plan to clean this plastic up will take nearly 50 years, but it will achieve nothing if we carry on dumping plastic.

The message is clear, the ocean is a very important part of life on Earth. It probably still has much to offer us but our use of it needs to be better managed in the future than it has been in the past.

Figure 5.0 Trawler fishing off the coast of The Netherlands.

5.1 The resource potential of the oceans

Oceans supply food and chemicals, including building materials, as well as providing an important route for the transport of goods, especially bulky ones, around the world. The ceaseless motion of the sea, in the form of wind-generated waves and the tides caused by the Moon and Sun, provide a largely untapped source of energy. The edge of the sea has always been attractive to humans and this, and increasingly the open ocean, is a source of tourism opportunities. Finally, in a world ever thirsty for safe water to drink, the oceans' vast reserves are increasingly being used for this purpose.

Food

By far the most important resource that humans obtain from the oceans is fish. This term can be used to include true fish, or finfish, but also shellfish and other animals that live in the sea and can be eaten. World fishery yields are about 90 million tonnes year^{-1}, with over 80 million tonnes of that coming from the sea. The main fisheries are located on the continental shelves. This is because the water is shallow there, so light can penetrate and there is more oxygen than further down. In addition, nutrients from the land are abundant on the shelf. All these features make the continental shelf a good place for the growth of plants and therefore the fish that depend on them.

Chemicals and building materials

As oceans cover 71% of the world's surface and 3.5% of seawater is made up of dissolved substances, it is hardly surprising that these water bodies are an enormous potential resource of chemicals. Compounds containing more than 60 chemical elements are dissolved in seawater.

Many materials in the oceans have been eroded from the land, where rain and wind break down rocks. These particles and dissolved substances are carried into the oceans via rivers. Some of these substances can be extracted directly, including:

- salt
- magnesium
- gold (in estuaries)
- tin
- titanium
- diamonds.

Figure 5.1 Salt collection.

In coastal sites such as the one shown in Figure 5.1, lagoons are made from sand. The sea is allowed in through a gap which is then blocked. The seawater is then left to evaporate over many weeks in the hot sun, leaving behind sea salt that can be collected.

The ocean floor is mined for many substances, diamonds, for example, are found in greater numbers on the ocean floor than on land. However, it is much harder to mine the ocean floor because it has to be dredged and then the sediment sifted.

Sand, gravel and crushed rock are mined for the construction industry, including housing and road building. Care must be taken with their removal, however, because physical damage can be caused to the seabed and associated habitats. In addition, fine particle clouds are produced that then resettle, and these interfere with photosynthesis and act as a source of heavy metals that can enter food chains.

As the mining of land depletes the sources of minerals there, mining the ocean floor will increase.

One of the most well-known chemicals derived from the sea is oil. Offshore drilling has become commonplace, with thousands of drilling rigs scattered around the oceans of the world. The world's largest offshore oilfield, in the Gulf of Mexico, has nearly 4000 active rigs. There is more about this in Section 2.5.

Wave and tidal energy

There is an enormous amount of energy in the waves that break on the shores all around the world. It is estimated that if this energy could be harvested it would be to twice the present world energy production, as much as that provided by 2000 large power stations. However, it is not easy to harness this energy; a number of devices have been trialled but only a few are in regular use. Examples include the Islay LIMPET (land-installed marine powered energy transformer) on the west coast of Scotland, and the Aguçadoura Wave Farm off northern Portugal. The latter is sadly non-operational at the moment but when it was in use generated 2.25 megawatts of power (2.25 MW) and was the biggest wave farm in the world. The Islay LIMPET produces 0.25 MW. The technology is still very much in its infancy but could become important in the future as fossil fuels run out.

There has been a little more success with tidal power. Because of the varying gravitational pull of the Sun and Moon, water in the sea moves up and down on a twice-daily basis. This causes it to come onto land and then later recede, and this movement can be harnessed to generate electricity. The first such power station was built at Strangford Loch in Northern Ireland, generating 1.2 MW of power. This has now been dwarfed by the Sihwa Lake Tidal Power Station in South Korea, the largest in the world generating 254 MW, and another at Rance in France, the second largest generating 240 MW. There are many proposed projects. At Penzhin Bay in North East Russia, the Penzhin Tidal Power Plant Project is a proposal that could generate up to 87 100 MW because of the 9 m tidal range in the bay.

Tourism

The seaside has been a major tourist attraction for centuries. The Romans enjoyed sea, sun and sand in Baiae when in Rome and on Mersae when in England, over 2000 years ago. Today, with the advent of cheap foreign travel by air, people in the more economically developed countries (MEDCs) of the world are attracted to marine sites of great natural beauty, especially coral reefs. Around the Caribbean, the Red Sea, the Indian Ocean (for example the Maldives) and on the Great Barrier Reef of Australia, visitors in their hundreds of thousands arrive every year. Diving, snorkelling, windsurfing and jet skiing are just some of the activities for the more adventurous, but many are content simply to sunbathe on the beach. Away from the shore, deep-sea fishing is a very popular pastime. In addition, there is big business in boat trips to view the creatures of the sea, especially whales and dolphins. Whale watching began in the mid-1950s off the coast of California as a chance event. It was not until whaling was banned in the early 1980s that people began to see watching whales as an economic alternative to killing them.

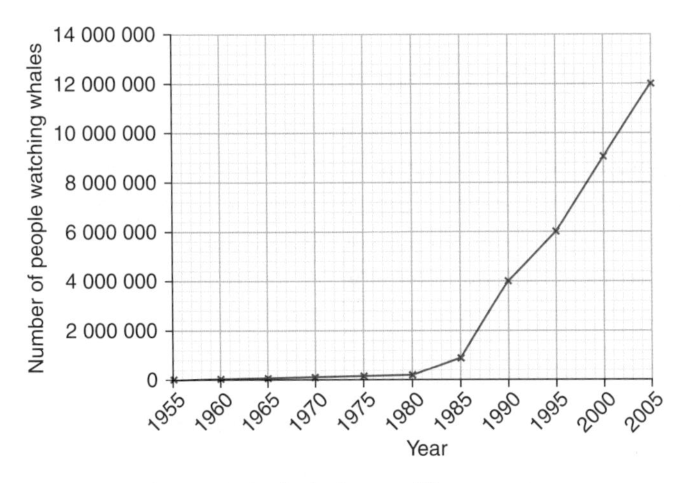

Figure 5.2 The growth of whale watching.

It is estimated that whale watching contributes over US$2 billion to the world economy (Figure 5.2). In 1880, the entire US whaling effort yielded $10 million, which is about $250 million today. There are few better examples showing the value of living things compared with dead things!

Transport

Ships have always been an important way of transporting people and goods. Today, shipping is less important for moving people because of the advent of aviation. However, pleasure cruises are still an important economic sector and bulk freight is still best transported from country to country on ships. There are currently over 50 000 merchant (goods-carrying) ships registered around the world. The level of shipping activity in the world is shown in Figure 5.3.

Table 5.1 lists different types of merchant ship.

Potential for safe drinking water

With the world's population now in excess of 7 billion, many essential commodities could become harder to obtain. Possibly the most essential of these is safe drinking water. Section 4.1 explained, however, that only a very small proportion of the water on Earth is safe to drink. Water that is salty is not safe to drink because your body has to remove the salt, which would require more water. It is possible to derive safe drinking water from salt water by desalination, as explained in Section 4.4.

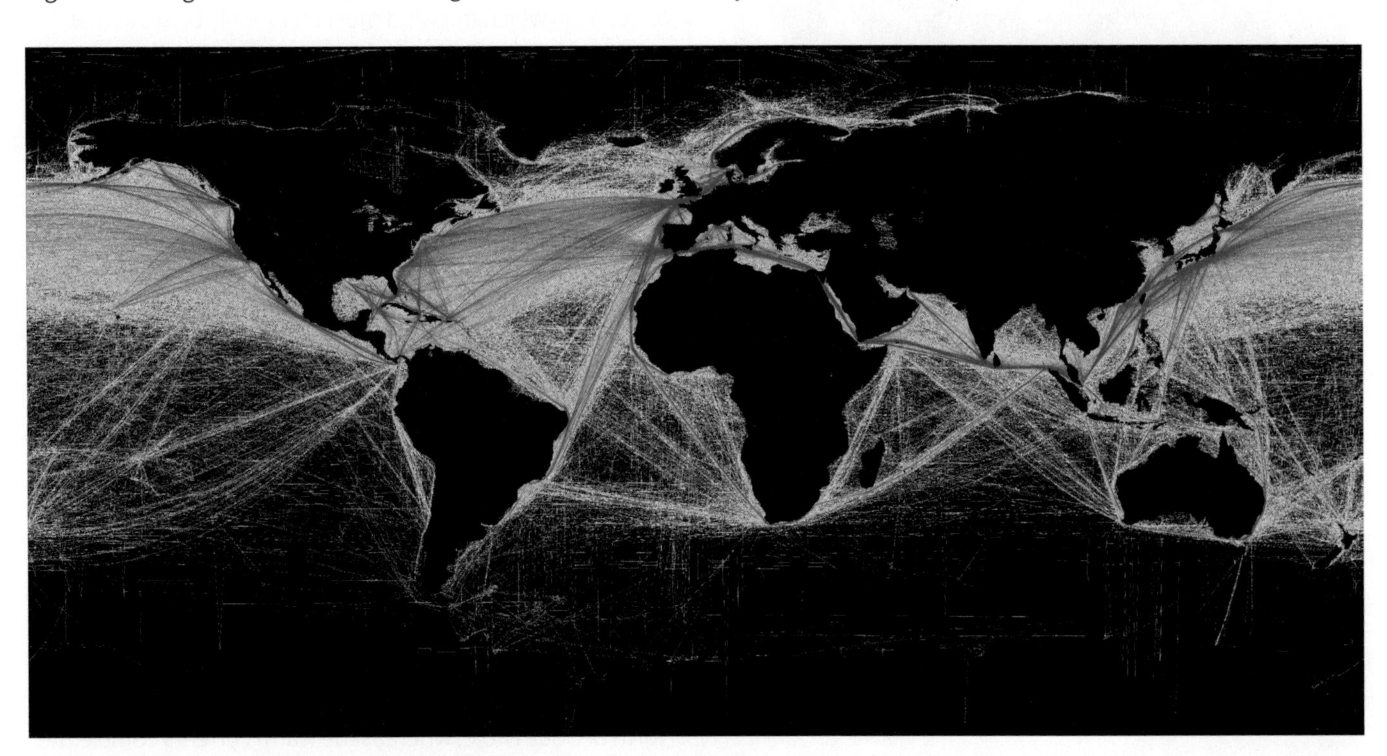

Figure 5.3 The level of shipping activity in the world. The busiest lines are east–west and vice versa, shown by the strength of the pink lines and through the Suez and Panama canals.

Ship type	Load or purpose
Bulk carriers	The transport of foods such as rice and wheat
Container ships	The entire load is carried in lorry-sized containers, this is known as containerisation
Tankers	The transport of fluids, especially oil and petroleum products, liquefied petroleum gas and liquefied natural gas. Also used for the transport of vegetable oils and wine
Refrigerated ships	The transport of perishable items such as vegetables, fruits, fish and dairy products
Roll-on / roll-off ships	The transport of vehicles, together with their loads, that can be driven on and off the ship
Coastal trading vessels	Used for trade between places that are close together, especially in island groups
Ferries	Used mainly for the movement of foot passengers, sometimes with their cars, mainly between islands or between a mainland and islands
Cruise ships	Used for pleasure voyages where the facilities on the ship are a crucial part of the trip
Ocean liner	Used to transport people from one port to another

Table 5.1 Types of merchant ship.

SELF-ASSESSMENT QUESTIONS

5.1 Explain the difference between wave and tidal energy.

5.2 Figure 5.4 shows a wave-driven power station. Explain how it can generate electricity 24 h day.

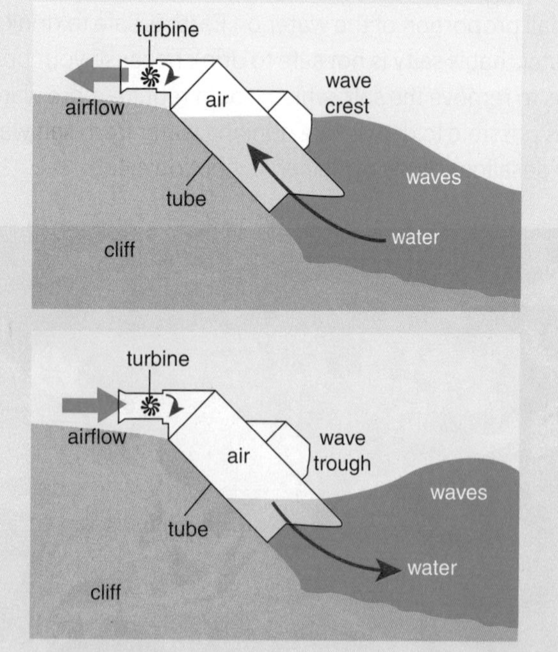

Figure 5.4 A wave-driven power station.

5.3 Contrast the ways in which water in a sewage-polluted lake and water from the sea are unsafe to drink.

5.2 World fisheries

As mentioned, over 90 million tonnes of fish (in the widest sense of the word) are harvested every year. Fish are always important as a source of protein for people, but are especially important in some countries of the world such as Japan. In order to understand where large numbers of fish can be found you need to study ocean currents and the food webs of the sea.

Major ocean currents

Currents, or strictly speaking **surface currents**, are caused mainly by wind. At any particular place in the world the nature of the **prevailing wind** can be described. This refers to the direction in which the wind most commonly blows at that place. Surface currents are ultimately caused by these winds. However, the final direction depends very much on the shape of the land around the ocean at any particular point.

Figure 5.5 shows the main prevailing winds around the world and the world's currents.

KEY TERMS

Surface currents: movement of the surface water of the sea in a constant direction

Prevailing wind: the direction from which the wind nearly always blows in a particular area

The currents in the Southern Hemisphere are generally anticlockwise as the winds blow from the south-east and force the western Australian, Benguela and Peruvian currents northwards. An important aspect of a current is whether it is warm or cold. Looking at the map of currents you will notice that cold currents come from the North or South Pole, whereas the warm currents come either from the tropics or flow along either side of the equator.

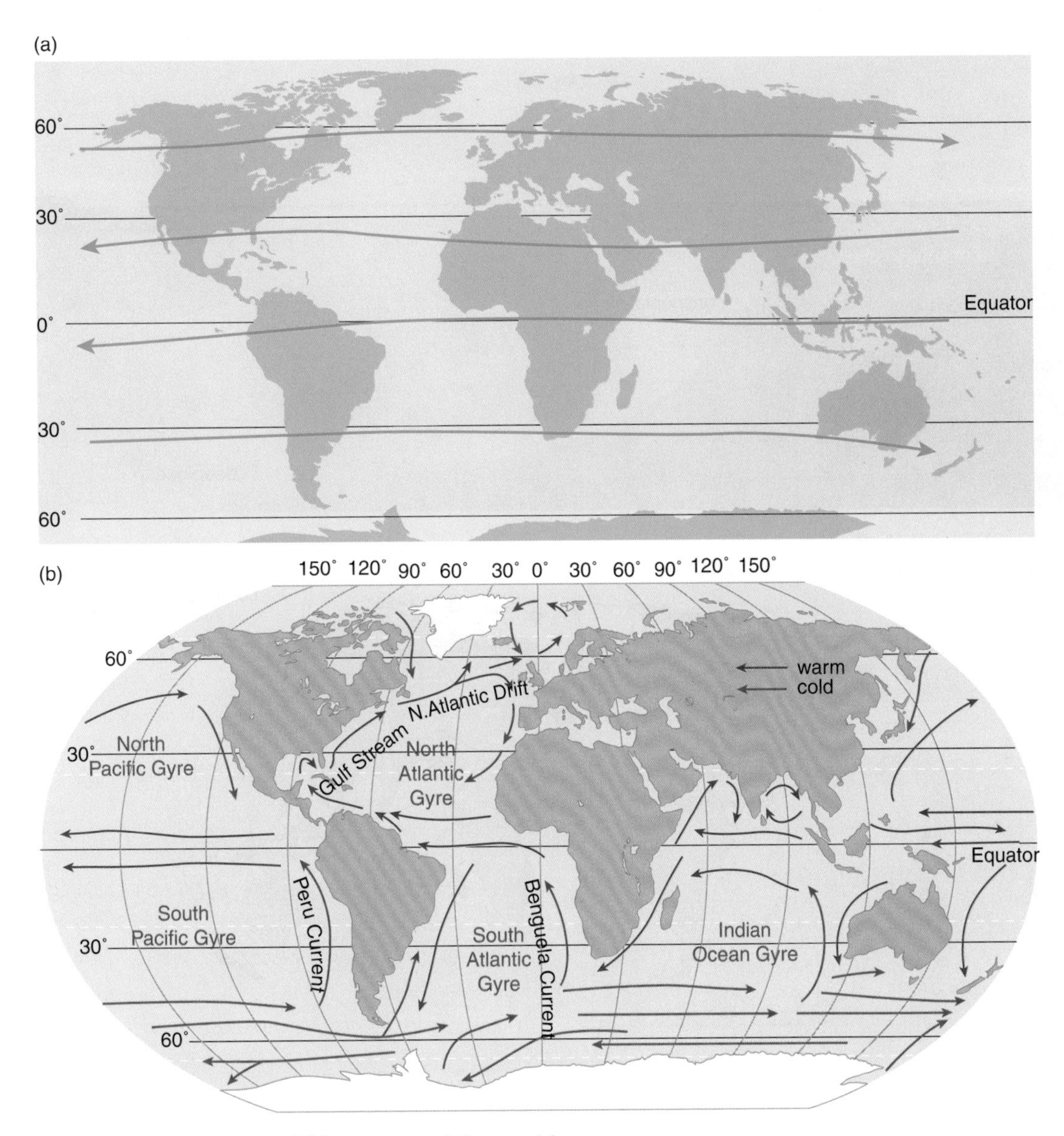

Figure 5.5 The (a) prevailing winds and (b) currents of the world.

Finding the fish

Fish are animals and so cannot make their own food. Herbivorous fish rely on the primary producers of the sea, which are nearly always green algae called **phytoplankton**. Carnivorous fish eat the herbivorous ones or other carnivores. They are part of a food web, starting with phytoplankton (see Section 9.1). So, fish are found where conditions are good for phytoplankton.

Phytoplankton make their own food by photosynthesis. This process requires light, water and carbon dioxide. Water is obviously available everywhere in the oceans and carbon dioxide easily dissolves in water from the atmosphere. Light is therefore likely to be the **limiting factor** for photosynthesis. Water absorbs light energy and most ocean water has absorbed all of the sunlight by a depth of only 200 m. This 200 m deep zone is called the **euphotic zone**. Below this photosynthesis will not happen. This is one reason why fish are found where the water is shallower. Shallow water is found over the continental shelves, which are usually no more than 150 m below sea level (Figure 5.6). Major fisheries are also found on these continental shelves (Figure 5.7).

KEY TERMS

Phytoplankton: small organisms in the sea that can make their own food and upon which almost all other sea creatures depend for their food

Limiting factor: of all the factors that might affect a process, the one that is in shortest supply

Euphotic zone: the top 200 m or so of seawater through which light can penetrate and in which photosynthesis can happen

Figure 5.6 The continental shelf.

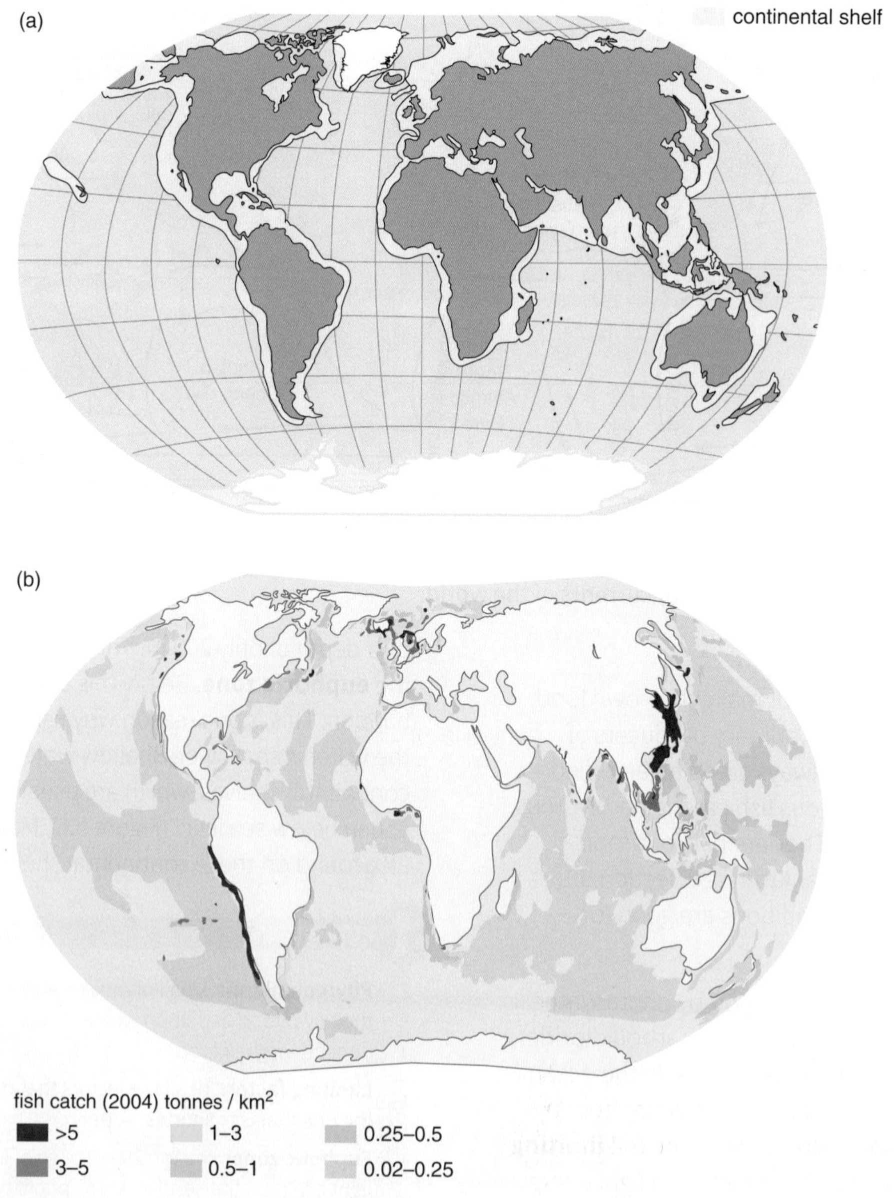

Figure 5.7 The distribution of (a) continental shelves and (b) major ocean fisheries.

You will notice that there are some areas where there are continental shelves but no significant fisheries. In addition to light, carbon dioxide and water, which allows the phytoplankton to make carbohydrates such as sugars, they also need mineral nutrients to make proteins. Making proteins requires a source of nitrogen and sulfur. Nucleic acids, which form the genes of living things, also require phosphorus. The green pigment chlorophyll, which is essential for photosynthesis in plants, requires magnesium. A lack of these mineral nutrients, even where there is plenty of light, water and carbon dioxide, will reduce the growth of phytoplankton. This in turn prevents there being very many fish. The most important fisheries of the world are where the current system stirs up decaying material from the seabed. This material is rich in mineral nutrients.

One of the most famous, and also the largest, fishery in the world is the Peruvian anchovy fishery off the west coast of South America. Here, cold water is forced upwards near the coast of Peru, leading to nutrient-rich surface water in this area; this is called **upwelling** (Figure 5.8). Because of its effect on phytoplankton growth, this area supports very large fish populations, mainly of the small herring-like fish, the anchoveta (*Engraulis ringens*).

At its peak, this single fishery yielded in excess of 12 million tonnes of fish. However, the fishery suffered an enormous collapse in the early 1970s. Part of the reason for this was **over-fishing**, which meant that the fish were being caught before they could breed, although this was not the only problem. Figure 5.9 shows fluctuations in Peruvian anchovy fishery between 1950 and 2000.

The upwelling described above is disturbed approximately once every 10–15 years by an event called the **El Niño Southern Oscillation**, also called the ENSO or just the El Niño. It is not fully understood why this change in the pattern of currents in this region occurs. However, it is known that there is a change to the normal trade winds. El Niño leads to warm, nutrient-poor water coming into the region from the equator. The effect of this is to stop the upwelling of the cold, nutrient-rich water that supports the anchovy fishery. A lack of

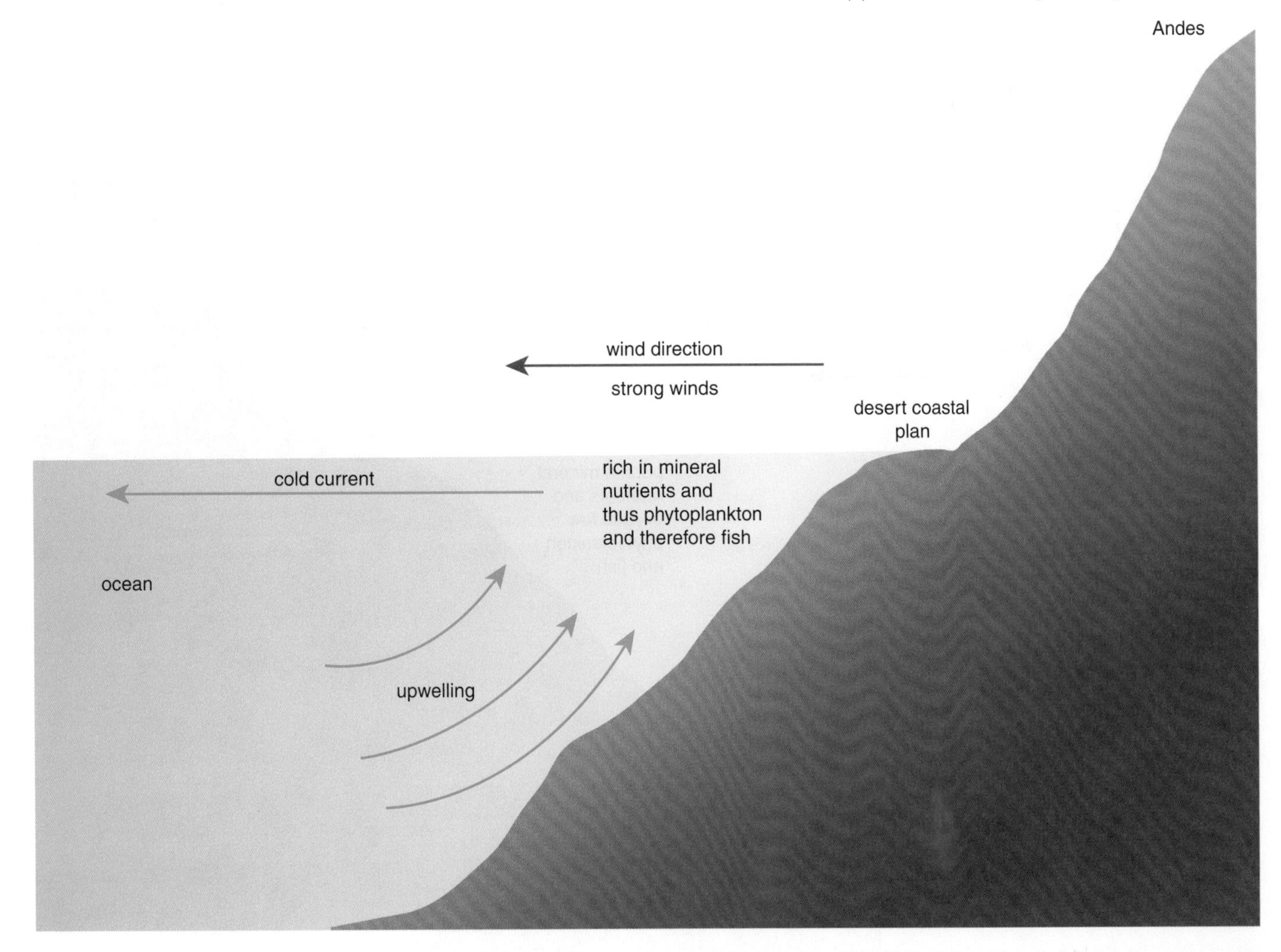

Figure 5.8 The basis of the Peruvian anchovy fishery.

nutrients means the phytoplankton do not grow well, so there is less food for the fish. The El Niño of 1972 was a very large one and, combined with over-fishing, led to the collapse seen in Figure 5.9.

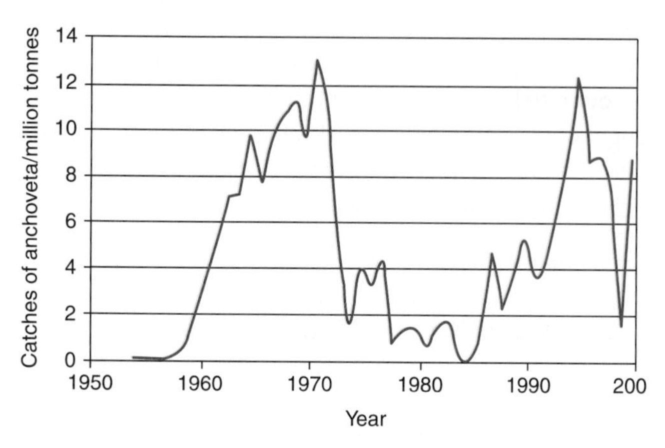

Figure 5.9 Yields of the Peruvian anchovy fishery.

In the 1970s, and still today, much of the production of the anchovy fishery was used for fishmeal. This fishmeal is used to feed farmed fish, and so countries where this is an important industry, such as the UK, are affected by a crash in the anchovy fishery. Compare Figure 5.10, showing the coast of Peru in an El Niño year, with Figure 5.8.

KEY TERMS

Upwelling: areas where minerals at the ocean floor are brought to the surface by currents

Over-fishing: when the number of fish that is caught is greater than the rate at which the fish reproduce, leading to a fall in fish numbers in an area

El Niño Southern Oscillation (ENSO): the change in the prevailing winds that leads to a change in the pattern of currents in the oceans of the south Pacific

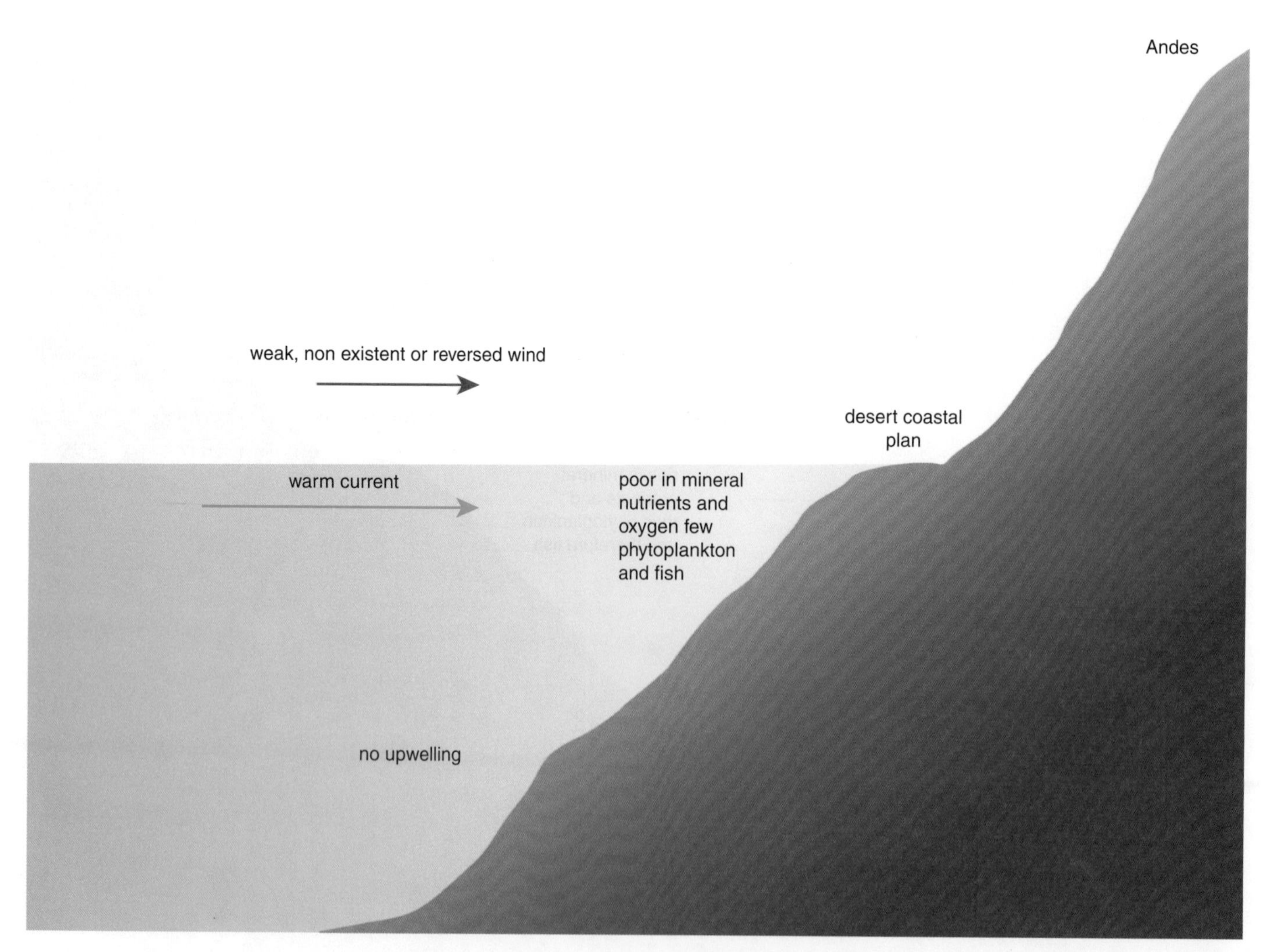

Figure 5.10 The Peruvian coast in an El Niño year.

SELF-ASSESSMENT QUESTIONS

5.4 State three reasons why most of the major fisheries in the world are found on continental shelves.

5.5 Explain why the reversal of ocean currents in an El Niño year causes a reduction in the catch from the Peruvian anchovy fishery.

5.6 Look at Figure 5.11.

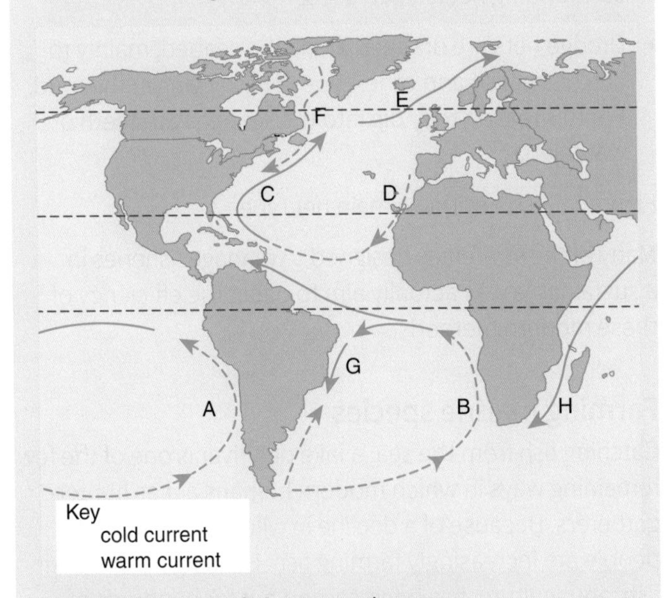

Figure 5.11 Ocean fisheries and currents.

a Copy and complete the key.

b Use the information in Figure 5.11 to explain why there is a large fishery at A and another at B.

5.3 Exploitation of the oceans: impact on fisheries

Over-fishing of marine fish species

The global fish catch grew every year from 1950 until the late 1980s. Since then there have been fluctuations but no trend of growth (Figure 5.12).

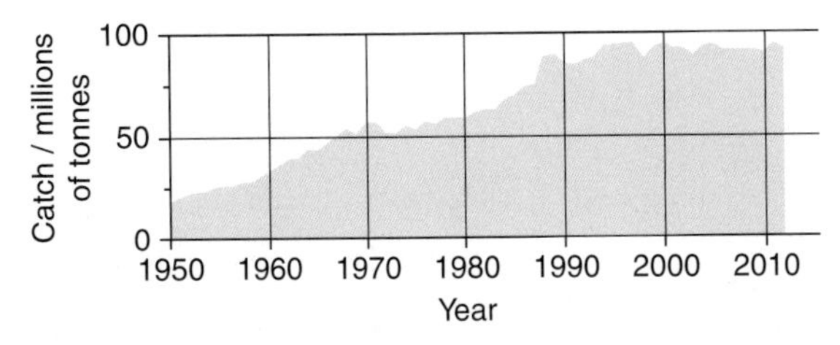

Figure 5.12 The change in total marine fish catches between 1950 and 2010.

This lack of growth is probably explained, at least partially, by over-fishing. At least 75% of the world's marine fisheries are threatened. The main reason for fishing used to be economic gain. This model leads to a fishery in which the number of fish caught is based on how many are available. Sustainable fishing involves monitoring how many fish are left in order to provide for the next generation of fishers and their customers.

The yield from world fisheries has only remained constant because it has been possible to switch to new species. A look at some of the major food providers of the past provides strong evidence for over-fishing. One of the best examples is the fate of the North Atlantic herring. It is estimated that, during the 1950s, 3000 million herring year^{-1} were caught and brought to ports in the UK. The stock of fish at that time is estimated to have been about 2 million tonnes. Fishing based on how many fish are available led to an increase in the size and power of the fishing boats. By the early 1970s, hardly any herring were left, the stock being less than 100 000 tonnes.

The symptoms of severe over-fishing are a reduced catch at the same time as an increased fishing effort. Another symptom is that the size of fish caught gets progressively smaller (Figure 5.13).

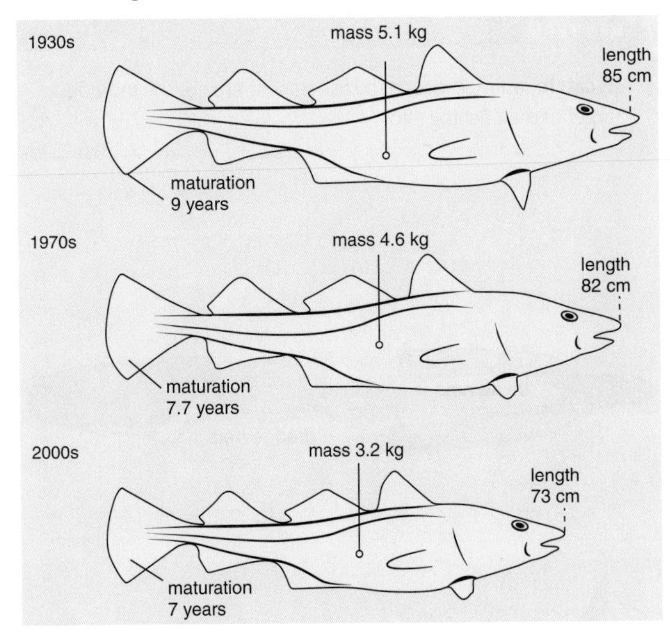

Figure 5.13 The decline in size of cod caught. Between the 1930s and the 2000s the average cod became 12 cm shorter and weighed nearly 2 kg less.

The target species is not the only casualty of over-fishing. Wherever fish are caught commercially, the wrong species, the wrong sex or individuals that are too small are also caught. These non-target individuals are referred to as

bycatch. Shrimp fisheries are known to have the biggest bycatch of all. Worldwide, it is estimated that for every shrimp caught nearly six other fish are also caught. Shrimp fisheries account for only 2% of the world fishery catch but more than 30% of the world's bycatch.

A very well-known example of bycatch is in the tuna fishery, where dolphins can become entangled in the tuna nets. The general public has become so concerned about this form of bycatch that tinned tuna often carries the label 'dolphin friendly' to reassure customers.

The most obvious cause of over-fishing is the increasing demand for fish as food. However, technology and improved fishing methods have also played a major part. Much bigger boats, which can work a long way from a port for many weeks, are used now than in the past. In addition, it is now possible to find fish very easily using SONAR and detailed weather data.

However, possibly the most important development has been the creation of huge nets. These nets can scoop up everything in an area, including unwanted fish and other species. Almost half of what is caught in such a net is regularly discarded as bycatch. The following list provides some examples of these huge nets.

KEY TERM

Bycatch: animals caught by fishers that are not the intended target of their fishing effort

- Trawl nets, including bottom trawl nets, catch all kinds of unwanted species and damage the seabed during their use.
- Drift nets, as their name suggests, drift with the current and are not anchored. These are often used in coastal waters
- Various kinds of seine net, including the purse seine, hang like a curtain in the water. A variant called the surrounding net is often used.
- Dredge nets are dragged along the seabed, mainly to catch shellfish and other types of fish living in the mud. For this reason they dig into the seabed with teeth or water jets.

Figure 5.14 shows these main net types.

Many of the strategies designed to manage fisheries in a sustainable way actually aim to offset the efficiency of these modern methods.

Farming marine species

Catching fish from the sea, a lake or a river is one of the few remaining ways in which modern humans act as hunter-gatherers. Because of a decline in wild fish populations, people are increasingly farming fish. Farming fresh-water fish, aquaculture, has been carried out for hundreds of years. Many central European countries have numerous fishponds that were constructed in the Middle Ages. Considering fish in the broadest sense, farming various

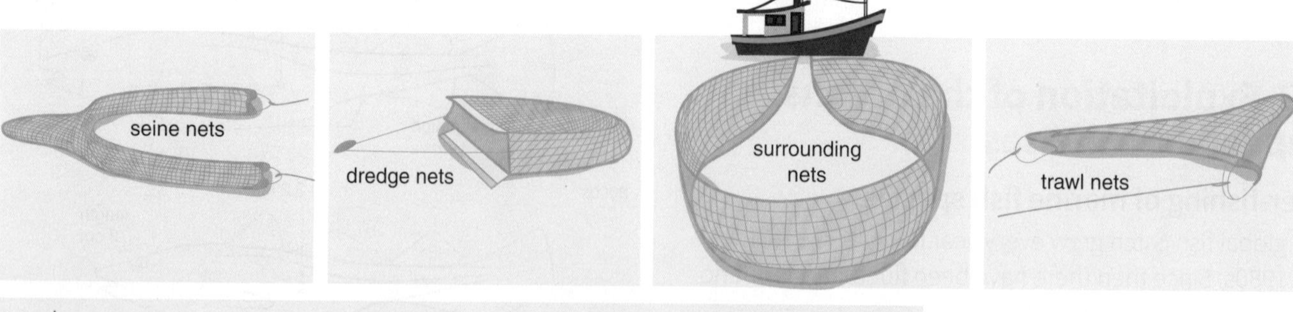

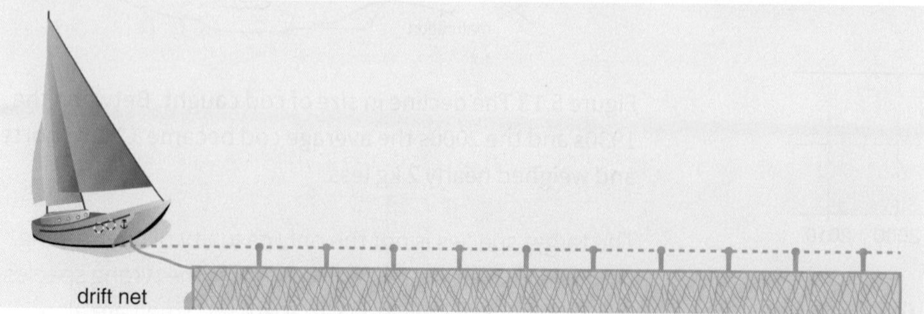

Figure 5.14 Some of the many types of nets used around the world to catch fish.

shellfish has also been practised for hundreds of years and can be a very important source of both income and food. With mussels, strings are hung from a raft and the mussels then grow on the strings. Yields as high 250 tonnes hectare^{-1} have been achieved.

Farming marine fish (mariculture) is generally much more difficult than farming fresh-water species and has not been enormously successful so far. One issue is that the species we prefer to eat are carnivorous fish. This means they are at the top of food chains and require a range of other species on which to feed. Furthermore, the food preferences of the young fish change as they get older.

Cobia (*Rachycentron canadum*) is one of the best candidates so far for warm-water aquaculture. It has a rapid growth rate and its high-quality meat achieves a good price.

Mariculture is carried out in the USA, Mexico and Panama as well as parts of Asia. Asia has the largest open-water fish farms in the world. However, the single largest such farm is found off the coast of Panama, using cobia. In 2013 the US Food and Agriculture Organization website reported 43 395 tonnes of cobia being cultured around the world.

Other marine fish being harvested include threadfin (*Polydactylis sexfilis*) and bigeye tuna (*Thunnus obesus*). The most productive form of mariculture is salmon farming, although the fish is only marine for part of its life. The biggest salmon fish farms are found in Chile, Norway, Scotland, Canada and the Faroe islands. By 1996 the production of farmed salmon exceeded that of wild caught fish. This apparent success is not without its problems, however. There are a number of concerns surrounding the farming of salmon. Farmed fish are much more susceptible to diseases and parasites than wild fish. Wastes from the cages in which the fish are kept can pollute the environment, and fish escaping from a farm can cause problems in the local environment (see the Extended Case Study at the end of this chapter).

5.4 Strategies for managing the harvesting of marine species

Every country with a coastline has a zone of 200 nautical miles around it designated by the United Nations (UN) Convention on the Law of the Sea as the **economic exclusion zone**. Inside this zone the country responsible must attempt to manage its fisheries so that they are sustainable. A variety of strategies exist to do this.

SELF-ASSESSMENT QUESTIONS

5.7 Figure 5.9 shows trends in the catches of anchoveta, or Peruvian anchovy, in the second half of the 20th century. There were strong El Niño events in 1957–58, 1965–66, 1972–73, 1982–83, 1986–87, 1987–88. Suggest explanations for the trends from:

- **a** 1950 until 1972
- **b** 1973 until 1985
- **c** 1986 until 1997

5.8 Give three reasons why some scientists think it is unlikely that mariculture will allow a significant reduction in over-fishing of wild stocks in the foreseeable future.

5.9 Suggest some advantages of mariculture compared with harvesting wild fish populations. Use the following headings:

- **a** the environment
- **b** fishers
- **c** consumers.

5.10 Figure 5.15 shows the status of world fisheries. Suggest what percentage of world fisheries could be described as unsustainable and explain your answer.

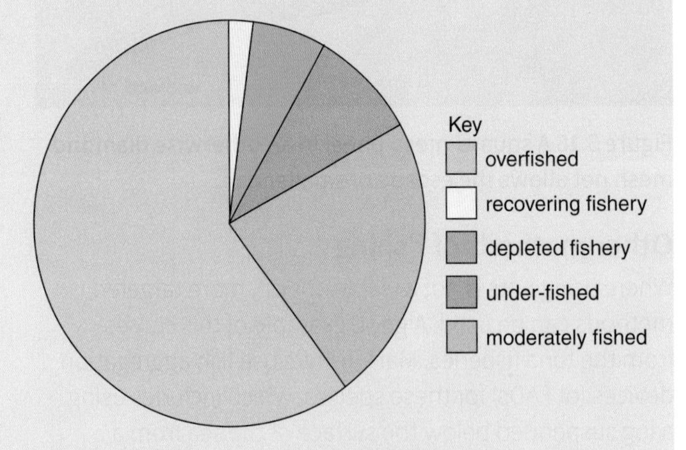

Figure 5.15 The status of the world fisheries.

Net types and mesh size and shape

Certain net types, such as the driftnet mentioned above, are now banned from use in certain areas. A more important consideration, however, is the mesh size of the net. If the mesh is too small, the net will catch juvenile fish. If this happens the number of fish available to grow to maturity and reproduce is reduced.

For example, the General Fisheries Commission for the Mediterranean (GFCM) adopted an agreement that stated a minimum 40 mm square-mesh **cod end** (the closed end of the net) or a diamond-mesh size of at least 50 mm should be used for all trawling activities exploiting demersal (bottom-living) fish and shellfish. A diamond-shaped mesh catches fish more easily and for this reason a square mesh panel is often included in an otherwise diamond net (Figure 5.16).

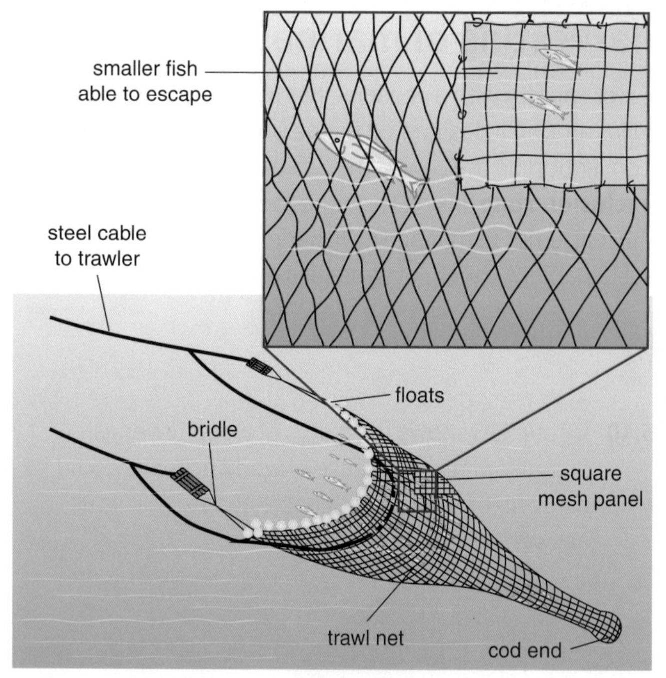

Figure 5.16 A square-mesh panel in an otherwise diamond-mesh net allows the escape of smaller fish.

Other methods of fishing

Where using nets is not a viable option, more targeted methods can be used. A good example of this comes from the tuna fisheries. Many fishers use fish aggregation devices (or FADs) for these species, which includes using a log suspended below the surface of the sea from a buoy. This attracts the tuna together with other species, including tuna predators. Once a good aggregation of fish has collected, they are gathered up in a giant net. This will take all the other species and younger tuna fish with it, leading to a large bycatch. A solution is to use the pole and line method for catching the tuna. Done properly, this method is highly selective with very little or no bycatch. For those conscious about the bycatch, which includes dolphins, in the tuna industry, canned tuna that clearly states that it is from a pole and line fishery is now available.

Quotas

Many fisheries scientists and others believe that the imposition of **quotas** is one of the most important ways in which fisheries can be managed. Legislators, usually governments but sometimes multinational organisations (such as the European Union), set limits on how many and what type of fish may be caught. Fisheries research scientists use a wealth of information gathered from networks across the world to help the legislators set sensible limits. If they get it right, enough fish should be left to reproduce and replenish the fishery for the following season. A 2008 study showed that a fishery managed with a quota system is half as likely to fail as one that is unmanaged.

KEY TERMS

Economic exclusion zone: the zone around a country's coastline that is under the control of that country

Cod end: the closed end of a fishing net

Quota: the legal limit on the amount of fish that can be caught

PRACTICAL ACTIVITY 5.1

Estimating fish population sizes

In order for quotas to work, a sensible figure must be set. The size of the quota will depend on the population of the target fish species. It is very important to have a good estimate of fish population size in order to decide on the quota.

The size of the yellowfin tuna population in an area of the Indian Ocean was estimated using a method called mark–release–recapture. Fish were captured and marked with a microchip. They were then released back into the sea. A month later fish were captured in the same area again. On the first occasion 127 fish were caught and marked. On the second occasion 174 fish were caught and 12 of these had a microchip. The formula for calculating the population from these results is:

$$\text{Population} = \frac{\text{number of fish caught on first capture} \times \text{number of fish caught on second capture}}{\text{number of marked fish caught on second capture}}$$

So, in this case, it is: 127 × 174 ÷ 12 = 1842

This method assumes that the proportion of marked fish in the whole population is the same as the proportion of marked fish in the second capture. So in this case, 12 is to 174 as 127 is to x, where x is the actual population.

You can simulate the mark–release–recapture method using some beans and a marker pen. This will allow you to practise your maths skills and think about real-life situations faced by fisheries scientists.

Materials

- A large quantity of beans
- A bag
- A marker pen

Method

- Put four handfuls of beans into a bag, without counting them.
- Take a handful of beans back out: this is your first capture.
- Count these beans and record the number (A).
- Mark these beans with a marker pen (Figure 5.17).
- Put these marked beans back into the bag.
- Shake the bag.
- Take a handful of beans from the bag without looking: this is your second capture.
- Count the total number of beans you took (regardless of whether they have a marker pen dot or not) and record your answer (B).
- Count the number of those beans that are marked and record this number (C).
- Return all the beans to the bag.
- Use the figures in the equation given above for yellowfin tuna, to calculate the size of the bean population in the bag.
- Count the total number of beans in the bag and compare this figure with your calculation.

Figure 5.17 Marked beans.

Question

1 Think of at least two other ways in which you might be able to get information about the size of a fish population.

Closed seasons and protected areas

In a way similar to the setting of quotas, governments and other legislative bodies can also pass laws that can close fisheries down for part of the year. This is most commonly done during the breeding season.

As with quotas and closed seasons, some fisheries are protected by preventing fishing in certain areas, often where the target species is known to breed.

International agreements and conservation laws

Some fisheries are protected by conservation laws. For example, the Magnuson–Stevens Fishery Conservation and Management Act is the main law governing marine fisheries in the USA. It was first passed in 1976 and has undergone numerous amendments. Its aims include controlling the country's territorial waters, conserving fishery resources and enforcing international fishing agreements. It also aims to develop under-used fisheries and protect fish habitats.

As mentioned above, an economic exclusion zone of 200 nautical miles surrounds most countries with a coastline. Inside such zones it is the right and responsibility of that country to manage its fisheries. However, to regulate fisheries in international waters, international agreements are needed. This led to the UN Convention on the Law of the Sea (UNCLOS). A good example of where such agreement is needed is the Mediterranean. In this narrow body of water, a 200 nautical mile exclusion zone has no meaning. The countries bordering the sea operate 12 nautical miles zones and beyond that agreements between them have to be reached.

These agreements are monitored to varying levels of success by different countries. A model system is that operated by the African country of Namibia. Here, larger vessels in its waters have onboard observers, air patrols detect and deter unlicensed vessels and all landings are monitored at the country's two fishing ports. In addition, all vessels in the exclusion zone must keep daily logs of their catches.

How well do these strategies work?

Any law or agreement is only as good as the level of enforcement that goes with it. Because of the vastness of the oceans it is difficult to monitor fishery laws and agreements. Monitoring organisations based in ports have more success.

Because fishing is important for both income and food for many people, there is a huge incentive for illegal activities. Quotas can easily be avoided by simply not declaring how many fish are being caught. Overstretched authorities may not be able to check every boat, and fishers may be willing to risk under-declaring the size of their catch and not being checked. It is not difficult to use a net with an illegally small mesh size, and in areas where patrols are inadequate, fishers frequently trespass in areas where they are not supposed to fish.

CASE STUDY

The Newfoundland cod fishery

Off the coast of western Canada is an area called the Grand Banks. Its location and some features are shown in Figure 5.18. For more than 500 years, this area was known for having huge numbers of fish, especially cod. Indigenous peoples and early settlers were able to feed themselves and make a living from this fishery. The stock never seemed to be affected and, after the Second World War, commercial fisheries were attracted to the area.

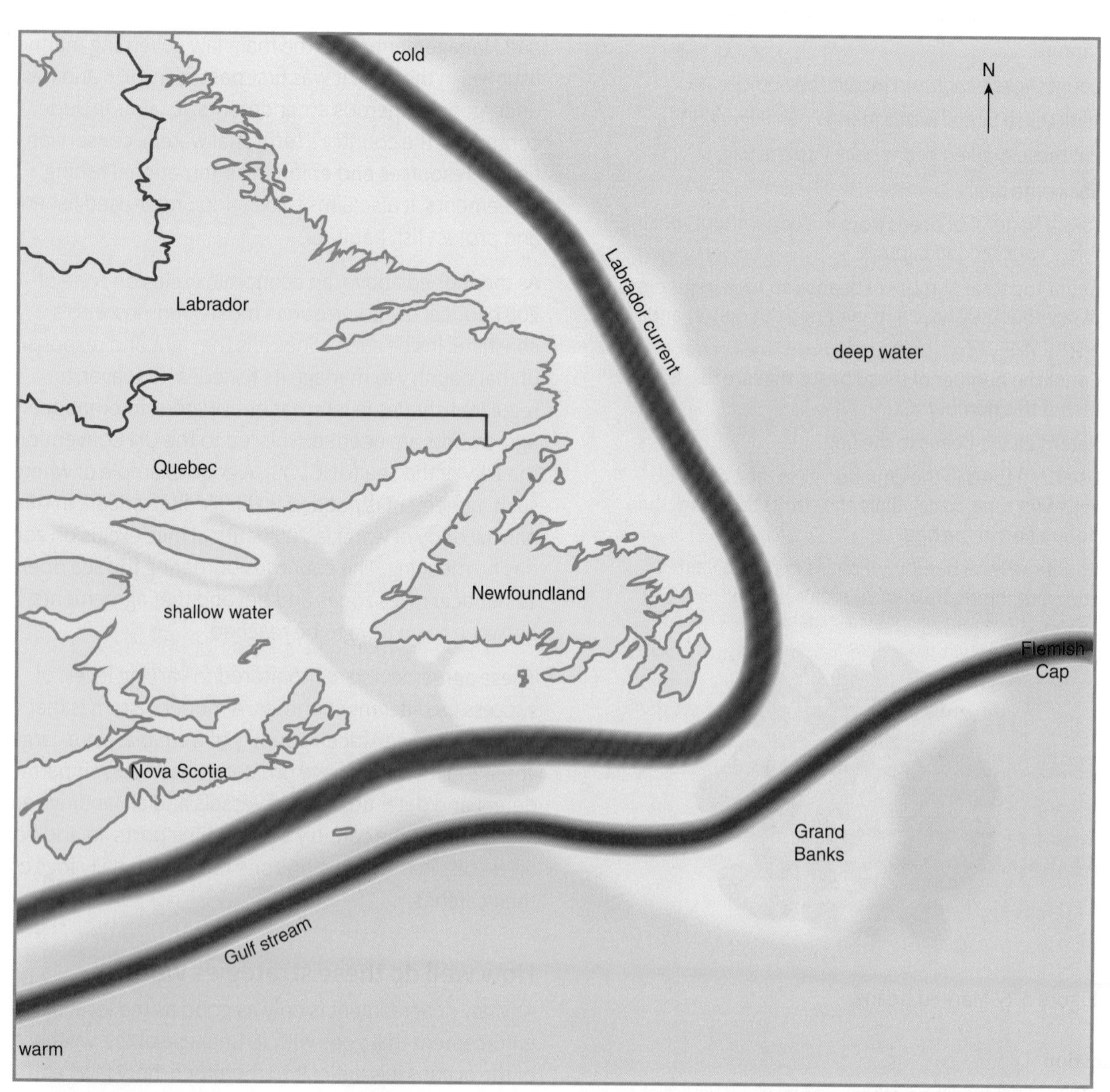

Figure 5.18 The Newfoundland cod fishery.

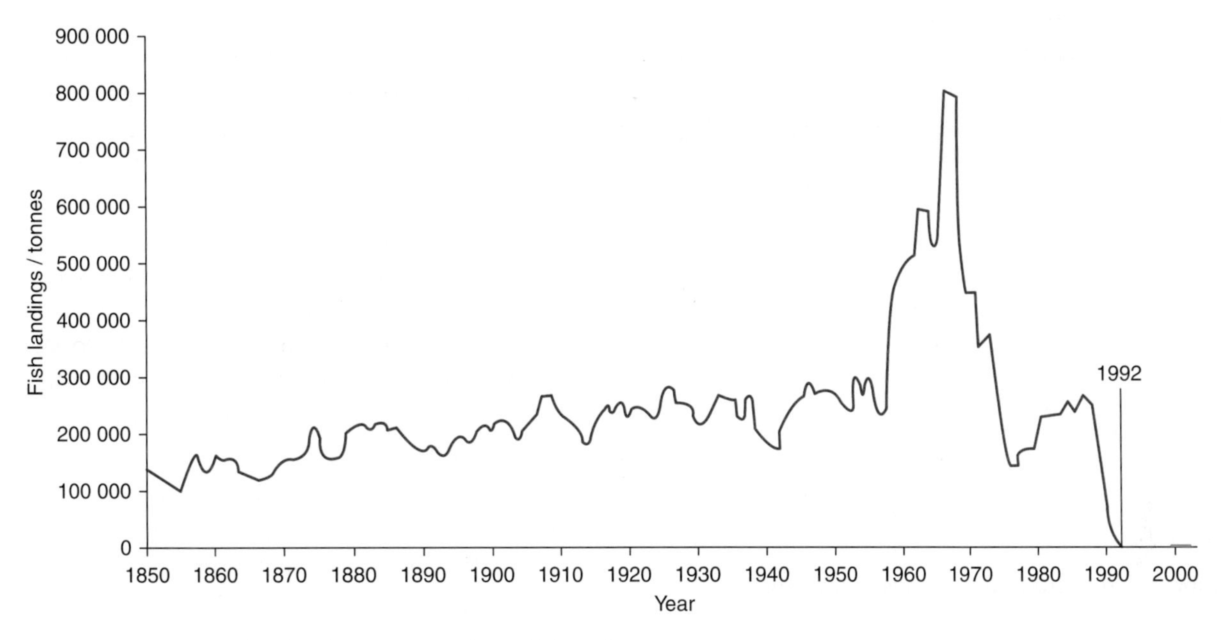

Figure 5.19 Cod catches by the Newfoundland fishery between 1850 and 2000.

Catches declined very quickly and the fishery collapsed completely in 1992 (Figure 5.19). A ban on fishing was hardly necessary, but the Canadian government did bring in a ban and paid pensions to many of the 40 000 people whose livelihood had disappeared. Despite this ban and the huge hardship that followed, the fishery is still very poor compared with its former status.

Until 1950 the fishery was not threatened because the technology simply did not exist to take the fish in unsustainable numbers. After this date, however, more and bigger ships started to trawl the area with huge nets. These took many more cod, a huge amount of bycatch, including smaller fish that are food for cod, and damaged the seabed bed where young cod feed. This pattern continued into the 1980s, but signs of the imminent collapse should have been seen much earlier, in the 1970s.

Today, nearly 25 years after the ban was implemented, cod catches remain very low. However, there is some encouraging news that suggests the stocks have grown well in a small part of the region called Smith Sound. Some researchers think that these healthy fish are about to recolonise the whole area. Time will tell.

Questions

1 Using the information in the case study, including Figure 5.18, suggest why the Grand Banks was the site of a huge fishery.

2 a Describe the pattern shown by the cod catch in Figure 5.19.
   b Calculate the percentage fall in the catch of cod in Newfoundland between its peak and 1976. Show and explain your working.
   c Give the date of the lowest catch between 1900 and the peak catch.

3 Devise a short explanatory paragraph to be read by people as an introduction and then a questionnaire to find out about the opinions of Newfoundlanders in the light of recent news about cod in Smith Sound.

SELF-ASSESSMENT QUESTIONS

5.11 Copy and complete Table 5.2. The first row has been done for you.

Reason for over-fishing	Possible solution
Large destructive nets	Control of net types
Large diamond-meshed nets	
Large boats	
Boats that can stay at sea for weeks	
Satellite location of shoals	
Human population growth	

Table 5.2 Reasons and solutions for over-fishing.

5.12 Tuna are fished in the Mediterranean. There are both traditional and large-scale fisheries there. In the traditional fishery, the tuna are forced into a net hung between boats. As the boats move in the tuna are trapped. The tuna are then killed and sold to produce several fish dishes in Asia. The fishermen operate from ports around the Mediterranean. In the large-scale operations, the ships use huge nets to catch the tuna, which are then put in cages and fed. They are then put onto ships at sea and taken to markets without ever going into a port.

Explain why a system of quotas operated by the European Union is not as successful in controlling the large-scale type of operation as it is for the traditional one.

Summary

After completing this chapter, you should know:

- the resource potential of the oceans
- the distribution of world fisheries
- the reasons for the location of fisheries
- about El Niño and its effects
- the impact of marine fisheries
- how to reduce the impact of marine fisheries with mariculture
- strategies for the management of fisheries.

End-of-chapter questions

1 Table 5.3 shows fish catches over a period of 8 years.

Year	Catch / thousands of tonnes
1997	68.0
1999	91.5
2001	88.0
2003	104.0
2005	131.0

Table 5.3 Data adapted from: *A Bioeconomic Analysis of Maldivian Skipjack Tuna Fishery*, Solah Mohamed. Idea adapted from FISHERIES SCIENCE Paper 2 5151/02 October/November 2010

a Plot a graph of these data. **[4 marks]**

b Using the graph, estimate the catch in 2000. **[2 marks]**

c Calculate the percentage increase in the catch between 1997 and 2005. **[2 marks]**

d Suggest reasons for the pattern shown by your graph. **[3 marks]**

2 In order for fish in the sea to thrive, they need food from plants. These plants need sunlight, water, carbon dioxide and minerals.

a State which of these requirements are needed for photosynthesis. **[1 mark]**

b Which of the above requirements is only found in low concentrations at the surface of the sea in most places away from the coast? **[1 mark]**

c Explain how upwelling brings this requirement to the surface in some coastal areas. **[2 marks]**

3 Shrimp are farmed along the coast of Honduras. Mangrove swamps have been cleared to create shallow ponds for shrimps.

a Explain why this process is thought of as non-sustainable by some scientists. **[4 marks]**

b Suggest how the sustainability of shrimp farming might be improved. **[3 marks]**

4 The following information was presented in support of the case for farming fish and other animals.

0.54 kg of food is needed to produce 0.45 kg of salmon. To make 0.45 kg of beef it requires 3.93 kg of food, 2.66 kg of food to make 0.45 kg of pork and 0.86 kg to make the same mass of chicken.

a Arrange this information into the table below. Pork has been done for you. **[6 marks]**

Food type	Feed Conversion Ratio
Salmon	
Beef	
Pork	5.9
Chicken	

b To what extent do you think this information supports the mariculture of fish? **[3 marks]**

c Apart from the possible increased food conversion efficiency, give other reasons for developing marine fish farming. **[3 marks]**

Atlantic salmon farming

After a 1970s peak of just over 15 000 tonnes, catches of wild Atlantic salmon have declined to not much more than 2000 tonnes.

Estimates of the number of fish available show that this has declined from about 10 million in the 1970s to fewer than 4 million now. There are a number of factors that are thought to be involved in this decline. A major factor are the salmon fisheries, which has led to the farming of salmon instead. The majority of Atlantic salmon eaten today is from farmed stock (Figure 5.20).

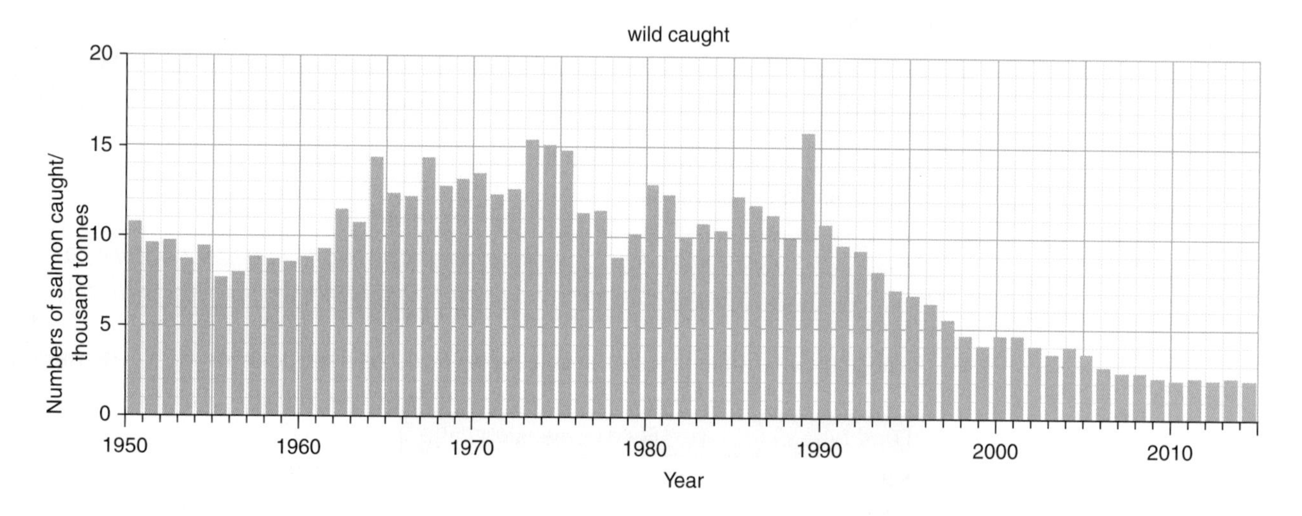

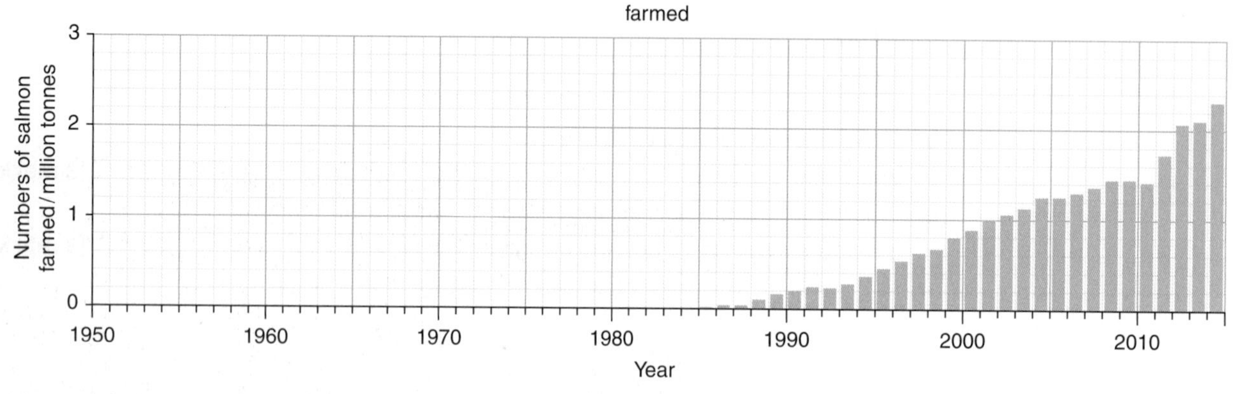

Figure 5.20 A comparison of the global numbers of farmed and wild-caught salmon. Note the difference in the scales on the vertical (*y*) axis.

A typical salmon farm holds up to a million fish in cages covering an area of about 3 hectares. At maturity, this many fish weighs more than 2000 tonnes, the weight of more than 400 elephants.

The culture of salmon was worth over US$10.7 billion globally by the end of the first decade of the 21st century. This represents a tenfold growth in production in the latter part of the 20th and early 21st centuries. The most important countries in this industry are Norway, with 33% of the product, Chile, with 31%, and European countries, excluding Norway, with 19%.

The fish are first hatched from eggs in tanks based on land and containing fresh water. This is because the species spends the first 2 years or so of its life in rivers. At about 18 months old, the young salmon (this smolt) are moved into floating cages at sea. These are usually located in sheltered coastal regions, fjords or sea lochs. Salmon are carnivorous in the wild and their food has to be mainly of animal origin. The fish are fed pelleted food made from fishmeal for the next 1–2 years, at which point they are harvested for market. It takes about 4 kg of fishmeal to produce 1 kg of farmed salmon. This is contrast to the 10 kg consumed by wild salmon for the production of 1 kg of fish.

The problems of mariculture of Atlantic salmon include the increased rate of infection with parasites such as sea lice compared with wild fish. Escapees from the cages pose a threat to wild populations of salmon as a result of competition and by infecting the wild fish with sea lice. Very young fish are especially susceptible to these parasites and many die. Various drugs are used to keep the farmed salmon healthy and these can have effects on the surrounding ecosystem. The growth of algae in pens can be a huge problem and a type of herbicide, called an algicide, is used to control this. The food pellets themselves can be a source of pollution, especially if overfeeding occurs and uneaten food is lost to the bottom of the cage. Along with other waste from the fish, the food waste can lead to eutrophication.

Questions

1 a What percentage of countries, in addition to the big three of Chile, Norway and the rest of Europe, are involved in the farming of salmon?

b Using the information in Figure 5.20, suggest the date when more salmon were produced in fish farms than were caught in the wild.

2 Suggest why wild salmon need 10 kg per 1 kg of salmon whereas farmed salmon needs only about 4 kg.

3 Use the diagram of a salmon cage in Figure 5.21 to draw a summary of the impacts of such a cage as described in the case study.

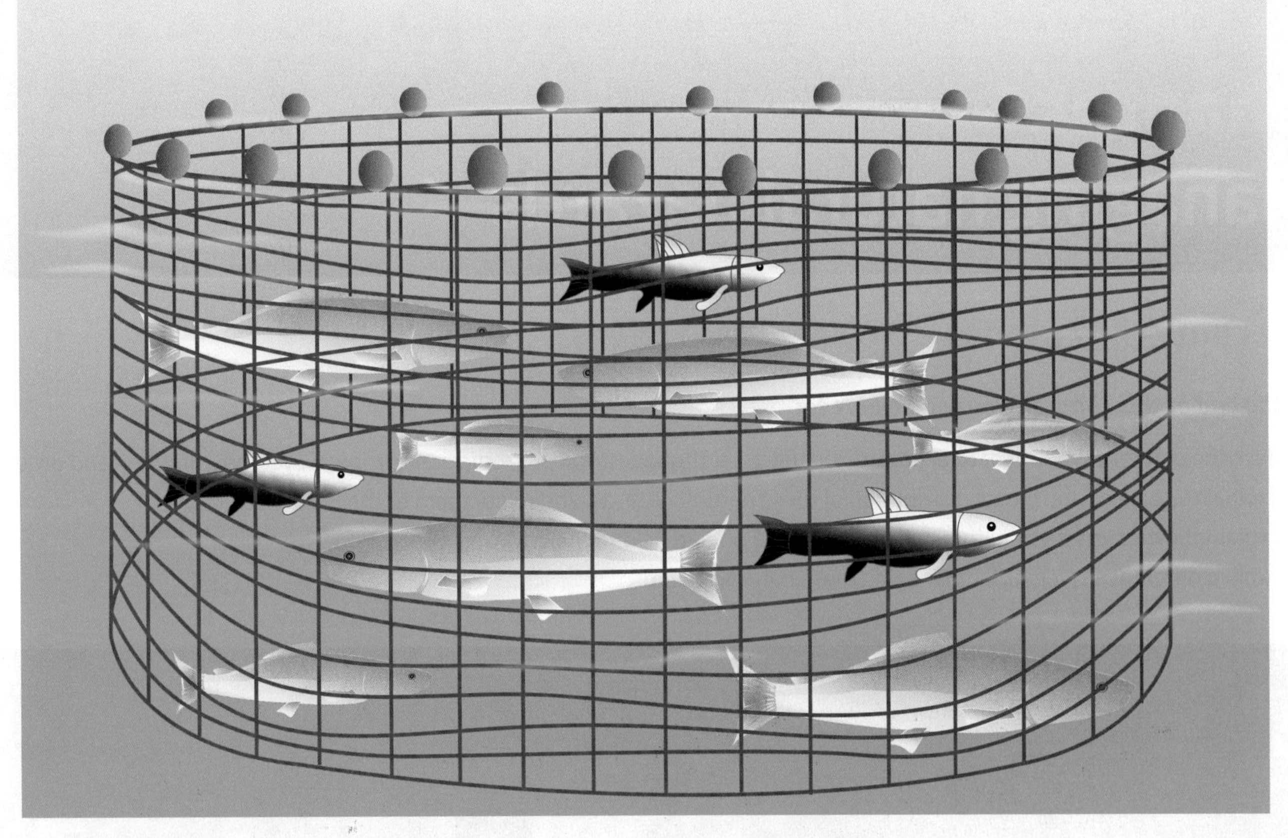

Figure 5.21 A salmon cage.

Chapter 6
Managing natural hazards

Learning outcomes

By the end of this chapter, you will be able to:

- describe different types of natural hazard, including earthquakes, volcanic eruptions, tropical cyclones, flooding and drought
- explain the causes and global distribution of these natural hazards, and relate them to the Earth's structure
- explain the impacts these natural hazards can have on people and the environment
- explain different strategies for managing these natural hazards.

Predicting the impossible?

In Yellowstone National Park, in the north-west of the United States, is a volcano. It is not just any volcano, but what scientists refer to as a **supervolcano**. A supervolcano is when an eruption measures magnitude 8 or more on the Volcano Explosivity Index and creates deposits that are greater than 1000 km^{-3}. If this volcano was to erupt today some of the suggested impacts are at least 90 000 people killed instantly and a 3 m layer of ash covering the Earth's surface for up to a 1000 km from the volcano. Global food shortages would occur as world temperatures drop. This volcano has had three supereruptions in the past: 2.1 million years, 1.3 million years and 640 000 years ago. The time period between these events ranges from 600 000 to 800 000 years, and some may think we are long overdue an eruption. However, scientists do not have sufficient data to establish a meaningful recurrence interval and no-one knows when the next eruption will be because we cannot predict it with any precision. In fact, one in ten people in the world live within 100 km of a volcano that could potentially erupt and, as world population grows, the exposure of human populations to **natural hazards** will only increase. Natural hazards have the capacity to kill, injure and disrupt lives. Between 2005 and 2015, natural hazards are believed to have killed over 700 000 people worldwide. Approximately 1.4 million people were injured, 23 million made homeless and the total economic loss was estimated at more than 1.3 trillion US$. The impact of a natural hazard can continue long after the event has passed. We cannot change when, where or how frequently natural hazards occur but we can try to predict, prepare and manage them so that we can minimise the impact.

Figure 6.0 Yellowstone National Park Grand Prismatic Spring.

6.1 What is a natural hazard?

A natural hazard is a physical event that has the potential to cause loss of life or injury and damage property and infrastructure. Livelihoods can be lost and the environment damaged. They can be short-term events that last just a few minutes or long-term events that can happen over several years. Natural hazards can be classified in a number of different ways. The most common classification is based on the cause of the hazard, including:

- geological hazards, for example earthquakes and volcanic eruptions
- climatic hazards, for example droughts, tropical cyclones, floods.

Other ways in which natural hazards can be classified are based on the:

- magnitude or intensity of the event
- speed at which the event takes place
- duration of the event
- frequency of the event.

The term natural hazard does not just mean physical events occurring in the natural world. People and property need to be put at **risk** by the physical event for it to be called a natural hazard. Volcanic explosions may look dramatic but it has been estimated that half of all deaths attributed to eruptions are from just five recorded events. The natural hazard that occurs most frequently is flooding, but between 1994 and 2014 it was earthquakes that killed the most people (Figure 6.1).

A **natural disaster** is when there is serious disruption to a community caused by a natural hazard, which can involve

KEY TERMS

Supervolcano: a volcano that erupts at least 1000 km^3 of material

Natural hazard: a naturally occurring event that will have a negative impact on people

Risk: the probability of a natural hazard occurring and the losses or damage that might result from that natural hazard

Natural disaster: when a natural hazard causes damage and the people affected are unable to cope

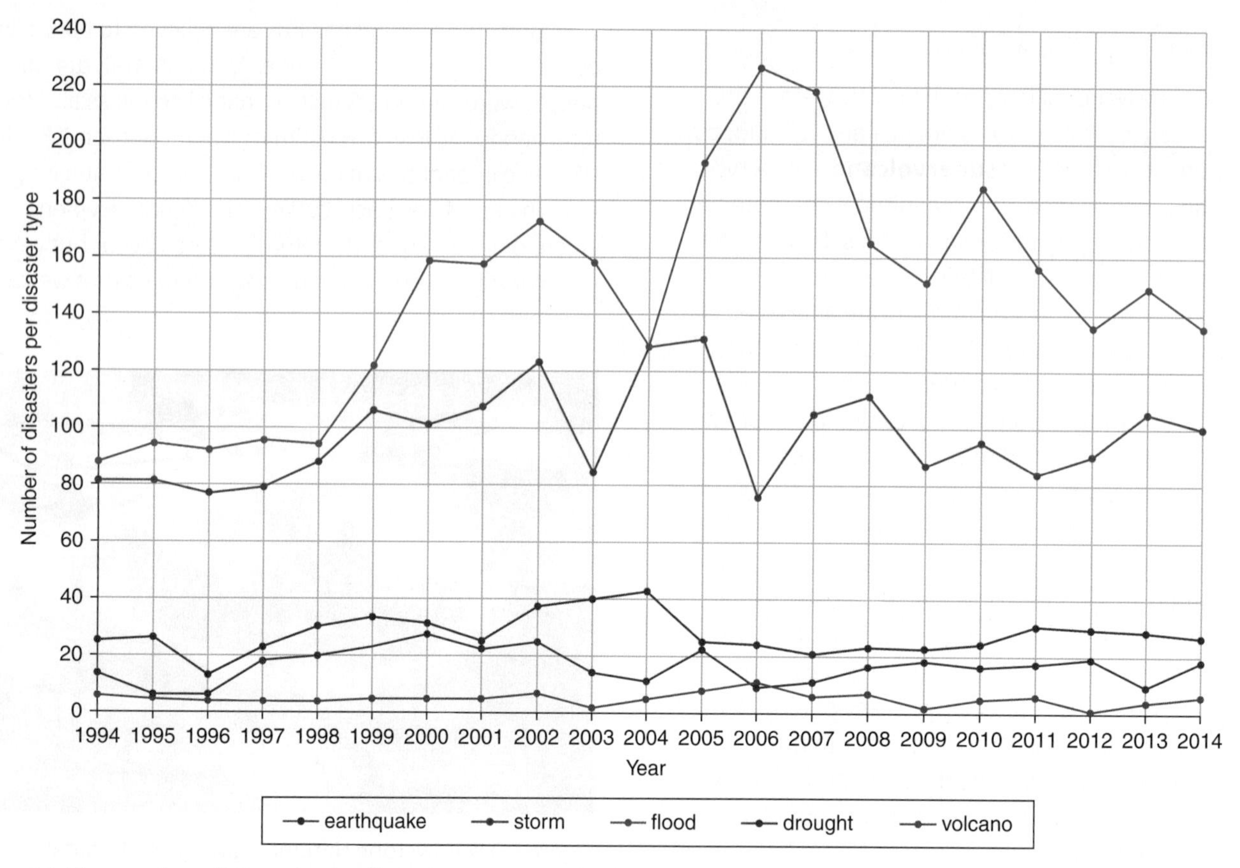

Figure 6.1 The number of disasters by disaster type, 1994–2014.

social, economic and environmental losses or impacts. A natural disaster follows a natural hazard.

natural hazard (for example flooding) **+** factors affecting possible risk (for example high population density) = natural disaster (for example many people killed)

For a disaster to be entered into the database of the United Nation's (UN) International Strategy for Disaster Reduction (ISDR), at least one of the following conditions must be met:

- a report of 10 or more people killed
- a report of 100 or more people affected
- a state of emergency declared by the government of the affected country
- a request by the relevant national government for international assistance.

The impact of a natural disaster on a community will depend on the:

- length of time people are exposed to the natural hazard
- **vulnerability** of the people affected
- people's ability to cope with the effects.

6.2 What causes earthquakes and volcanic eruptions?

The theory of **plate tectonics** was developed in the 1960s and helps us understand the movement of the Earth's surface. It also helps explain the global distribution and causes of features and landforms such as volcanoes, earthquakes and mountain ranges called **fold mountains**.

KEY TERMS

Vulnerability: the characteristics and circumstances of people in a community that make them susceptible to the impacts of a natural hazard

Plate tectonics: a theory developed in the 1960s that helps explain the formation of some of the important features on the Earth's surface and how the continents move

Fold mountains: mountains created where two or more tectonic plates are pushed together, compressing the rocks and folding them upwards

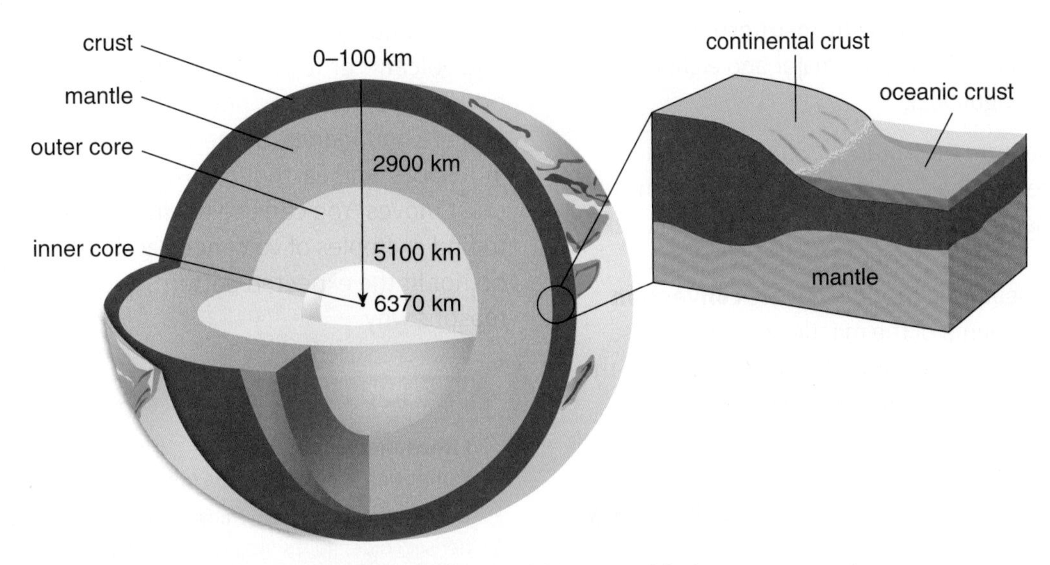

- Inner core: temperatures are 5000–6000 °C. It is solid because of the intense pressure from overlying rocks. Pressure is 3 million times greater here than at the surface. It is made of iron and nickel.
- Outer core: temperatures are 4000–5000 °C. It is liquid and made of iron and nickel.
- Mantle: accounts for more than 80% of the volume of the Earth. Made up of mainly silicate minerals. Lower mantle is sometimes called the **asthenosphere** and has a temperature of 1000–1200 °C. It behaves like a plastic and flows slowly due to convection currents created by heat from the core. The upper part of the mantle is more brittle and joins with the top layer of the earth (the crust). This is called the lithosphere.

Figure 6.2 The structure of the Earth, showing the two types of crust: oceanic and continental.

To understand the theory of plate tectonics it is important to know about the structure of the Earth, as shown in Figure 6.2.

There are two types of crust (Figure 6.2) and their different features are summarised in Table 6.1.

Oceanic crust (**sima**)	Continental crust (**sial**)
Mainly made of a rock called **basalt**	Mainly made of a rock called **granite**
Thinner, average depth is 6 km	Thicker, average depth is 35 km but it can be over 100 km under mountain ranges
Denser (heavier), 3 g cm^{-3}	Lighter, 2.6 g cm^{-3}
Younger	Older
It can sink and is continually being renewed and destroyed	It cannot sink and is neither destroyed or renewed

Table 6.1 The main features of oceanic and continental crust.

It is important to try and remember the differences between oceanic and continental crust because it will help you understand the processes you are going to learn about in the theory of plate tectonics. The Earth's surface is not a continuous layer. It is fractured and the sections are called **tectonic plates**. The plates are made up of crust and

KEY TERMS

Asthenosphere: the layer of the Earth below the lithosphere, it is hotter and weaker than the lithosphere above and is capable of plastic flow (deformation of material that remains rigid)

Sima: another name for the oceanic crust, which is rich in silicate and magnesium minerals

Sial: another name for the continental crust, which is rich in silicate and aluminium minerals

Basalt: a fine-grained extrusive igneous rock formed by the cooling of lava at constructive plate margins

Granite: a coarse-grained intrusive igneous rock comprising the minerals quartz, feldspar and mica, it is formed at destructive plate margins

Tectonic plate: A piece of lithosphere that moves slowly on the asthenosphere, seven major, eight minor and numerous micro plates have been identified

upper mantle. This is called the **lithosphere**. The surface of the Earth is divided into seven major and eight minor plates, shown in Figure 6.3.

The largest plates are the Antarctic, Eurasian and North American. Plates can be continental, oceanic or a mixture of both. Continental plates are on average 100 km thick and lighter than oceanic plates. Plates float like rafts on the mantle. Heat from the core creates **convection currents** in the magma of the mantle and these cause plates to move. Where the convection currents rise to the surface the plates move away from each other. Where convection currents sink, plates move towards each other. Most plates only move a few millimetres each year. The place where two plates meet is called a **plate boundary** or plate margin. Plates can move away from, towards or sideways past each other.

Look carefully at the map of plate boundaries and the distribution of volcanoes and earthquakes (Figure 6.3). What do you notice about the distribution of earthquakes and volcanoes? Most earthquakes and volcanic eruptions occur along or close to plate boundaries. However, not all tectonic hazards are found at plate boundaries. Some volcanoes are found above 'hot spots' and earthquakes can occur wherever the crust moves. You can use the internet and textbooks to find examples of volcanoes and earthquakes that do not fit the expected pattern, and investigate the reasons why.

KEY TERMS

Lithosphere: the outer and rigid layer of the Earth, comprising the crust and the upper part of the mantle

Convection currents: transfer heat from place to place, denser colder fluid sinks into warmer areas, heat from the Earth's core causes convection currents in the mantle

Plate boundary: where two or more plates meet, the three main types of plate boundary are constructive, destructive and conservative

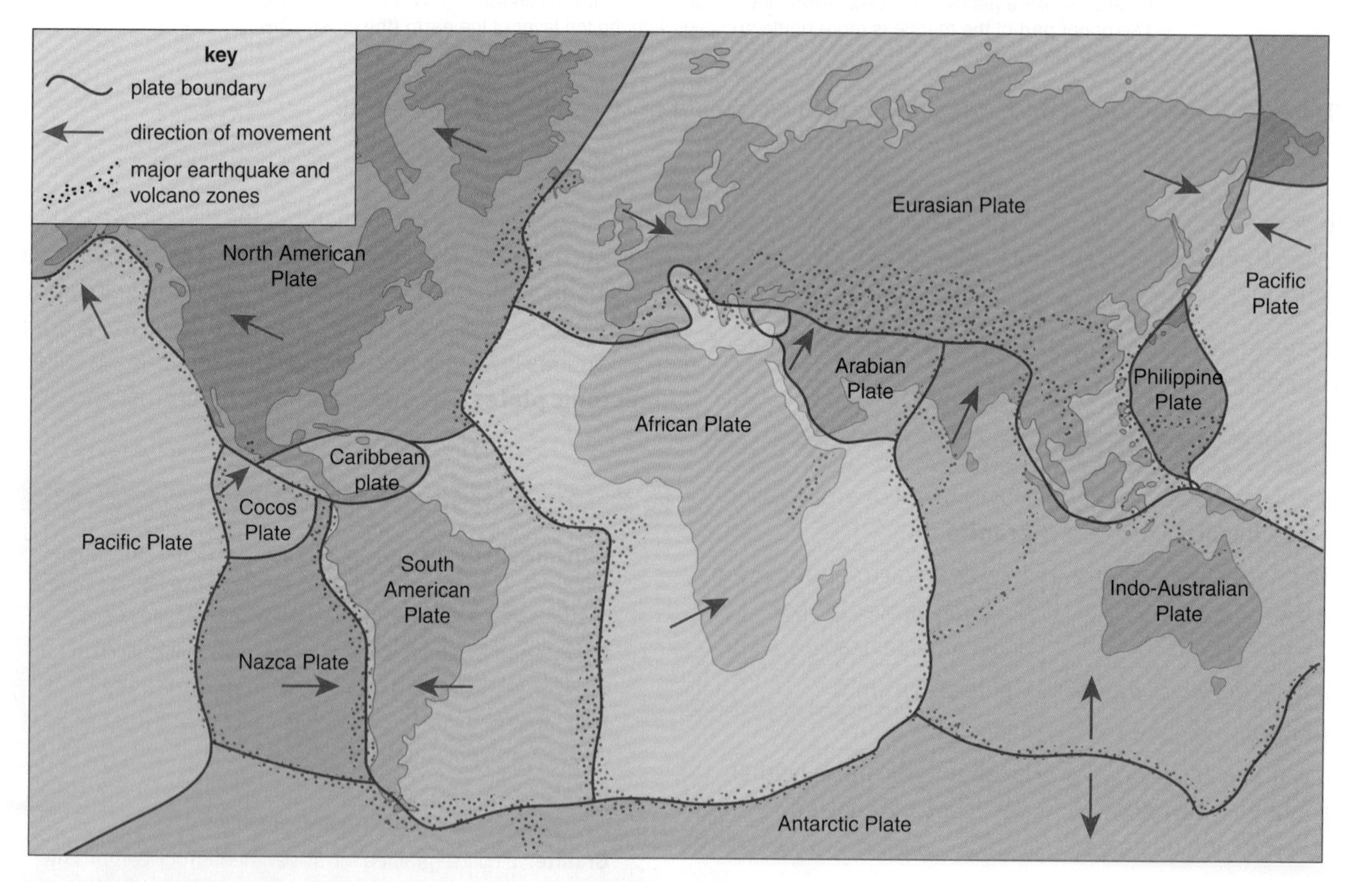

Figure 6.3 The distribution of tectonic plates and zones of tectonic activity.

SELF-ASSESSMENT QUESTIONS

6.1 Draw a diagram to show the structure of the Earth. Use the following labels: crust, mantle, inner and outer core.

6.2 State three differences between oceanic and continental crust.

6.3 What is a tectonic plate?

6.4 Look at Figure 6.3. What is the name of the plate that you live on?

6.5 What is meant by a plate boundary?

6.6 What process causes the tectonic plates to move?

Plate boundaries

There are three types of plate boundary:

- constructive (divergent)
- destructive (convergent)
- conservative.

Constructive (divergent)

At a constructive plate boundary (Figure 6.4a), two oceanic plates are pulling away from each other. A gap or weakness is formed and magma from the mantle rises to the surface because of convection currents. The magma solidifies when contact is made with the cold ocean water. The magma turns to lava and forms new basaltic ocean

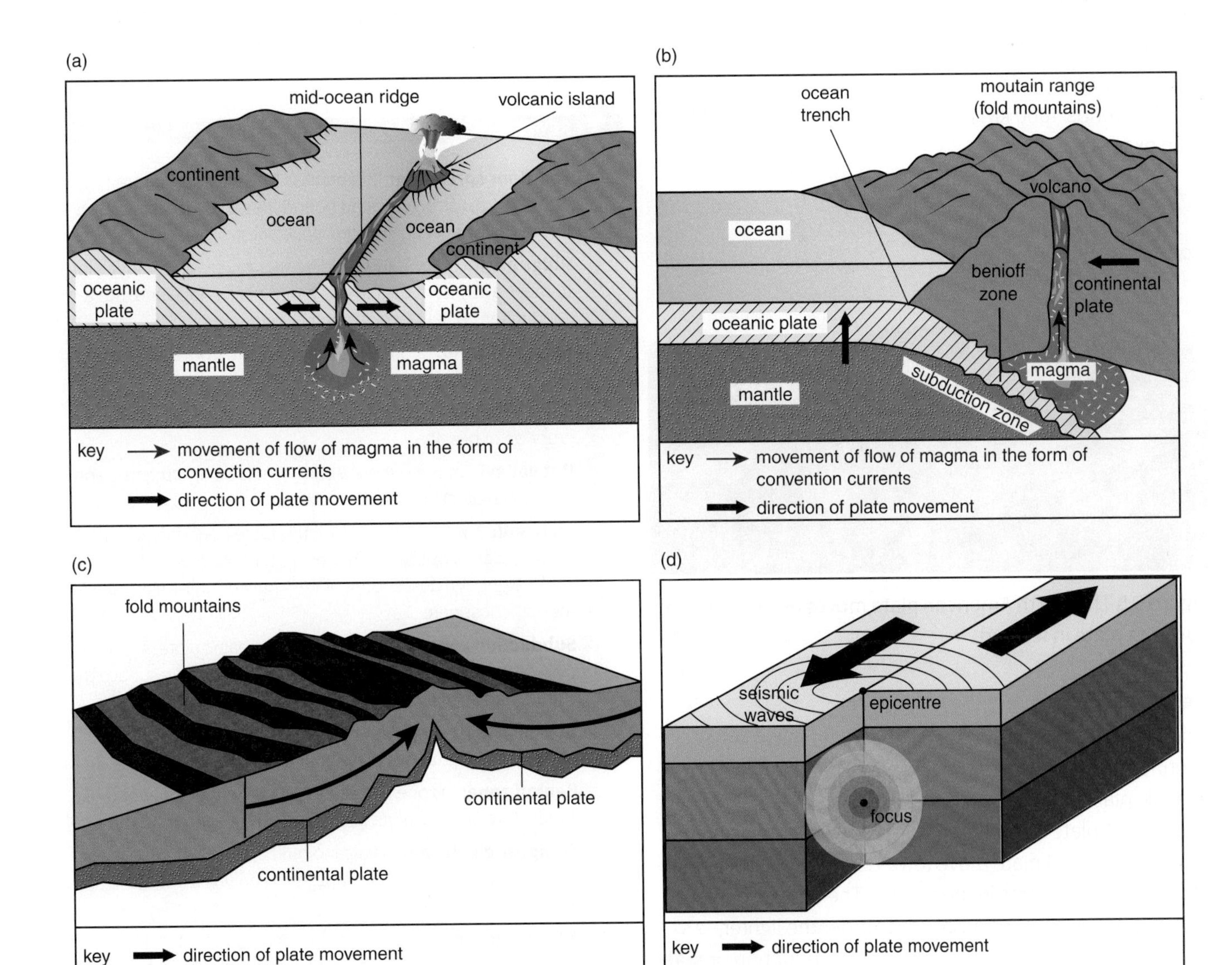

Figure 6.4 (a) A constructive plate boundary; (b) a destructive plate boundary; (c) a collision zone; (d) a conservative plate boundary.

crust. This whole process is called **sea-floor spreading** or **ridge push**. Small earthquakes are triggered. The new ocean crust builds up to form mid-ocean ridges and can also form submarine volcanoes, which may grow and appear above sea-level as volcanic islands. These volcanoes are called **shield** or **basic volcanoes** and usually have non-explosive eruptions because there is little pressure build up. Radiometric dating and fossil evidence show that the ocean floor becomes progressively older in both directions away from mid-ocean ridges. An example of this type of plate boundary is where the Eurasian plate moves away from the North American plate along the Mid-Atlantic Ridge at a rate of 3 cm $year^{-1}$ (Figure 6.5). Iceland is located on the Mid-Atlantic Ridge and is entirely made up of lava and other volcanic rocks. It has 35 active volcanoes.

If two continental plates move away from each other, a **rift valley** may form as the central block of land drops down between the faults. The East African Rift Valley, which extends 4000 km from Mozambique to the Red Sea, is an example.

Figure 6.5 The North American plate moves away from the Eurasian plate in Iceland.

Destructive (converging)

A destructive plate boundary can be found between a continental plate and an oceanic plate, between two oceanic plates and between two continental plates. At a destructive plate boundary (Figure 6.4b) an oceanic plate and a continental plate move towards each other because of convection currents in the mantle. The denser, oceanic plate is forced down, or subducted, under the lighter, continental plate. This process is called subduction or **slab pull** and it takes place in the **subduction zone**. An **ocean trench** is formed where the oceanic plate is subducted. These trenches are the deepest part of oceans. The Mariana Trench in the western Pacific Ocean has a known depth of nearly 11 km at an area called Challenger Deep. As the oceanic plate moves downwards, pressure and friction trigger severe earthquakes in the **Benioff zone**. The heat produced by friction turns the descending plate into magma and by 700 km down the plate has completely disintegrated. The magma then starts to rise and, because of the release of pressure, it can erupt through a weakness in the crust as an explosive **composite (strato)** or **acidic volcano.** Fold mountains are also formed on the continental plate as the sediments get pushed upwards and folded. An example of this type of plate boundary is where the Nazca plate moves towards the South American plate. The Peru–Chile Trench has been formed at the subduction zone and the movement of the plates together explains the formation of the Andes Mountains and the resulting 194 volcanoes found along the length of the mountain range.

KEY TERMS

Sea-floor spreading: the process by which oceans are formed at constructive plate boundaries, new oceanic crust is formed as two oceanic plates move apart

Ridge push: a gravitational force that causes an oceanic plate to move away from the crest of a mid-ocean ridge and into a subduction zone, it works together with slab pull

Shield volcano: a broad volcano built up from the repeated eruption of basalt

Basic volcano: a broad volcano built up from the repeated eruption of basalt

Rift valley: an area where a continent is being stretched and the central block moves downwards

Slab pull: the force at a destructive plate boundary, where the oceanic plate sinks beneath the adjacent plate, as a result of its own weight, the descending plate is pulled by gravity through the asthenosphere

Subduction zone: a zone where the oceanic plate is deflected (subducted) down into the mantle, at the surface the subduction zone coincides with ocean trenches

Ocean trench: a depression of the ocean floor that runs parallel to a destructive plate boundary

Benioff zone: a zone of earthquake foci in the upper part of a subducting oceanic plate at a destructive plate boundary

Composite volcano: a volcano built up by alternating layers of lava and ash, conical in shape. Also known as a strato volcano.

Acidic volcano: a volcano that is made up of just lava, it is steeped sided as the lava does not flow easily, and it builds up into a convex cone-shape

When two oceanic plates move towards each other, the older and denser plate is subducted. The magma that rises upwards and erupts at the surface forms a chain of volcanic islands called an **island arc**. The Japanese islands are an example of an island arc.

If two continental plates move towards each other, this is called a **collision zone** (Figure 6.4c). The sediments between the two plates are squeezed together and pushed upwards to form fold mountains, such as the Himalayas. Earthquakes occur but no volcanic activity because there is no subduction of an oceanic plate.

Conservative

At a conservative plate boundary (Figure 6.4d), no plate is being destroyed or created. The plates are sliding past each other. An example of this is along the San Andreas Fault in California, USA, where the Pacific plate is moving past the North American plate in the same direction but at a different speed. The Pacific plate is moving north-west at a rate of 6 cm $year^{-1}$, whereas the North American plate is moving north-west at 1 cm $year^{-1}$. The plates get locked together and pressure builds up until it is eventually released as an earthquake.

SELF-ASSESSMENT QUESTIONS

6.7 Look again at the map of plate boundaries (Figure 6.3). What type of plate boundary is found between the:

a Nazca and South American plates

b Indo-Australian and Eurasian plates

c Pacific and North American plates

d South American and African plates

e Eurasian and Pacific plates?

6.8 Why do earthquakes occur along:

a destructive plate boundaries

b conservative plate boundaries?

6.9 Why do volcanoes occur along:

a destructive plate boundaries

b constructive plate boundaries?

6.10 Research the location of the following fold mountains using an atlas or the internet: Himalayas, Andes, Rockies. Between which two plates do each of the fold mountains lie?

Characteristics of earthquakes

An earthquake is when the ground shakes or moves in sudden jerks. Earthquakes result from a build up and sudden release of tension, usually along a fault line. The **focus** is where the earthquake begins underground, and the point on the Earth's surface, directly above, is called the **epicentre**. The release of tension sends out shock waves (seismic waves) that travel outwards from the focus (see Figure 6.4d). The magnitude of an earthquake is measured on the **Richter scale** by an instrument called a seismometer. During an earthquake, faults or cracks may appear on the Earth's surface, the ground may suffer from **liquefaction** if it is made of loose sediments, and aftershocks can occur. A **tsunami** can also be created if an earthquake occurs under the sea or in a coastal area.

The number of deaths and injuries caused by an earthquake does not just depend on the magnitude. Other factors that must be considered are:

- the location of the epicentre, because the closer to the epicentre the greater the damage
- the time of the earthquake, because if the earthquake occurs during winter months or at night there is often a greater loss of life
- the geology of the area, which determines whether liquefaction takes place
- the relief of the area, because, for example, mountainous areas can suffer from landslides and coastal areas can suffer from tsunamis

KEY TERMS

Island arc: a chain of volcanoes, generally with an arc shape, that run parallel to an oceanic trench at a destructive (oceanic–oceanic) plate boundary

Collision zone: a destructive plate boundary between two continental plates, resulting in fold mountains

Focus: the location under the Earth's surface where an earthquake originates

Epicentre: the point on the Earth's surface directly above the focus of an earthquake

Richter scale: a measure of the magnitude of an earthquake, taken with a seismograph and with a scale of one to ten, ten being the most powerful, it is a logarithmic scale which means that if an earthquake measures two on the scale it is ten times more powerful than an earthquake that measures one

Liquefaction: the process where loose sediments with a high water content behave like a liquid when shaken by an earthquake

Tsunami: a large wave created by ocean floor displacement or landslides

- the severity of aftershocks, which can cause already damaged buildings to collapse
- the level of development of the human settlement, which will affect its ability to cope with the impact
- the population density and associated building density
- building strength.

SELF-ASSESSMENT QUESTIONS

6.11 What is an earthquake?

6.12 What is the difference between the focus and epicentre of an earthquake?

6.13 What scale is used to measure the magnitude of an earthquake, and with what instrument?

Characteristics of volcanoes

There are two types of volcanic activity:

- intrusive, when magma cools underground to form igneous rocks
- extrusive, when magma flows out onto the Earth's surface as lava.

A volcano is a hole or crack (fissure) through which magma erupts onto the surface. Gases and **pyroclastic material** can also be erupted. Most volcanoes are a mixture of solidified magma and ash, which build up over time with each eruption to form a volcanic mountain or cone. A cross-section through a volcano is shown in Figure 6.6. There are many hazards associated with an eruption such as **lahars**, which are also shown in Figure 6.6.

When magma erupts at the surface it can form different types of volcanoes depending on the viscosity (stickiness) of the magma and the amount of gas in it. Table 6.2 shows the difference between two contrasting types, and Figure 6.7 illustrates a shield volcano.

KEY TERMS

Pyroclastic material: very hot gases, ash and volcanic bombs, pyroclastic flows can reach speeds of over 100 km h^{-1} at temperatures of 200 to 700 °C

Lahars: mudflows of volcanic material, caused when ash mixes with heavy rain or water from melting snow

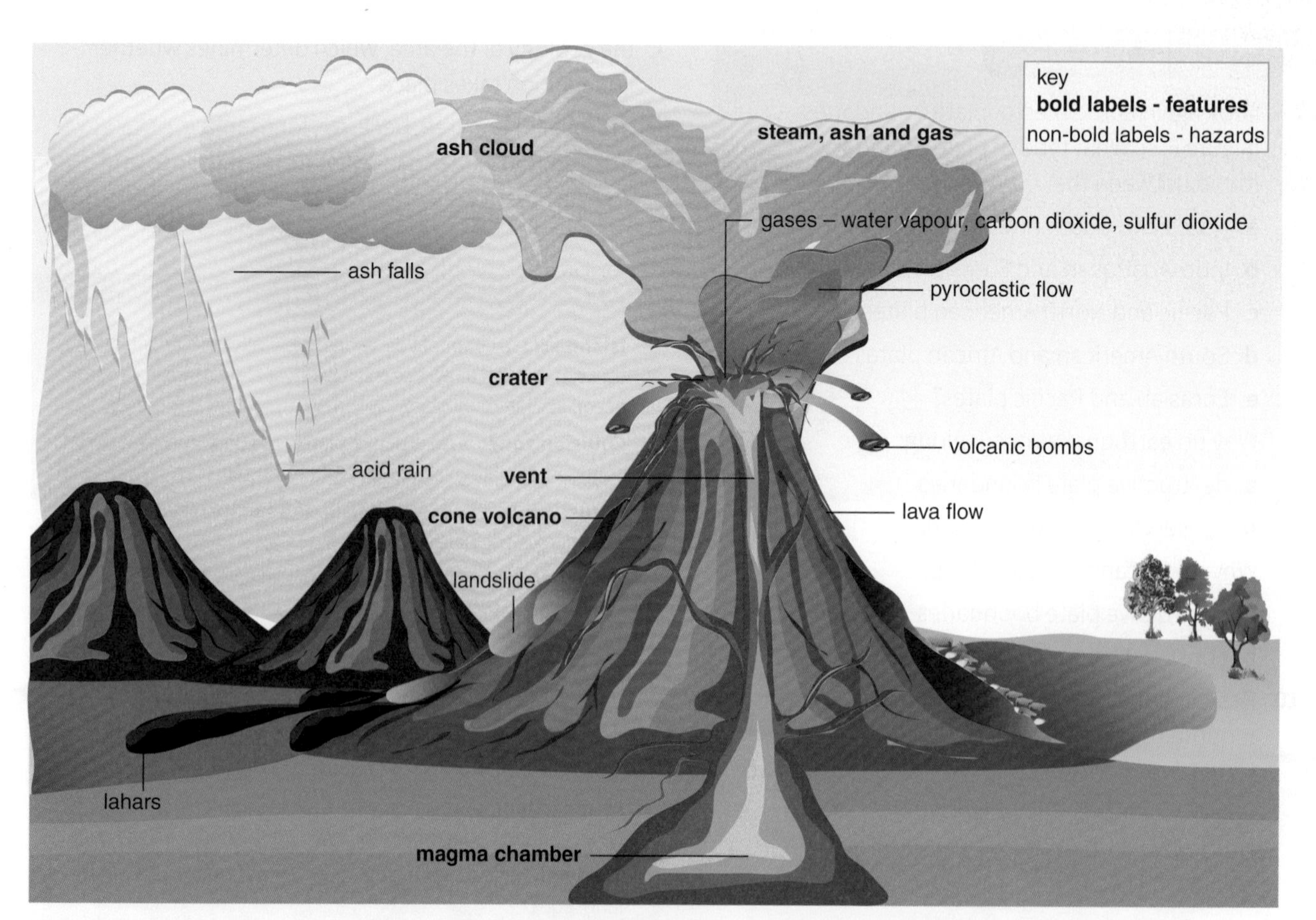

Figure 6.6 Features of a volcano and some hazards associated with a volcanic eruption.

Shield volcanoes	Composite (strato) volcanoes
• Examples include Mauna Loa in Hawaii and volcanoes in Iceland • Found on constructive plate boundaries and hotspots • Cover a wide area with gentle slopes (2° to 10°) • Up to 900 m in height • Formed by lava flows • Magma has a low viscosity • Eruptions are usually non-explosive and consist of mainly basalt lava flows from a vent	• Examples include Mt St Helens, USA, and Mt Pinatubo in the Philippines • Found on destructive plate boundaries • Conical in shape with steep slopes (10° to 30°) and narrow bases • 100–3500 m in height • Formed by alternating layers of ash and lava • Magma is viscous • Eruptions are explosive but infrequent and consist of ash, shattered lava, volcanic bombs and gases. Lava flows are limited in extent because of the high viscosity of the magma

Table 6.2 Characteristics of contrasting type of volcanoes.

Figure 6.7 A shield volcano.

SELF-ASSESSMENT QUESTIONS

6.14 What is a volcano?

6.15 Which of the following is the odd one out? Explain why.

lahar pyroclastic flow liquefaction landslides ash volcanic bombs

6.16 What is the relationship between lava and magma?

6.3 What causes tropical cyclones?

Tropical cyclones, hurricanes and typhoons are found in different parts of the world but they are all the same weather feature. Cyclones are found in the Indian Ocean and Australia, hurricanes in the Atlantic Ocean and eastern Pacific Ocean and typhoons in the western Pacific Ocean (Figure 6.8). Tropical cyclone is a common term that is used for this weather feature.

Tropical cyclones are large areas of very low pressure with wind speeds of over 119 km h^{-1}. They are categorised using the Saffir–Simpson hurricane wind scale, which rates wind speed on a scale of 1 to 5. Category 1 is when the wind speeds are between 119 and 153 km h^{-1} and category 5 is reached when the speeds are over 252 km h^{-1}. In the western North Pacific, the term 'super typhoon' is used for tropical cyclones with winds exceeding 241 km h^{-1}. Since 1953, tropical cyclones had been given girls names but in 1979 boys names were included. The list of names is rotated over a 6 year period. If the storm is very destructive, the name is removed from the list and is not used again. Figure 6.8 shows the distribution and time of year when tropical cyclones occur in different areas of the world.

Certain conditions are needed for tropical cyclones to form.

- The ocean surface temperature must be at least 27 °C. Warm water provides the energy for increased evaporation of water, which rises, condenses and releases huge amounts of energy.

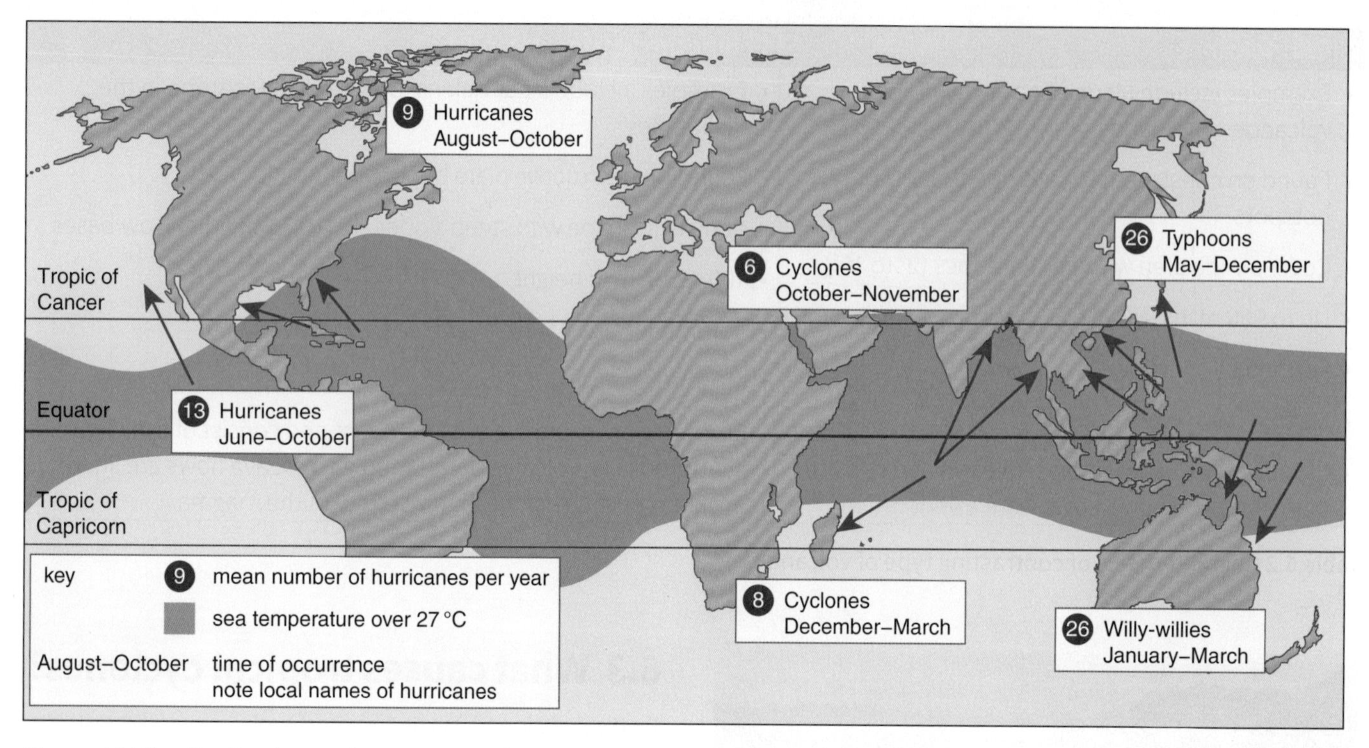

Figure 6.8 The distribution and occurrence of tropical cyclones, hurricanes and typhoons.

- The warm ocean water must be at least 60 m deep.
- These conditions must occur between latitudes 5° and 20° north and south. Any closer to the equator, and there is insufficient Coriolis force (rotation of the Earth) to make the air spin, at higher latitudes the oceans are too cold.
- There should be very little wind shear (a change in wind speed or direction with height in the atmosphere). Strong wind shear can stop the vertical development of a storm.

These conditions exist between May and November in the Northern Hemisphere and between November and May in the Southern Hemisphere. Tropical cyclones start as clusters of thunderstorms that grow in size and start to spin. The air rises as it is heated from below. It cools, condenses and releases latent heat. This causes the air to rise even faster, intensifying the low pressure area and more air is sucked in towards the centre of the storm. Cumulonimbus clouds are formed. The air cools at high altitudes and sinks, forming the eye of the storm. A tropical cyclone therefore derives its energy by evaporating moisture from a warm ocean; when it passes over land or a cold ocean current it loses the source of energy and the speed decreases.

Characteristics of tropical cyclones

A tropical cyclone can be up to 800 km in diameter and up to 20 km in height. Tropical cyclones usually last for a week, moving 17–32 km h^{-1}. They rotate in an anti-clockwise direction around the eye (the calmest part of the storm) in the Northern Hemisphere and in a clockwise direction in the Southern Hemisphere.

The typical weather expected as a tropical cyclone passes over an area is listed below and shown in Figure 6.9.

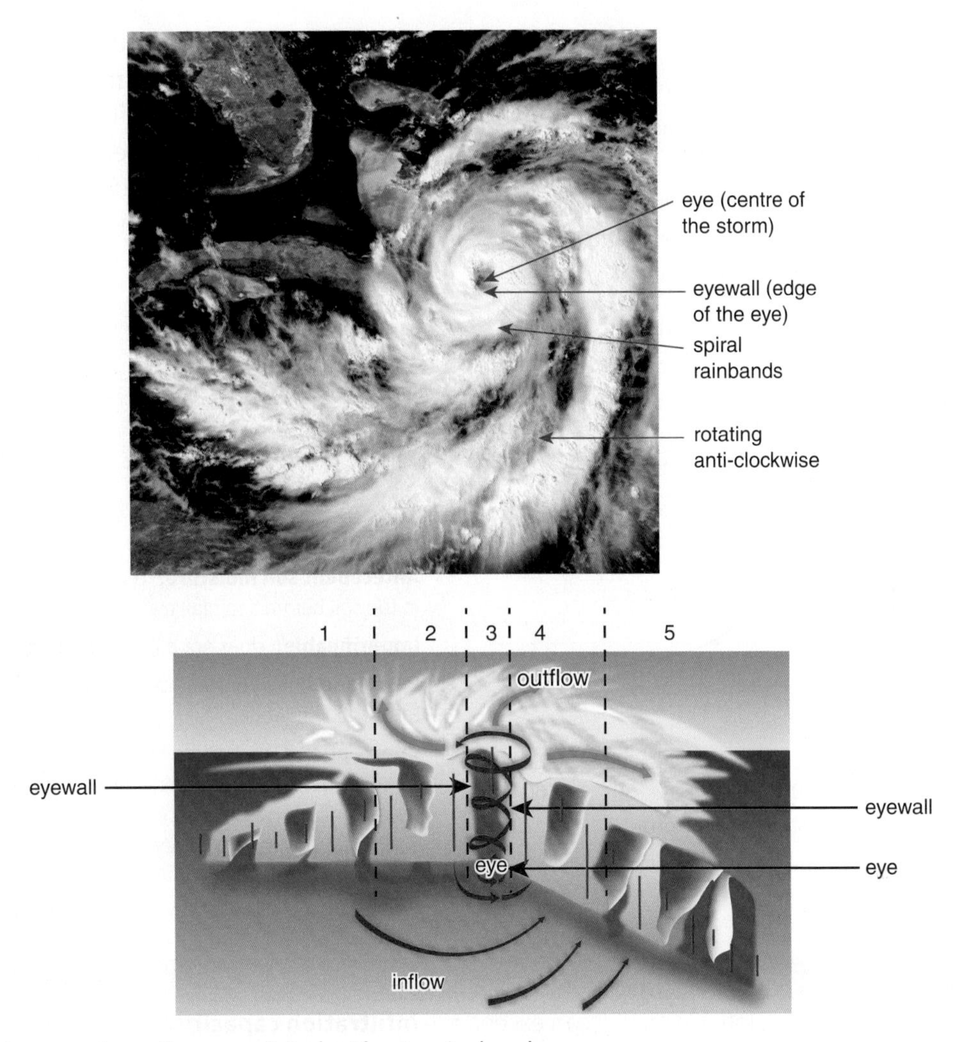

Figure 6.9 The features and weather associated with a tropical cyclone.

- Sky becomes cloudy, wind speed increases, rain with sunny intervals.
- Air pressure falls, wind speed continues to increase to over 119 km h^{-1}. Large cumulonimbus clouds form and very heavy rain falls. This is the eyewall or vortex.
- In the eye of the storm the sky is clear, winds are light and there is little rain. Temperatures are warm.
- After the eye has passed cumulonimbus clouds form again, with the return of heavy rain and strong winds.
- Wind speed and rainfall decreases. Sunny intervals.

Tropical cyclones create the following hazards:

- strong winds can cause structural damage to buildings
- heavy rainfall can lead to river flooding and landslides
- storm surges can lead to flooding in low lying coastal areas, the intense low pressure can raise sea levels and strong winds can push waves up to 5 m high inland.

SELF-ASSESSMENT QUESTIONS

6.17 Study Figure 6.8 and describe the distribution of tropical cyclones.

6.18 Describe three conditions needed for the formation of tropical cyclones and explain why the conditions are needed.

6.19 What weather conditions would you expect to encounter as a tropical cyclone passes over an area?

6.20 Why does a tropical cyclone lose its strength when it passes over land or a cold ocean current?

6.4 What causes flooding?

Between 1995 and 2015, floods caused 47% of all weather-related disasters, affecting 2.3 billion people and killing 157 000 people worldwide. Flooding is when the **discharge** of a river exceeds the capacity of the river's channel. When this occurs, the river overflows the banks and covers the adjacent floodplain. Heavy rainfall is the cause of most floods.

Storm hydrographs

A storm hydrograph shows how quickly a river responds to a rainfall event (Figure 6.10). The water can reach the river by overland flow, throughflow and groundwater flow (see Section 4.2).

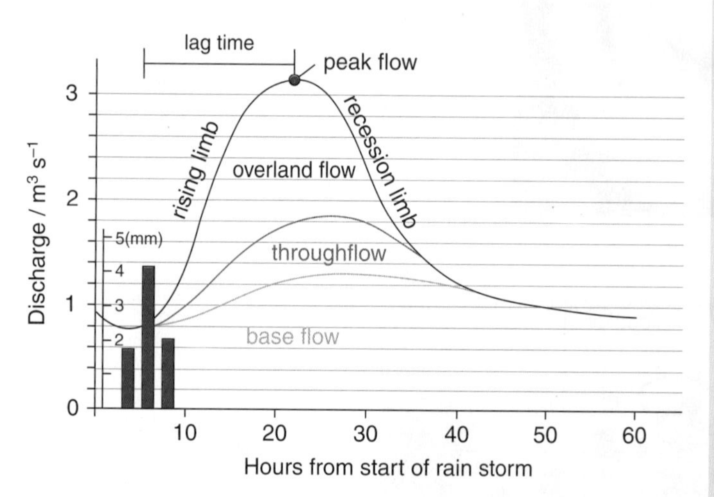

Figure 6.10 A storm hydrograph.

The shorter the **lag time** and the steeper the rising limb, the quicker the water reaches the river (flash response) and the greater the chance of flooding. The shape of storm hydrographs vary between river drainage basins and are useful for planning against future flooding and times of drought. The causes of flooding can be seen in Table 6.3.

> **KEY TERMS**
>
> **Discharge:** the volume of water passing a measuring point or gauging station in a given time, measured in cubic metres per second (cumecs)
>
> **Lag time:** the time difference between peak rainfall and peak discharge
>
> **Infiltration capacity:** the maximum rate that water enters soil
>
> **Antecedent soil moisture:** the amount of moisture present in the soil before a rainfall event
>
> **Impermeable:** does not allow water to pass through
>
> **Percolation:** the vertical movement of water from the soil into the underlying rock
>
> **Interception:** the process by which vegetation prevents rainfall from reaching the surface directly, the intercepted rainfall is temporarily held as interception storage and then either falls directly to the ground or is evaporated back to the atmosphere

Physical causes	Impacts
Weather	Heavy, intense rainfall can exceed the **infiltration capacity** of the soil and lead to an increase in overland flow. Steady, prolonged rainfall can saturate the soil and cause the water table to rise, reducing infiltration capacity. Overland flow will occur if snowmelt is rapid and the ground beneath frozen
Previous weather	**Antecedent soil moisture** refers to the amount of water in the soil before a rainfall event. The more saturated the soil, the less infiltration and the more overland flow
Soil and rock type	**Impermeable** soils and rocks, such as clay or granite, have a low infiltration capacity and **percolation** rate, which leads to greater overland flow
Relief	Steeper gradients can lead to faster overland flow and water has little time to infiltrate
Earthquakes, volcanoes and tropical cyclones	These natural hazards can produce tsunamis and storm surges that flood low-lying coastal areas.
Human causes	
Deforestation	Cutting down trees reduces **interception** and infiltration
Urbanisation	Concrete and tarmac are impermeable surfaces that lead to more overland flow. Storm drains speed up the movement of water to the nearest river
Agriculture	Overgrazing and leaving soil exposed reduces interception. Ploughing down rather than across slopes quickly channels the water downwards. Heavy farm machinery compacts the soil, making it impermeable
Climate change	Enhanced global warming may lead to a rise in sea-levels, as well as more rainfall and storms in certain parts of the world

Table 6.3 The causes of flooding.

PRACTICAL ACTIVITY 6.1

Interpreting storm hydrographs

Storm hydrographs are an important tool in helping to predict the possibility of flooding. Look again at Figure 6.10: a storm hydrograph is drawn with two vertical axes. One is used to plot a line graph showing the discharge of a river in cumecs (cubic metres per second) at a given point in time. The second is used to plot a bar graph of a rainfall event that causes the discharge to rise. The scale on the horizontal axis is usually in hours or days and allows the rainfall event and river discharge to be recorded.

Materials

- A copy of Figure 6.11
- Pen and paper

Method

- On a copy of Figure 6.11 draw bar graphs to show rainfall using the data in Table 6.4. Call this hydrograph B.

Questions

1 Work out the lag time for hydrograph A and hydrograph B.

2 State three ways in which hydrograph A differs from B.

3 Decide which hydrograph (A or B) represents an urban drainage basin and which hydrograph (A or B) a rural, wooded drainage basin.

4 Is flooding more likely in hydrograph A or B? Explain your answer as fully as possible.

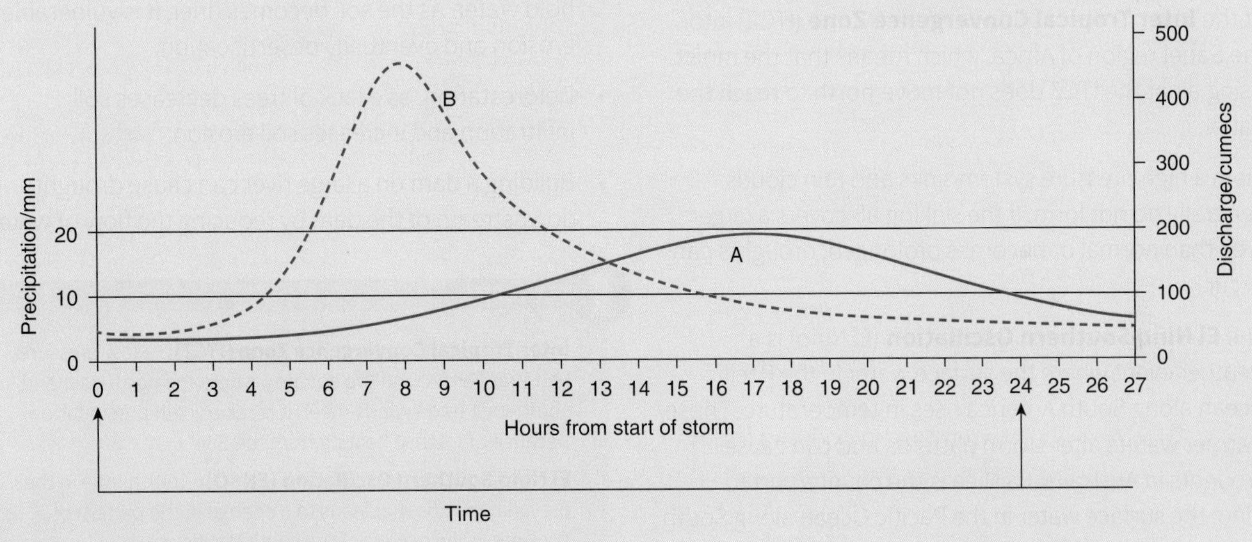

Figure 6.11 Storm hydrograph A.

Hours from the start of the rainfall	Millimetres of rainfall
1	3
2	3
3	15
4	20
5	5
6	4
7	3

Table 6.4 Rainfall data.

6.5 What causes droughts?

Drought is when there is a lack of rain or less rain than normal over a long period of time. It can lead to a deficit in the water supply, with insufficient water to support plants, animals and people. Droughts can occur anywhere but they are particularly common in Africa. Between 1995 and 2015, 136 droughts were recorded in Africa, and 77 of those were in East Africa For more details look on the UN website (www.cambridge.org/links/scspenv4001).

Most droughts occur when regular weather patterns are interrupted and evaporation exceeds precipitation. There are various reasons why this can happen.

- Changes in atmospheric circulation patterns altering storm tracks and wind patterns. An example of this is patterns that prevent the northwards movement of the **Inter Tropical Convergence Zone** (ITCZ) into the Sahel region of Africa, which means that the moist rising air at the ITCZ does not move north to reach the Sahel.
- Air in a high pressure system sinks and rain clouds generally do not form. If the sinking air covers a larger area than normal or becomes prolonged, droughts can occur.
- The **El Niño Southern Oscillation** (El Niño) is a weather event where the surface water in the Pacific Ocean along South America rises in temperature. These warmer waters alter storm patterns and can cause droughts in Australia. La Niña is the counterpart to El Niño: the surface water in the Pacific Ocean along South America decreases in temperature. The cooler waters contribute to drier conditions in parts of North and South America. While El Niño usually lasts less than a year, La Niña can last for 1–3 years.
- There is a lot of debate about the connection between drought and the current period of climate change. Some scientists predict that warmer worldwide temperatures will mean decreased rainfall in some parts of the world, leading to more drought events.

Human activity can influence the effect that drought has on a region.

- Agricultural practices can make land more vulnerable to drought. Irrigation techniques have increased farmers' dependence on water. Overcultivation and overgrazing can lead to soil compaction, and the soil is less able to hold water. As the soil becomes drier, it is vulnerable to erosion and eventually desertification.
- Deforestation, as a lack of trees decreases soil infiltration and increases soil erosion.
- Building a dam on a large river can cause drought downstream of the dam by reducing the flow of water.

KEY TERMS

Inter Tropical Convergence Zone (ITCZ): a low pressure belt that lies around the equator, where the north-east and south-east trade winds meet, it receives high precipitation because of intense heating from the Sun

El Niño Southern Oscillation (ENSO): the change in the prevailing winds that leads to a change in the pattern of currents in the oceans of the south Pacific

SELF-ASSESSMENT QUESTIONS

6.21 Arrange the following factors which explain the characteristics of a storm hydrograph under the following two headings:
flash response and **slow response.**
urban permeable rock ploughing downslope wet soil forest rural dry soil light rainfall impermeable rock ploughing across the slope heavy rainfall rapid snowmelt

6.22 Use the internet to research the causes of a recent flood event in the country where you live. Think about the physical and human causes of the flood. Use Table 6.3 to help you with the possible causes.

6.6 Impacts of natural hazards

The impact of natural hazards can be social, economic or environmental, and can be short and long term (Figure 6.12). Some impacts are the same for nearly all natural hazards, such as fatalities, injuries, loss of livelihoods and destruction of property and infrastructure, while other impacts are unique to certain events. The impact is usually greater on communities at lower levels of economic development because of a lack of finance to rebuild the infrastructure, lack of insurance cover, and a lack of technology and expertise to deal with the event. Such communities are more dependent on emergency aid.

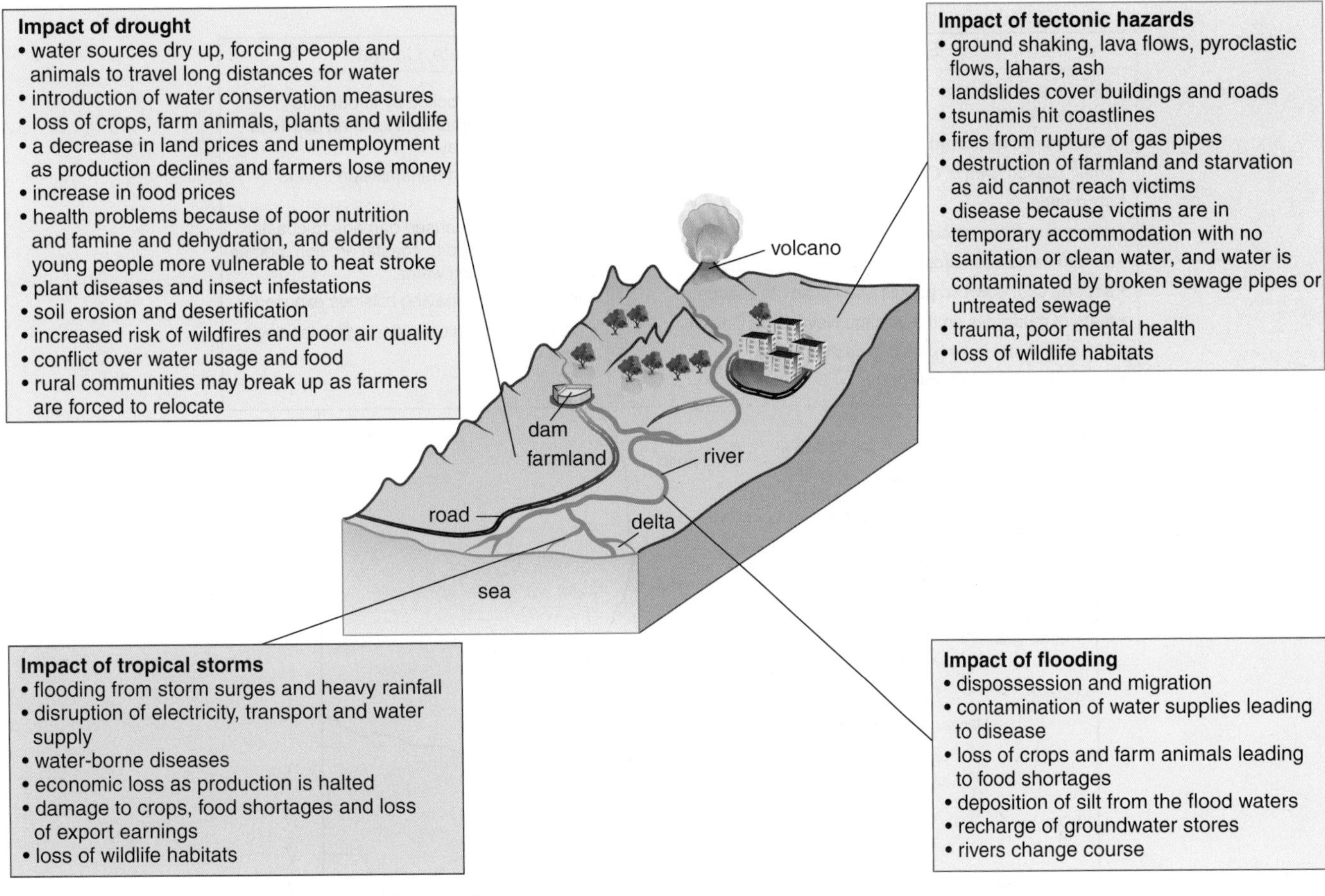

Figure 6.12 Some impacts of natural hazards.

CASE STUDY

Hurricane Patricia: the impact of a tropical cyclone

Hurricane Patricia was a tropical cyclone that formed in the eastern Pacific Ocean and rapidly intensified into a category 5 hurricane (Figure 6.13). On 23 October 2015 it became the most powerful tropical cyclone ever measured, as the maximum sustained winds reached an unprecedented 320 km h^{-1}. It also set the record for the lowest pressure recorded in a tropical cyclone in the western hemisphere, with a minimum central pressure of 879 millibars. Even more quickly than it had gained strength, the hurricane rapidly weakened over the Sierra Madre mountains of Mexico.

The hurricane was a compact storm, with the most intense winds extending just 16 km out from the eye. Landfall was in a rural area of Mexico with a low population density and where the coastline rises steeply. Tourism is important to the local economy. The management strategies used to deal with the event proved to be very successful because there was no loss of life.

The government was well prepared, and a 'warning-alert-evacuate' strategy was used effectively. Regular warnings were issued before the event, 1782 shelters were opened, 8500 people were evacuated and sandbags were distributed to prevent flooding. Food was stockpiled, property boarded up and electricity was shut down to avoid electrocutions and fires. The army, navy and police were all deployed.

→

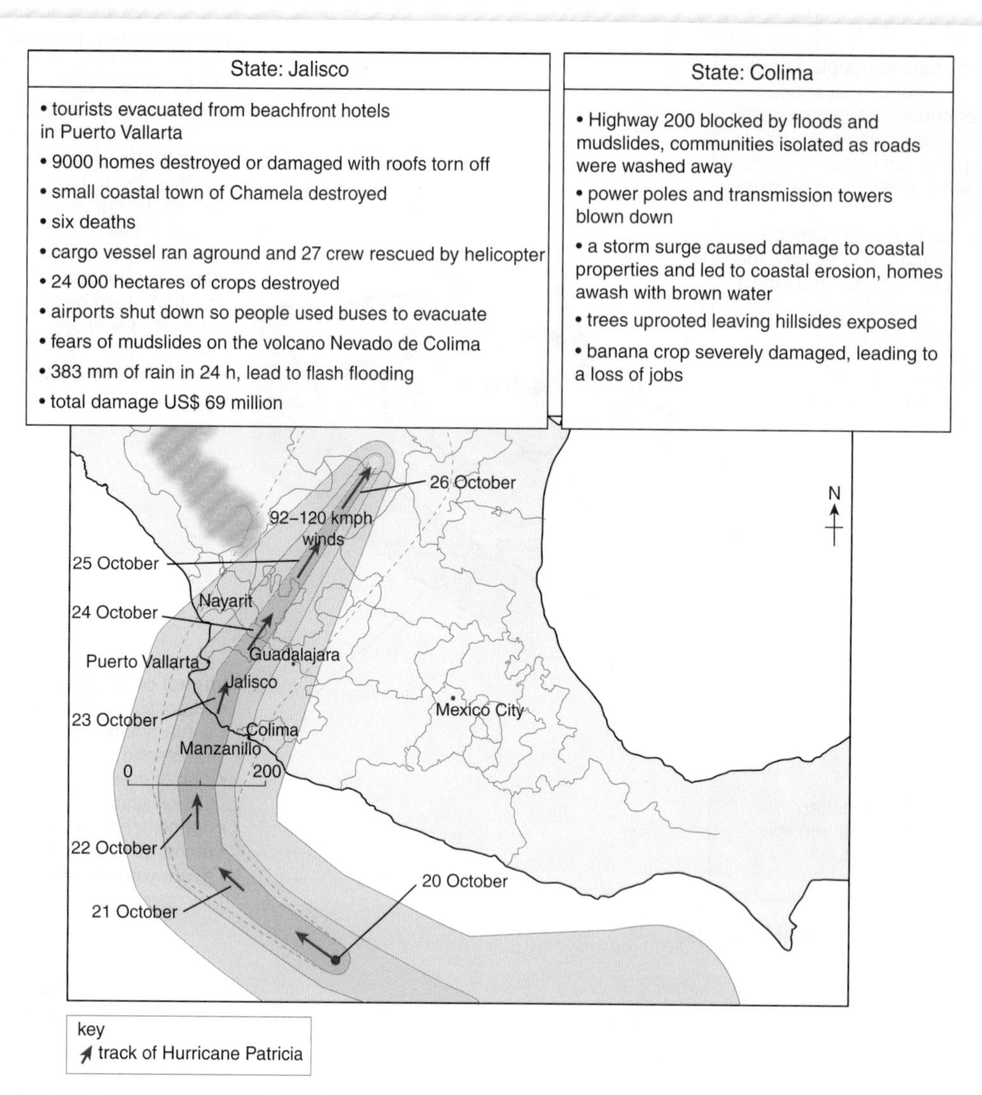

Figure 6.13 The track and impacts of Hurricane Patricia on the west coast of Mexico.

Questions

1 a Why do you think Hurricane Patricia formed where and when it did?
  b Describe the track of the hurricane using the dates provided.
  c Identify the state where the main track of Hurricane Patricia reached land.

2 a What strategies did the government take to manage the hurricane before its arrival?
  b Suggest reasons why people in the affected Mexican states had to be evacuated.

3 a Describe different ways in which the hurricane affected the transport and infrastructure.
  b Explain why some people were worried about the long-term impacts of Hurricane Patricia on the local and national economy of Mexico.
  c Why do you think Hurricane Patricia killed fewer people than expected?

6.7 Strategies to manage the impact of natural hazards

Management strategies focus on prediction, prevention or protection (the three Ps), in other words trying to deal with a natural hazard before, during and after the event. The strategies used can be short term (such as warnings by text messaging, television or radio, rescuing people, providing food, water supplies and temporary shelter) and long term (such as training emergency services, providing education and awareness so people can stockpile essential items or evacuate safely). Strategies should be sustainable, and improvements in technology mean that it is increasingly possible to predict and protect against natural hazards.

However, this is usually expensive and the provision of aid, whether national or international, is often needed for the rebuilding process. International aid can come from governments or charitable organisations, which offer various forms of assistance such as medicine, food and shelter.

Earthquakes

Regions at risk from earthquakes can be identified by studying plate tectonics but predicting earthquakes is very difficult and prevention probably impossible. Table 6.5 highlights what can be done.

Prediction	Preparation and protection
• Instruments such as seismometers can monitor tremors. Groundwater levels and radon gas can also be measured • Epicentres and the frequency of past events can be mapped to see if a pattern is developing • Measurement of local magnetic fields • A hazard zone map can be drawn based on geological information and ground stability • Unusual animal behaviour	• Earthquake proof or aseismic buildings (Figure 6.14). Older buildings can be retrofitted • Smart meters that cut off gas supplies to prevent fires • Land-use planning: important services such as schools and hospitals are built in low risk areas

Table 6.5 Managing the earthquake hazard.

Some features of an earthquake-proof building (Figure 6.14) include:

- rubber shock absorbers at the base to absorb tremors
- foundations sunk deep into bedrock
- cross-bracing steel beams allowing the building to move as a rigid structure
- computer-controlled weights on the roof to reduce shaking
- construction using fire-resistant materials
- flexible piping for electricity, water and gas
- no bricks or concrete blocks.

Volcanoes

We know where volcanoes are located but eruptions are often unpredictable in terms of magnitude and timing. Table 6.6 highlights some management strategies that can be used.

Prediction	Preparation and protection
• Seismometers monitor tremors caused by rising magma • Satellites using heat-seeking cameras can measure increasing ground temperatures • Tiltmeters and global positioning systems monitor changes in volcano shape • Emissions of steam and gas (sulfur dioxide) can be monitored	• Study past eruptions of a volcano and create a volcano hazard map • Plans such as lava diversion channels, lava barriers, spraying lava with water and halting lava advance by dropping concrete slabs into the flow • Building reinforcements, for example sloping roofs to protect against ashfall

Table 6.6 Managing the volcano hazard.

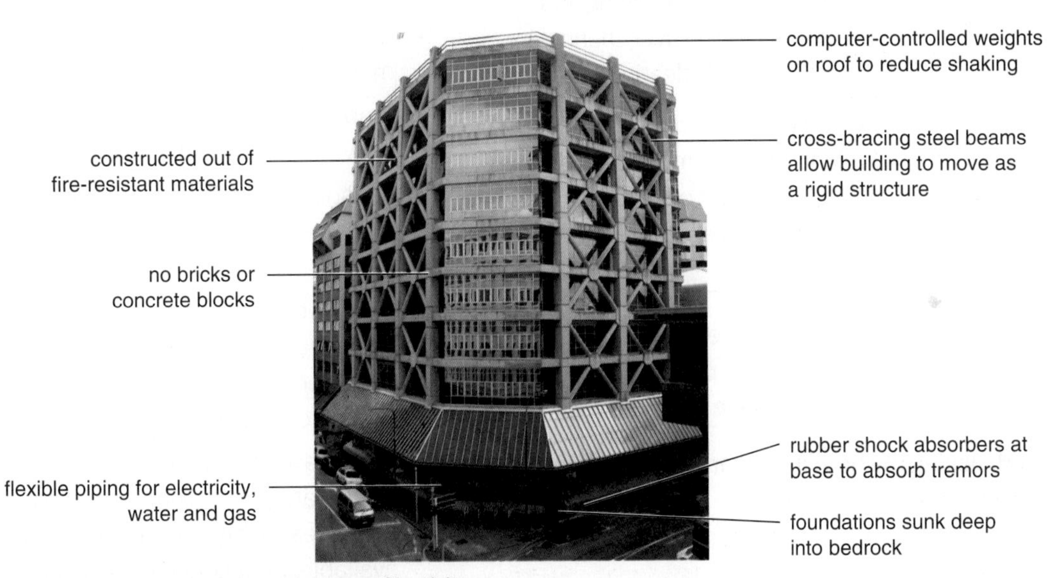

Figure 6.14 Some features of an earthquake-proof building.

Tropical cyclones

Tropical cyclones are the most predictable of natural hazards. We know when they will form, we can track their movements and we know what the impacts will be. Table 6.7 lists some of the management strategies that can be used.

Prediction	Preparation and protection
• Tropical cyclones are tracked using satellites	• Cyclone shelters • Buildings on stilts so not flooded by storm surge • Embankments built along coast • Preserve mangrove swamps to absorb the energy of storm surges

Table 6.7 Managing the tropical cyclone hazard.

Flooding

Managing flood risks involves not only in the river channel but also the drainage basin. Table 6.8 highlights some management strategies that can be used.

Prediction	Preparation and protection
• Monitoring the amount of rainfall and the change in river discharge • Knowledge about the characteristics of the drainage basin and type of storm is valuable for determining the possible severity of the flooding	• Hard engineering projects (physical structures that are permanent, often expensive and can impact on the environment) such as levees, flood barriers, flood control channels and dams • Soft engineering projects, such as afforestation, controlled flooding of meadowland and storage basins • Straightening, widening and deepening the river channel by dredging and clearing vegetation • Land-use planning to use higher land for settlements, restrict development on floodplains or increase green space • Use of sandbags and pumps • Adapt houses, for example positioning power sockets to 1.5 m above ground level

Table 6.8 Managing the flooding hazard.

Drought

Table 6.9 lists strategies for managing droughts.

Prediction	Preparation and protection
• Monitoring precipitation and temperature	• Increase water supplies by dams and reservoirs, percolation ponds, wells, pumps and use of aquifers, water transfer by pipeline, desalination • Water conservation such as using storage tanks, spray irrigation, planting drought-tolerant crops, reducing deforestation and increasing water recycling • Agricultural improvements such as planting shelterbelts to reduce wind and evaporation, building low banks across a slope (bunds) to encourage infiltration and fencing to control overgrazing • Government stockpiling supplies of water, food and medicine

Table 6.9 Managing the drought hazard.

6.8 Opportunities presented by natural hazards

Despite the known risks of living in areas prone to natural hazards, many millions of people around the world continue to do so. Why is this?

- Individuals may have lived in an area all their life and want to be near family and friends. They do not perceive the risk to be very high, particularly if they have never experienced a natural hazard.
- Confidence in prediction, preparation and protection methods.
- Employment opportunities, such as in tourism as souvenir sellers and guides, or in fishing.
- An individual may have no choice in moving if there is pressure on land, or it is too expansive to move.
- In the case of volcanoes, fertile soils are created that produce high crop yields. The scenery can be spectacular, geothermal power can supply a cheap form of power and there is the possibility of mining minerals such as sulfur, diamonds and gold.
- In the case of flooding, rivers may provide a source of food, water for drinking and irrigation, communications maybe easier and flat land either side of the river is available for building on.

PRACTICAL ACTIVITY 6.2

Finding out whether there is a relationship between two sets of data

Scattergraphs are used when you have two sets of data and you want to see if there is a relationship (correlation) between them so that a hypothesis can be proved or disproved. The data are not continuous like a line graph. The two variables are plotted on the *x*- and *y*-axes and each plot is marked by a cross or dot. A best fit line is drawn between as many of the plots as possible. The three possible results as shown in Figure 6.15.

Materials

- Pen and paper

Method

Use the data in Table 6.10 to draw a scattergraph to see if there is a relationship between the number of deaths and the magnitude of an earthquake. Make sure you label the axes.

Questions

1. Which earthquake led to the greatest loss of life?
2. Which earthquake had the strongest magnitude?
3. What conclusion can be drawn about the relationship between the magnitude of an earthquake and the number of deaths? Use data from your figure to support your answer.
4. Explain why earthquakes of the same or similar magnitude cause different numbers of deaths.

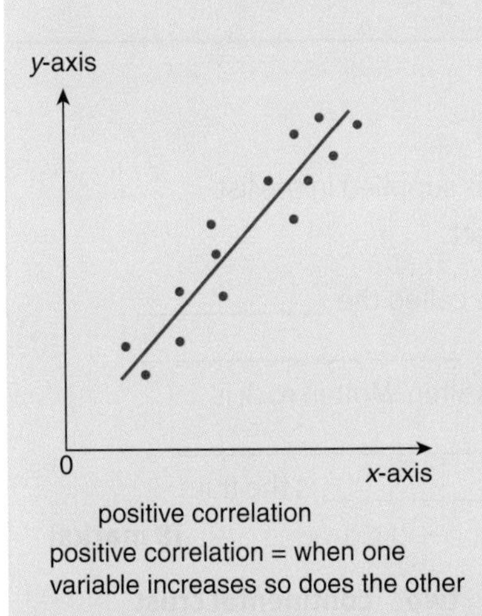

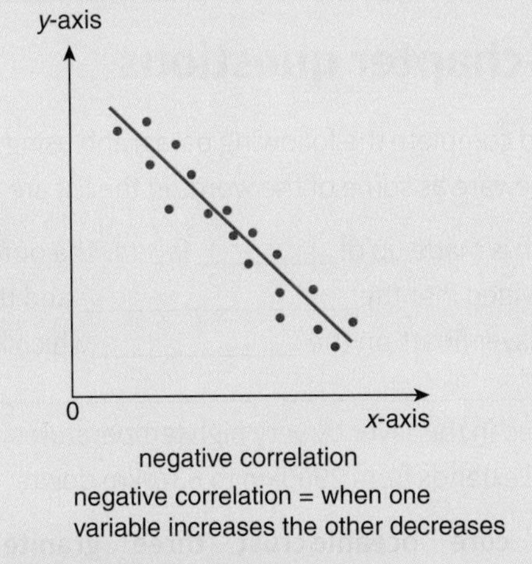

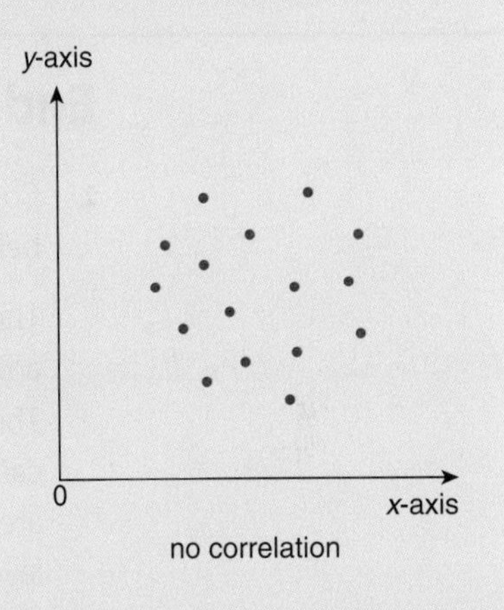

Figure 6.15 Three scattergraphs showing types of correlation.

Country	Number of deaths	Magnitude of earthquake on the Richter scale
Nepal 2015	9000	7.8
China 2013	196	7.0
Japan 2011	21 000	9.0
Chile 2010	500	8.8
Indonesia 2009	1214	7.6
China 2008	68 000	8.0
Pakistan 2005	79 000	7.6
Iran 2003	26 271	6.6
Afghanistan 2002	1000	6.1
India 2001	20 000	7.7

Table 6.10 The number of deaths associated with earthquakes.

Summary

After completing this chapter, you should know:

- how to describe the distribution of earthquakes, volcanoes and fold mountains in relation to the plate tectonics theory
- the three types of plate boundaries and the effects of these movements
- the causes and effects of earthquakes and understand the strategies that can be used to lessen the impacts
- the formation of different types of volcanoes and volcanic activity and how we can manage the impacts of eruptions
- where and how tropical cyclones are formed, the threats posed by them and strategies that can be used to reduce the impacts
- explain why flooding occurs, know the positive and negative effects of flooding and explain the different measures used to reduce damage from flooding
- what the causes of drought are and be able to explain the impacts on people and the environment, and describe the strategies used to deal with drought.

End-of-chapter questions

1 Copy and complete the following paragraph using the words supplied in the list below. Beware as some of the words in the list are not correct.

The Earth is made up of ________ layers. The outer layer is called the ___________ and is divided into the ________________ and the ___________________________. The top layer floats on the ____________ which is semi-molten. Molten rock is called ________________. _______________________ ____________________ are formed in this layer by very high temperatures. The ____________ is the third layer and extends from 2900km to 6370km down. **[8 marks]**

magma core oceanic crust three granite crust two continental crust tectonic plates convection currents subduction

2 For each of the following features decide if it is found at a constructive, destructive or conservative plate boundary. Some of these features maybe found at more than one plate boundary.

a Fold mountains
b Subduction zone
c Shield volcano
d Earthquakes
e Mid-ocean ridge
f Composite volcano
g Rift valley **[7 marks]**

3 In 1995 there was a volcanic eruption on the island of Montserrat.

a Describe three possible impacts of the volcanic eruption on people living close to the volcano. **[3 marks]**
b To what extent do you think it is possible to protect nearby settlements from such an eruption? **[3 marks]**

4 Why are tropical cyclones dangerous to people? **[4 marks]**

5 The following five statements contain an error. Re-write the statements correctly.

- **a** Drought is when there is rain over a long period of time.
- **b** Droughts only occur in Africa and South America.
- **c** Droughts in the Sahel region of Africa occur when the ITCZ moves northwards.
- **d** Drought is associated with low-pressure systems.
- **e** El Niño brings droughts to South America and floods to Australia. **[5 marks]**

6 State two short-term and three long-term problems caused by flooding. **[5 marks]**

7 The impact of some natural hazards is greater for those who live in urban areas than those who live in rural areas. How far do you agree with this statement? **[5 marks]**

8 Read the newspaper report below.

16th April 2016

A major earthquake of 7.3 magnitude shook the island of Kyushu in southern Japan at 1.30 am yesterday, the focus was very shallow at only 10 kms in depth. The island has a population of over 13 million and it was the second major earthquake in 2 days. 34 people have been killed and 1,500 injured mainly by collapsed buildings. Heavy rain is forecast and temperatures are due to fall with further strong aftershocks predicted.

An earthquake with a magnitude 7.8 also hit the coast of Ecuador in South America at 7 pm yesterday. The focus was 20.6 kms down and has killed over 661 people with 30, 000 people injured. Poor infrastructure in the region is slowing down rescue efforts.

a Using the information in the report complete the table comparing the two earthquakes.

	Japan	Ecuador
Local time		
Magnitude		
Number of people who died		
Number of people injured		

[8 marks]

b All earthquakes have a focus and an epicentre. Explain the meaning of

focus **[1 mark]**

epicentre. **[1 mark]**

c The Japanese earthquake was caused by conservative plate movement, the Ecuador earthquake by destructive (convergent) plate movement. Describe the movement of the plates at these boundaries. **[4 marks]**

d What information in the report could explain why thousands of people have refused to return to their undamaged homes in Japan? **[1 mark]**

e Suggest two items that were needed immediately after the earthquakes in Japan and Ecuador and explain why each item is needed.

Item 1... **[1 mark]**

Item 2... **[1 mark]**

A comparison of two earthquake events

Study the information about two earthquakes in contrasting areas of the world, Nepal and New Zealand.

Nepal

Figure 6.16 The impact of the earthquake in Nepal.

At 11.56 a.m. on Saturday 26 April 2015, an earthquake of magnitude 7.8 on the Richter scale struck the mountainous country of Nepal (Figure 6.16). The depth of focus was 11 km, which is relatively shallow but results in worse ground shaking than when an earthquake's focus is deeper. The epicentre was 80 km to the north-west of the capital city, Kathmandu. Severe aftershocks continued for many days. Avalanches were triggered on Mt Everest, killing 18 climbers, and landslides blocked roads, leaving rural areas isolated. Entire villages were destroyed. In Kathmandu there was extensive damage to buildings, historic temples, roads, communications, water supply and electricity. The country's only international airport was shut down temporarily. Food, medicine and clean water were in short supply. Nine thousand people died, 23 000 were injured and over 8 million people were affected, including many tourists. The monsoon rains were due to start soon after the earthquake and many farmers were unable to harvest and store the wheat crop and plant the next rice harvest. An estimated $4.1 billion of aid was donated by foreign governments and charities but the distribution of the aid was slow because of the limited infrastructure in Nepal. The airport was too small to take the large planes used for the delivery of emergency teams and equipment, and it had been damaged. Remote villages were cut off for weeks because of road failures on the steep mountain slopes, and 6 months after the earthquake many thousands were still living in temporary shelters.

Christchurch, New Zealand

At 12.51 p.m. on Tuesday 22 February 2011, an earthquake of magnitude 6.3 hit the South Island of New Zealand. The depth of focus was 5 km down and the epicentre was 10 km from the city of Christchurch. The same area of New Zealand had been hit by a slightly stronger earthquake in September the previous year. Severe liquefaction occurred and much of the city centre was destroyed. One hundred and eight-five people were killed, 115 when the Canterbury Television building collapsed. Suburban residents were evacuated and there was no electricity or water for 7 days, although chemical toilets and bottled water were brought in. The local Earthquake Recovery Authority (ERA) is now responsible for demolition and rebuilding to higher standards in safer areas of Christchurch over a 10 year period at a cost of $30 billion.

Figure 6.17 The impact of the earthquake in Christchurch, New Zealand.

Questions

1 Copy and complete the following paragraph.
At Nepal the ____________________ plate is colliding with the ________________ plate. It is a ______________plate boundary. New Zealand has many earthquakes because the _____________ plate meets the __________________ plate. At Christchurch these plates slide past each other.

2 Explain the reason for the earthquakes at these different locations.

3 Copy and complete Table 6.11 using the information provided in the text.

	Nepal	New Zealand
Date of earthquake		
Time		
Magnitude on Richter scale		
Depth of focus		
Distance of nearest city from epicentre		
Short-term impacts		

Table 6.11 A comparison of two major earthquakes.

4 How might the number of deaths in Nepal and New Zealand have been affected by the time at which the earthquake struck?

5 What are the possible long-term impacts for Nepal and Christchurch? Explain why Nepal is likely to suffer more long-term consequences than Christchurch.

6 What three management strategies could be taken to minimise the impact of a future earthquake in Nepal?

7 The management strategy of the ERA is to have higher building standards in preparation for future earthquakes in Christchurch. Which earthquake-proof strategies for buildings would you advise the ERA to use in the rebuilding of Christchurch?

Chapter 7
The atmosphere and human activities

Learning outcomes

By the end of this chapter, you will be able to:

- explain the composition and structure of the atmosphere
- explain the greenhouse effect
- describe the causes of atmospheric pollution and its impact on people and the environment
- explain how the effects of atmospheric pollution can be reduced.

The man who survived a supersonic freefall

The Earth's atmosphere extends 1000 km upwards from the Earth's surface, and the Karman line occurs at an altitude of 100 km above the Earth's sea-level. The Karman line represents the boundary between the Earth's atmosphere and what is referred to as 'outer space'. On 24 October 2014, a former Google Executive, Alan Eustace, took 1 h and 45 min to rise up through the atmosphere with a helium-filled balloon to a height of 41.4 km. He then jumped from the balloon and fell at speeds of up to 1287 km h^{-1}. Fifteen minutes later he was back on Earth. Doing this, Eustace broke the world record for the highest freefall parachute jump by just over 2 km, which had been set 2 years before by Felix Baumgartner. Eustace faced many dangers on his ascent and descent and wore a specially designed pressurised spacesuit with a built-in life support system. Pressure decreases with height, so if his suit had failed above 19.2 km (the Armstrong limit) fluids in his exposed body would have boiled. Oxygen levels also fall as pressure decreases, and he faced the risk of hypoxia (lack of oxygen) and freezing to death.

Although Eustace did not jump from the edge of space, he did jump from above the ozone layer and above the height that civilian aircraft fly at. At 41.4 km up, he had 99% of the Earth's atmosphere below him and he fell through two of the four layers of the atmosphere: the stratosphere and the troposphere.

Figure 7.0 Alan Eustace parachutes back to Earth from the stratosphere.

7.1 The structure and composition of the atmosphere

Composition

The atmosphere is a layer of gases held to the Earth by gravitational force. Gravity and compression mean that 50% of the atmosphere lies within 5.6 km of the Earth's surface. When the Earth was first formed, it is believed it had no atmosphere but, as the planet cooled, gases were released and an atmosphere began to form. Today's atmosphere is composed of nitrogen (mostly the product of volcanic eruptions), oxygen, argon (an **inert** or **noble gas**), carbon dioxide (cycled through photosynthesis, respiration and burning of fossil fuels) and ozone. Carbon dioxide and ozone are referred to as variable gases because their quantity can change as a result of processes such as evaporation and transpiration and, in the case of ozone, because of varying rates of formation, pollution and seasonal change. There are minute traces of other, mostly inert, gases, such as krypton. Besides these gases the atmosphere contains **aerosols** or solid particles (minute particles of dust such as salt, fine sand and volcanic ash) and water vapour. Table 7.1 shows the composition of the atmosphere.

KEY TERMS

Noble gas: a gas that rarely reacts with other elements because it is stable, previously referred to as inert gases

Aerosols: sprays containing fine particles and/or droplets that become suspended in the atmosphere

The natural balance of gases in the atmosphere is maintained by various cycles, for example the nitrogen cycle and carbon cycle (see Section 9.1). However, human activities can alter the composition in many ways. Carbon dioxide is added by burning fossil fuels and deforestation. Growing rice and keeping cattle both increase methane levels. We can also reduce some gases by afforestation or releasing ozone-destroying chlorofluorocarbons (CFCs).

Component	% in atmosphere	Importance to life on Earth
Permanent gases Nitrogen (N_2) Oxygen (O_2)	78.09 20.95	Needed for the growth of plants Produced by photosynthesis and used in respiration
Variable gases Water vapour (H_2O) Carbon dioxide (CO_2) Ozone (O_3)	0.2–4 0.03 0.00006	Source for all types of precipitation. Provides most of the natural greenhouse gases. Vital to the existence of life Used by plants in photosynthesis. As plants are primary producers they support other life. CO_2 is a greenhouse gas Absorbs ultra-violet radiation
Inert gases Argon (Ar) Helium (He), neon (Ne), krypton (Kr)	0.93 Trace	Can create an inert atmosphere that protects materials from reacting with oxygen or other gases
Non-gaseous particles Dust	Trace	Absorbs and reflects incoming short-wave radiation. Water vapour condenses on particles, forming droplets or ice crystals, which are the basis of cloud formation
Pollutants Sulfur dioxide (SO_2), nitrogen dioxide (NO_2), methane (CH_4)	Trace	Can lead to smog, acid rain, ozone depletion and the enhanced greenhouse effect

Table 7.1 The composition of the atmosphere.

Structure

Atmospheric pressure decreases with height in the atmosphere but temperature changes are more complicated. Based on temperatures changes, the atmosphere can be divided into four layers, as shown in Figure 7.1.

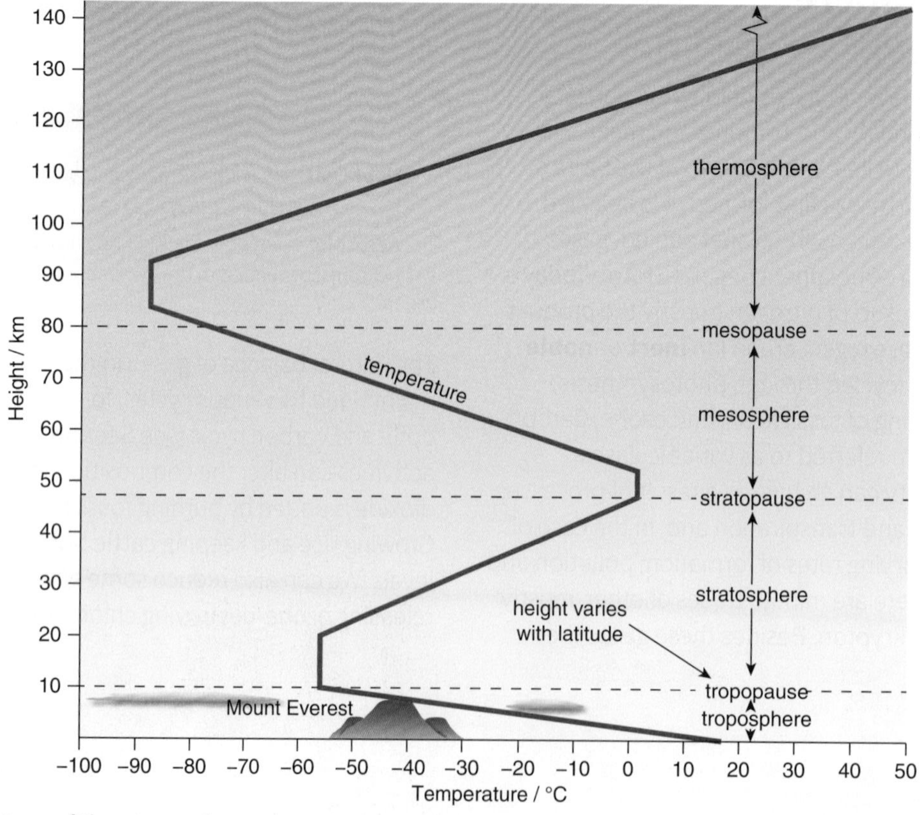

Figure 7.1 The structure of the atmosphere.

The troposphere

Temperature decreases with height (averaging 6.4 °C km^{-1}), because the warming effect of the Earth's surface through conduction and convection diminishes as altitude increases. The strength of the Earth's gravitational pull declines with altitude, and pressure declines too. In contrast, wind speeds increase with height. The top of this layer is marked by the **tropopause**, where temperatures remain fairly constant. This boundary occurs at a height of about 8 km at the poles and 17 km in the tropics, and marks the upper limit to the Earth's weather and climate.

The stratosphere

This layer extends to nearly 50 km above the Earth's surface. Pressure continues to fall but temperatures increase steadily with height. This situation is called a **temperature inversion** and is caused by the concentration of ozone, which absorbs the incoming ultraviolet radiation from the Sun. This layer also acts as a shield against incoming meteorites, which burn out when they enter the Earth's gravitational field. The ozone layer is discussed further in section 7.3. The upper limit of the stratosphere is marked by the **stratopause**.

The mesosphere

This layer is 50–80 km in height. Pressure continues to decrease and temperatures fall rapidly to below −80 °C because there is no water vapour, dust or ozone to absorb the incoming short-wave radiation. Winds can reach speeds up to 3000 km h^{-1}. The **mesopause** marks the upper limit of this layer.

The thermosphere

This layer is 80–1000 km in height and temperatures rise rapidly to as high as 1500 °C because of the absorption of ultraviolet radiation by atomic oxygen. The **thermopause** marks the upper limit of this layer.

KEY TERMS

Tropopause: the upper limit of the troposphere

Temperature inversion: when temperatures increase with altitude

Stratopause: the upper limit of the stratosphere, temperatures remain constant in this boundary layer

Mesopause: the upper limit of the mesosphere, temperatures remain constant in this boundary layer

Thermopause: the upper limit of the thermosphere, temperatures remain constant in this boundary layer

SELF-ASSESSMENT QUESTIONS

7.1 Copy and complete the following paragraph using the words supplied in the list below. Beware as some of the words in the list are not correct.

The Earth's atmosphere is a mixture of _________, with some liquids and solids, held to Earth by _____________ . ____________ is the most abundant gas (_______%) . This is followed by _________________________.
A gas which makes up less than 0.93% is _____________ . Another gas which is __________________ and makes up ______% . Plants make food from this gas via photosynthesis. _____________ is a gas found in the ___________________ that absorbs potentially harmful ultra-violet radiation.

ozone 78.09% oxygen gases nitrogen thermosphere krypton pressure argon gravity carbon dioxide 20.95% 0.03% stratosphere

7.2 Why is carbon dioxide an important gas for life on Earth?

7.3 Using Figure 7.1, state the name of the layer in which weather and climate occur.

7.4 Describe and explain how temperature changes with altitude through the four layers of the atmosphere.

The natural greenhouse effect

The natural greenhouse effect is the process that helps keep the Earth's surface and atmosphere warm (Figure 7.2).

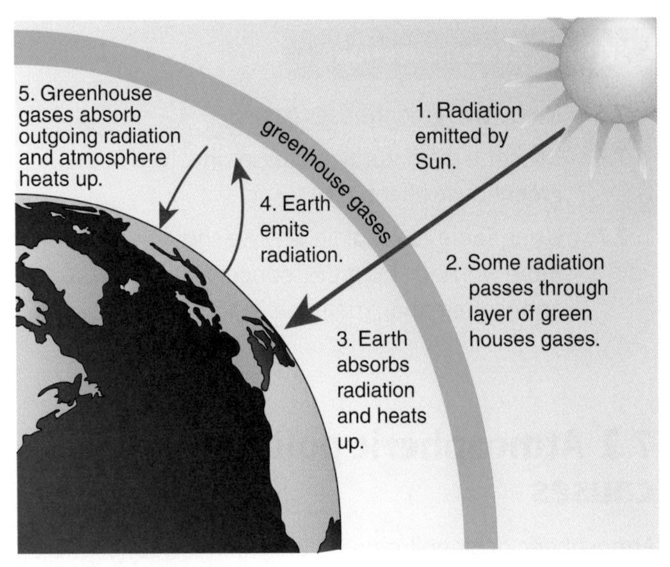

Figure 7.2 The processes involved in the natural greenhouse effect.

The Earth receives incoming **short-wave radiation** from the Sun. About half of this radiation is absorbed by the Earth's surface, around 20% is absorbed by the atmosphere and 30% is reflected by clouds and the Earth's surface, back into space.

As the Earth's surface warms, outgoing **long-wave radiation** or infrared radiation is emitted back into the atmosphere. Greenhouse gases absorb some of this radiation and deflect it back to the Earth's surface. These greenhouses gases make up a small proportion of the atmosphere but they act like a blanket trapping the radiation. The greater the concentration of greenhouse gases, the more effectively they return radiation back to the Earth's surface. This process maintains the Earth's temperature at around 33 °C warmer than it would otherwise be, allowing life to exist. Aside from water vapour, the main greenhouse gases are carbon dioxide, methane and nitrous oxides. The CFCs (chlorofluorocarbons; gases containing fluorine, chlorine and carbon) are also greenhouse gases but are artificial. Ozone is a greenhouse gas. These gases stay in the atmosphere for differing amounts of time, as shown in Table 7.2.

Name of greenhouse gas	% contribution to the greenhouse effect	Number of years gas stays in the atmosphere
Carbon dioxide	65	200
Methane	17	12
CFCs	12	1000
Nitrous oxides	6	114

Table 7.2 Some of the greenhouse gases.

SELF-ASSESSMENT QUESTIONS

7.5 Name two greenhouses gases.

7.6 Describe the natural processes involved in the greenhouse effect.

7.7 Using Table 7.2, explain why we should be more worried about CFC concentrations in the atmosphere than methane.

7.2 Atmospheric pollution and its causes

Atmospheric or air pollution occurs when the atmosphere contains gases and substances in harmful amounts. The substances that cause atmospheric pollution are called pollutants. Pollutants that directly pollute the atmosphere are called **primary pollutants**. If the primary pollutants in the atmosphere undergo chemical reactions the resulting compounds are called **secondary pollutants**.

Smog

Smog (smoke and fog) occurs where the burning of fossil fuels in industry, homes and vehicles provides additional particles that act as condensation nuclei for fog to form around. Smog is a problem associated with industrial and urban areas and is more frequent during winter months as people use more heating (Figure 7.3).

Figure 7.3 Smog in Beijing.

Photochemical smog involves chemical reactions induced by sunlight on certain pollutants that converts them into harmful substances such as ground-level or tropospheric ozone. This type of smog occurs during warm and sunny conditions. Vehicles are a major source of **particulate matter** (PM) and

KEY TERMS

Short-wave radiation: incoming or short-wave solar radiation, visible light and ultraviolet radiation are commonly called shortwave radiation

Long-wave radiation: outgoing or terrestrial radiation, as the Earth produces very little visible light or ultraviolet radiation, all radiation from the Earth is infrared

Primary pollutant: a pollutant that is emitted directly from the source

Secondary pollutant: a pollutant that forms through chemical reactions with primary pollutants

Photochemical smog: air pollution in the atmosphere accompanied by high levels of ozone and nitrogen oxides from vehicles and caused by the action of sunlight on the pollutants

Particulate matter (PM): a mixture of very small particles and liquid droplets suspended in the air

volatile organic compounds (VOCs), which cause photochemical smog. Particulate matter is categorised by the size of the particles (for example PM2.5 comprises particles with a diameter of less than 2.5 μm). They can be derived from both human (for example fuel combustion, engine emissions, tyre wear, mining, quarrying and construction) and natural (for example sea spray, soil and dust) sources. Volatile organic compounds comprise a wide range of organic compounds, including hydrocarbons, that evaporate and exist as vapour in the atmosphere. Emissions of volatile organic compounds result from the incomplete combustion of fuel, leakages from petrol tankers and fuel tanks, etc. Methane, produced by certain agricultural practices, is also a volatile organic compound. Agricultural smog can form when ammonium nitrate from fertilisers and manure is carried in the air.

Certain physical conditions can create a temperature inversion that then traps and increases the concentration of smog, as shown in Figure 7.4. The smog may be thick enough to block out the Sun, which gives rise to what is known as the 'dustbin lid effect'. The conditions needed for a temperature inversion include:

- high air pressure (anticyclone), which causes the upper air to sink
- calm conditions resulting from high pressure (winds will disperse smog)
- valleys surrounded by steep-sided hills, which trap the smog.

KEY TERM

Volatile organic compounds (VOCs): chemicals that easily enter the atmosphere as gases, mainly from evaporation

Acid rain

Acid rain is precipitation with a pH value of less than 6 (see Section 4.8). The acidity results from burning fossil fuels in factories and power stations, which release sulfur dioxide and nitrogen oxides into the atmosphere. Vehicle emissions add further nitrogen oxides. This is dry deposition. If these gases mix with water vapour and oxygen in the atmosphere, weak solutions of nitric and sulfuric acids are created, which can then be moved by winds. These solutions will eventually fall to Earth as acid rain and can occur at some distance from the source. This is wet deposition.

Ozone depletion

In 2010 a report from the United Nations (UN) claimed that levels of stratospheric ozone between 1996 and 2009 were 4% lower than before 1980. Ozone is a greenhouse gas that can be found in both the troposphere ('bad' ozone) and stratosphere ('good' ozone) but it is concentrated at a height of about 25 km in the stratosphere. The ozone layer exists because oxygen filtering from the top of the troposphere reacts under the influence of ultraviolet radiation to form ozone. This screens the Earth from the Sun's harmful radiation. The stratosphere's ozone is continually being produced, destroyed and replaced by this chemical process, creating a dynamic balance between our atmosphere and ultraviolet radiation. This chemical reaction is greatest above the equator and tropics, where solar radiation is strongest and more direct, and ozone is distributed to other regions by wind in the stratosphere. This natural balance has been disrupted by human activities, causing the concentration of ozone to fall. The main danger is chlorine, which reacts with oxygen

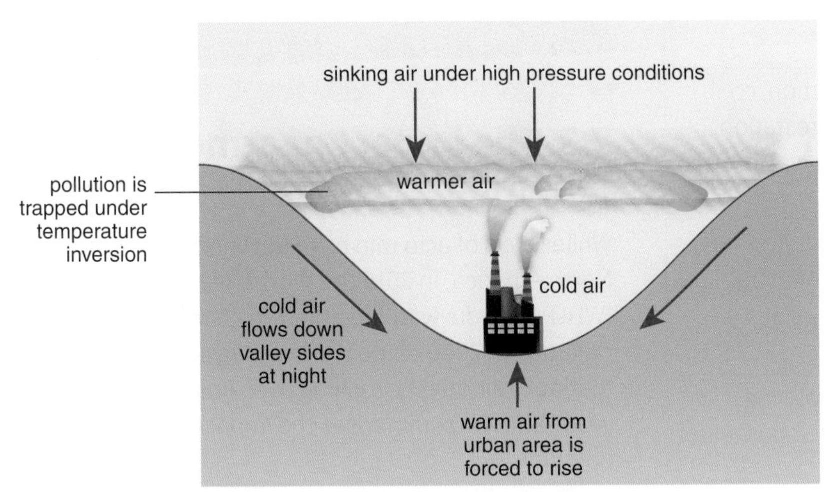

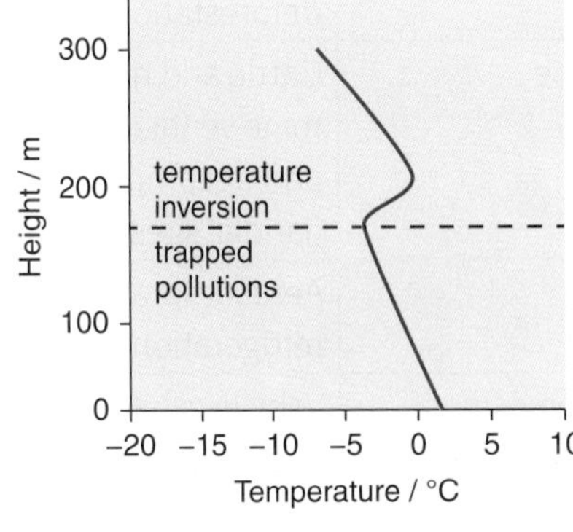

Figure 7.4 Formation of smog under a temperature inversion.

in a destructive process. Chlorine is found in the CFCs released by plastic manufacturing, air cooling systems, refrigeration fluid and aerosol sprays. CFCs are long lived (see Table 7.2) and eventually reach the stratosphere, where ultraviolet radiation breaks them down, releasing chlorine. As ozone **depletes** in the stratosphere, it forms a 'hole'. In 1985 a seasonal depletion in the layer of ozone was found above Antarctica. This hole allowed harmful ultraviolet radiation to enter the Earth's atmosphere. In the Southern Hemisphere winter, air over Antarctica is cut off from the rest of the atmosphere by the **polar vortex**, strong winds sweeping around the continent. High in the stratosphere, clouds form from tiny ice particles in the intense cold, and on their surfaces chemical reactions involving CFCs take place, releasing chlorine, which reacts with the oxygen in the ozone layer. Destruction of the ozone layer begins when the spring Sun arrives; in summer the clouds evaporate and chlorine converts into other compounds and the hole fills in until next year. The ozone hole is more developed over Antarctica than the Arctic because Antarctica is separated from the rest of the world by the polar vortex.

The enhanced greenhouse effect

The enhanced greenhouse effect is created by the addition of greenhouse gases to the atmosphere through human activities. It results in more heat being retained in the atmosphere and an increase in the Earth's temperature (look back at Table 7.2). This is leading to global warming and global climate change. The increase in these gases is because of human activities, as illustrated in Table 7.3.

Greenhouse gas	Human activities that increase their abundance
Carbon dioxide	Burning of fossil fuels, deforestation
Methane	Cattle and rice production, coal mine ventilation, deforestation and decomposition of waste (landfill sites)
CFCs	Aerosol sprays, fire extinguishers, refrigeration, air conditioning
Nitrogen oxides	Vehicle exhausts, chemical fertilisers
Tropospheric ozone	Chemical reactions involving nitrogen dioxides and unburnt fuel vapours

Table 7.3 Sources of some of the main greenhouse gases.

KEY TERMS

Depletion: a reduction or loss

Polar vortex: a circulation of strong upper level winds that surround Antarctica and keep cold air locked in above the continent

Carbon dioxide is the single largest contributor to the enhanced greenhouse effect. Deforestation can increase the amount of carbon dioxide in the atmosphere because it reduces the number of plants available to take carbon dioxide out of the atmosphere. Increases in carbon dioxide emissions account for approximately 70% of the enhanced greenhouse effect. Scientists estimate that the concentration of carbon dioxide in the atmosphere before the Industrial Revolution in the late 18th century had a value of approximately 280 parts per million (ppm). Measurements in 2015 put it at over 400 ppm, the highest ever recorded.

SELF-ASSESSMENT QUESTIONS

7.8 What is meant by atmospheric pollution?

7.9 Match the pollutant gas to the source.

Gas	Source of pollutant
1 Methane	A Burning fossil fuels
2 CFCs	B Keeping cattle
3 Sulfur dioxide	C Leakage from petrol tankers
4 VOCs	D Using aerosols

7.10 Which gas causes a depletion of ozone in the atmosphere?

7.11 Define the terms; smog, the enhanced greenhouse effect.

7.3 The impact of atmospheric pollution

While levels of acid rain have declined in Europe and North America, in 2016 the World Health Organization (WHO) issued a warning about the levels of atmospheric pollution in 2000 of the world's biggest cities. It is claimed that poor air quality is killing over 7 million people each year. Table 7.4 summarises the impacts of atmospheric pollution.

Pollutant	Potential impact on people	Potential impact on the environment
Smog Pollutant molecules: VOCs and NO_2	• Irritation of eyes and throat, increasing respiratory diseases such as asthma • Fine particles carried into the lungs leading to lung cancer. Strokes and heart attacks • Breathing difficulties	• The ability of plants to make and store food through photosynthesis is reduced • Growth, reproduction and general health of plants decline, making them more prone to disease and pests
Acid rain Pollutant molecules: SO_2 and NO_2	• Acidification of groundwater makes water undrinkable and can cause diarrhoea and stomach upsets • Aluminium leached from the soil into the groundwater has been linked with pre-senile dementia. • Limestone buildings are chemically weathered • Crop yields decline	• Trees affected as foliage dies • Acidification of groundwater damages tree roots • Nutrients such as calcium are leached out of the soil • Aquatic and animal life in lakes is poisoned and decreases as acidity levels increase
Ozone depletion Pollutant molecules: CFCs	• Higher levels of ultraviolet radiation causes sun burn, skin cancers, retina damage and cataracts (a disease of the eye that clouds the eye's lens) • Immune system can be suppressed	• Extra ultraviolet radiation inhibits the reproductive cycle of phytoplankton, which make up the lowest layer of some food webs. This could affect the populations of other animals • Changes in biochemical composition makes some plant leaves less attractive as food • Melting ice sheets, glaciers and permafrost can lead to a rise in sea-levels
Climate change Pollutant molecules: various greenhouse gases	• Damage to low-lying countries such as Bangladesh from flooding would be disruptive with high financial costs. Forced migration as people lose their homes and farmland from rising sea-levels • Warmer weather may mean farmers grow different crops and have longer growing seasons. Increased droughts could lead to desertification and famine • Negative impact on certain economic activities, e.g. the skiing industry	• Sea-level rise will lead to the loss of coastal land and increased erosion • Animal and plant species would not be able to adapt fast enough to the changes, leading to a loss of biodiversity, habitat or extinction • More severe storms and droughts • Changes to fishing industries if fish species move to different waters • Ecosystem change could mean plant and animal species move into new areas and new (invasive) species emerge • Warmer temperatures could allow diseases such as malaria to spread

Table 7.4 Some impacts of atmospheric pollution on people and the environment.

SELF-ASSESSMENT QUESTIONS

7.12 Describe the effects of acid rain on people and the environment.

7.13 Why should people be concerned about a hole forming in the ozone layer?

7.14 Using the internet, research the possible impacts of an increase in global temperatures for the country in which you live.

PRACTICAL ACTIVITY 7.1

Testing the effect of different levels of acidity on the germination of seeds

Materials

- Filter paper
- Five Petri dishes
- Measuring cylinder
- Distilled water
- Beaker
- 100 seeds (e.g. mung beans or cress, but make sure the seeds are of the same species and the same age)
- Pen
- 0.5 mol dm^{-3} sulfuric acid
- Syringe

Method

- Place some filter paper in a Petri dish. Using a measuring cylinder, pour 20 cm^3 of distilled water into a beaker.
- Now carefully pour the 20 cm^3 of distilled water into the Petri dish. Spread 20 seeds over the filter paper. Replace the Petri dish lid and label it 'distilled water'. This is your control.
- Prepare the second Petri dish with filter paper as above and pour 19 cm^3 of distilled water into a beaker. Add 1 cm^3 of 0.5 mol dm^{-3} sulfuric acid to the water (see Table 7.5) using a syringe. Stir well. Pour into the second Petri dish, spread 20 seeds over the filter paper and label it '5% acid rain'.

Amount of distilled water/cm^3	Amount of sulfuric acid/cm^3	Total volume/cm^3
20	0	20
19	1	20
18	2	20
17	3	20
16	4	20

Table 7.5 Dilution table.

- Repeat the procedure with three more Petri dishes. Work down the dilution table for the correct concentration of distilled water and sulfuric acid. Label the Petri dishes'10% acid rain', '15% acid rain' and '20% acid rain' accordingly.
- Place the Petri dishes in a warm, dark place for 7 days. Temperature, water and light must be kept the same for all five Petri dishes.
- Draw up a suitable table to record your results. Count the number of germinated seeds in each Petri dish and record the results as a %.

Questions

1. Why would you use a control dish?
2. List two factors that should have been kept the same in this experiment.
3. Apart from germinated seeds, what else could possibly be recorded in this experiment?
4. How could you improve this experiment?

7.4 Managing atmospheric pollution

The international community

The serious nature of the problems that atmospheric pollution creates, and the fact that they cross international borders, means that international co-operation is needed to combat them. There is a realisation that solutions can only be achieved by countries working together, not least because the countries that produce pollution are often not the main recipients of pollution. Table 7.6 summarises some of the main international conferences and resulting laws and procedures on atmospheric pollution.

However, international agreement is not always easy to achieve. Some less economically developed countries (LEDCs) want to develop their industry and do not want to reduce emissions. These countries may not have the money to implement costly strategies to reduce pollution or use more renewable energy sources instead of burning fossil fuels.

Governments

There are many different schemes that governments can implement to tackle rising levels of air pollution. To reduce sulfur dioxide emissions and hence acid rain, governments can use low sulfur coal and crush and wash it before it is burnt in power stations. Flue gas desulfurisation measures such as scrubbers can remove up to 95% of sulfur dioxide emissions, and lining chimneys with lime also helps. Catalytic converters reduce sulfur emissions from vehicles,

Date	International agreement	Details
1979	Geneva Convention on Long Range Transboundary Air Pollution	Controlling and reducing air pollution across borders by international corporations
1987	Montreal Protocol	Ban and controlled use of CFCs to slow down ozone depletion
1992	Rio Earth Summit	Agreement Agenda 21 passed with aim to cut environmental pollution and conserve resources and wildlife habitat
1997	Kyoto Protocol	Signed by over 100 countries to cut carbon dioxide emissions by 5%, compared with 1990 levels. Each MEDC was allotted a target on emission reductions. Some LEDCs such as China were given no targets and allowed to increase emissions
1999	Gothenburg Protocol	Aimed to reduce pollutants and levels of acid rain and tropospheric ozone
2009	Copenhagen Conference	MEDCs and some LEDCs agreed to limits on greenhouse gas emissions. To assist LEDCs with the reduction, $30 billion was offered as aid by MEDCs, increasing to $100 billion by 2020. However, not legally binding
2015	Paris Climate Conference	195 countries agreed to limit rise in global temperature to 2 °C. EU will cut carbon dioxide emissions by 40% by 2030, the USA by 28% by 2025, and China agreed their emissions will peak in 2030. Countries will meet every 5 years to discuss progress

Table 7.6 A summary of major international conferences that have taken place on atmospheric pollution.

as can the use of low-sulfur vehicle fuels. Particulate filters can be fitted on diesel vehicles.

To combat ozone depletion there has been a global reduction in the use of CFCs. Alternative processes have been introduced, for example pump action sprays, or alternative materials are used, for example alcohols and hydrochloroflorocarbons (HCFCs). Safe disposal of items containing CFCs, such as old refrigerators, has also been encouraged.

To reduce other pollutants, such as carbon dioxide, governments can implement a comprehensive public transport policy, with the creation of cycle lanes, bus lanes, metro systems and trams. Electric or hybrid cars can be encouraged, as can the use of biofuels. A higher road tax discourages more car ownership and vehicles can be deterred or banned from certain parts of cities by actions such as pedestrianisation or the congestion charge in London. To reduce the level of PM10 particles in Paris in 2015, only vehicles with odd-numbered number plates or carrying more than three people were permitted to enter the city. The speed limit for vehicles in Paris was 20 km h^{-1} in the city. To encourage people to leave their vehicles at home, public transport and residential parking were free.

Increased use of renewable energy (see Section 2.1) and nuclear energy can be attempted through government policy, as can an increase in carbon sinks through reforestation and afforestation. Carbon capture and storage can be implemented: this is when waste carbon dioxide from power stations is transported via pipelines to storage sites. Laws can also be passed to reduce emissions from industries, and new industrial areas can be located on the downwind side of urban areas.

Individuals

Governments can encourage individuals through campaigns and advertising to be more energy efficient in their homes (see Section 2.4) and to be aware of personal carbon footprints. A carbon footprint is a measure of the impact our activities have on the environment. It calculates all the greenhouse gases we are expected to produce through our activities and measures them in units of carbon dioxide. Reduce, reuse and recycle (the 3Rs) should be encouraged. In agriculture, farmers can replace chemical fertilisers with organic fertilisers.

CASE STUDY

Acid rain in China

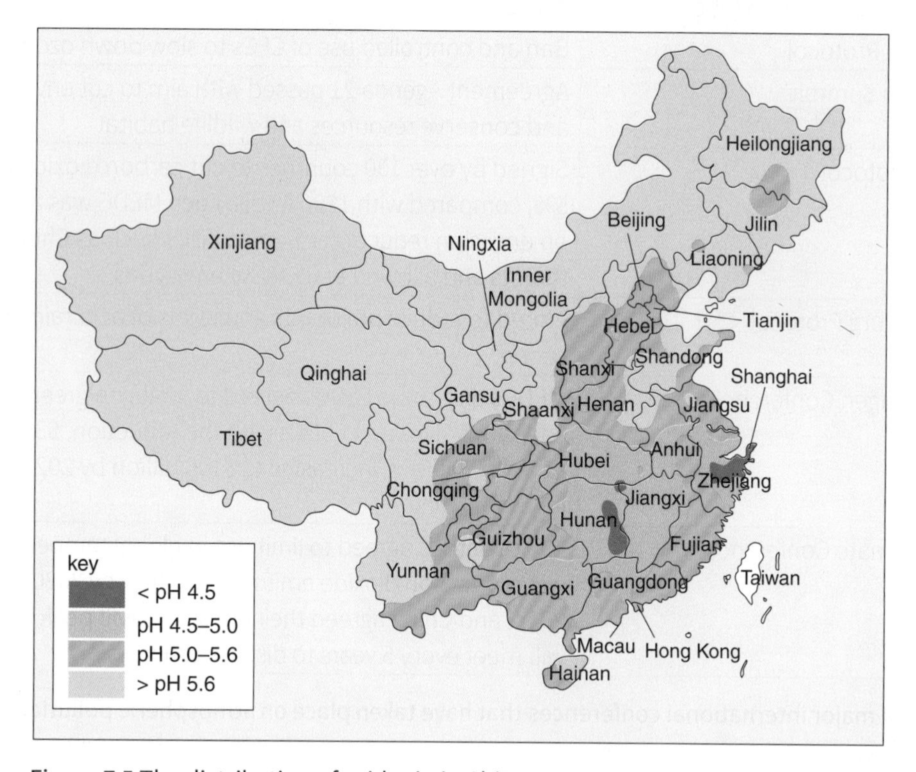

Figure 7.5 The distribution of acid rain in China.

China is experiencing rapid industrialisation. In 2011 China's government published a report that claimed that 258 Chinese cities were suffering from the effects of acid rain. The acid rain falls in the south and east of the country, where the majority of the population, industry and power stations are located (Figure 7.5). In 2014 China was the world's largest energy consumer, accounting for 23% of all global energy consumption, and the dominant fuel is coal, providing 66% of the country's energy consumption. When the coal is burnt in factories and power stations, it releases sulfur dioxide and nitrogen oxide, which form acid rain. Expanding car ownership is also leading to high emissions of these gases.

The effects of acid rain in China are numerous. Lakes and rivers have become more acidic, killing fish, crop yields are lower and commercial timber is being lost as trees die. Structural damage to buildings is being caused by chemical weathering. The 71 m high and 28 m wide Leshan Giant Buddha, which has stood for more than 1000 years, has been badly affected (Figure 7.6).

China first attempted to reduce sulfur dioxide emissions in 2007, before the 2008 Beijing Olympics. In 2011, as part of the government's Five-Year Plan, ambitious targets for emission reductions were set. Several

Figure 7.6 The Leshan Giant Buddha is starting to show the effects of acid rain.

strategies were used: flue gas desulfurisation methods, such as switching to coal with a low sulfur content and crushing and washing it, installing scrubbers and using lime spray. Small coal-fired power stations were closed in favour of less polluting energy sources (nuclear, wind, and solar), and in their homes people were encouraged to change their fuel type and use cars less. While sulfur dioxide levels over China remain the highest in the world, the implementation of these strategies and a slowing of the Chinese economy led to a 50% reduction in emissions of acid rain-producing gases between 2012 and 2014. However, China's acid rain problem has become the world's problem. Sulfur dioxide and nitrogen oxides from China's coal-fired power stations fall as acid rain on South Korea, Japan and Taiwan.

Questions

1 Using Figure 7.5, describe and explain the distribution of acid rain in China.

2 a Using Figure 7.7 and your own knowledge, explain how acid rain is formed.

b Should people outside China be worried about acid rain, and, if so, why?

3 The Chinese government has implemented various strategies to try and reduce acid rain levels in its country. Choose one of these strategies and describe how it might help reduce acid rain levels in China.

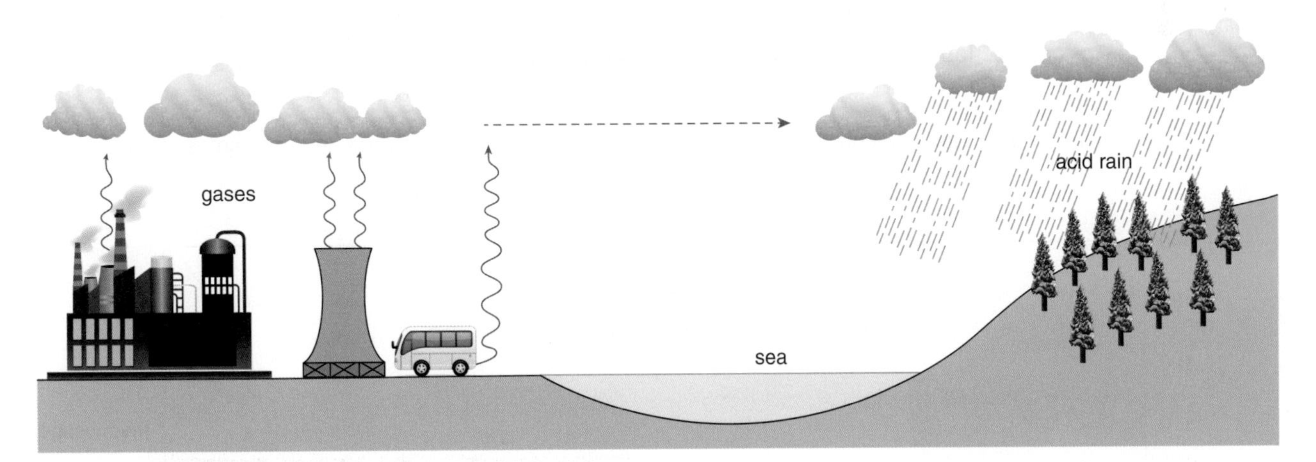

Figure 7.7 The formation of acid rain.

Summary

After completing this chapter, you should know:

- the composition of the atmosphere
- the causes of atmospheric pollution, including smog, acid rain, ozone depletion and the enhanced greenhouse effect
- how to carry out a simple experiment to show the effect of different pH levels on seedling growth
- about the impact of various atmospheric pollutants on people and the environment
- about strategies for the management of atmospheric pollution that can be used by the international community, governments and individuals.

End-of-chapter questions

1 Table 7.7 shows the composition of the atmosphere. Copy and complete the missing gases, formulae and abundance. **[10 marks]**

Gas	Formula	Abundance
	N_2	78.09%
Oxygen		
Argon		
	H_2O	
Carbon dioxide	CO_2	
	CH_4	Trace
Ozone		0.00006

Table 7.7 The composition of the atmosphere.

2 Look at Figure 7.8. It has axes of temperature against altitude and the names of the four layers in the atmosphere.

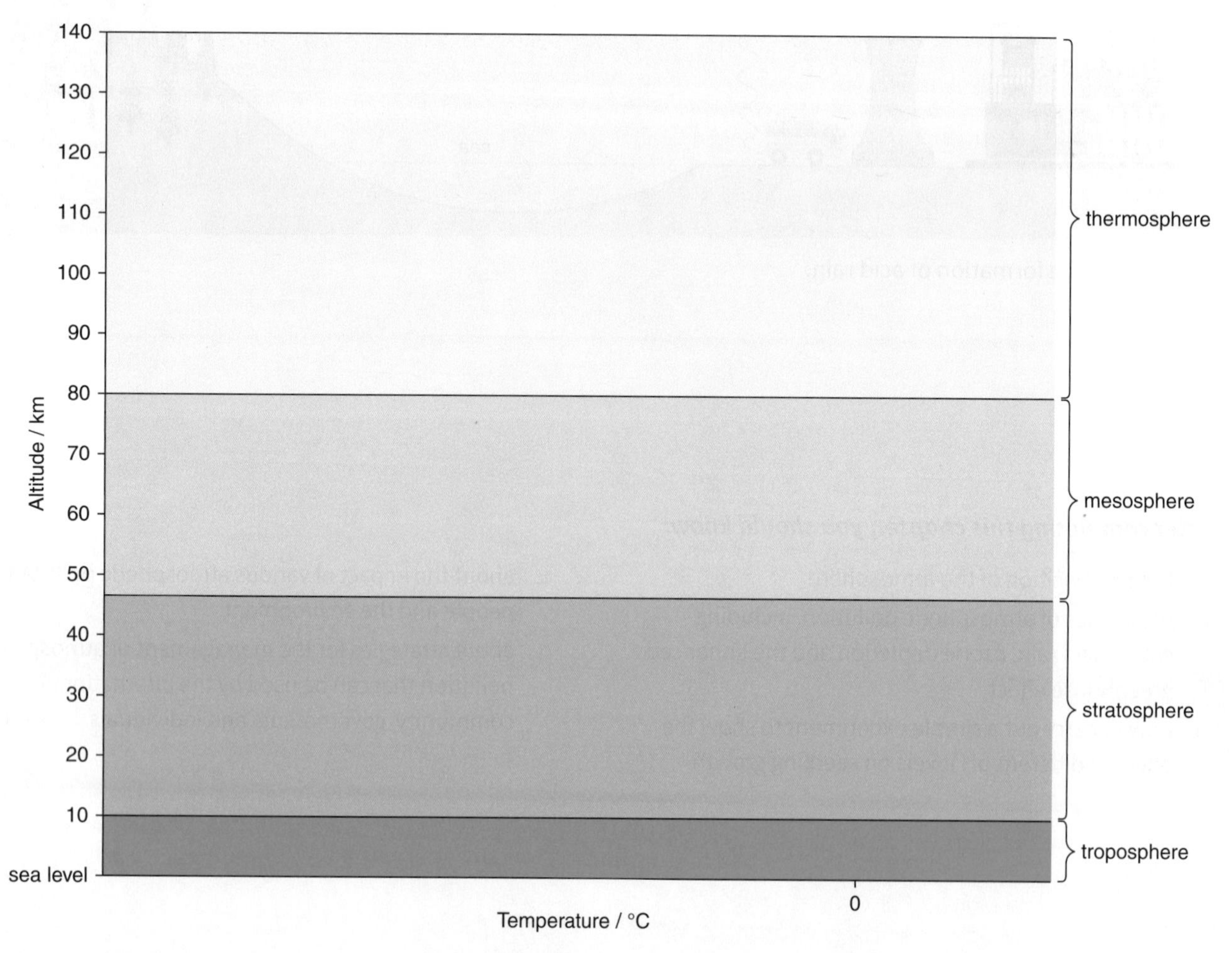

Figure 7.8 Graph showing temperature against altitude.

Copy the diagram and draw a line to represent the changes in temperature with increasing altitude in the atmosphere. On your diagram label a temperature inversion. **[2 marks]**

3 **a** Explain why there are high levels of air pollution in many urban areas. **[3 marks]**

b Describe three different problems caused by air pollution in urban areas. **[3 marks]**

c Describe three ways agriculture can cause air pollution. **[3 marks]**

4 Copy and complete Table 7.8, which shows the differences between ozone depletion and the enhanced greenhouse effect. **[12 marks]**

	Enhanced greenhouse effect	Ozone depletion
Type of radiation involved		
Atmospheric layer that absorbs the radiation		
Direction of radiation when absorbed		
Pollutant gas		
Action of pollutant gas		
International agreement to combat problem		

Table 7.8 A comparison of ozone depletion and the enhanced greenhouse effect.

5 Suggest four reasons why people are concerned about increases in global temperatures. **[4 marks]**

6 Why are international attempts to reduce atmospheric pollution not always successful? **[4 marks]**

Atmospheric pollution in the Arve valley, Chamonix, France

Figure 7.9 Atmospheric pollution in the Arve valley.

Chamonix is a long established, all-year-round tourist town. In winter the area is famous for skiing and in summer people visit for the scenery and activities such as walking, mountain biking, hang gliding and climbing. However, it also has some of the worst air quality in France (Figures 7.9–11). The daily limits set by the European Union (EU) for certain atmospheric pollutants are exceeded on a regular basis in the Arve valley. The pollution comes from three main sources.

1. Nitrogen dioxide generated by vehicle emissions. The main motorway link between France and Italy runs through the valley and up through the Mt Blanc tunnel, just south of Chamonix. Up to half a million trucks use the route each year and over 5 million people visit the valley annually. Skiing at Chamonix is split into five separate resorts, which means vehicle transport is needed to access the ski areas.
2. Particulates from domestic activity, such as heating from wood fires and burning green waste. The valley also contains a dense concentration of metal working industries that supply parts for the aviation and vehicle industry.
3. Benzo(*a*)pyrene(BaP) released from industry, vehicle exhausts and domestic wood and coal fires.

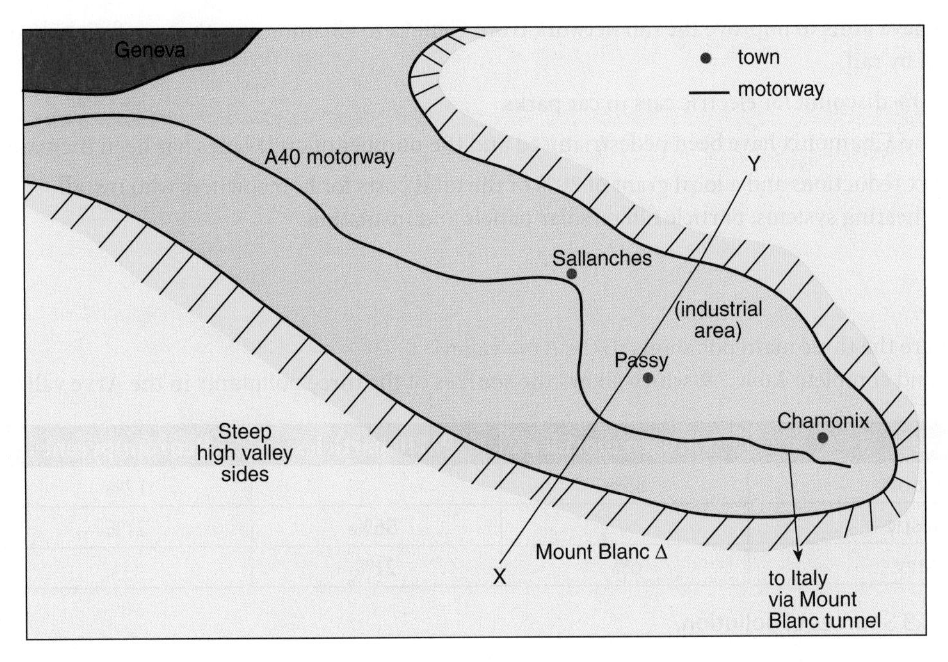

Figure 7.10 The Arve valley.

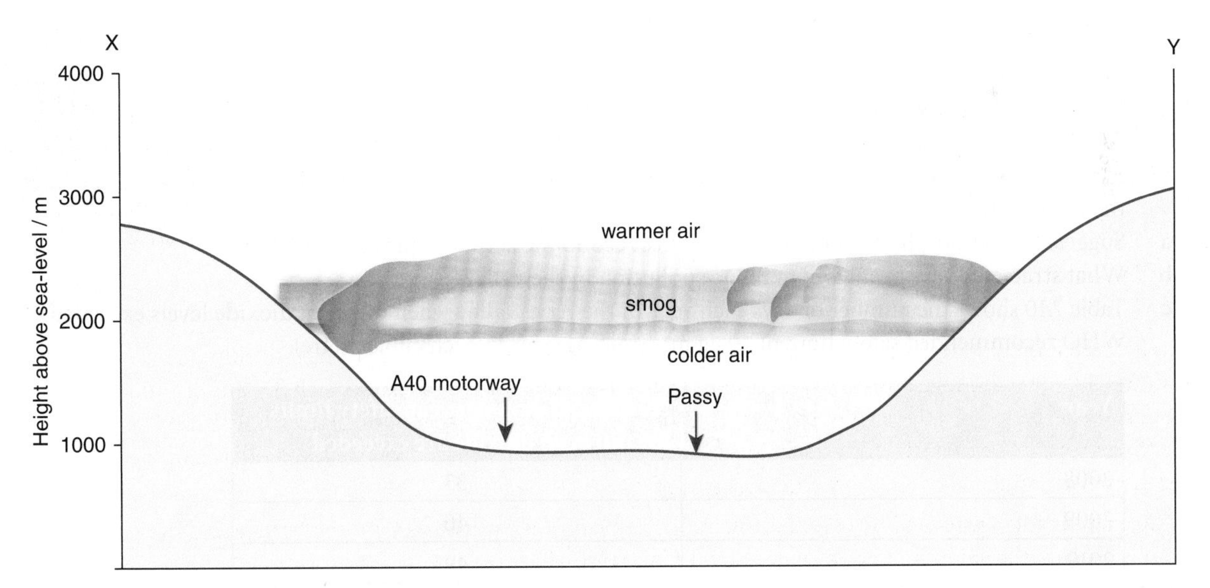

Figure 7.11 Cross-section through the Arve valley.

The pollution is made worse by the geography of the valley. When there is high pressure and low wind speeds, and during the night in winter, the steep valley sides trap the pollution, as shown in Figure 7.11. In the Arve valley, between 60 and 80 premature deaths are caused by air pollution each year, from a population of 155 000. The effects on human health caused by the pollution include increased eye irritations, breathing difficulties and asthma. The pollution can also lead to coronary illnesses, strokes and lung cancer. If people are ill they cannot work, so there is an economic loss involved as well as increased healthcare costs. Tourism can start to decline because visitors stay away.

A Plan of Protection of the Atmosphere was devised in 2010 to reduce pollution.

- Public transport is free in the valley and carries up to 3 million people each year. Many buses are electric.

- Grande Geneva aims to improve the rail network from Geneva to Chamonix with more freight being transported by rail.
- There is a 50% discount for electric cars in car parks.
- Some areas in Chamonix have been pedestrianised and the number of cycle lanes has been increased.
- There are tax reductions and a local grant of 20% of the total costs for homeowners who install sustainable heating systems, particle filters, solar panels and insulation.

Questions

1 a What are the three main pollutants in the Arve valley?

b Copy and complete Table 7.9, which shows the sources of the three pollutants in the Arve valley.

Source	Nitrogen dioxides	PM10 particles	Benzo(*a*)pyrene
Transport	85%		12%
Domestic		56%	21%
Industry	6%	21%	

Table 7.9 Sources of pollution.

c Using Table 7.9 match the three main pollutants to the main sources.
Nitrogen dioxide =
Particle PM10 =
Benzo(*a*)pyrene=

2 a Using Figure 7.11, what is the name of the phenomenon shown?

b At what height does this phenomenon occur in the valley?

c Explain how the geography of the valley makes pollution worse and why pollution is often worse in winter in the Arve valley.

3 a Suggest how atmospheric pollution might affect economic activities in the Arve valley.

b What strategies have been used to reduce pollution in the valley?

c Table 7.10 shows the number of days each year in the Arve valley when nitrogen dioxide levels exceeded the WHO recommended safety limit of 40 $\mu g\ m^{-3}$ (micrograms in each cubic metre).

Year	Number of days per year safety limits for nitrogen dioxide are exceeded
2008	33
2009	40
2010	49
2011	53
2012	57
2013	52
2014	49
2015	37

Table 7.10 Number of days per year safety limits for nitrogen dioxide are exceeded.

Draw a bar graph to show the data. Remember to label your axes and give your bar graph a title.

d Using evidence from your bar graph, how successful do you think the strategies used to reduce atmospheric pollution in the Arve valley have been?

Chapter 8
Human population

Learning outcomes

By the end of this chapter, you will be able to:

- explain that human populations grow in a similar way to those of other species
- describe changes in human populations in terms of birth rates, death rates and migration
- describe where in the world people live
- explain differences in population structure between different countries
- discuss the need to control human population growth, and the strategies that could be used to do this.

The population bomb

In the Philippines on 31 October 2011, Danica May Camacho was born and was designated by the United Nations (UN) as the world's 7 billionth human. A cake with '7B Philippines' written on it was made to commemorate this event. She also received a voucher for some free shoes.

Knowing that she actually was '7B' was not easy, with a daily global birth rate of over 350 000. On 12 October 1999, the UN secretary Kofi Annan visited Fatima Nevic, who had been proclaimed the 6 billionth human, but it is now thought that that particular milestone had already been passed a year before. However, these symbolic events are designed to focus attention on the growth of world population.

With 350 000 births, but only about 155 000 deaths, every day, the population is growing at about 73 million year^{-1}. Can the Earth support this rapid growth in population? Furthermore, the problem is greater than just the numbers involved. There is also the issue of wealth and advancements in technology that lead to people's continuous desire to be better off.

Estimates for the future world population vary. The highest estimate suggests 14 billion by 2100, while the lowest gives a figure of only 6 billion. Wealth is expected to double by 2020. Some believe that the impact of this rapid growth in size of the human population is already as significant as past major events, such as those that lead to the extinction of the dinosaurs 65 million years ago.

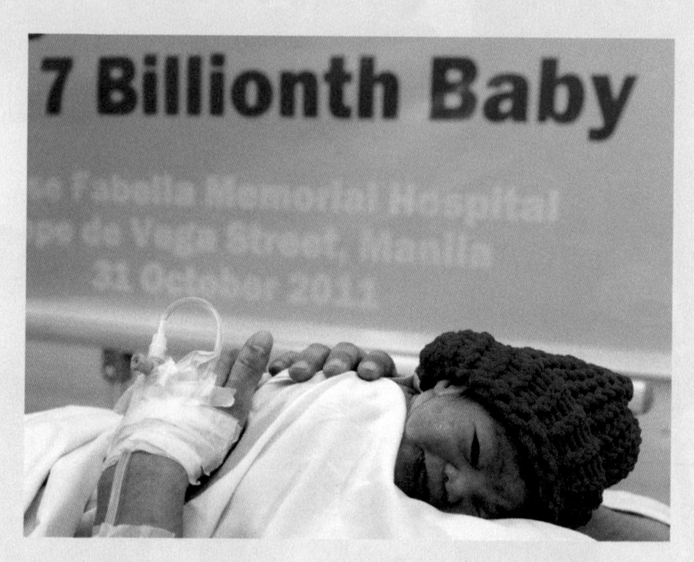

Figure 8.0 Danica May, the 7 billionth baby.

8.1 Changes in population size

Growth

With an organism that reproduces by splitting into two, you can easily see how **exponential growth** occurs. If you assume that the splitting into two happens every 30 min, then you can estimate **population** growth over time. After 10 h (600 min) of this doubling, the numbers will be as shown in Table 8.1.

Time/min	Population number
0	1
30	2
60	4
90	8
120	16
150	32
180	64
210	128
240	256
270	512
300	1024
330	2048
360	4096
390	8192
420	16 384
450	32 768
480	65 536
510	131 072
540	262 144
570	524 288
600	1 048 576

Table 8.1 Population growth.

KEY TERMS

Exponential growth: when the growth rate of a population increases rapidly over time

Population: all the organisms of one species living in a defined area

Figure 8.1 shows how this growth looks like as a graph.

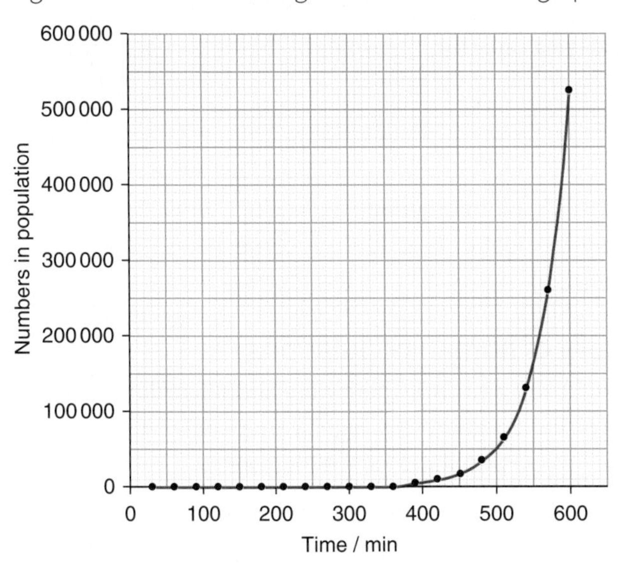

Figure 8.1 Population growth over 600 min at a division rate of once every 30 min.

Is this what population growth looks like in nature? This is not actually often been seen in nature, because most populations have reached their maximum size long before scientists start investigating them. One study followed 29 reindeer released onto St Matthew Island, near Alaska, in 1944. By 1963 there were 6000 reindeer. The graph of reindeer growth is shown in Figure 8.2.

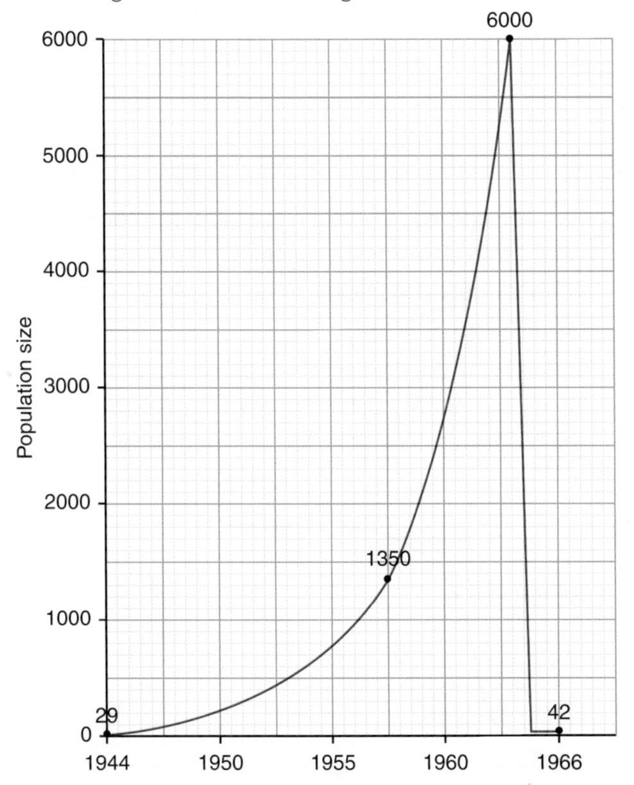

Figure 8.2 Change in population size of reindeer on St Matthew Island with a starting population of 29 in 1944.

The reindeer had no predators on the island, which meant they could undergo very rapid population growth, but in doing so they damaged the environment and their food supply. After 1963 the population crashed to almost none by 1966.

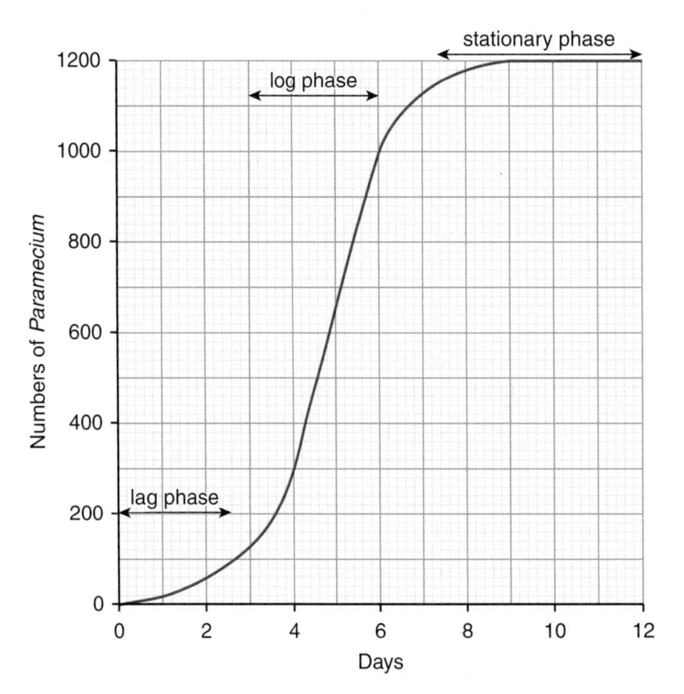

Figure 8.3 Growth in a laboratory study of a single-celled organism called *Paramecium.*

In the laboratory many studies have investigated population growth, and all show this pattern. In the ideal curve for the population growth of any organism, the **lag phase** happens as the organism becomes used to a new environment. The **log** or **exponential phase** occurs while all requirements are in superabundance. The **stationary phase** is when the population is in equilibrium and has reached the carrying capacity of the environment

Carrying capacity

All studied populations show an S-shaped curve with a number of identifiable stages, as seen in Figure 8.3.

KEY TERMS

Lag phase: the period of time in population growth when an organism is adapting to its new environment and growth is slow

Log growth: when the growth rate of a population increases rapidly over time

Stationary phase: when the growth of a population has slowed to zero

In nature, the environment can only provide a limited amount of resources such as food, shelter and nest sites. It is said to have a **carrying capacity**. The carrying capacity is the maximum population size of any species that the environment can support without damage. Populations are therefore expected to stop growing at some point. The *Paramecium* laboratory study shows this (Figure 8.3). In the *Paramecium* experiment, exponential growth started to slow down at about 6 days and population growth stopped altogether after just over 8 days. After population growth stopped there was neither growth nor decline. In nature, after the exponential growth phase the population fluctuates up and down rather than remaining steady as in laboratory examples.

Sometimes, if natural limits on population growth are not present, the population size might exceed the carrying capacity. The reindeer population shown in Figure 8.2 shows this. The consequences of exceeding the carrying capacity can be devastating. Humans have consistently managed to exceed the natural carrying capacity of virtually every area in which they live. This is because of our use of technology, especially that associated with agriculture. In 1798, Thomas Malthus predicted that the human population would actually grow faster than its food supply. This has not proved to be true, because the advances that have been made since then could not have been predicted by Malthus. Food production has grown much more rapidly than he expected, largely due to advances in plant breeding, the use of chemical fertilisers, improved irrigation and all kinds of mechanisation (see Section 3.4)

KEY TERM

Carrying capacity: the maximum size of a population that an environment can support in terms of food, water and other resources

History of human populations

About 10 000 years ago there were about 5 million people living as hunter-gatherers. Significant points in the growth of the human population since then are:

- about 6000 years ago humans started to grow crops and keep animals, which provided more food and allowed the population to begin to grow
- by the time the modern system of counting years started (just over 2000 years ago), the population was about 250 million
- it then took another 1800 years to reach 1 billion (1 billion = 1000 million)
- after this, growth became very rapid
- by 1930 it was 2 billion (just 130 years to double)
- by 1975 it was 4 billion (doubling in just 45 more years)
- at time of writing (2016) it is well over 7 billion, a rise of 3 billion in just 37 years.

SELF-ASSESSMENT QUESTIONS

8.1 Figure 8.4 shows the change in size of a human population and a small mammal population over time. Compare the two graphs and explain any differences you can see.

8.2 In 1937, in the Machakos Reserve in Kenya, much of the natural woodland was removed and replaced by sparse grassland. Livestock numbers were considered to be far in excess of the carrying capacity. Explain what is meant by 'livestock numbers were considered to be far in excess of the carrying capacity'.

8.3 Suggest why the population of a herbivore introduced on to an island may grow to a size at which it starts to damage its own food supply.

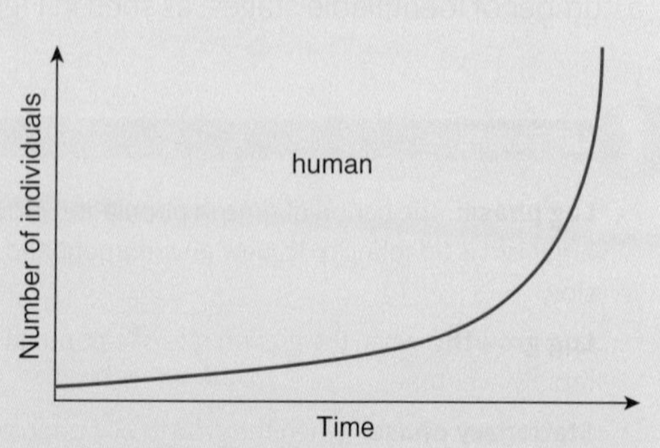

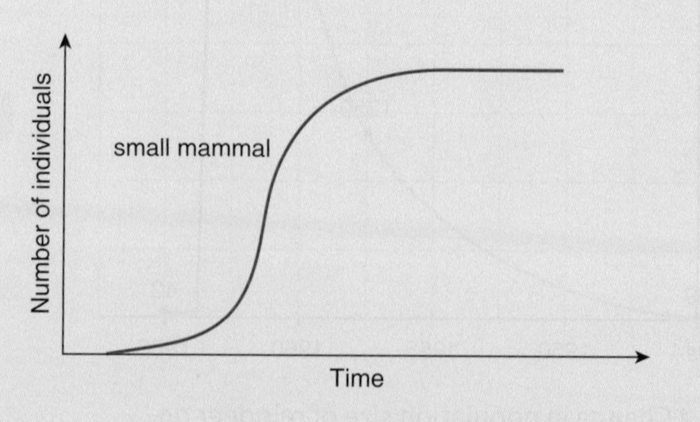

Figure 8.4 Two population growth curves.

This growth is shown in Figure 8.5.

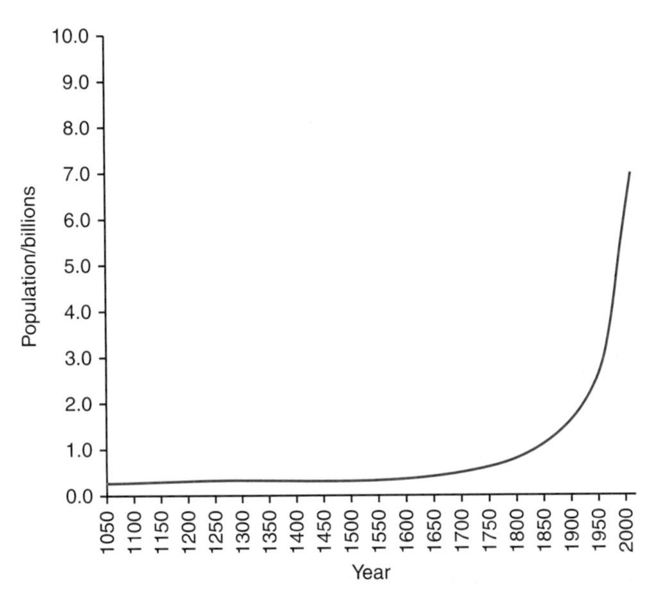

Figure 8.5 Human population growth from 1000 years ago to the present day.

The most striking feature of Figure 8.5 is how similar the pattern of growth in the human population is to that shown in animal studies. The only difference between this graph for humans and that for other animals is that there is no sign of levelling off. The similarities in growth curves suggest that future trends in human populations will be like those found in other animals. Human population growth is therefore expected to slow down and settle into an equilibrium, that is level off.

The UN predictions for the human population in 2100 based on all the evidence available are shown in Figure 8.6.

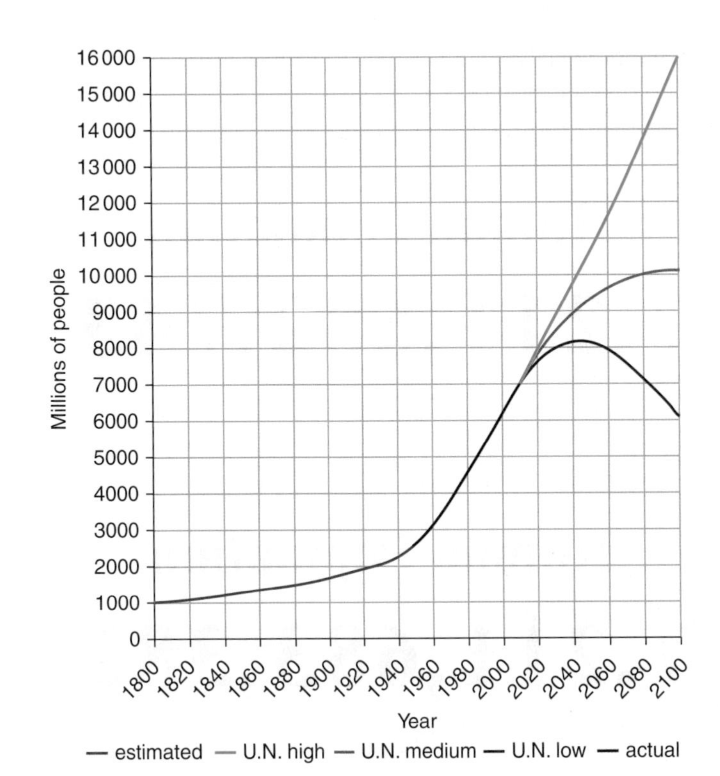

Figure 8.6 The three scenarios predicted by the UN for the world population in 2100.

Birth rate and death rate

Individuals are born and others die every day. In 2015 about four babies were being born every second, which is about 350 000 every day. This is the **birth rate**. The birth rate is partially balanced by the **death rate** which, in 2015, was about 150 000 every day. The difference between these two rates is the **rate of natural increase**. For the world in 2015 it was approximately:

$350\,000 - 150\,000 = 200\,000 \text{ day}^{-1}$

This is about 73 million extra people in a year.

> **KEY TERMS**
>
> **Birth rate:** the total number of live births over time
>
> **Death rate:** the total number of deaths over time
>
> **Rate of natural increase:** the birth rate minus the death rate

Figure 8.7 shows a 5 min period on the evening of 1 January 2016. It also shows a population prediction, made on 1 January 2016, of what the population will be on 1 January 2017. Other population clocks may show slightly different estimates.

Rates of increase are often expressed as a percentage. Using the figures given above, the rate of natural increase is:

$$\text{increase} = \frac{73\,000\,000}{7\,000\,000\,000} = 0.01 \times 100 = 1\% \text{ per annum}$$

The official figure in 2012 was 1.103%, with a birth rate of 1.915 and a death (mortality) rate of 0.812%.

Factors affecting birth rate and death rate

A wide range of factors affect birth rate:

- in countries with a high death rate for the very young (the infant mortality rate), birth rates are also high
- in agrarian (farming) economies of many less economically developed countries (LEDCs), more people are needed for manual labour, and so families tend to be larger
- in more economically developed countries (MEDCs) it is expensive to have children and pensions are provided by the state

- many social and political factors result in low use of birth control in LEDCs, whereas in MEDCs birth control is widely used, so both birth and death rates are lower.

Human Population

7,211,682,743

Un/Freeze

January 1, 2016 19:05:21 Do this time

Human Population

7,211,683,382

Un/Freeze

January 1, 2016 19:10:24 Do this time

Human Population

7,278,451,803

Un/Freeze

January 1, 2017 19:10:24 Do this time

Figure 8.7 Screenshots from the world population clock at http://galen.metapath.org/popclk.html (accessed July 2016).

Migration

Population growth (or decline) is the result of the balance between birth and death rates. Table 8.2 summarises the three possibilities.

When …	The population …
birth rate = death rate	stays the same
birth rate > death rate	grows
birth rate < death rate	declines

Table 8.2 Different population growth scenarios.

In real populations, however, the situation is more complicated because of the movement of people into and out of an area. This is called **migration**. Taking this into consideration, the population growth equation changes from:

population growth = birth rate – death rate

to:

population growth = (birth rate + immigration) – (death rate + emigration)

where:

- immigration means people entering an area from outside
- emigration means people leaving an area from inside.

Push and pull factors

How population change can affect the environment is considered later in the chapter. Here, how environmental factors can drive population change is discussed. The most common form of human movement, worldwide, is from rural areas to urban areas. This is largely because there are often more problems in rural areas that people want to move away from (**push factors**) and a perception, by people living in the countryside, that life will be better in the city (**pull factors**). There are other types of migration, including urban to rural, which is now more common in some parts of the world, for example in Botswana. Table 8.3 shows some of the major rural push factors and urban pull factors.

<table>
<tr><th>Push from rural to urban</th><th>Pull from rural to urban</th></tr>
<tr><td>Drought/famine</td><td>Good supplies of food whatever the weather</td></tr>
<tr><td>Poverty</td><td>Well-paid jobs</td></tr>
<tr><td>Poor links with outside world</td><td>Good roads</td></tr>
<tr><td>Poor services</td><td>Hospitals, schools, water, electricity</td></tr>
<tr><td>Work on the land only, subsistence</td><td>Factory, shop, office work for a wage</td></tr>
<tr><td>Desertification</td><td rowspan="3">no comparable pull factors</td></tr>
<tr><td>Sea-level rise</td></tr>
<tr><td>Seasonal weather events such as monsoons, cyclones, etc.</td></tr>
</table>

Table 8.3 Major rural push factors and urban pull factors.

KEY TERMS

Migration: the movement of people into (immigration) or out of (emigration) a region, country or other area

Push factors: factors that encourage people to move away from an area

Pull factors: factors that encourage people to move into an area

Density: the number of people living in a population in a defined area

Distribution: where populations of people either do or do not live

Some of the factors listed are directly environmental (for example drought, sea-level rise, weather events and desertification) or are induced by environmental change (for example famine). In this way environmental problems can cause population change, resulting in growth of the urban population as a result of immigration, and a fall in the rural population as a result of emigration. In the future it is likely that climate change (see Section 7.2) will lead to dramatic changes in the environment and thus create environmental migrants as a consequence.

SELF-ASSESSMENT QUESTIONS

8.4 Figure 8.8 shows the global human population over the last 2000 years.

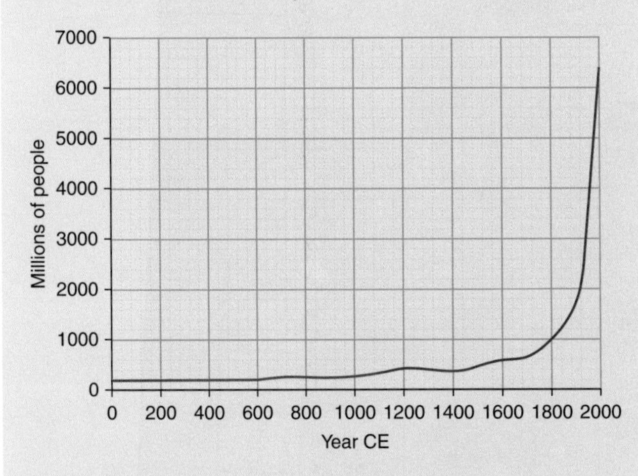

Figure 8.8 The human population of the world over the last 2000 years.

a Suggest possible reasons for the change in the population between common era (CE) 1200 and CE 1400.

b Calculate how many times bigger the population was in CE 2000 compared to its size in CE 1800.

c Explain why the population grew so rapidly between CE 1800 and CE 2000.

8.5 List two push and two pull factors that could lead to migration.

8.6 Explain why the population of an area may be declining even though the birth rate exceeds the death rate.

8.2 Human population distribution and density

Density

The **density** of a population is worked out by dividing the number of people living in a place by the area of that place, but it is important to remember that these figures just provide an average value. The population density of the USA at the 2013 census was estimated to be 33 km^{-2}. However, Figure 8.9 shows the current density in different regions of the country. In some parts of the USA the density is as high as 467 km^{-2} while it is as low as 2.3 km^{-2} in the state of Wyoming, for example. Figure 8.10 shows that even the figures given above hide a lot of variation too, with some parts of the state of Wyoming having densities of over 5 000 km^{-2} and others densities of less than 1 km^{-2}.

Across the world as a whole, the average density of humans is about 50 km^{-2} of land (that is, not counting the oceans). The highest density for any country or territory is that of Monaco at nearly 26 000 km^{-2}, while the lowest is that of Greenland at 0.03 km^{-2}. The population and population density of the ten most populous and the ten least populous countries in the world are shown in Table 8.4.

Distribution

The population **distribution** of an area is how the population is spread over that area. Worldwide, there are vast areas, such as deserts and mountains, where very few or no people live. On the other hand on coasts, especially where there is a port or near sources of fresh water, populations are very high. Figure 8.11 shows the areas of high population density around the world.

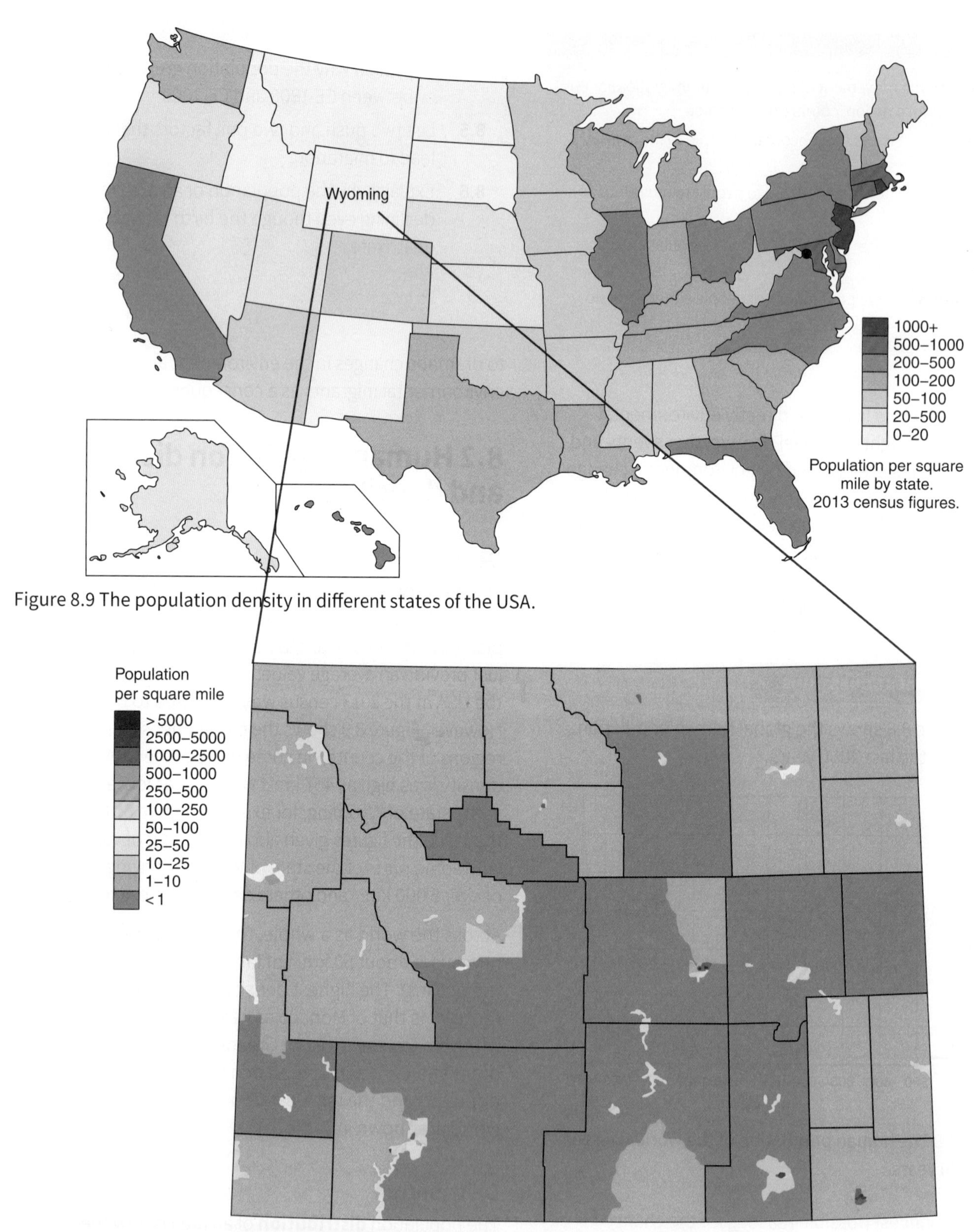

Figure 8.9 The population density in different states of the USA.

Figure 8.10 Population density in different regions of Wyoming, USA. Source: U.S. Census Bureau.

Population rank of 233	Country	Population	Density per km^{-2}	Density rank of 233
1	China	1 401 586 609	146.05	80
2	India	1 282 390 303	390.11	28
3	United States of America	325 127 634	33.77	176
4	Indonesia	255 708 785	134.26	83
5	Brazil	203 657 210	23.92	186
6	Pakistan	188 144 040	236.33	53
7	Nigeria	183 523 432	198.67	68
8	Bangladesh	160 411 249	1,113.98	12
9	Russian Federation	142 098 141	8.32	215
10	Japan	126 818 019	335.61	39
224	Wallis and Futuna Islands	13 153	65.77	142
225	Nauru	10 122	482	23
226	Tuvalu	9916	381.39	31
227	Saint Pierre and Miquelon	6049	25	184
228	Montserrat	5176	50.75	153
229	Saint Helena	4124	33.8	175
230	Falkland Islands (Malvinas)	3058	0.25	232
231	Niue	1273	4.9	219
232	Tokelau	1250	104.17	101
233	Vatican City	800	1818.18	7

Table 8.4 Countries ranked by population as at 2015 (source http://statisticstimes.com/population/countries-by-population-density.php) (accessed July 2016).

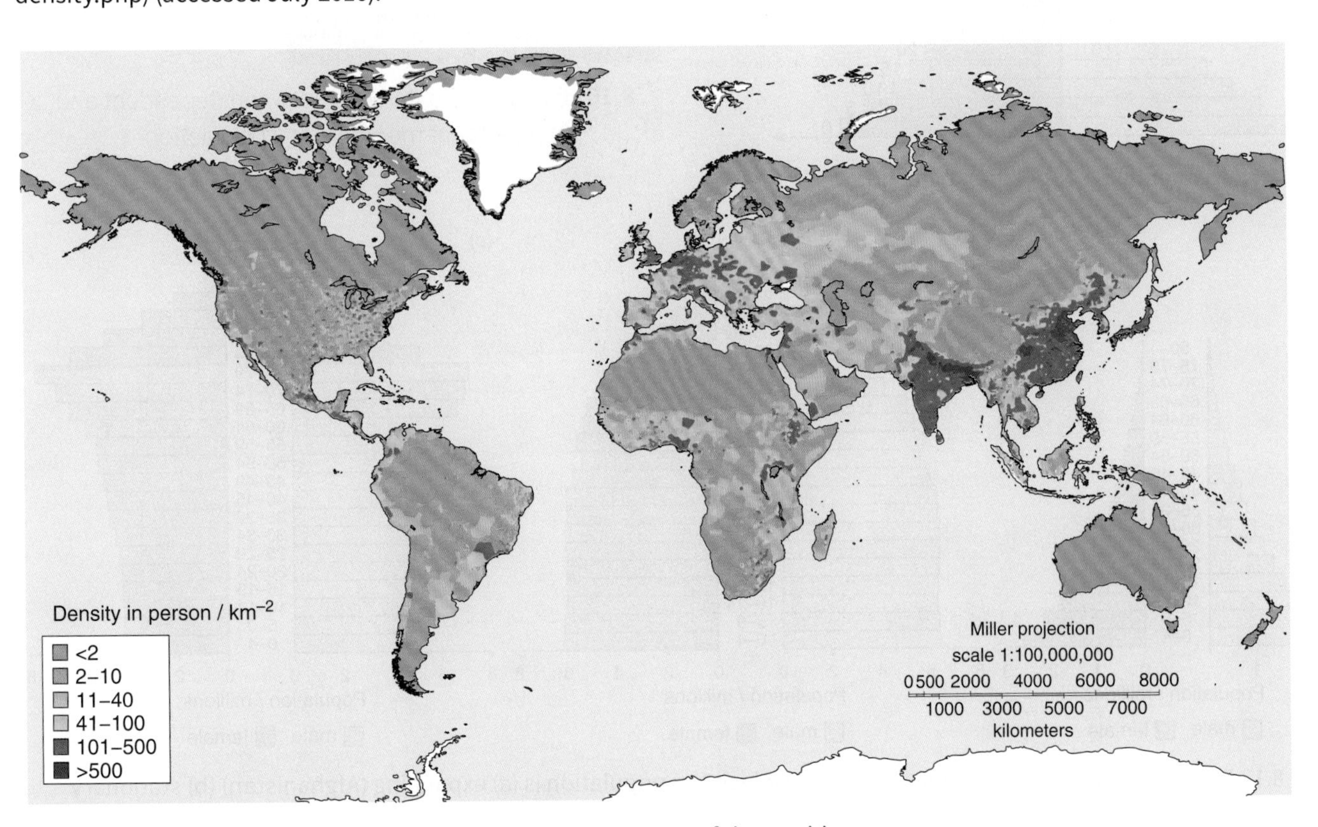

Figure 8.11 The human population density in different regions of the world.

> **SELF-ASSESSMENT QUESTIONS**
>
> **8.7** Explain the difference between population density and population size.
>
> **8.8** Use Table 8.4 to answer the following questions.
>
> **a** Calculate the area in km² of the USA.
>
> **b** Which country in the world has the lowest population?
>
> **8.9** Explain why Table 8.4 shows the world's most populous country but not the one with the most dense population.

8.3 Population structure

In addition to their size, populations have a structure. The structure describes how the population is made up in terms of age and sex, and can be displayed in a diagram called a **population** or **age pyramid**. Figure 8.12 shows an example, with males and females, one on each side, and 5 year age groups going vertically.

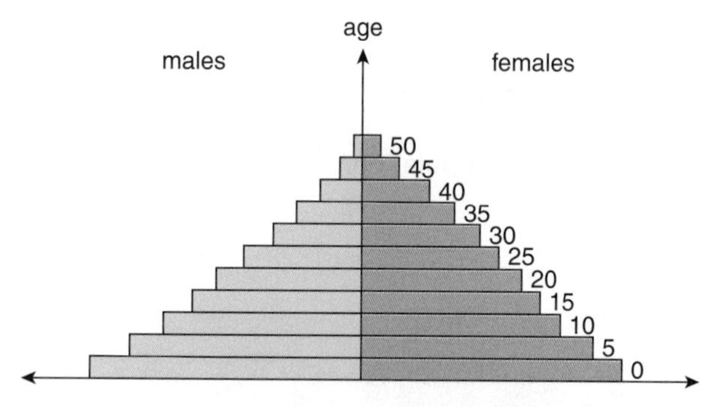

Figure 8.12 A generalised population pyramid.

Population pyramids fall into three main categories: expanding (or young) populations, stationary populations and contracting (or old) populations (Figure 8.13). Afghanistan has a typical pyramid for a LEDC, with a high proportion of young people because of a high birth rate. The USA has a population that is almost stationary, with a rectangular shape, except at the top when older people die. In Japan, the population is declining because of low birth rates, and its pyramid is top-heavy because of low death rates.

Looking at a pyramid, from bottom to top, it can be divided conveniently into three groups. The young, up to about school age (14–16 years old, depending on country), the 'middle aged' (about 16–65) and then the old, over 65. In practical terms the young and old are **dependent**, whereas the middle aged are **independent** and working. The young use money, in the form of taxes paid by the middle aged, for education. These taxes support the old as well.

The differences in age structure present different challenges for governments of LEDCs with young populations and MEDCs with older populations. In LEDCs with a young population, provision of school places for the many children who will be reaching school age is likely to be a priority. In MEDCs, the ageing population will put a strain on hospital and care-home places, making those a priority. Money from taxes paid by the middle aged may need to be used to address these priorities.

> **SELF-ASSESSMENT QUESTIONS**
>
> **8.10** Explain the difference between dependent and independent members of a population.

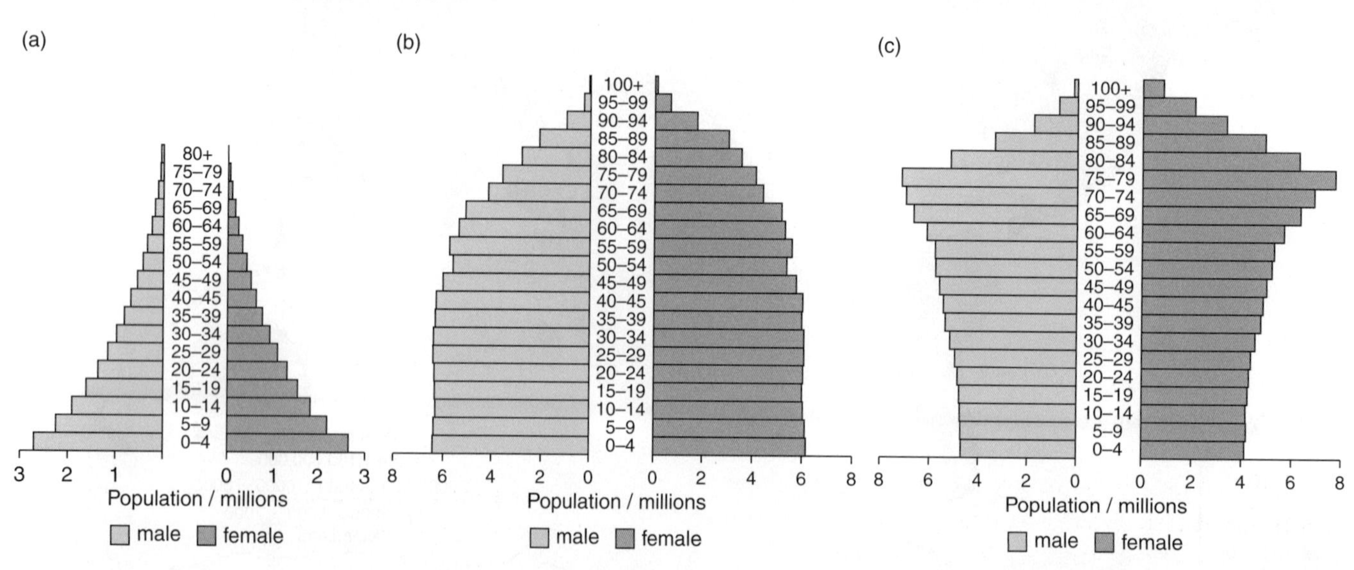

Figure 8.13 Population pyramids showing countries in which the population is (a) expanding (Afghanistan) (b) stationary (USA) and (c) declining (Japan).

8.11 Draw a sketch to show the shape of a population pyramid in a:

a LEDC

b MEDC.

8.12 Explain why a population pyramid is unlikely to be exactly the same on either sides of the central axis.

8.13 Sketch the shape of a population pyramid for:

a a country in which the population is expanding

b a country in which the population is stationary.

8.4 Managing human populations

Human population growth can be seen as a problem. Usually, the concerns are about the impact of the increasing numbers of humans on global resources and the environment, as discussed elsewhere (for example Sections 3.5 and 7.3).

However, there are cases where population growth is thought to be too slow. There have been many attempts at various levels of society, for example in cities or countries, to manage population size.

Family planning

Family planning is the strategy a couple uses to plan how many and when to have children. Although family planning is sometimes taken to just mean **contraception**, other methods are involved. In its widest sense family planning also includes sterilisation and abortion. The application of assisted reproductive techniques (*in vitro* fertilisation or IVF) can also be thought of as a form of family planning. Although family planning is usually associated with the choices couples make, governments can intervene in many ways. Some governments provide free contraception to all couples, while in other nations contraception may be generally unavailable.

Improved health and education

An obvious effect of improved health care and education would seem to be a rise in the population, because it is likely to lower the death rate. However, this is often not the case. Education makes people more aware of methods that can be used to limit family size. In addition, educated women may plan a career as well as having children, the former frequently limiting how many children are born. Education can also lead to a tendency for later marriage and thus later child bearing. Health care, especially of young under the age of 5, tends to reduce growth as well. When infant mortality is high, the response is for couples to have many children. When it is reduced by better health care and sanitation, the trend goes the other way.

National population policies

In countries where the population is declining, the government may try to remedy the situation with a **pronatalist policy**. Where the population is becoming too large, **antinatalist policies** may be used.

Pronatalist policies

In France, the government had concerns that the country's population was declining and would be unable to sustain itself. It decided to try and raise the birth rate by encouraging couples to have more than two children, and so increase the population. Parents are paid the equivalent of the minimum wage for a year after they have a third child. In addition, they enjoy subsidised train fares, pay less tax the more children they have, and subsidised day-care. The birth rate has now increased to be one of the highest in Europe.

Antinatalist policies

A more widespread problem outside the MEDCs is a population that is increasing too fast. In such countries, antinatalist policies are often used. These policies take many forms, from quite weak measures such as the provision of family planning, contraceptives and education, to laws encouraging couples to only have one child. Some countries have no population policies at all and their birth rates are usually very high.

KEY TERMS

Population pyramid: a diagram that shows the proportion of the population that is male and female in different age groups (usually 5 year intervals)

Age pyramid: a diagram that shows the proportion of the population that is male and/or female in different age groups (usually 5 year intervals)

Dependent: those people in the population who are not economically active (working) and so rely on the those who are working for their needs

Independent: those people in the population who are economically active (working)

Family planning: methods used by a couple to decide when and how many children to have, may be practised by couples and encouraged by governments

Contraception: a range of methods used to prevent pregnancy

Pronatalist policy: a national or regional policy that aims to encourage couples to have children

Antinatalist policy: a national or regional policy that aims to discourage couples from having children

CASE STUDY

The one-child policy in China

By the early 1970s the population of China had reached almost 1 billion. The response of the government was quite simple. Couples who had only one child were rewarded with money and other benefits. Those who had more children than this received no such rewards and, in many cases, were fined. It is estimated that about 300 million fewer Chinese are alive today (2016) than there would have been if the policy had not been implemented. Predictions suggest that the population of China will begin to fall in about 2030.

It can be concluded that the policy has been successful, but there have been many problems. In rural areas, people rely on young family members to work in the fields. This meant that the one-child policy had to be relaxed in such areas. As a result the plan to limit the population to 1.2 billion was not achieved. There will also be problems in the future, when one person may have both parents and four grandparents to look after alone. In the past most older people lived with their family, but it is likely to become more common for older people to live in some type of nursing home.

The natural preference for boys in rural communities has meant that many girls were abandoned and have been raised as orphans. Men now outnumber women in China by many millions.

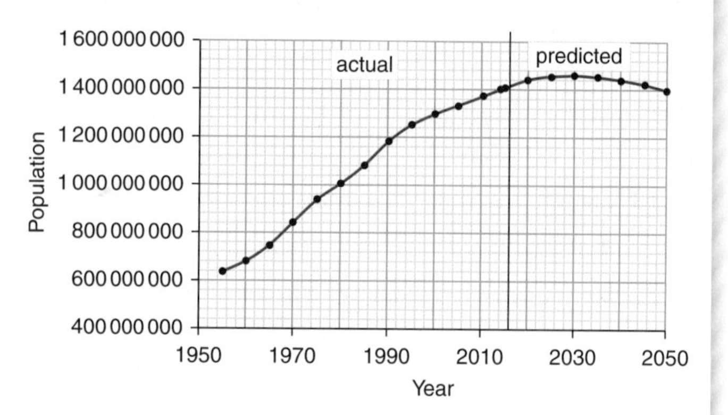

Figure 8.14 The actual and predicted growth of the population of China from 1955 until 2050.

Questions

1 Use the information in Figure 8.14 to:
   a calculate the predicted increase in the population of China from 2020 until it starts to fall
   b calculate what the population of China would have been in 2015 if the one-child policy had not been implemented.

2 In late 2015 it was announced that the one-child policy was to be abolished and people would be allowed to have two children. Suggest three reasons why you think this was done.

3 Suggest why the one-child policy may have been more successful in China than it would have been in other countries.

PRACTICAL ACTIVITY 8.1

Seven billion and counting

The world population is assumed to have reached 7 billion in October 2011. Danica May Camacho of the Philippines was designated as the 7 billionth human.

Materials

- Access to the internet
- A3 or larger sheet of paper
- Marker pens

Method

- If you go to the BBC website (www.cambridge.org/links/scspenv4002) you can find out what number in the world's population you were when you were born.
- On a large sheet of paper (at least A3), draw the world population size from 1500 to the present day. You can get help with this on the website.
- Mark your birth number on the world population time line.
- Choose five historical world events and five events from your country's history. Mark these events on your poster.

Question

1 Estimate the world's population at the time your chosen historical events happened. For example, when the Second World War ended, the world population was about 2 300 000 000.

Summary

After completing this chapter, you should know:

- how populations grow in nature and that the human population is no exception to this pattern
- what limits the size of natural populations
- the pattern of human population growth over the last 10 000 years
- what the birth and death rates are and what factors affect them
- that population size can change because of immigration and emigration, and the push and pull factors involved
- what the density of a population is (as opposed to its size)
- how human populations are distributed across the globe
- how populations are structured in relation to gender and age
- how and why human populations are managed.

End-of-chapter questions

1 Why does the birth rate need to be above 2 in order to maintain human populations at a constant size? **[2 marks]**

2 Distinguish between the density and the distribution of a population. **[3 marks]**

3 Explain why Russia is the world's 9th largest country by population size but 215th out of 233 for density. **[2 marks]**

4 Explain why Tuvalu is the world's 226th country for population size but has a density that places it at 31st. **[2 marks]**

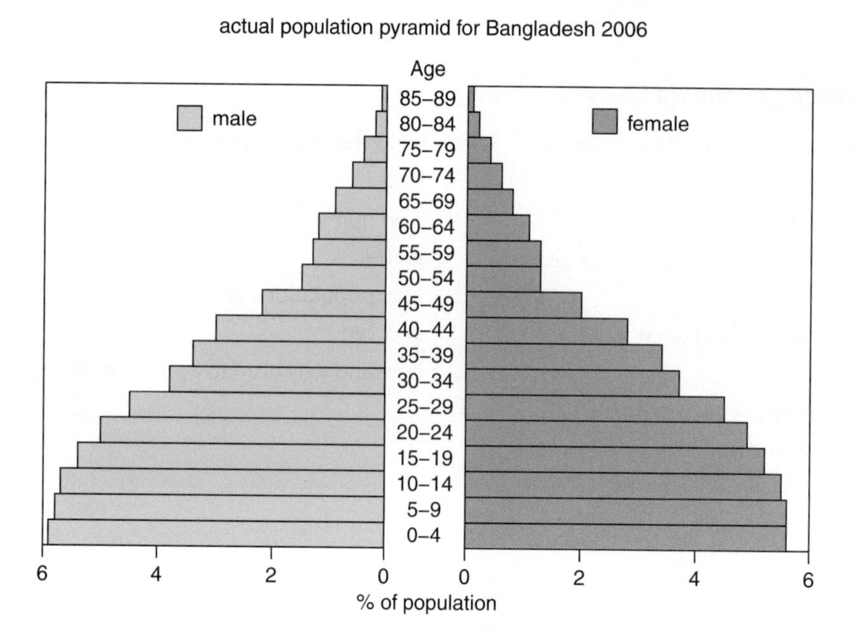

Figure 8.15 Population pyramids for Bangladesh

5 Figure 8.15 shows the population pyramid for Bangladesh in 2006 and the predicted shape for 2026.

a What do the two pyramids show about the Bangladeshi population? **[4 marks]**

b What strategies might the Bangladeshi government use to prepare for the changes predicted for 2026? **[3 marks]**

EXTENDED CASE STUDY

Population control in Kerala

In the Indian state of Kerala, the birth rate is about 1.7 children per woman whereas in the rest of India it is 2.6. Life expectancy is 74, compared to 64 in the rest of the country. It is believed that these differences are almost entirely due to the education of women in the state. Generally, each year of female education in a population reduces the birth rate by 10%. In addition, education to secondary level leads to later marriages. In Kerala, the average age of women getting married is 21, whereas it is 17 in the rest of India.

Between 1951 and 2009 the birth rate in Kerala dropped from 5.6 children per woman to only 1.7. The replacement rate is 2.05, which means the population is declining. It is thought that the provision of family planning would not have achieved such a dramatic fall had it not been for the high literacy rate of the women. In India, female literacy is about 50% and in men it is 86%. In Kerala, the literacy rate is 94% overall, with a 96% rate for men and 92% for women.

Infant mortality is also very low, at 12 per 1000 births in Kerala, compared with 50 per 1000 for the rest of India. It is thought that education has benefited the women in Kerala because it has:

- led to more job opportunities for them
- taught them about contraceptives, where to get them and how to use them
- given them more status within the family and more control over how many children to have.

Unfortunately, this is not all good news for Kerala. With the decline in birth rate the population is beginning to age. The population pyramids for 1991 and projected for 2021 are shown in Figure 8.16.

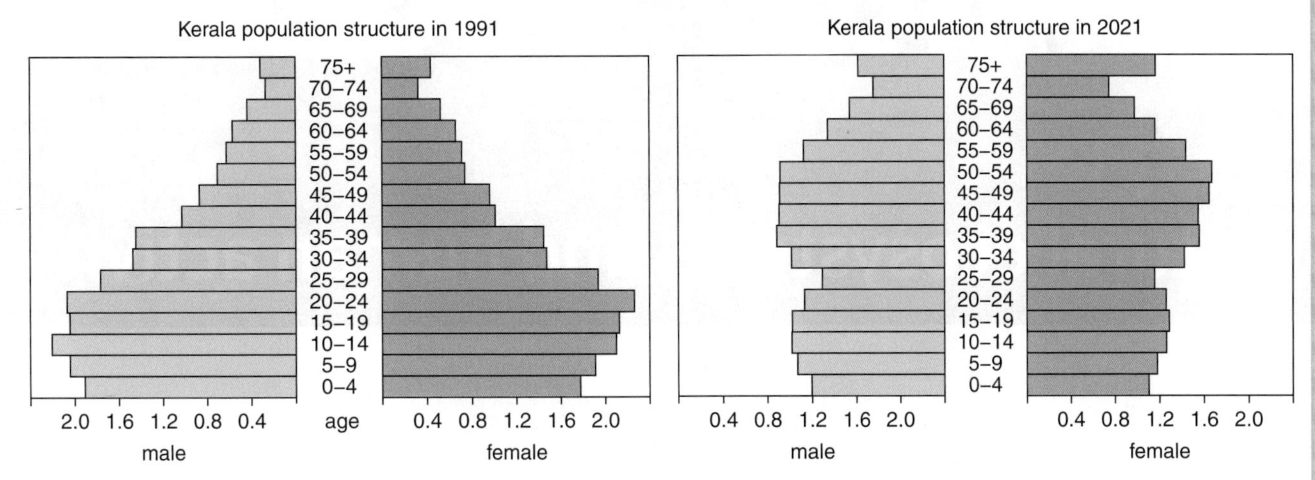

Figure 8.16 The predicted changes in the age structure of the population of Kerala, India.

Questions

1. Use the information in the case study to draw bar charts comparing life expectancy and birth rate between India in general and Kerala.
2. In the same way draw a diagram to show a comparison of literacy rates in men and women between Kerala and India in general.
3. Explain three ways in which the provision of education for women can help to lower birth rates.
4. Explain why later marriage lowers birth rate.
5. a. Calculate the percentage fall in birth rate in Kerala and in India as a whole between 1951 and 2009. Assume the birth rate was 5.6 in both regions in 1951.
   b. How many years of female education would these falls in birth rate take if that were the only factor?
6. Compare the population pyramids for Kerala in 1991 and 2021.
7. Describe the new problems that will arise as a result of the change in age structure in Kerala between 1991 and 2021.

Chapter 9
Natural ecosystems and human activity

Learning outcomes

By the end of this chapter, you will be able to:

- explain which physical factors affect and are affected by the living things in an ecosystem
- explain some of the relationships between living things within an ecosystem
- explain how energy flows along food chains and webs within an ecosystem
- use pyramids of numbers and pyramids of energy to describe food chains
- describe photosynthesis and respiration as key processes in plants
- explain how nutrients cycle within an ecosystem in general, and for carbon in particular
- describe how habitats are lost and the consequences of their loss
- explain why forests are removed and the consequences of their removal
- explain why we need strategies for the sustainable management of forests
- estimate biodiversity using a variety of methods together with random and systematic sampling
- explain the advantages and disadvantages of various strategies for conserving ecosystems and the species within them.

The sixth extinction?

Life on Earth arose more than 3000 million years ago. The number of species that have gone extinct over that vast period of time far outnumber those alive today. So extinction is normal: species are only expected to exist for a geologically short period of time. Geological evidence suggests that, on average, mammalian species exist for only about 1 million years. The so-called background level of extinction of species is about 10 $year^{-1}$. One of the greatest dilemmas for humans in the early 21st century is the current extinction rate, which stands, according to some estimates, at 27 000 species $year^{-1}$! The world's species have experienced five mass extinctions in the past. The largest of these was the Permian extinction, or Great Dying, 280 million years ago, when 96% of all species extant then were lost. All life on Earth now is descended from the 4% of species that survived the Permian extinction. However, even if the Permian was the biggest, the Cretaceous–Tertiary extinction of 65 million years ago is the most well-known. This is when the dinosaurs, which had existed for millions of years, were wiped out.

So, why are we worried if mass extinctions are part of the natural process? The possible sixth extinction event, which we are living through, is different in a number of ways. First, the rate is much faster than any of the previous five. It is estimated that we could have lost as many as 67% of all species by 2100, compared with the number that existed at the end of the 19th century. That is a huge loss in just 200 years. The other five great extinction events took place over many thousands of years.

In this chapter you will learn why there are so many species and how they interact with each other and the non-living environment. You will find out about the threats to these species, and the places in which they live. Finally, you will study strategies for conserving species and their environment.

Figure 9.0 Life in the sea in the Devonian period, 419 to 358 million years ago. The trilobites, eurypterids, blastoids, crinoids, caryocrinites and graptolite dictyonemans are all extinct.

9.1 The ecosystem

An **ecosystem** is defined as all the living things (**biotic** components) together with all the non-living things (**abiotic** components) in an area. These biotic and abiotic components interact with each other.

Ecosystem structure

The living things in an ecosystem can be described at a number of different levels.

Populations are made up of all the individuals of the same species in an area. Examples of populations include all the frogs in a pond, all the drongos in a forest or all the elephants in a national park.

Communities are made up of all the species characteristic of a particular ecosystem. Examples include all the different species of animal in the Arctic tundra or all the plants in the Arctic tundra, representing the animal and plant communities respectively.

KEY TERMS

Ecosystem: all the living things (biotic components) together with all the non-living things (abiotic components) in an area

Biotic: living components of the environment that may affect other living things

Abiotic: non-living components of the environment that may affect living things

Population: all the organisms of one species living in a defined area

Community: a group of populations of different species that live together in an area and interact with each other

Living things are found in a **habitat** within the ecosystem. A habitat is the place where the population of an organism lives, finds food and reproduces. Within its habitat, the population of an organism has a particular role in terms of its interactions with other species and its effect on the environment. This is called its **niche**. The fact that there are so many niches to fill in the ecosystems of the world is the reason why there are so many species. This may seem to be something of a paradox. For example, all plants make food from sunlight. However, plants that can make food in a desert climate are very different from those that do the same thing on the floor of a rainforest, which are different again from those that do it in the canopy of the same forest.

So, an ecosystem consists of communities of living things that live in single-species populations in particular habitats where they perform particular functions within their niche.

Abiotic factors

Most of the concepts above are about the living things (biotic factors), but habitats and niches include non-living or abiotic factors too. These affect living things and are affected by them. The major abiotic factors are describe below.

Temperature

Temperature is usually expressed as degrees centigrade (°C). Living things have a range of temperatures within which they can survive. For example, species of flatworms from the genus *Planaria* are distributed in mountain streams according to how hot or cold the water is. One planarian species lives high up in the mountains where the water is colder, and another lives lower down where the water is warmer.

Humidity

Humidity is a measure of how damp the air is: how much water vapour it holds. It is usually expressed as relative humidity (RH). RH expresses the humidity as a percentage of the amount of water vapour the air could hold if fully saturated. This can range from 0% in dry desert environments to 100% in humid rainforests. Some living things simply cannot survive in dry air, for example many species of fungi.

Water

Water is essential for all life. It is a raw material for photosynthesis and a medium for chemical reactions. However, living things can survive without water in liquid form. For example, some beetles that live in stored products like flour only use the water they make themselves during respiration.

Plants obtain water from the soil and the water content of soil can be a very important factor in determining exactly where a plant species lives. For example, cacti are adapted to survive in soil with very little water. Those plants that live in soil that is saturated with water (waterlogged), such as rushes and rice, have roots that are adapted to function in low oxygen conditions.

Oxygen

The oxygen level is nearly always about 20% of the gas in air, the rest of the gas in air is mainly nitrogen. However, the absolute quantity decreases as altitude increases. At the top of a high mountain, there is much less oxygen than at sea-level. In water, the amount of oxygen is usually expressed as parts per million (ppm).

Oxygen is not very soluble in water so all aquatic organisms have special adaptations to get enough, for example gills in fish. Plants with their roots in waterlogged soil have adaptations to get oxygen to the roots. For example, rushes have a spongy stem that allows oxygen to move down from the air to the roots.

Salinity

Salinity, how salty something is, is measured as parts per million (ppm) or parts per thousand (ppt) of salt, or as a concentration (for example milligrams^{-1} litre).

This is mainly a factor that affects aquatic animals. All marine species live in water that has 35 ppt of salt, whereas in fresh water there is none. Water with a salinity that is less than 35 ppt, but more than zero, is referred to as **brackish water**.

In some cases, the water in soil is saline, for example in salt marshes. Plants that live in saline water are adapted in various ways, for example mangroves secrete the excess salt from their leaves. Salty soil can arise as a result of poor irrigation practices (see Section 3.4) and this can be a serious problem for farmers trying to grow crops.

Light

Light is measured in various ways and expressed as lumens. It is essential for photosynthesis and therefore nearly all living things depend on it. With no light there will

KEY TERMS

Habitat: the place within an ecosystem where an organism lives

Niche: the role of a species within the ecosystem

Brackish water: water that is salty but not as salty as seawater be no food. However, some plants are adapted to living in low light levels and can support a community of animals.

pH

pH is a measure of how acid or alkaline water, or an aqueous solution, is. It is expressed as a number without units on the pH scale (see Section 4.8). The pH of the sea is relatively stable but pH can vary a lot in fresh water. Decomposing leaves, for example, add humic acid to the water, reducing the pH to less than 7. The pH of soil water is a very important factor for plants. Some plants are acid loving, requiring a soil with an acidic water content. Other plants cannot survive in the acidic soils at all.

SELF-ASSESSMENT QUESTIONS

9.1 A species of plant is found growing in a narrow zone at the edge of woodland bordering an open field. Suggest two biotic and two abiotic factors that may be involved in restricting it to this zone.

9.2 Copy and complete the following passage using these words:

population species community niche habitat

An ecosystem contains a number of ____________ of animals and plants each of which has a ___________, lives in a particular ____________ and occupies a __________. They all live together in a __________.

Ecosystem processes

A key feature of the way in which the living world works is that organisms interact with each other. The best way to see this is in a diagram called a **food chain**. Green plants make food in a process called **photosynthesis** and are called **producers**. Animals, called **herbivores**, eat the plants and animals called **carnivores** eat the herbivores. Both these kinds of animals are called consumers, one consuming (=eating) plants and the other consuming animals. A plant-eating consumer is a **primary consumer** and animal-eating one is a **secondary consumer**. If an animal eats an animal that itself eats an animal, it is called a **tertiary consumer**. If the animal (or other organism, for example fungi) consumes dead bodies of plants or animals it is called a **decomposer**. This simple relationship can be shown in a food chain.

producers → herbivores (primary consumers) →
1st carnivores (secondary consumers, predators) →
2nd carnivores (tertiary consumers, also predators)

However, if you look at a real example, you will see that the full picture is not so simple. In a garden there might be plants with leaves that, when they fall to the ground, are eaten by earthworms. In turn the earthworm is eaten by a bird, which could be eaten by a snake.

leaves → earthworm → bird → snake

However, the leaf might also be eaten by a slug or a woodlouse, the worm by a fox or a shrew, and the bird by a fox as well. If you put all of these relationships, and more, into a diagram you will have a much more accurate picture of real life. Such a diagram is called a **food web** (Figure 9.1).

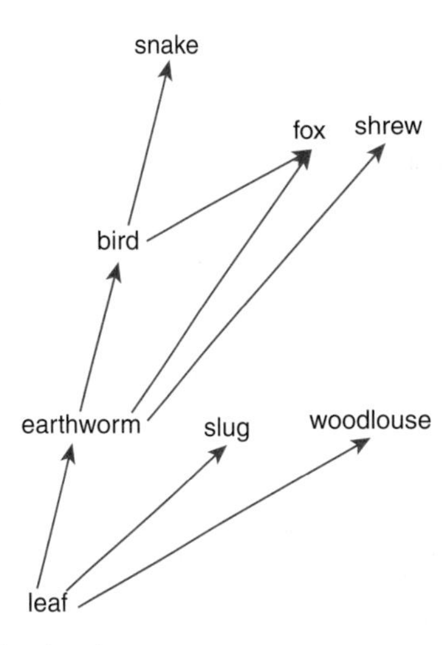

Figure 9.1 A food web.

KEY TERMS

Food chain: a diagram showing the relationship between a single producer and primary, secondary and tertiary consumers

Photosynthesis: the process by which plants or plant-like organisms make glucose in the form of carbohydrate from carbon dioxide and water using energy from sunlight

Producers: organisms within an ecosystem that can carry out photosynthesis

Herbivore: another name for primary consumer

Carnivore: another name for secondary and tertiary consumers

Primary consumers: organisms within an ecosystem that derive their food from producers

Secondary consumers: organisms within an ecosystem that derive their food from primary consumers

Tertiary consumers: organisms within an ecosystem that derive their food from secondary consumers

Decomposers: organisms within an ecosystem that derive their food from the bodies of dead organisms

Food web: a diagram showing the relationship between all (or most) of the producers, primary, secondary and tertiary consumers in an ecosystem

Any change in one part of the food web can cause changes in any other part. So, if the weather is poor and plants do not grow so well, everything will be affected. If snake numbers fall because they are killed by humans, this could lead to an increase in the numbers of birds, which might then eat more earthworms, causing their numbers to fall. It is often impossible to predict what one change in one part of a food web might lead to elsewhere.

Even this is not likely to be the whole story: what eats the woodlice, the slugs and the shrews? What else do the snakes, foxes, birds and earthworms eat? Real food webs are very complicated. A way of simplifying this information is to think of the numbers of producers and consumers found in the ecosystem. In a lake, millions of tiny microscopic plants are being fed on by thousands of tiny animals. In turn, these are eaten by hundreds of small fish, which in their turn are eaten by dozens of large fish. Standing by the side of the lake might be a few herons and egrets, eating the big fish. This information can be represented in a diagram called a **pyramid of numbers** (Figure 9.2). The pyramid shape reflects the loss of energy at each **trophic** (feeding) **level**.

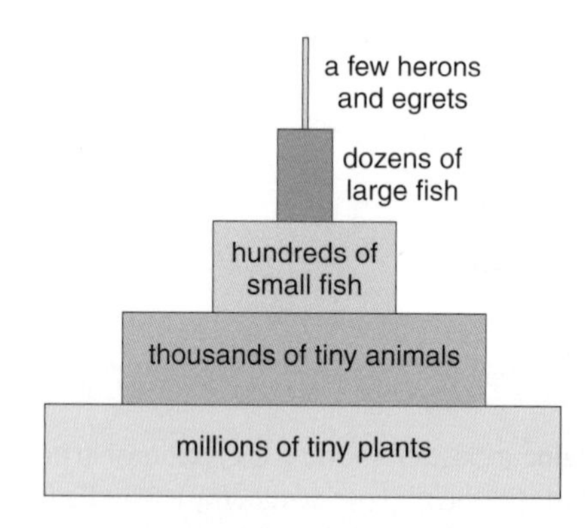

Figure 9.2 A pyramid of numbers for a lake ecosystem.

Photosynthesis

Plants trap energy in the form of light from the Sun in a process called photosynthesis. Photosynthesis is a complicated process but can be summarised as if it was a single-step chemical reaction:

$$\text{carbon dioxide} + \text{water} \xrightarrow[\text{chlorophyll}]{\text{light}} \text{glucose} + \text{oxygen}$$

Glucose is a sugar used by plants in the process of respiration to release energy, and is also converted by the plant to make other substances it needs, such as starch, cellulose, proteins and many more. Some of these substances are very important for humans as medicines.

Other elements (minerals) from the soil, such as nitrogen, are needed to form some of the substances, such as proteins, but in every case, chemical energy remains stored in the substance.

Plants obtain the carbon dioxide (CO_2) from the atmosphere through pores in their leaves (stomata). They obtain the water from the soil through their roots. A green pigment in the leaves called **chlorophyll** absorbs the light. The light energy is used to split the water into hydrogen and oxygen. The hydrogen is added to carbon dioxide to make glucose. The oxygen not used in **respiration** is given off to the atmosphere.

Interactions between living things – biotic interactions

Living things interact in a variety of ways, including those discussed below.

Competition

Living things need a range of resources from the environment, including other living things and non-living components like water and oxygen. Many more young are produced than will survive, so there is often competition for the resources. Those individuals that are least well adapted to the current conditions will die earlier or fail to reproduce.

Predation

When one animal eats another it is called a predator. Examples of familiar predators include tigers and lions. However, there are also many predators in the insect world and in the sea. Many beetles eat earthworms and insect larvae, and marine predators range from small fish to the great white shark.

Pollination

The male gametes (sex cells) of many animals (including humans) swim through an aqueous (watery) environment to the female gamete (egg cell). However, flowering plants do not reproduce like this. The male sex cells are found in a structure called a **pollen grain**, made in the anther. The pollen grain is

KEY TERMS

Pyramid of numbers: a diagram that represents the numbers of organisms at each feeding (trophic) level in an ecosystem by a horizontal bar whose length is proportional to the numbers at that level

Trophic level: a feeding level within a food chain or web

Chlorophyll: the green pigment in plants that traps light energy

Respiration: the process by which living things release energy from food to carry out the processes of life, such as movement

Pollen grain: the structure in plants that contains the male sex cell, it is carried to the female organ by pollination either blown about by the wind (as in many grasses and trees) or carried by insects, bees, birds and mammals. The anther is in the flower, which attracts the animals with bright colours, scent and the production of nectar. The pollen grain lands on the stigma of another flower and sends out a tube. This tube grows down to where the female gamete (egg) is. Here, the egg is fertilised and from this an embryo in a seed, egg, develops. This embryo can grow into a new plant.

SELF-ASSESSMENT QUESTIONS

9.3 The following questions refer to the drawing of a woodland ecosystem in Figure 9.3.

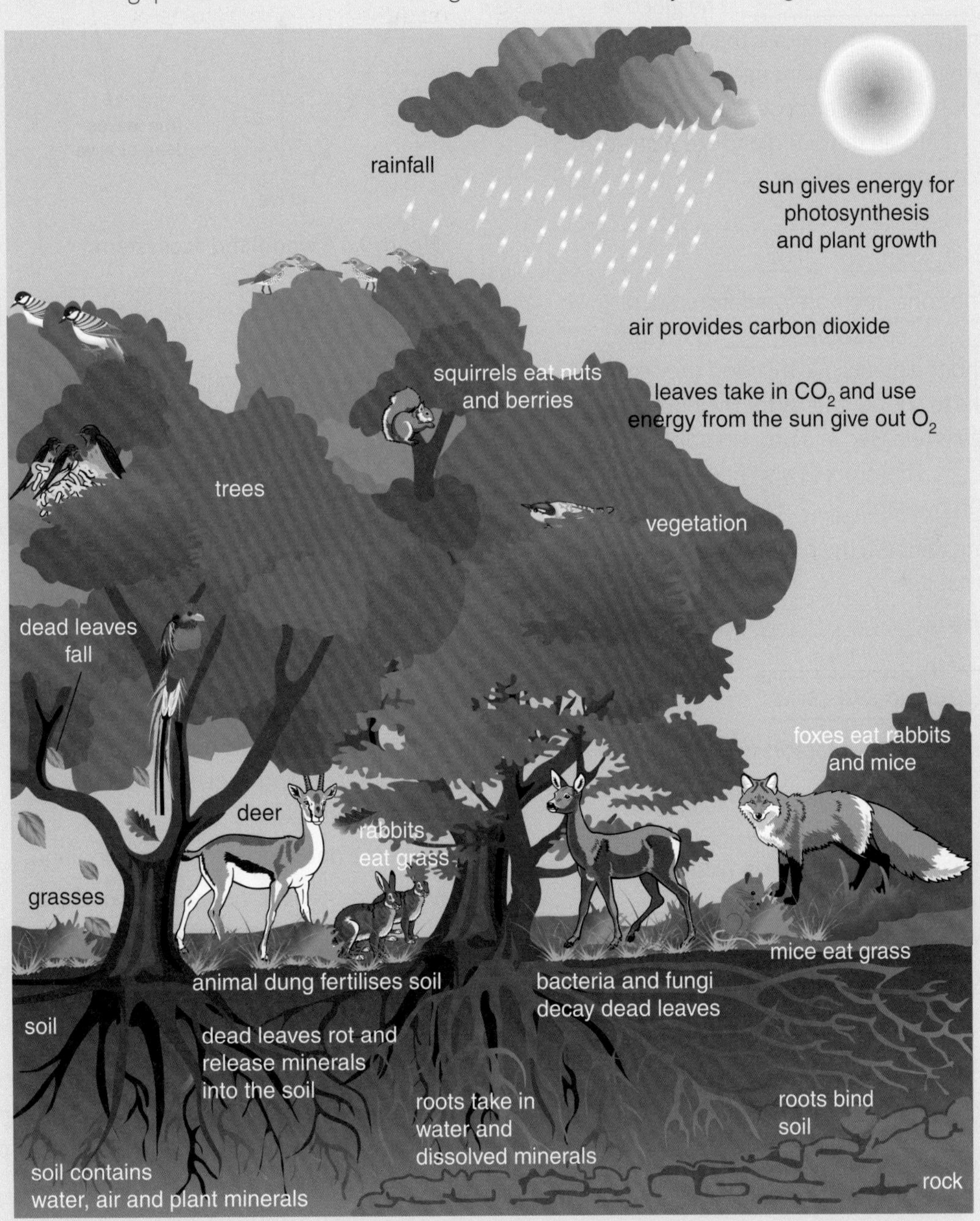

Figure 9.3 A woodland ecosystem.

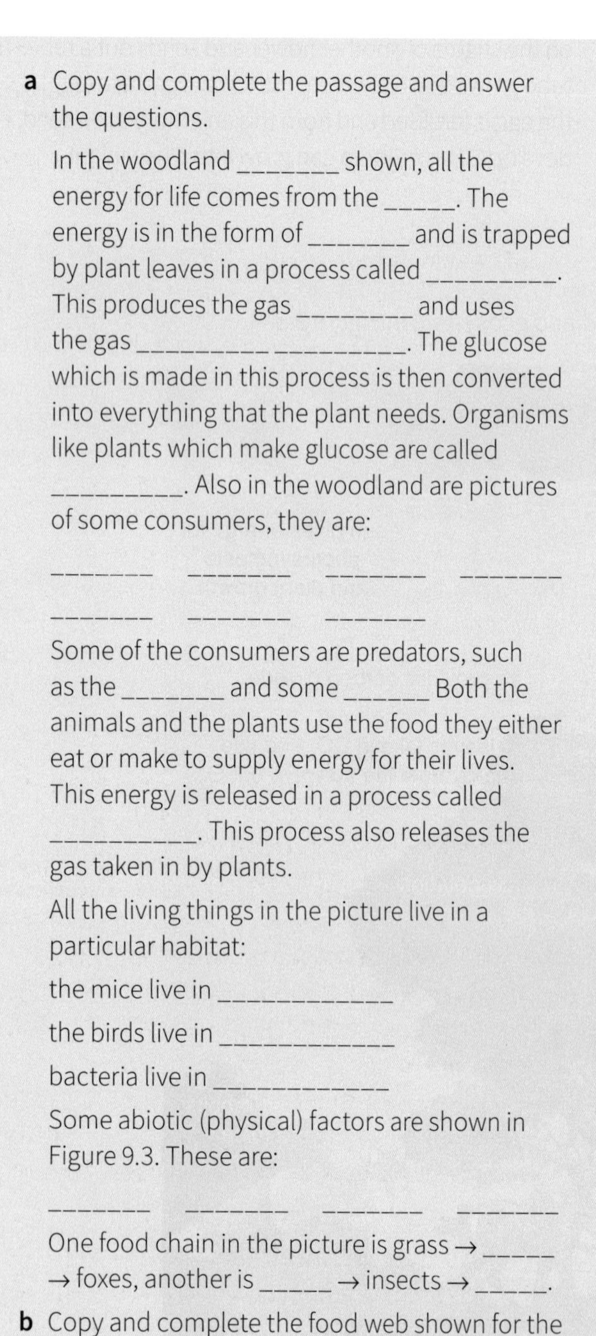

a Copy and complete the passage and answer the questions.

In the woodland _______ shown, all the energy for life comes from the _____. The energy is in the form of _______ and is trapped by plant leaves in a process called _________. This produces the gas ________ and uses the gas _________ _________. The glucose which is made in this process is then converted into everything that the plant needs. Organisms like plants which make glucose are called _________. Also in the woodland are pictures of some consumers, they are:

_______ _______ _______ _______

_______ _______ _______

Some of the consumers are predators, such as the _______ and some ______ Both the animals and the plants use the food they either eat or make to supply energy for their lives. This energy is released in a process called __________. This process also releases the gas taken in by plants.

All the living things in the picture live in a particular habitat:

the mice live in ____________

the birds live in ____________

bacteria live in ____________

Some abiotic (physical) factors are shown in Figure 9.3. These are:

_______ _______ _______ _______

One food chain in the picture is grass → _____ → foxes, another is _____ → insects → _____.

b Copy and complete the food web shown for the whole woodland in Figure 9.4.

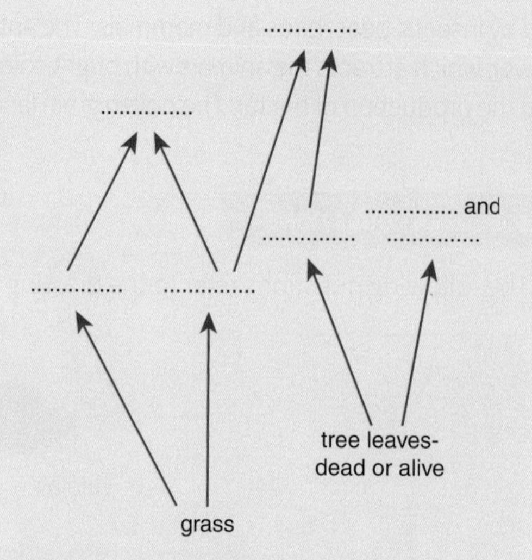

Figure 9.4 A woodland ecosystem.

The one animal not shown on this web is the __________.

There are five populations of animals in this woodland: deer, rabbits, foxes, squirrels and mice. In addition there will be many populations of insects and birds of different species. All the animals in the woodland live in a __________.

c **i** Choose two animal species from the woodland shown and say what you think their niche is.

ii Name two animal species that might be in competition with each other in this woodland and suggest what they are competing for.

iii Name one predator in the woodland.

iv Name one living thing in the woodland that needs to be pollinated and suggest a pollinator, also shown in this woodland picture.

Energy flows and nutrient cycles

When a consumer eats a plant it gets two things:

- chemical energy from the starch, simple sugars and other compounds
- various materials, such as nitrogen, that are also present in these substances.

Consumers use some of the chemical energy for their own life processes, converting it into heat. This heat is given off to the environment and lost to living things. However, the minerals are not lost because, when consumers die, their bodies break down. The minerals in the dead bodies are released and become available again to living things. It is important to know this difference: energy flows through ecosystems but minerals cycle round ecosystems.

Energy flow

How much of the energy in a plant is available to a consumer? The plant needs some energy for its own life processes. It gets this energy not from the light it traps but from the chemical energy it has stored. Plants store light energy as chemical energy in the sugars and other substances they make. A plant gets the energy that it needs for its own life processes from a process called respiration. The overall equation for respiration is:

glucose + oxygen → carbon dioxide + water + (energy)

Note that in the equation, energy is placed in brackets because it is not a substance.

Glucose and oxygen are used up during respiration and water and carbon dioxide are produced as waste products.

The energy is used for the processes the plant needs (for example transporting food and making proteins) and given off to the environment as heat. Only the energy that is left in the material a plant does not use is available to a consumer. This is about 10% of the energy that was fixed from sunlight by the plant. This energy flow can be shown in a simple diagram, as in Figure 9.5a. The same relationship occurs at the next trophic level, shown in Figure 9.5b. Together, the two parts of Figure 9.5 form a **pyramid of energy** (Figure 9.6).

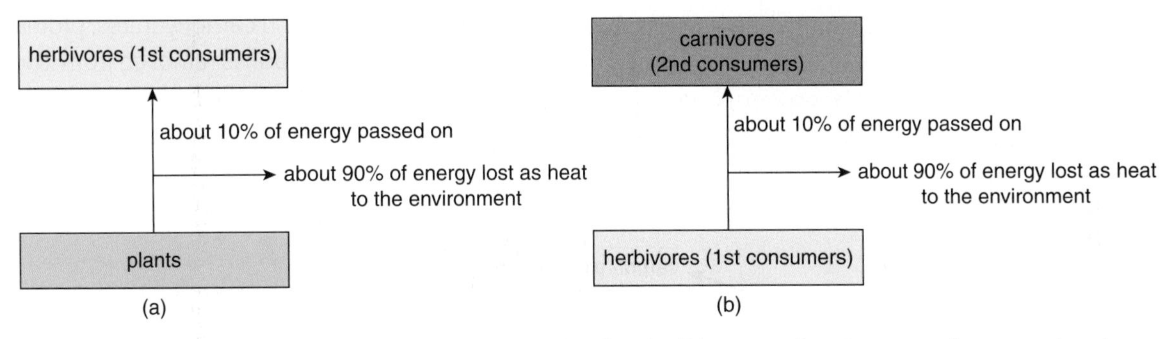

Figure 9.5 (a) Energy flow between the first and second trophic levels. (b) Energy flow between the second and third trophic levels.

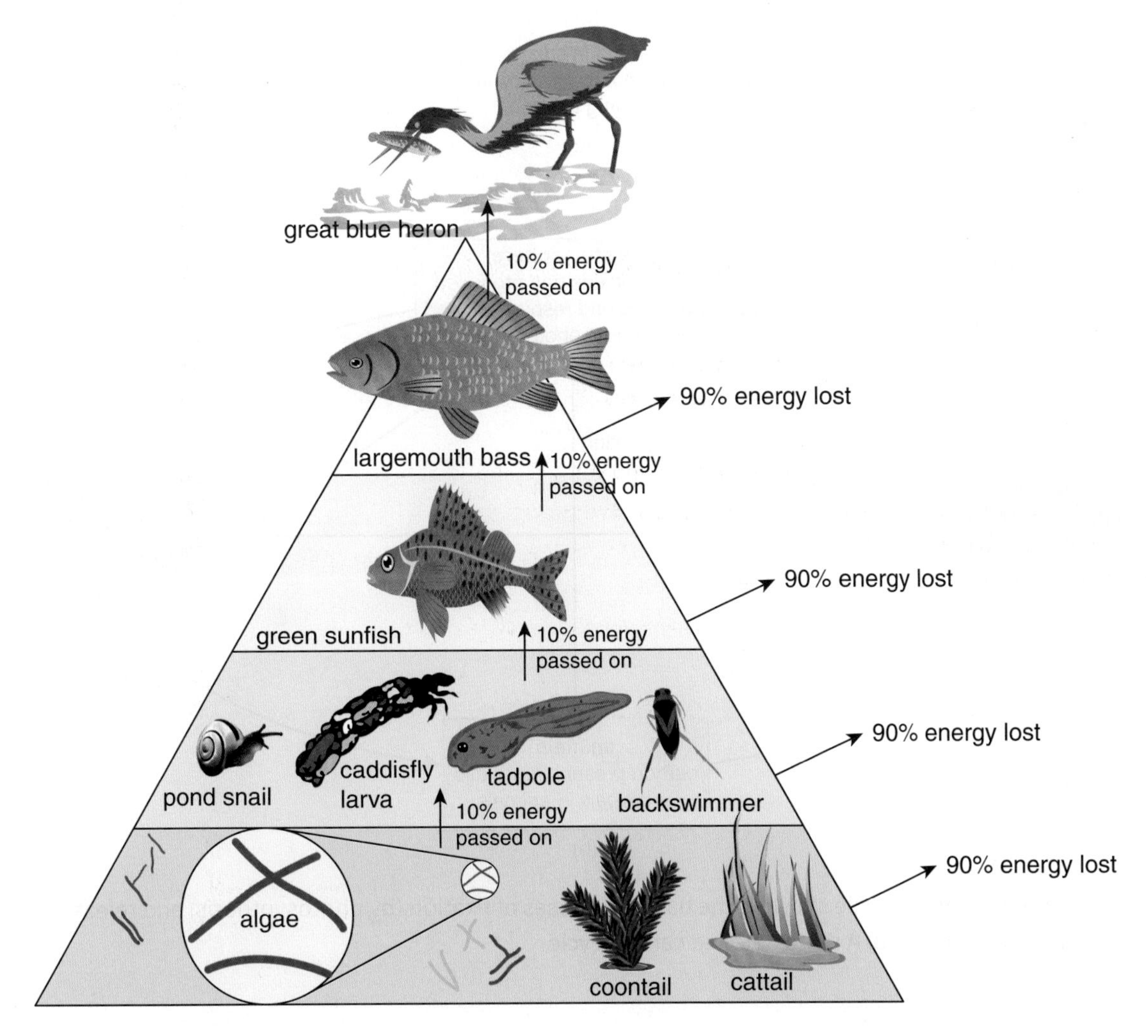

Figure 9.6 A pyramid of energy for a lake.

So, after just two steps the amount of energy available to a consumer is 10% of 10% of that available from the Sun, which is only 1%. After three steps it is only 0.1%. This explains why food chains never have more than four, or sometimes five, links: there is just not enough energy left to support another trophic level. The quantity of energy present in each level, and flowing between them, is measured in kilojoules (kJ).

Mineral cycles

At the same time as a consumer is obtaining energy from the level below, it is acquiring the minerals that it needs. These include carbon, oxygen, sulfur, phosphorus and nitrogen, among many others. All cycles have the same basic pattern (Figure 9.7).

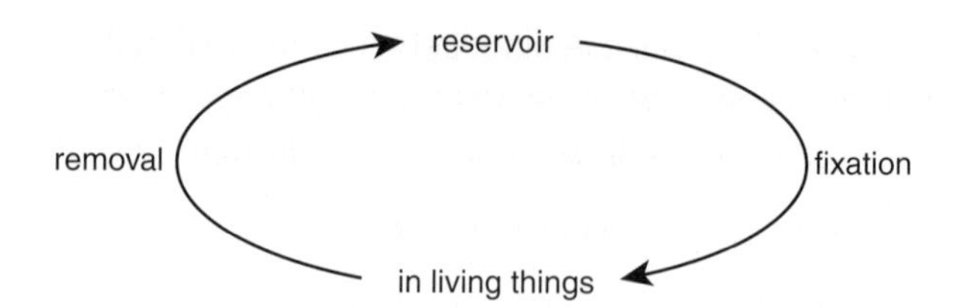

Figure 9.7 General diagram of mineral cycles.

For carbon, the reservoir is carbon dioxide in the atmosphere. Fixation is by photosynthesis. Carbon is found within living things in carbohydrates, proteins, fats and other chemicals. Carbon is removed from living things by respiration, which returns the carbon dioxide to the atmosphere (Figure 9.8).

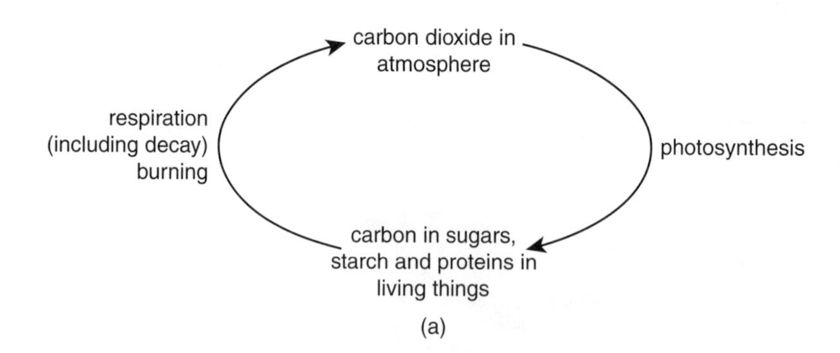

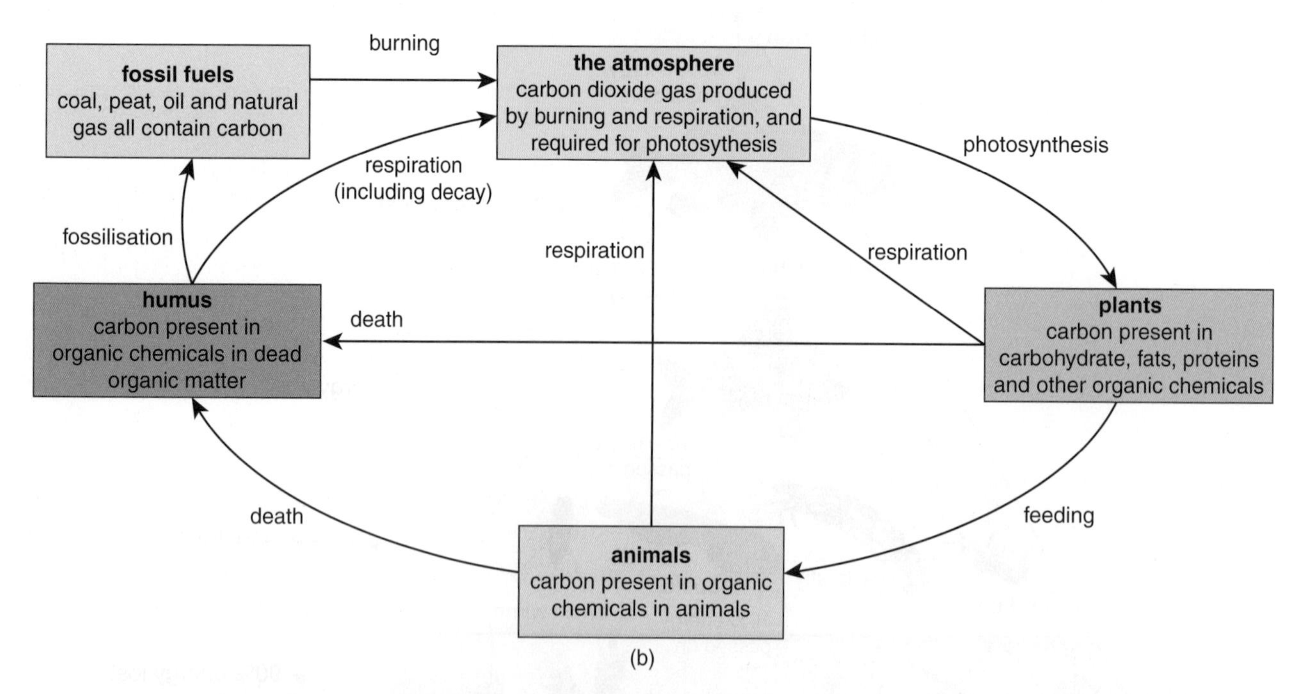

Figure 9.8 (a) A simplified carbon cycle showing the basic processes of fixation (by photosynthesis) and release (by respiration, decay and burning). (b) A more detailed carbon cycle.

Respiration occurs in all living things, including microorganisms that break down dead organisms. When microorganisms break down dead organisms, the process is called decay or decomposition. Carbon dioxide is also returned to the atmosphere by burning (combustion). This is important in relation to the removal of forest, when much of the forest material that is cut down is burnt.

SELF-ASSESSMENT QUESTIONS

9.4 State the location of the reservoir of carbon in the carbon cycle.

9.5 State two examples of substances in living things that contain carbon.

9.6 Compare and contrast respiration and decay.

9.7 In a study of the organisms in a food web it was found that 3000 kJ of energy were present in the herbivores, 450 kJ in the carnivores and 40 000 kJ in the plants.

a Sketch a pyramid of energy for this food web.

b Calculate the percentage efficiency of energy transfer from:

i plants to herbivores

ii herbivores to carnivores.

Show your working for both parts of the question.

9.2 Estimating biodiversity in ecosystems

Biodiversity refers to all the species within an ecosystem as well as all the variation within a species (genetic diversity) and the many different ecosystems in an area. There are good reasons for managing the biodiversity of ecosystems. However, before biodiversity can be properly managed it needs to be measured.

The populations of individual organisms and numbers of different species can be huge. This means it is impossible to count all of them. For this reason, scientists use sampling methods to count a subset of the whole; it is assumed that the subset reflects the whole population size or species diversity. There are two main groups of methods for sampling and measuring biodiversity. One group uses techniques for sampling organisms that do not move about (sedentary organisms), for example plants and animals such as barnacles and limpets on a seashore. The second group uses techniques for sampling non-sedentary organisms, which usually involve some sort of trap to catch the organisms.

Sampling sedentary organisms: quadrats and transects

When an area of land has to be surveyed, it is usually necessary to sample it. If the subject of the survey is plant species, the sampling can be done with a **quadrat**. A quadrat is a frame of known area that can be placed over part of the site to be sampled. The plants enclosed within the quadrat can then be counted. In some cases, counting individual plants is still not possible so an estimate has to be made. The most common of way of estimating plant numbers is to use an estimate of cover, for example using a simple scale such as ACFOR. This provides a qualitative estimate:

- A = abundant
- C = common
- F = frequent
- O = occasional
- R = rare.

In the example in Figure 9.9, plant species C would be A(bundant) and both plant species A and B would be C(ommon). Use of a gridded quadrat, however, allows a more quantitative measurement to be made.

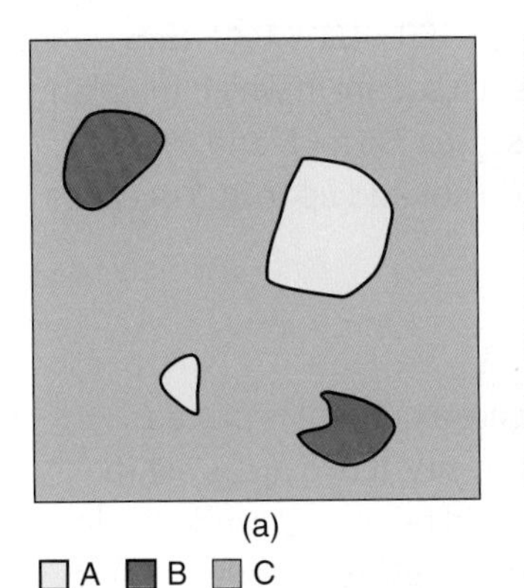

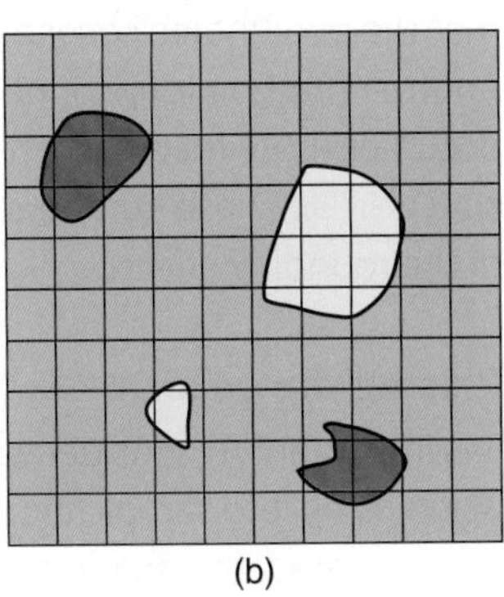

A B C

Figure 9.9 An area of grassland (C) with patches of other plants (A and B). It is difficult to estimate percentage cover, but if a gridded quadrat, as shown on the right, is placed over the area it is easier to make this estimation.

KEY TERM

Quadrat: a frame of known area used to sample organisms that do not move, such as plants

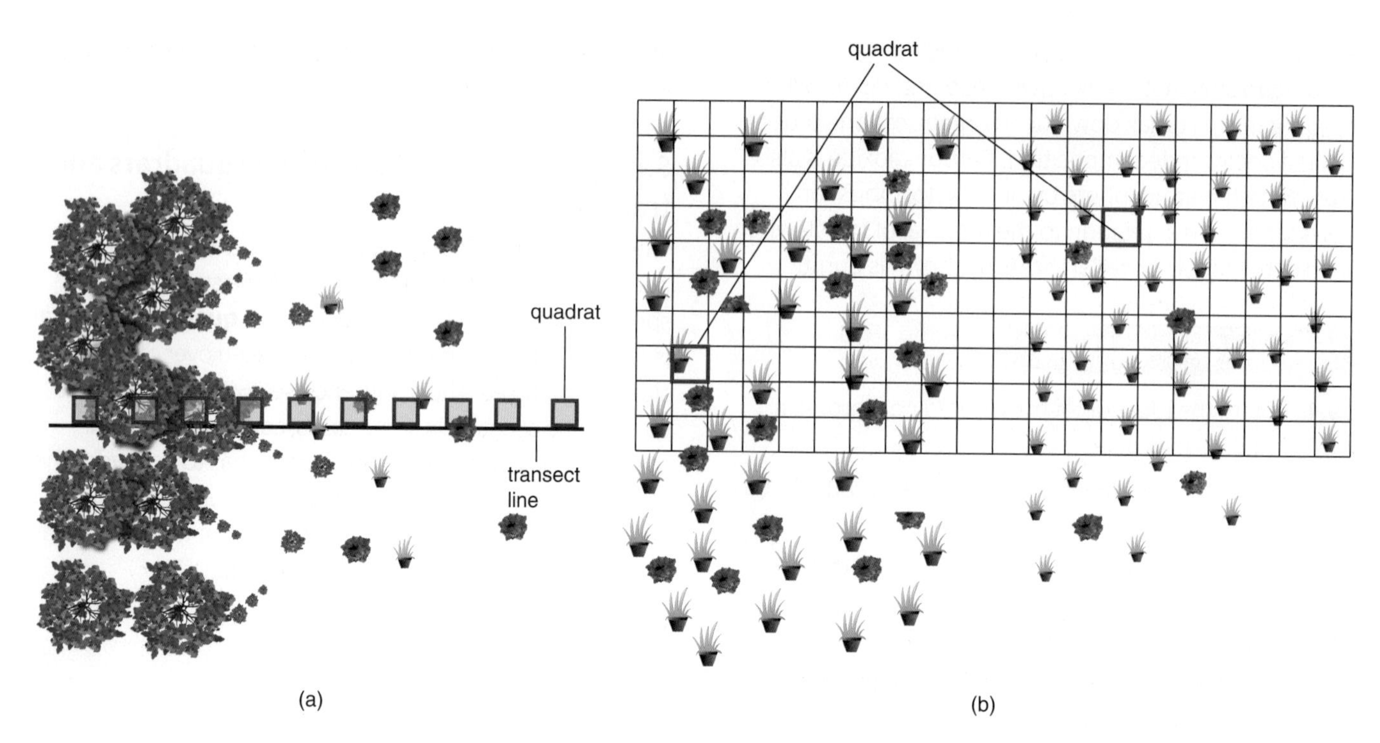

Figure 9.10 Systematic sampling using quadrats along a transect is appropriate in the situation shown in (a). Random sampling, placing quadrats using random number tables in a pre-marked grid, is appropriate in the situation shown in (b) in which area 1 is being compared to area 2.

One way to use a gridded quadrat is to count the number of squares that the plant appears in and take the total to be the percentage cover. In the example in Figure 9.9, this would give 11% for B and 14% for A. You can then say that the percentage cover of C is 100 − (11 + 14) = 75%. Another method is to count each square in which the plant occupies more than half. This gives 7% for B and 9% for A, so C is 87%. These numbers do not add up to 100 because of the rounding effect.

Placing the quadrat

It is important to consider where a quadrat is placed when using it to sample biodiversity. If two areas are to be compared, the quadrat should be placed randomly in each, which is called **random sampling** (Figure 9.10b). If the aim is to see how the species change along a gradient in the environment, the quadrat should be placed along a line called a **transect**, which is **systematic sampling** (Figure 9.10a). An example of an environmental gradient is the change in light intensity from the shade of a woodland into an open field.

In the case of systematic sampling, the quadrat is placed along the transect line at either regular or irregular intervals. Figure 9.10a shows them placed at regular intervals. When carrying out random sampling, the best method is to lay out a gird in each of the areas to be sampled. The position of the quadrats is then determined using random coordinates from a set of random number tables or by throwing dice. For example the coordinate generated might be 4, 2. The quadrat would then be placed 4 units (say metres) along one axis (say *x*) and 2 along the other, *y*. This is shown in Figure 9.11.

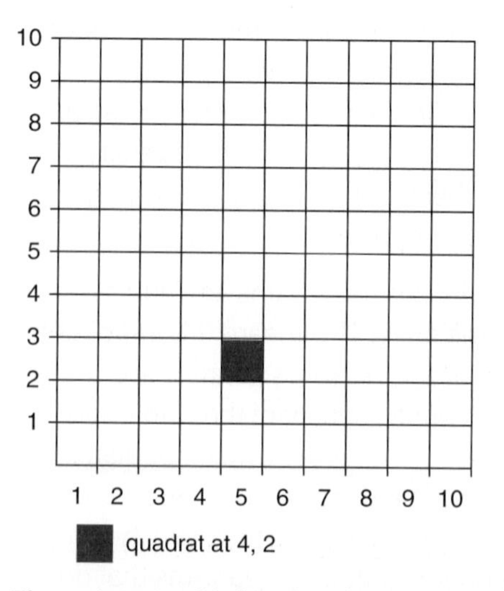

Figure 9.11 A grid showing the position of quadrat at coordinates 4, 2.

> **KEY TERMS**
>
> **Random sampling:** a sampling method in which the sampling device is placed using random number tables or the roll of dice
>
> **Transect:** a sampling method in which sampling devices are laid out along a line already placed across an area
>
> **Systematic sampling:** a sampling method in which the sampling device is placed along a line or some other pre-determined pattern, the most common pattern being the line of a transect
>
> **Pooter:** a device for retrieving small animals from devices such as nets and pitfall traps

Sampling mobile organisms: pitfall traps and pooters

For organisms that move, a variety of trapping methods are used to estimate biodiversity as well as population size. One very common device, used for small animals moving about on the ground, is the pitfall trap (Figure 9.12). A pitfall trap consists of a jar sunk up to its rim in the soil. The top may or may not be covered, depending on the predicted likelihood of rainfall, and the trap should be inspected and emptied regularly.

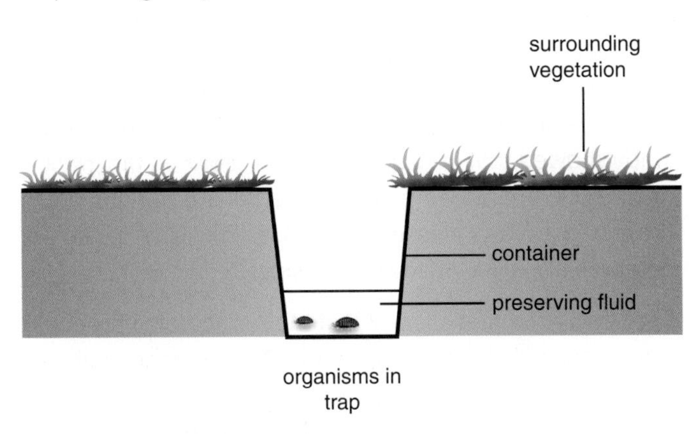

Figure 9.12 A pitfall trap without a cover.

Traps can be placed systematically, for example along a transect, or randomly, for example in places selected on a grid with random numbers. Therefore, a transect line or random set of samples as set out for plants can also be used to sample this type of animal. However, one problem with the pitfall trap is that it measures the level of activity of the animals as well as their numbers.

Other techniques for sampling small animals, such as insects in short vegetation or on trees, often involve catching them in a net of some kind. The animals will often then need to be transported back to a laboratory for careful identification. The **pooter** is simple piece of equipment for getting the animals out of the net and into a specimen container (Figure 9.13).

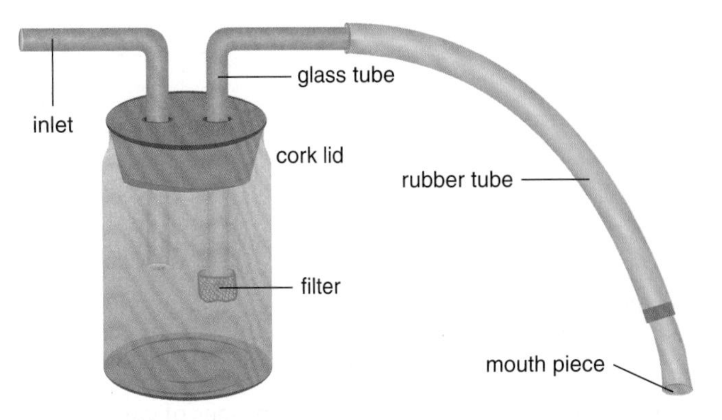

Figure 9.13 A pooter.

For larger animals, such as small mammals like mice and voles, other kinds of traps can be used. For very large animals, such as zebras and wildebeest, counting is used, often from an aeroplane.

When to use random or systematic sampling

When designing an ecological investigation, scientists have to decide whether the quadrats or traps should be positioned in a systematic or random fashion. As a general rule, if the investigation is looking at how distribution changes over an environmental gradient, systematic sampling will be used. For example, if you wanted to look at the effect of a road on vegetation, you would use this method (Figure 9.14).

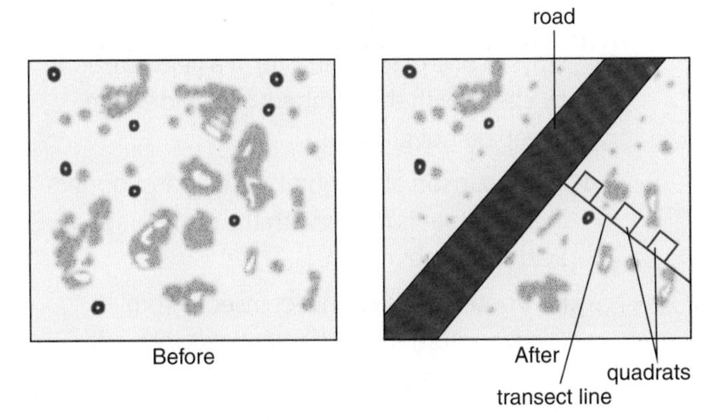

Figure 9.14 To investigate the effect building a road has had on the plants growing on either side, a transect with quadrats laid at regular intervals along it can be used to sample the plants.

If your investigation requires you to compare areas, then random sampling using a grid is the most suitable method. For example, to compare the insect populations between an area grazed by animals and an area that is not grazed, pitfall traps could be set out randomly in both areas using a grid and random number tables. However, there are advantages and disadvantages to any method used, as shown in Table 9.1.

Method	Advantages	Disadvantages
Quadrats	• Quick • Inexpensive • Portable	• Not always very accurate • Unless many quadrats are placed, the sample can be unintentionally biased
Transects	• Quick • Inexpensive • Portable	• Often used in inappropriate situations, so care must be taken when deciding whether or not to us a transect
Pitfall traps	• Inexpensive • Easy to set up and use	• Often kill the organisms captured • May oversample or undersample

Table 9.1 The advantages and disadvantages of various sampling methods

SELF-ASSESSMENT QUESTIONS

9.8 Match the following studies with the sampling methods that could have been used for them from the list below. The first one (a) has been done for you.

a The distribution of ground-living beetles along the side of a road heading from the countryside into a town. (iii)

b The distribution of plants on either side of a heavily used footpath across a field. (....)

c A comparison of the numbers of scale insects (an insect that sucks sap from plants and stays in one place all its life) in a field grazed by sheep with the numbers in a field where sheep do not graze. (....)

d A comparison of the numbers of grasshoppers in a field that is mown with the numbers in a field that is not mown. (....)

i Pooters used to collect insects from quadrats in two different fields, placed using coordinates generated from the throw of dice.

ii Quadrats placed in two different fields using coordinates generated from the throw of dice.

iii Pit-fall traps placed in a line a fixed distance apart.

iv Quadrats placed 10 m apart in a line.

9.3 The causes and impacts of habitat loss

As discussed above, a habitat is the place where the population of an organism lives, finds food and reproduces. Therefore, the loss of a habitat means the loss of those species that live, find food and reproduce within it. Habitat loss is the single most important cause of species **extinction**. Many scientists believe that species extinction is happening at a faster rate than at any time in the past. What are the implications of this? It is a difficult question to answer because we do not know enough about the impact of species loss on an ecosystem. A recent study showed that 80% of the beetles captured from just 19 trees in Panama were new to science! So, working out the consequences of losing species is difficult, because we do not really know what we are losing.

The latest estimates suggest that the current rate of species extinction could be as much as 10 000 times higher than the natural rate. How many species this actually means is, again, difficult to estimate. So far, fewer than 2 million different species have been named, and the estimates of how many species there currently are range from a few million to maybe as many as 100 million. If the latter estimate is correct, an extinction rate of just 0.01% $year^{-1}$ means that 10 000 species are lost every year. If the rate is 0.1% $year^{-1}$ then that would mean a loss of a 100 000 species. But this still does not answer the question: does this matter?

KEY TERM

Extinction: the process by which a species or other named group ceases to exist on the Earth or in a named area

Causes of habitat loss

There are three major causes of habitat loss and, therefore, species extinction.

The drainage of wetlands

Some wetlands are found inland and some are coastal, and the total area is hard to estimate. The most widely accepted figure is that there are about 7-9 million km^2 of wetlands around the world. Three million km^2 of wetlands are found at the poles, just under 1 million km^2 in temperate regions, about 1.9 million km^2 in the tropics and 1.5 million km^2 are rice paddies. This represents somewhere between 4 and 6% of the Earth's land surface. The area of wetlands is difficult to estimate because of their scattered distribution. However, there are some major wetland areas, such as the Pantanal in Brazil (140 000 km^2), the Llanos of Venezuela and Colombia (about 500 000 km^2) and the Pearl and Yangtze river deltas in China (650 000 km^2 between them).

Wetlands have traditionally been regarded as wasteland and therefore relatively worthless. However, it is now realised that they have a variety of benefits, including the provision of a range of environmental services. These environmental services include shoreline protection, maintenance of water quality, flood control, recharging of aquifers (see Section 4.4) and biological productivity. They also provide habitats and are a source of a variety of products such as fish, wildfowl, fuel and fibres.

Unfortunately, the current global area of wetlands is half what it was in 1900. There are many causes of wetland loss, including:

- drainage for agriculture, forestry and mosquito control
- dredging for flood protection
- use for disposal of waste created by road construction
- discharge of pollutants
- peat removal
- removal of groundwater.

Wetland is drained for a variety of reasons, including the provision of tourism facilities and agricultural land. As discussed in Section 4.7, many diseases are water related and one way of reducing or eliminating these is to drain the water in which the causative organism or its vector lives. This is an especially important way to control the spread of malaria. The state of Minnesota in the USA provides a good example of the rate of wetland loss over the last two centuries. The loss there is estimated to be well over 50% since the early 1800s.

Intensive agricultural practices

The main reason for the drainage of wetlands is to provide land for agriculture. It is estimated that about 75% of this has occurred in temperate latitudes (that is, outside the topics and subtropics). The remaining 25% of loss has been within the tropics.

Much land that is not wetland has also been used for agriculture. Agriculture poses the greatest threat to species survival because it results in so much habitat loss. It is estimated that the threat of extinction to 63% of vertebrates comes from agricultural practices. In south-east Asia it is estimated that more than 80% of bird species have been lost as a result of clearing native forest for the production of palm oil.

Other aspects of intensive agriculture, including the use of pesticides and fertilisers, can have far-reaching effects on habitats. The agrochemicals used are soluble in water and can be carried away from the farms where they are applied. For example, the fish in coastal areas of Mexico have been badly affected by agrochemicals entering the Gulf of Mexico down the Mississippi River from farms in the centre of the USA.

Deforestation

Perhaps the most obvious cause of habitat loss is deforestation. In many parts of the world, at a wide range of altitudes, forest forms the **climax community**. In these areas trees form a continuous cover and provide habitats for a wide range of tree- and ground-dwelling species. In temperate regions these species are mainly birds but squirrels and various reptiles are also found.

In the tropics and subtropics of both Africa and South America, primates are adapted to living in forested habitats. These areas are also home to a huge variety of tree-dwelling birds. In both of these regions, and others, millions of insects depend on the forest for their survival. The most biodiverse habitats on Earth are thought to be in the tropical rainforests of South America and Central Africa. In these regions, hundreds of thousands, or possibly millions of species exist. Loss of this habitat, or just its fragmentation, is likely to lead to the loss of very many species. Deforestation is discussed further in Section 9.4.

KEY TERM

Climax community: the stable community characteristic of an area that persists as long as the climate does not change

Impacts of habitat loss

The impact of habitat loss is mainly the loss of species within it.

Loss of biodiversity and genetic depletion

As recently as 10 000 years ago, people were still gathering plants and hunting animals as their source of food. Then, at around 10 000 years ago, some human populations learned to plant seeds. At first the plants grown from these seeds would have given an unpredictable and often small yield. Quite unintentionally, those plants that gave a good yield would be selected for the next generation. This was an early form of selective breeding (see Section 3.4). Since those times, which were the beginning of the agricultural revolution, intentional selection has been carried out. Modern crop plants, such as wheat, rice and maize, are therefore the product of 10 000 years of this artificial selection. The process has been hugely beneficial in providing food for a growing population of humans. There are worries now, however, that modern strains of crop plants may not be able to adapt to changes in the future, such as those anticipated as a result of climate change. Efforts have been made to retain populations of ancient strains of important crop plants. However, no matter how successful these projects are, it is very important to retain biodiversity in the wild. The characteristics of wild varieties of modern crop plants may prove useful in the future. For example, because of climate change, in an area beginning to suffer more frequent and more severe droughts, drought-resistant strains are needed. The wild plants may not produce very good yields but may be able to withstand drought, and their genes can be incorporated into modern high-yielding strains. The wild-type resistance to drought is given to the plants by the genetic instructions (genes) they contain. Recent advances in our understanding of genetics have allowed scientists to transplant a gene, for example for drought resistance, into a plant that does not already have it. So, for example, using the techniques of genetic modification (see Section 3.4), modern strains can be 'given' drought resistance.

In addition, the species and genetic diversity that exist in the wild may have many currently unknown uses. A large proportion of the medicines currently used have come from wild plants and animals. It is possible that further medicines and other useful products may exist in the wild. Habitat loss, leading to the loss of biodiversity, could mean valuable products are never discovered. The loss of species containing potentially useful genes is called genetic depletion. As discussed earlier in this chapter, habitat destruction reduces genetic diversity and may even lead to species becoming extinct, when the genetic loss becomes irretrievable.

SELF-ASSESSMENT QUESTIONS

9.9 Habitat destruction causes a loss of biodiversity, and therefore loss of genetic depletion. Explain why this is a problem.

9.10 Explain some possible consequences of draining a wetland area.

9.4 The causes and impacts of deforestation

Causes of deforestation

Deforestation is a major cause of habitat loss, but how extensive is deforestation and what causes it? In Africa, South America (especially Brazil) and Indonesia, very significant forest losses occurred in the early part of the 21st century. Over 8 million hectares year^{-1} were lost during this period, with Brazil losing 3.1 million hectares year^{-1} and Indonesia 1.9 million hectares year^{-1}. Over the same time period over 5 million hectares year^{-1} were gained. However, the losses mainly occurred in the tropics and the gains in temperate regions.

The most obvious cause of deforestation is the need for the wood itself. In some parts of the world, timber is another name for wood, but in other places timber refers to the products made from that wood in the form of boards and planks. Where the term wood means timber, the planks and boards are called lumber. Essentially lumber and timber are the same thing: wood processed to be ready for human use. Logging, in its broadest sense, is the process by which wood is extracted from a forest and made into timber. This timber is needed by more economically developed countries (MEDCs) for products ranging from luxury furniture to paper, which are all in enormous demand.

Wood is a remarkable material and has been used by humans for thousands of years. It can be used for building and furniture making, but also for papermaking, and is source of energy when burnt.

Another reason for deforestation is to clear land for farming, roads and settlements. In tropical forests, the logging itself is not necessarily very damaging. Only some species are suitable for creating timber, and so logging tends to be selective and such a process can be beneficial to the forests. However, often logging and timber extraction involves opening up the forest. Creating roads for the vehicles associated with the logging process is probably the single most damaging aspect of logging. Logging itself may lead to only 10% of the deforestation in an area. It is the agriculture and settlement that follow, encouraged by the logging roads, that cause the greatest loss of trees. As people establish themselves in an area, other activities follow. If economic deposits are found, rock and mineral extraction may occur, which can lead to further deforestation.

Figure 9.15 shows that agriculture in all its forms (subsistence and commercial, together with pasture for animals) is the cause of about 80% of all deforestation, while the construction of settlements and mining cause only a small faction (as part of 'other'). Roads only lead directly to a small amount of deforestation, but are instrumental in opening up the forest to other activities.

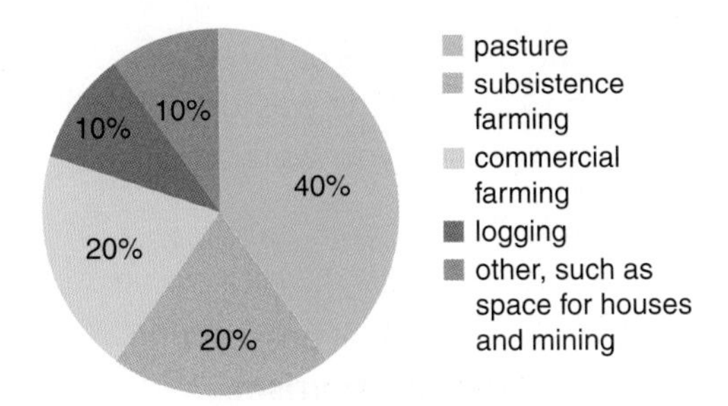

Figure 9.15 The causes of deforestation.

Impacts of deforestation

Deforestation is one of the most important causes of habitat loss. As well as the loss of forest habitats, its impact on the soil can lead to further habitat loss. Soil erosion, and often desertification, are frequent results of wholesale deforestation. Climate change, largely thought to be caused by changes in the atmosphere (see Section 7.2), could also be caused by deforestation.

Habitat loss

Biodiversity is lost when habitats are lost, as discussed earlier. Tropical forests in particular are centres of great biodiversity, so the loss of habitats in these forests is especially serious. In addition, the huge volume of trees in these forests acts as a massive carbon store and they are home for many rare species that may be useful to us.

Soil erosion and desertification

When forests are lost, soil erosion inevitably becomes a problem. The forest reduces the impact of heavy rainfall on the ground, reducing soil erosion. In addition, tree roots hold the soil in place and the layer of fallen leaves and branches protects the soil. Over time, after deforestation, the area that once supported luxuriant growth may become a desert, as a result of desertification (see Section 3.5).

Climate change

Climate change is a consistent change in long-term weather patterns. In the context of environmental management, climate change usually refers to on-going changes that are thought to be caused by changes in the levels of various **greenhouse gases** in the atmosphere. The main greenhouse gases are carbon dioxide and methane. It is currently thought that greenhouse gas levels are rising and so are atmospheric temperatures (global warming) and that this, in turn, is leading to climate change.

KEY TERM

Greenhouse gas: a gas that stops energy in the form of heat from being lost from the atmosphere

That the levels of greenhouse gases, especially carbon dioxide, are rising is agreed by almost all scientists, but why is it happening? The main cause of the rise in carbon dioxide is the burning of fossil fuels (see Section 7.1), which accounts for about 87% of all human carbon dioxide emissions. Following that come changes in land use, most importantly deforestation, at about 9%, and then other industries at about 4%.

Trees remove carbon dioxide from the atmosphere during photosynthesis. As deforestation reduces the number of trees, it also reduces how much carbon dioxide the Earth's forests can remove. However, it must be remembered that trees also respire and give out carbon dioxide. If the rate of photosynthesis and the rate of respiration are the same, then the removal of the trees will have no effect on the atmospheric carbon dioxide level. However, the permanent removal of trees leads to large quantities of carbon dioxide being released when they are burned or when they decompose. In addition, the machinery of deforestation burns fossil fuels, releasing more carbon dioxide.

Loss of biodiversity and genetic depletion

Because forests, and rainforests especially, are such centres of biodiversity and genetic diversity, their loss causes particularly dramatic examples of habitat, biodiversity and genetic loss. The situation is even more worrying when you consider that we are probably unaware of the identity of the majority of species that live in these forests.

SELF-ASSESSMENT QUESTIONS

9.11 A large area of mature rainforest has been cleared to plant fast-growing oil-palm trees. Suggest how this might affect:

a the level of carbon dioxide in the atmosphere

b biodiversity in the area.

9.12 Table 9.2 shows the results of a study of the reasons for deforestation in the Amazon in 2006.

Reason	Percentage
Cattle grazing	60
Subsistence farming	30
Commercial agriculture	2
Logging	4
Other	4

Table 9.2 Reasons for deforestation in the Amazon in 2006.

a Copy and complete Figure 9.16 using the data from Table 9.2.

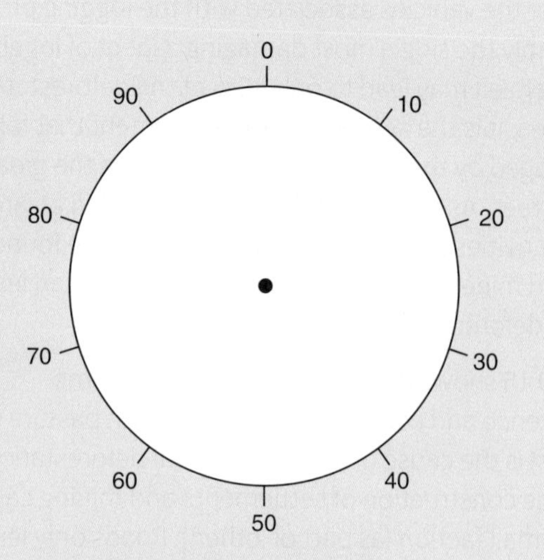

Figure 9.16 Reasons for deforestation in the Amazon in 2006.

b In 2006, 14 285 km^2 of the Amazon forest were lost. Calculate how much of this was lost due to subsistence farming. Show your working.

9.5 The need for sustainable management of forests

Forests are vital for the lives of many animals, plants and other organisms because of the habitats they provide. These organisms, in turn, represent a huge genetic resource as well as a source of food, medicine and raw materials for industry. In addition, forests perform a variety of ecosystem services. They are involved in the carbon and water cycles and help to prevent soil erosion. Pristine, biodiverse forests are also a huge attraction for tourists, who bring money into the countries that possess the forests, a phenomenon known as **ecotourism**.

Carbon sinks and carbon stores

When a forest is growing because most of the trees in it are relatively young, it takes in more carbon dioxide in photosynthesis than it gives out in respiration, so it is a **carbon sink**. A mature forest in which all of the trees are old and not growing actively, takes in and gives out the same quantity of carbon dioxide and is a **carbon store** (Figure 9.17).

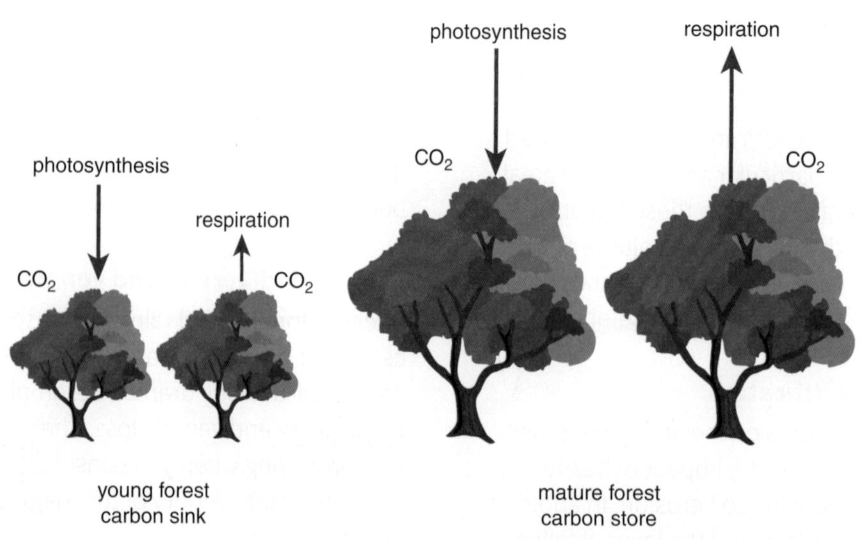

Figure 9.17 Movements of carbon dioxide into (in photosynthesis) and out of (in respiration) trees in a young and a mature forest.

KEY TERMS

Ecotourism: tourism in which the participants travel to see the natural world, ideally in a sustainable way

Carbon sink: a vegetated area where the intake of carbon dioxide from the atmosphere in photosynthesis exceeds its output from respiration, so the net flow of carbon is from the atmosphere into plants

Carbon store: a mature vegetated area where the intake of carbon dioxide from the atmosphere by photosynthesis equals its output from respiration, so the mature plants store carbon

Role in the water cycle

Forests add water to the atmosphere in the process of transpiration (see Section 4.2). This leads to the formation of clouds. Eventually the clouds release the water back as precipitation. When forests are cut down, this process is reduced, which can lead to local droughts in the area of deforestation. Forests generate moisture in the atmosphere that can also affect rainfall around the world. For example, deforestation in the Amazon is now thought to influence the rainfall from Mexico to Texas. The level of precipitation in the American Midwest seems to depend on the state of the rainforest in Central America, and that of China and the Balkans is influenced by deforestation in Asia.

Prevention of soil erosion

Forests help prevent soil erosion in a number of ways.

- By intercepting rain, the forest reduces heavy rainfall on the forest floor, thus reducing soil erosion.
- Debris such as tree leaves on the floor of the forest slows run-off, again reducing soil erosion.
- The roots of trees hold the soil in place.
- Forests on the coast reduce erosion by absorbing energy from storms.

Figure 9.18 illustrates what happens when trees are removed.

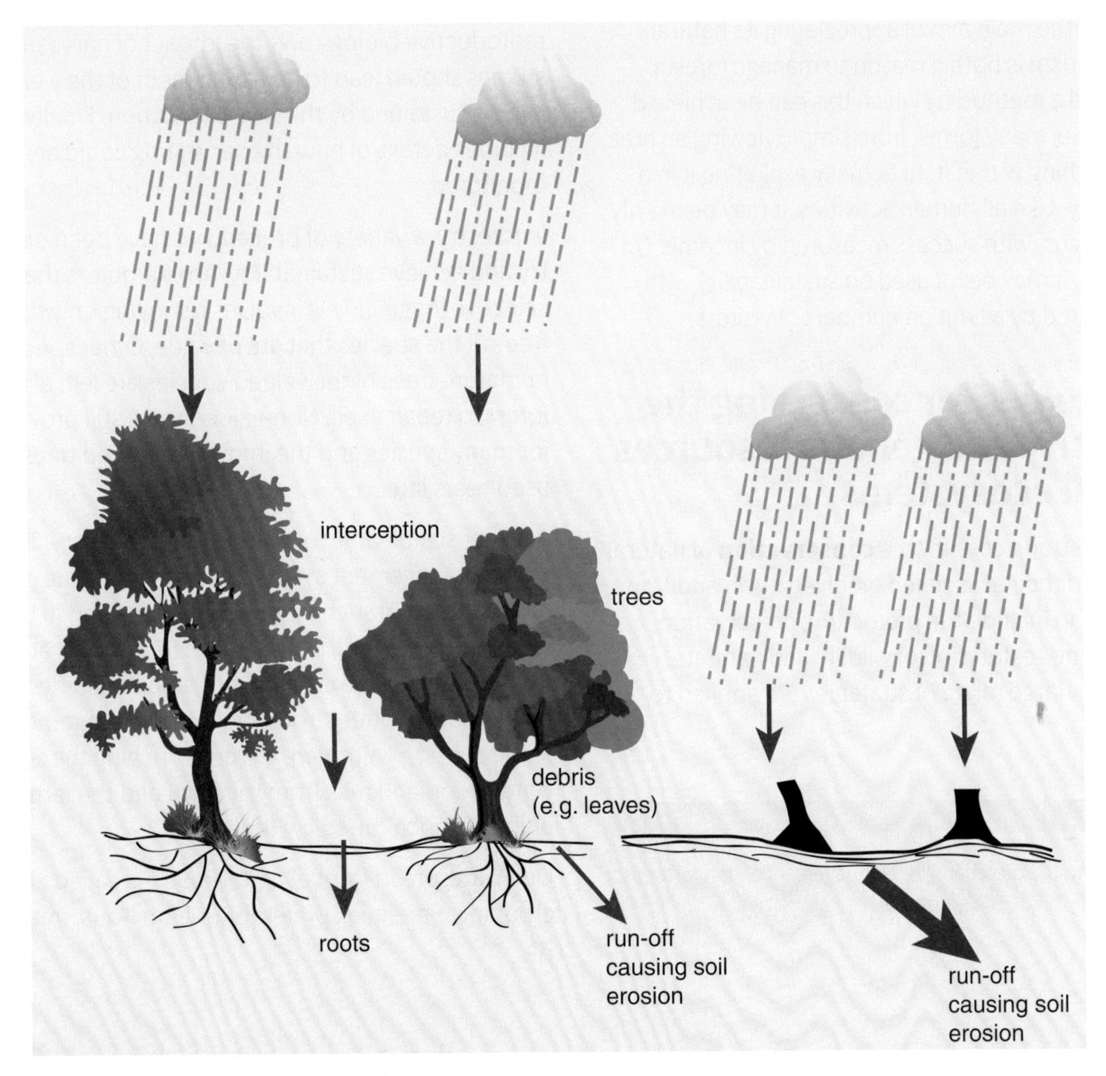

Figure 9.18 The effect of tree removal on soil erosion.

SELF-ASSESSMENT QUESTIONS

9.13 One very popular form of ecotourism is whale watching. People travel to areas where whales can be found, stay in local accommodation and then go out in boats on day trips to see the whales. One description of ecotourism is that it involves travelling to natural areas that conserve the environment and improves the welfare of the local people. Suggest ways in which whale watching as described meets this description and ways in which it does not.

9.14 Draw an annotated sketch to show how trees might reduce the erosion of soil by wind and water.

Ecotourism

Ecotourism is responsible travel to a natural area that promotes conservation of the environment. Visitors travel to an area with the main aim of appreciating its natural beauty. Ecotourism is both a reason to manage forests sustainably and a method by which this can be achieved. Ecotourism takes many forms, from simply viewing an area, to doing something within it, to actually exploiting it in a sustainable way. Like all human activities, it may be mainly economic in focus, with success measured by income. On the other hand, it may be focused on sustainability with success measured by a limit on numbers of visitors.

9.6 Strategies for conserving the biodiversity and genetic resources of natural ecosystems

There is a very strong case for the **conservation** of natural ecosystems and their associated biodiversity; in addition, conservation can include the protection, preservation, management and restoration of wildlife and habitats. Consequently, a large range of strategies are applied to conservation.

KEY TERM

Conservation: the protection and management of natural areas

Sustainable harvesting of wild plant and animal species, sustainable forestry and agroforestry

Any action described as sustainable must meet the needs of the present without denying the needs of future generations. This means we need ways of taking the wild animals and plants are required now and still leave enough for people in the future. Perhaps the most well-known examples of harvesting wild animals and plants are fisheries, forestry and medicinal plants. The successes and failures of harvesting wild fish are covered in Chapter 5.

Many plants have medicinal properties because of the secondary metabolites they produce. In many cases, wild plants are the preferred source because cultivated varieties only produce small quantities, or even none, of the chemicals we want to use. There have been many attempts to control the harvesting of wild-grown medicinal plants, generally involving a management plan. Such a plan involves assessing the abundance of the plant (see Section 9.2) then investigating the species' growth rate, reproductive biology and the impact of harvesting. Such studies should lead to an assessment of the yield that can be sustained by the wild population. Finally, the plan includes details of how the harvesting could and should be monitored.

In forestry, a variety of procedures have been devised to try and achieve sustainability. An example is the practice of selective logging. This involves removing only the mature trees of the species that are of value. Other species and immature trees of the valued species are left, allowing the forest to repair itself. Non-valued trees still provide habitat for many species and the immature valued trees can be used years later.

Another sustainable technique is agroforestry. This is a land management system in which crops are grown around trees. In such systems, the trees enrich the soil when the leaves fall, provide food for animals and firewood for people. In some cases they also provide medicines. In addition, the trees' roots hold the soil together and, in some cases, fix nitrogen, further enriching the soil. Farmers obtain food and milk from the farm and the farmers' animals enrich the soil with manure.

One widespread form of agroforestry is called alley cropping. Perennial, preferably leguminous, trees or shrubs are grown with an arable crop. The trees are grown in rows with big gaps between them. The crops are planted in an alley between the rows of trees. The trees are pruned and the prunings used to improve the soil and provide minerals to the crop. If the tree is a legume, these minerals will include nitrate. Mineral recycling and the suppression of weeds by the trees are combined with cropping on the same land. This allows the land to be farmed for much longer than would otherwise be possible.

National parks, wildlife and ecological reserves and corridors

A common response by governments to the need to protect an area and its wildlife is to designate them as specially protected regions covered by certain laws. National parks and wildlife and ecological reserves differ mainly in size. Wildlife corridors have a special role, of linking protected areas that otherwise would become isolated from each other.

The world's first national park was designated in 1872 in the USA. Yellowstone Park has an area of 898 318 ha (8983 km^2) that protects nearly 2000 species of plants and nearly 60 large mammals, including the grey wolf, lynx and bison. America now has 59 national parks, with a total area of 210 000 km^2, 2.18% of the country's total area. Canada, itself a very large country, has the largest area of land protected by national parks, at 377 000 km^2, representing 3.78% of the country's land. In contrast, the Central American countries of Costa Rica and Belize have 25.1% and 38%, respectively, of their land area protected by national parks. The largest national park in the world is the Northeast Greenland National Park, covering 972 001 km^2.

Worldwide there are about 113 000 national parks, which cover about 6% of the Earth's land surface, or about 149 million km^2. Governments have been slower to protect marine ecosystems in a similar way, but a start has been made. The largest marine park in the world protects the Chagos Islands and their surrounding waters in the Indian Ocean. This park has a total area of 544 000 km^2. The Great Barrier Reef marine park off the east coast of Australia protects an area of 345 000 km^2.

Once an area has been designated as a national park, it should be protected from damage. Laws are usually implemented that ban or limit activities such as hunting and logging. Even the collection of wildflowers is restricted or banned. However, it is sometimes difficult to stop these activities and enforcement can require a combination of regular inspection and the threat of hefty fines or imprisonment for breaking the law. Although the focus of national parks is not tourism, extensive facilities for tourists are usually provided, which can include a system of roadways, car parks and nature trails. An entry fee is sometimes charged and this money can be used for conservation work. A guidebook or leaflet is often provided with the purchase of an entrance ticket, which can include information about what can and cannot be done in the park.

Many iconic areas of the world only remain today because they have been given having national park status. These include the Pantanal Matogrossense National Park in Brazil, the Everglades National Park in Florida, USA, Redwood National Park in California, USA, and the entire Galapagos Islands off the coast of Ecuador. National parks have detailed management strategies that will vary according to the nature of the park.

Wildlife and ecological reserves are areas where the focus is management of the area for the wildlife and ecology. People actually living in such areas can feel they are in competition with the world around them. An example of this situation arose in Australia when attempts were made to set up ecological reserves on rivers. The opinions of different stakeholders ranged from those who thought the water is there for the creatures that live in it, to those who thought that too much was being spent on protecting fish and other wildlife. The ultimate goal of a successful ecological / wildlife reserve is to balance the needs of people and wildlife. This can only be achieved with a strategy that protects the wildlife and is part of a system people want and need.

Wildlife corridors are areas of land that link large reserves or other wildlife areas. When natural habitats are fragmented, the remaining areas may be acquired and set up as reserves. However, it has been shown that many species are not be able to maintain a viable population in smaller areas. For example, some species are so dependent on trees that they never come down to the ground. Therefore, even if another forested area is only a few tens of metres away, individuals within the two areas may not be able to mate or interact in other ways. A corridor of trees between the otherwise isolated areas can provide a solution to this problem.

Extractive reserves

Extractive reserves attempt to find a balance between destroying the forest for short-term benefit and stopping all economic activity, which can have an impact on local people. A poor rubber tapper called Chico Mendes suggested the creation of protected areas in the Amazon Forest in which local people would manage the land, and then have the right to take products from the area. A rancher was so outraged by Mendes' ideas that he shot Mendes dead in 1988. Ultimately, this tragedy led to the establishment of the first extractive reserve, i at Alto Juruá in the Brazilian province of Acre in the western part of the Amazon rainforest. The Chico Mendes extractive reserve was set up soon after. Brazil now has 88 such reserves covering an area of about 200 000 km^2. Rainforests preservation is linked to the necessity of ensuring justice and opportunities for the people who live there. As Chico Mendes said 'At first I thought I was fighting to save rubber trees, then I thought I was fighting to save the Amazon rainforest. Now I realise I am fighting for humanity.'

World biosphere reserves

Biosphere reserves represent another way of trying to strike a balance between conservation while at the same time meeting peoples' needs. Figure 9.19 shows the basic model on which all biosphere reserves are based.

The ecosystems that need protection are located in the core area. Human activities here are restricted to monitoring and possibly some research. The buffer zone is an area where more research is carried out, together with education and tourism. This area may therefore contain field stations with laboratories and recreational facilities. The transition (or multiple-use) zone is where local communities and conservation organisations work together to manage the area for the benefit of the people who live there.

One advantage of biosphere reserves is that they are recognised internationally via the United Nations Educational Scientific and Cultural Organisation (UNESCO). This can improve the success of the reserve because it makes it easier to attract funding and the support of experts in the conservation community. The benefits of biosphere reserves are many and affect local people, local government, scientists and the world in general. There are currently 669 biosphere reserves in 120 countries around the world (Figure 9.20).

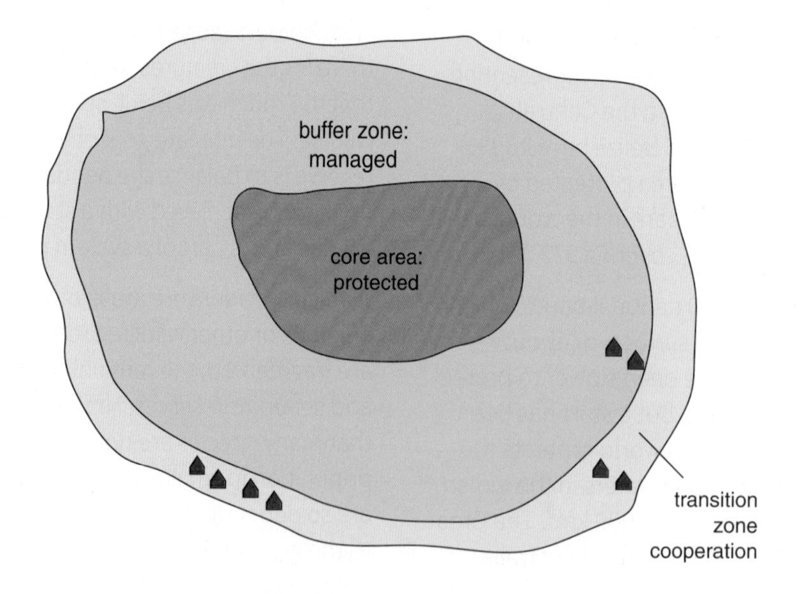

Figure 9.19 The general structure of a biosphere reserve, with a core area protected by a buffer zone, which is managed, and a transition zone, where the authorities cooperate with people who live there.

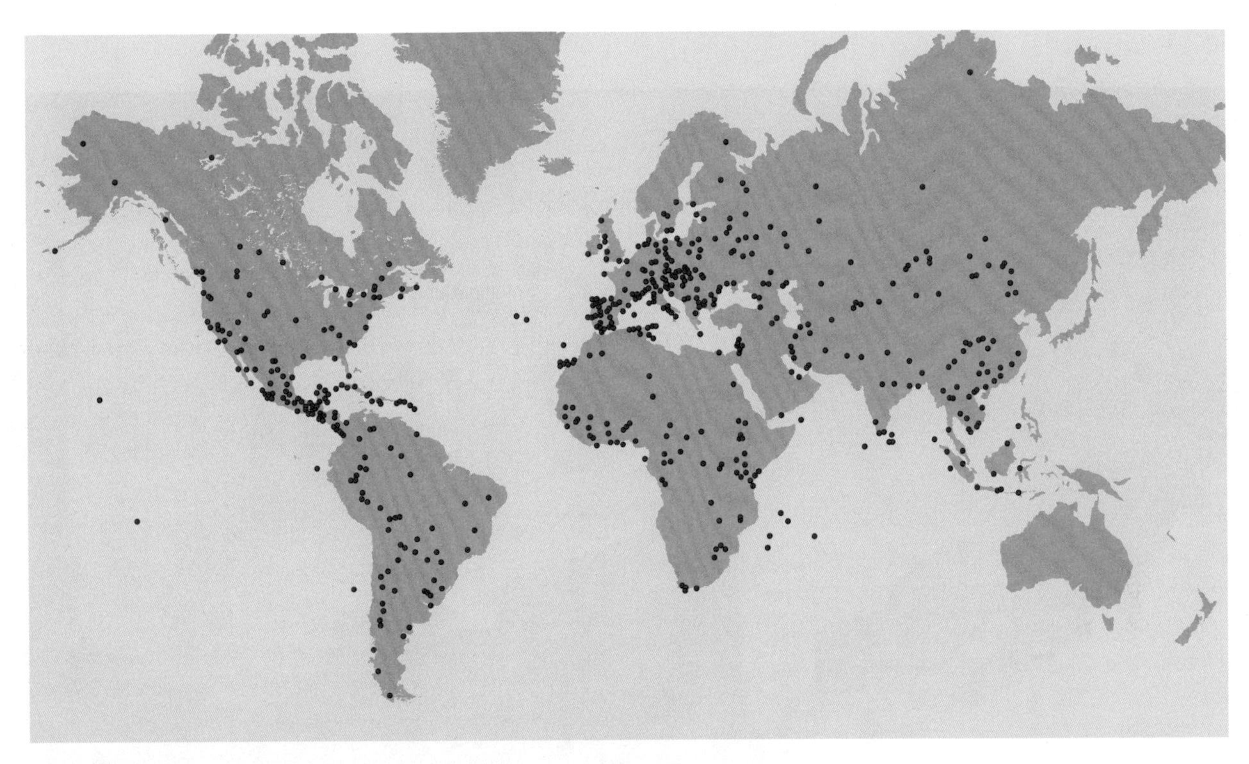

Figure 9.20 The distribution of biosphere reserves around the world in 2016.

CASE STUDY

Mayan Biosphere Reserve, Guatemala

The Mayan Biosphere Reserve in northern Guatemala contains part of one of the largest areas of tropical forest in Central America. In line with the general model of a biosphere reserve, the Mayan reserve has core areas, which include national parks and wildlife reserves (Figure 9.21). The reserve contains lowland forest, savannah, pine forest, lakes, lagoons, rivers, wetlands and some mangrove forests. The core areas are the only part of the reserve where laws govern the conduct of people.

The transition zone consists of mainly tropical forest dedicated to the harvesting of xate palms, chicle gum, allspice and timber. These activities are encouraged as a way of giving the locals a livelihood that does not involve slash and burn. With slash and burn, vegetation is cut down and burnt and then crops can be grown on the land for a few years afterwards (see the extended case study at the end of this chapter).

The buffer zone in the south is an agricultural landscape with some forest. The population of this area has grown during the last 30 years, most in regions south of the reserve. Archaeological sites in the reserve include Tikal, a Mayan city, which gets as many as 180 000 visitors $year^{-1}$.

In 2008, President Alvaro Colom of Guatemala announced the Cuatro Balam initiative to increase tourism in the reserve, focusing on the archaeological sites. The plan is designed to help the conservation of biodiversity and archaeology, at the same time as encouraging economic development in the region. One aim is to attract 12 million visitors to the region. Key features of the plan include a small train that will carry tourists to and from the archaeological sites, and a new university that will promote the study of the region's biodiversity and genetic material, as well as Mayan studies. Colom said that some of the planned objectives could be achieved within just 2 years, while others would take up to 15 years to realise. He also said that to achieve any of this, the region would have to

→

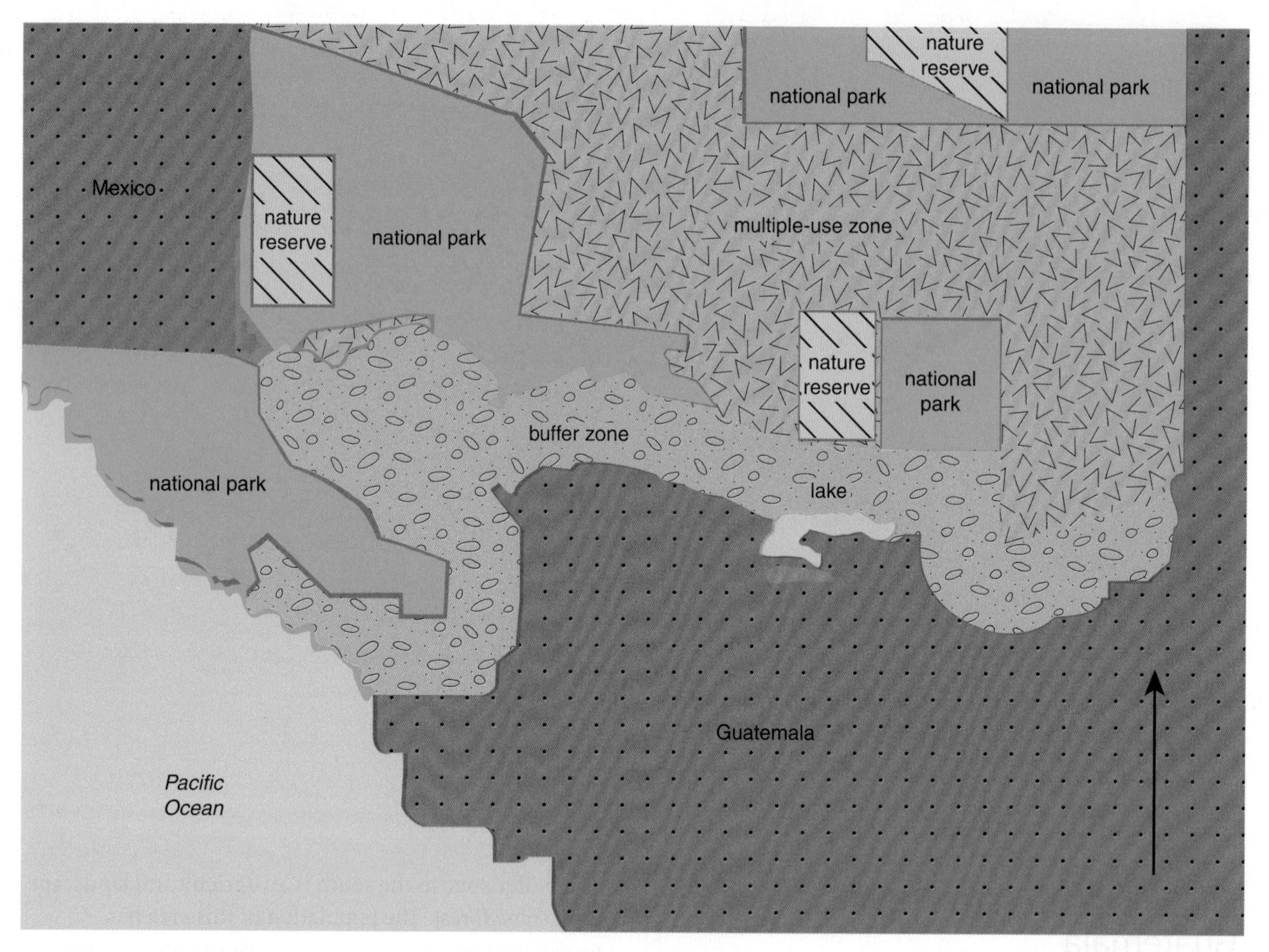

Figure 9.21 Map of the Mayan Biosphere Reserve in northern Guatemala.

be protected from invasive farmers, ranchers and drug traffickers, who are concentrated in the western part of the reserve.

Research carried out in the Mayan reserve includes:

- population studies of the Mexican crocodile (*Crocodylus moreletii*)
- the ecology of various bird species
- the biology and conservation of parrots
- measuring the abundance of fauna
- fishery pressures in the San Pedro River
- management of natural resources
- the impacts of tourism
- the impacts of subsistence hunting on populations of jaguar and pumas
- the biodiversity and potential uses of vascular plants in the rainforest
- development of communities near Flores, through the hunting and conservation of the turkey (*Pavo ocelado*)
- the harvesting of traditional non-timber forest products such as chicle (*Manilkara zapota*) and xate (*Chamaedorea* spp.).

Questions

1. Suggest the possible benefits of the Cuatro Balam plan to:
   a. local people
   b. the world in general.
2. Suggest how 'hunting and conservation' of *Pavo ocelado* can both be achieved in the same area.
3. Explain how the biodiversity of plants in the rainforest can be studied.

Seed banks, zoos and captive breeding

When habitats become severely threatened or even destroyed, the last resort for conserving the species within them maybe to put them into zoos (in the case of animals) or seed banks (in the case of plants).

Seed banks

Wild plant populations can be destroyed by habitat destruction caused by, for example, floods, fire, climate change and over-harvesting. Wild plants may carry genes that could be used in crop plants to confer resistance to pests and diseases.

If it is not possible to protect the area where the plants live, the plants can be preserved as seeds in seed banks.

Seeds are stored rather than living plants because less space is required, so more species can be held in the available space. Also, most plants produce large numbers of seeds so collecting small samples of seeds is unlikely to damage the wild population. Finally, seeds are easier to store than whole plants because they are dormant and need minimal care. Figure 9.22 shows the process of seed storage and Figure 9.23 shows the Global Seed Bank on the island of Svalbard at about 78 °N.

Zoos and captive breeding

Zoos have three main roles in conservation. First, they are very good at providing education about the illegal trade in animals and products and the need to maintain biodiversity. Secondly, zoos are involved in scientific research on the control of diseases, animal behaviour and techniques to improve breeding success. Third, zoos have a very important role in captive-breeding programmes to increase species numbers, thus reducing the risk of extinction, with a view to releasing captive-bred animals into the wild when habitats have been restored. Such programmes try to maintain the genetic diversity of a species, because inbreeding can lead to a reduction in diversity and therefore reduced adaptability if and when the species is placed back in the wild. However, some zoos only have a small number of individuals, so zoos try to avoid inbreeding and reduced adaptability in a number of ways:

- organisms are not allowed to breed repeatedly with the same partner
- a variety of partners for an organism can be achieved by *in-vitro* fertilisation and inter-zoo swapping of individuals
- all zoos use a database called a studbook to record the breeding history of individuals in captivity.

Sustainable tourism and ecotourism

Tourism can be a very important source of income for a country or a region. However, tourism can also be very damaging. Habitats are destroyed to provide accommodation, such as hotels, for tourists. The often huge but temporary increase in the population of an area leads to increased pollution and other problems. If tourism is managed in a sustainable way to prevent

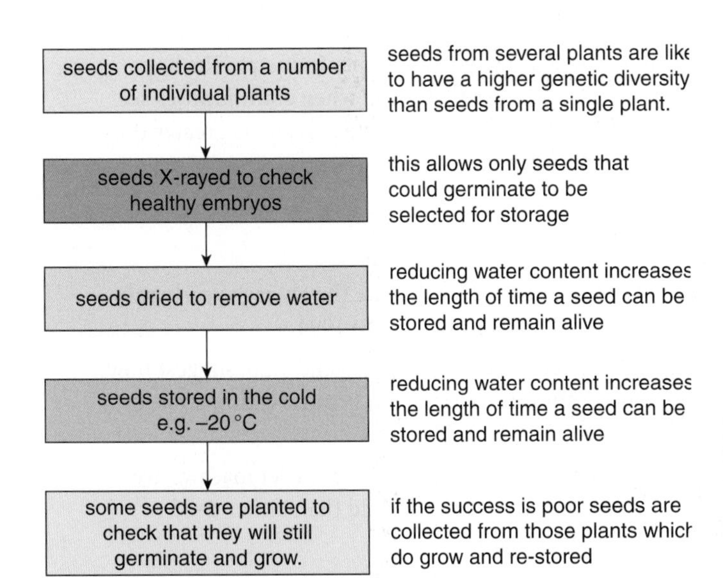

Figure 9.22 The stages in the storage of seeds in a seed bank.

Figure 9.23 The Global Seed Vault on the island of Svalbard, Norway. The site is dug in to a mountain on land inside the Arctic Circle at 78 °N.

damage to habitats and provide what people want, it is called sustainable tourism. Ecotourism is a form of sustainable tourism that is guided by environmental principles. Measures are taken to safeguard the wildlife of the area and the natural resources are used in a sustainable way. The key to successful sustainable ecotourism is realising that the growth of the tourist industry depends on maintaining the environment. One definition of ecotourism is responsible travel to natural areas that conserves the environment and improves the welfare of the local people.

SELF-ASSESSMENT QUESTIONS

9.15 List the advantages of agroforestry as a series of bullet points.

9. 16 Explain the differences between land management in the core area of a biosphere reserve with that in an extractive reserve.

9. 17 Suggest why plants are often conserved by creating a seed bank whereas animal conservation is often carried out in a zoo.

CASE STUDY

The scarlet macaw in Costa Rica

Of 146 species of new world parrots, over 40 are threatened. The scarlet macaw (*Ara macao*) is one of these (Figure 9.24). In Costa Rica, by the late 20th century, they occurred in only two areas, the Osa Peninsula and the Central Pacific Conservation Area (CPCA). Populations in a 560 km^2 area of the CPCA were monitored from 1990 until 2003 and managed from 1995 until 2003.

The birds are most visible during their daily flights between nocturnal roosting areas and feeding sites. For this reason, counts of the birds were made during their daily flights, from May 1990 until October 1994. The results of this monitoring are shown in Figure 9.25.

Figure 9.24 A pair of scarlet macaws in flight.

The study at this stage confirmed a decline in numbers and a macaw conservation strategy was developed at a workshop in 1994. The strategy focused on minimising chick poaching, the enhancement of habitats and community education. Subsequently, nest boxes were constructed and natural nests were protected. This was done under the auspices of the association for parrot protection, LAPPA. This organisation worked with ranchers, park workers, scientists, the local community and ecotourism organisers. The strategy also included raiding poachers' homes, confiscating poached chicks and tree-climbing equipment, arresting poachers and writing newspaper articles criticising named poachers. The effect of this strategy on macaw numbers is shown in Figure 9.26.

The Central Pacific scarlet macaw population is important for ecotourism. In 1994, more than 40 000 tourists spent US$6 million during visits to the area. It was reported that most of the tourists came to see the scarlet macaw. It was also reported that less than 10% of the money generated by tourism went to the local community. More recently it has been reported that tourism in the Central Pacific region employs more adult Costa Ricans than any other industry. The hope is that chick poaching will stop when communities see that the income from conserving macaws is greater than from poaching them.

Questions

1 Using Figure 9.25, calculate the average yearly rate of loss of birds from 1990 to 1994.

2 Using data from Figures 9.25 and 9.26, suggest how successful the experimental conservation strategy started in 1994 has been.

3 Explain why it is claimed that scarlet macaws are worth more alive in the wild than either dead or caged in a house.

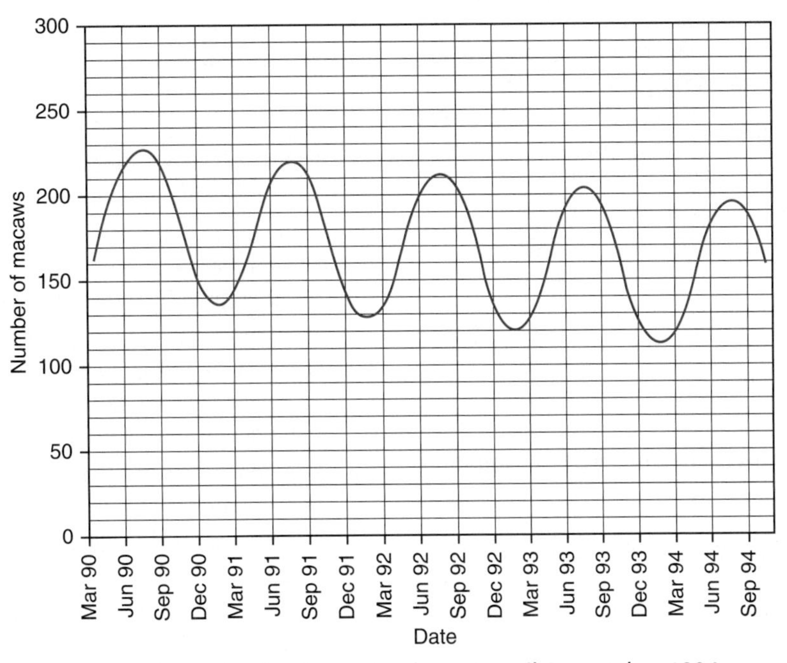

Figure 9.25 Scarlet macaw numbers in Costa Rica from March 1990 until September 1994.

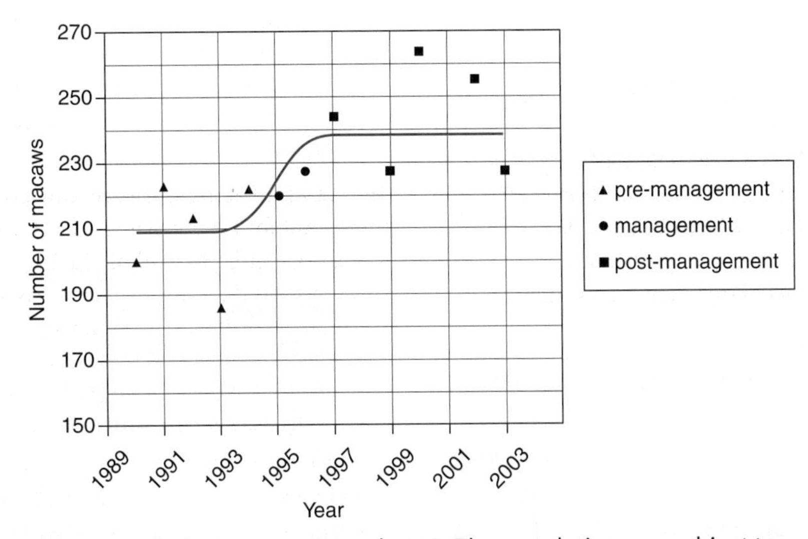

Figure 9.26 Scarlet macaw numbers between 1989 and 2003. The population was subject to management between 1995 and 1997.

PRACTICAL ACTIVITY 9.1

Estimating plant coverage using quadrats

To carry out this practical, ideally you need to find a place outside where there is either a gradient from one environment to another (for example at a woodland edge or across a footpath) or two areas that are different (for example one grazed by an animal and one not). If you are looking at a gradient you will need to place your quadrats systematically along a line (a transect) that crosses the gradient (see Figure 9.10a). If you are looking at two areas, then you need to place your quadrats randomly (see Figure 9.10b).

→

If you do not have commercially bought quadrats, it is easy to make one. You will probably want to make one 50 cm on each side (a square), but it can be any size depending on what you are studying. Four (or even two) rulers can be used to make a quadrat. For a 50 cm quadrat you will need two 0.5 m or larger rulers (Figure 9.27).

Figure 9.27 Two metre rules used to make a 50 cm quadrat.

Materials

- Quadrats
- Two 0.5 or 1 m rulers
- Random number table
- Pen and paper

Method

- If you are using a transect, lay your line across the area to be studied and put your quadrat at the first position.
- If you are comparing two areas, lay your quadrat at the coordinates generated with numbers from a random number table Figure 9.11 shows how to place quadrats.
- Once you have placed your quadrat, you need to count or estimate the plant coverage. If the plants can be seen as individuals they can be counted, if not you should use percentage cover (see Figure 9.9).
- Record your results. (For advice on creating an appropriate results table, see the Key skills in Environmental Management chapter).

Present your results in an appropriate format, then write a conclusion.

Summary

After completing this chapter, you should know:

- different levels of organisation in ecosystems, including population, community, habitat and niche
- the difference between biotic and abiotic factors within an ecosystem
- about some of the relationships between living things within an ecosystem
- how energy flows along food chains and food webs within an ecosystem
- how to use pyramids of numbers and pyramids of energy
- that photosynthesis and respiration as key processes in plants
- how nutrients, especially carbon, cycle within an ecosystem
- why habitats are lost and the consequences of their loss
- why forests are removed and the consequences of this removal.
- why we should try to keep forests
- some strategies for the sustainable management of forests
- how to estimate biodiversity using a variety of methods together with random and systematic sampling
- the advantages and disadvantages of various strategies for conserving ecosystems and the species within them.

End-of-chapter questions

1 Forests are often cleared for agriculture. In some cases the cleared land is used to grow plants, which are then used for the production of biofuels. One scientist said this was a good idea as the fuel produced was carbon neutral. Another disagreed with this statement. Explain your view on this. **[2 marks]**

2 Explain the importance of chlorophyll to the ecosystems of the world. **[4 marks]**

3 Figure 9.28 shows changes in an area of wetland in the US state of Minnesota over the past 150 years.

   a Describe the changes that have occurred between these three periods. **[3 marks]**

   b Suggest one strategy that could be used to conserve the remaining wetlands, and one that be used to extend wetland cover in this state. **[4 marks]**

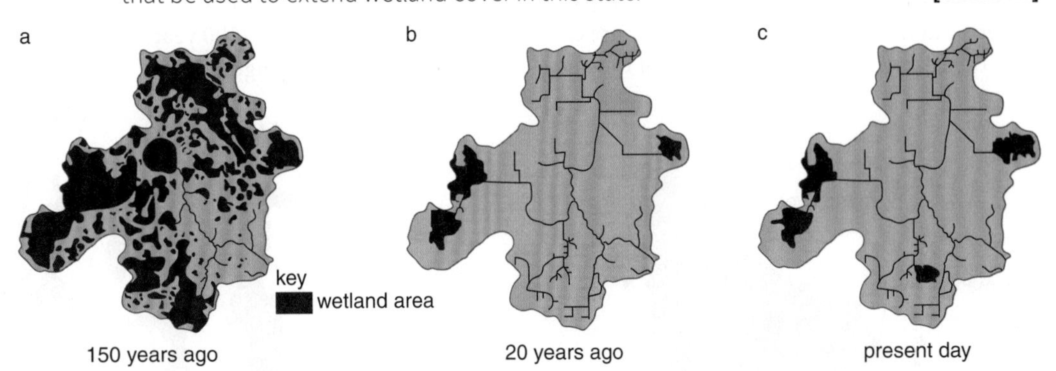

Figure 9.28 Changes in an area of wetland in the US state of Minnesota.

Source: Cambridge IGCSE Environmental Management 0680 Paper 1 Q6 June 2007

4 Two species of flatworm, A and B, were studied. They were found living in streams both alone and together. When alone they were found in the temperature ranges as follows: A, 8.5-19 °C, and, B, 8.5-23 °C. At temperatures above 23 °C, neither was found. In streams where both flatworms occurred, A was not found at all in temperatures above 14 °C. Suggest and explain a reason for this, assuming that both species eat the same food. **[4 marks]**

5 Figure 9.29 represents the numbers in each of four trophic (feeding) levels in a woodland ecosystem.

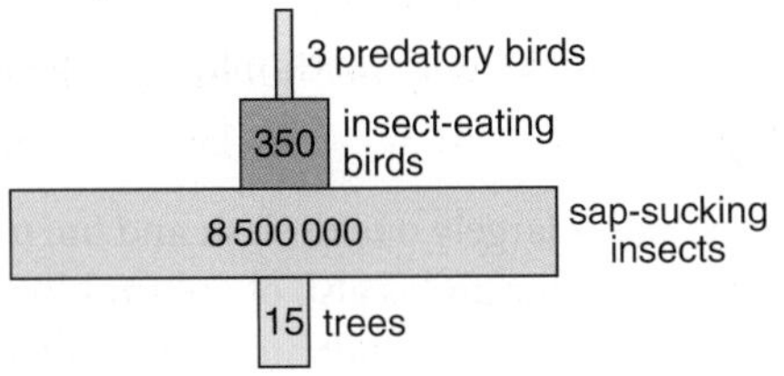

Figure 9.29 The numbers in each of four trophic levels in a woodland ecosystem.

   a To which trophic level do the sap-sucking insects belong? **[1 marks]**

   b Some students told their teacher they were surprised that the diagram did not form a pyramid shape. Write down what you think the teacher might have said to them to explain why it is not a pyramid. **[3 marks]**

   c The information below was collected about the organisms in Figure 9.29. Using this information and Figure 9.29, draw an annotated pyramid of energy for this woodland food web.

   average mass of one tree = 1000 kg
   average energy content of trees = 5 kJ g^{-1}
   average mass of one sap-sucking insect = 0.01 g
   average energy content of sap-sucking insects = 8 kJ g^{-1}
   average mass of one insect-eating bird = 5 g
   average energy content of insect-eating birds = 10 kJ g^{-1}
   average mass of one predatory bird = 100 g
   average energy content of predatory birds = 10 kJ g^{-1} **[10 marks]**

Deforestation in Madagascar

Madagascar is a large island off the east coast of southern Africa. It became isolated from all other land masses about 90 million years ago. During most of the time between then and the present day, the animals and plants have been left alone. This means that over 90% of the organisms living on the island live only there and nowhere else on Earth: they are endemic to Madagascar. About 2500 years ago, humans arrived on the island. Since then over 90% of the once lush forest has been lost (Figure 9.30).

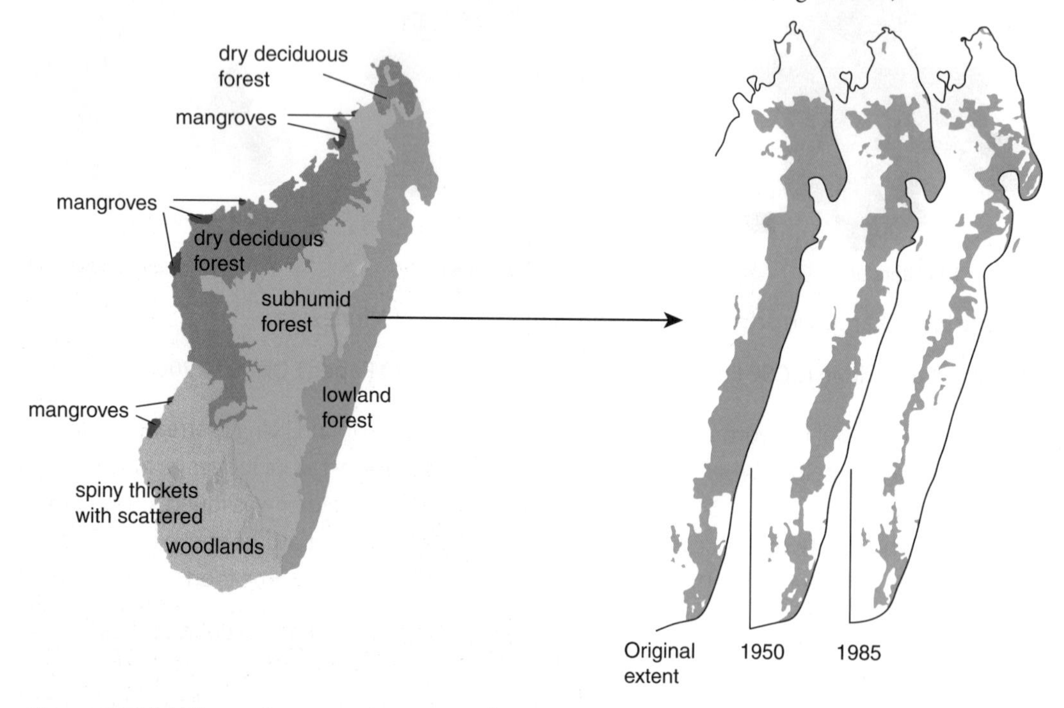

Figure 9.30 (a) The main vegetation zones of Madagascar. (b) Loss of eastern humid forests since human colonisation 2500 years ago.

Much of this deforestation has occurred quite recently, and is largely due to slash and burn, a practice called *tavy* in Madagascar. This is a valued agriculture technique and is also of cultural significance. Parcels of land pass from the family who first cleared them to the descendants of those people. The areas are carefully selected by taking account of the species already there and the colour of their leaves, both indicators of how fertile the soil is. A hectare or so of forest is cut down and then burned. No trees are left. Burning turns the cleared vegetation into ash, which is rich in minerals. It also destroys potential pests and weeds. The resulting area is planted, usually with rice. The cleared land can usually support a rice crop for only 2 years, giving a yield of about 900 kg hectare^{-1} year^{-1}. It is then left to recover, usually for 4 years. The vegetation that has grown in those 4 years is cut and burned again, and rice is cultivated for 2 more years. This sequence can be repeated once more, but after that the area is useless for further cultivation.

There is also quite a big world market for timber from Madagascar. The eastern part of the island has a band of tropical rainforest, and it is from here that most of the valuable trees are taken. The most important of these are ebony and rosewood, which can be worth US$ 1000–2000 tonne^{-1}.

Many of the profoundly poor people of the country can earn a little money from the sale of charcoal. This is made from many types of wood, leading to further deforestation. In this case, it is the spiny forests of the south-west which are very badly affected.

Tavy is a very controversial practice both inside Madagascar and internationally. Primary rainforest, much valued for reasons already discussed, is turned into secondary growth and, ultimately, grassland. Deforestation leads to desertification, extensive soil erosion and nutrient loss. Minerals are lost because of leaching and are taken out in harvested crops, together with some (mainly carbon and nitrogen) that is burnt off.

In the short term, levels of soil minerals increase, but they soon decline again. Over the long term, nutrient loss is on-going. One study has shown that nutrient levels in the soil had increased by about 25% 2 years after *tavy* and were back to the starting point within 6 years. The same study showed that after 160 years of *tavy* cycles, nutrient levels had fallen by 25% from the beginning of the cycle and that the trend was consistently downward.

The soils of Madagascar, like those in most tropical regions, are laterites. These soils are rich in iron compounds and deep red in colour. From space, astronauts have seen red-stained water at many river estuaries, prompting them to describe the island as 'bleeding to death' (Figure 9.31).

Figure 9.31 (a, b) Laterite soils of Madagascar. (c) The estuary of the River Betsiboka showing silt from the lands in the interior being washed out sea.

Along with the forests and their soils, many of the large animals that once lived in Madagascar have been lost. The biggest of these includes the giant elephant-birds, of which there used to be eight species. The list also includes two species of hippopotamus, a large species of fossa and over twelve species of lemurs.

Lemurs are a group of primates that are endemic to Madagascar. There are currently thought to be about 100 species left, but eight are critically endangered, 18 are endangered, 15 are vulnerable and four are near threatened. Of the remaining 55, eight are of least concern but for the rest there is simply not enough information to decide their status.

Questions

1 Explain what is likely to happen to lead to the recovery of a plot that has undergone *tavy.*

2 If the level of nitrate in a soil before *tavy* was 5 g kg^{-1}, use the information in the case study to calculate what it would be:

 a 2 years after *tavy*

 b 160 years after *tavy*

3 Explain the causes and consequences of the observation by astronauts that Madagascar is 'bleeding to death'.

4 Calculate the total yield from a hectare of land cleared by *tavy* after 18 years of this process.

5 Suggest two reasons why it might be difficult for the Madagascar government to control deforestation.

6 Suggest why the loss of animal species may be an issue for the people of Madagascar.

Answers to Self-assessment questions

All questions and sample answers have been written by the authors.

Chapter 1

1

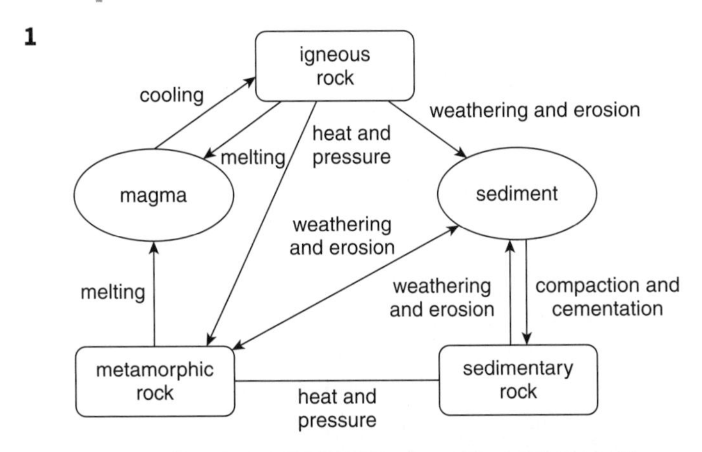

2

Description	Rock type
Rocks formed in the sea from particles of eroded rock	Sedimentary
Rocks changed by heat	Metamorphic
Rocks formed from the cooling of other molten rock	Igneous

3 To include:

- size of deposit
- geology
- accessibility of site, transport links (existing or future)
- likely cost benefit (worth of deposits versus costs of extraction)
- safety
- world price.

4 Much less costly to remove overburden than to drill down. Deposits are easier to find on surface. Safety issues may need more consideration and cost more in a sub-surface mine.

5 If it is illegal to mine then the other legal factors are unlikely to have been considered. So, safety requirements will have been ignored, putting anyone in the mine at risk. Environmental laws will also be ignored, so there will be no control on the impact of the mine. This is likely to include pollution aspects as well as landscape effects.

6 Plants are the primary producers in nearly all ecosystems. This means they make all the food that all other organisms in the system rely on. Reduced plant growth will thus mean less food for herbivores and, in turn, for carnivores. They provide more than food though. They also provide habitat for other organisms, including other plants. In addition, reduction in the growth of plants may lead to a reduction in their ability to protect the soil. Soil erosion may be another consequence of the reduction of plant growth.

7 The treating of waste *in situ* (on site) will involve much less cost, especially that of transport.

The treating of waste *ex situ* (off site) has the advantage of taking any contaminants, which the waste may contain, away to somewhere that is more suitable.

8 It will reduce the necessity for mining and extracting more material, which will reduce the environmental effect of these activities.

Obtaining materials early always involves the expenditure of energy and it may be that recycling would reduce the energy costs.

The recycling of waste can create jobs.

Chapter 2

1 **a** 188/22 560 × 100 = 0.83%

b Iceland and the USA are both industrialised (developed), they also both have colder climates so more energy is used in heating and lighting.

2 Water is pumped underground where it is heated by the hot rocks. As the water reaches the surface the change in pressure turns the water to steam. The steam turns a turbine, which rotates the generator to produce electricity. The cooling water can then be reheated by the rocks underground.

3 Healthy economies produce more goods (more energy used), they also consume more goods (needing greater transport to supply them) and have more wealth to buy non-essential items (using energy in their manufacture). People also travel more in their leisure time.

4 Examples could include the following.

Government forcing a change:

- planning laws on energy use for new buildings
- banning energy-inefficient designs
- banning use of energy sources that are particularly polluting, etc.

Government encouraging change:

- grants to scrap inefficient machinery
- taxes on fuel (encouraging machines with low running costs and energy use)
- education
- providing alternatives such as public transport.

5 It might be unfair because it does not take into account:

- climate (the need for heating)
- geography (distances that have to be travelled)
- economy (some countries depend on industries that need large amounts of energy)
- demographics (the age of the population, the rate of growth) and the impact this may have on energy use.

6 The largest spills have all happened on land. Oil is not able to spread so widely on land as it does on the sea, where it forms a thin layer. A smaller amount of oil can impact a far larger area at sea.

7 Lack of light will kill organisms that photosynthesise (such as marine plants and phytoplankton). These are the producers in the food web. If these are removed, there is an impact on the food supply of all other organisms in this environment. This impact is potentially larger than for those animals that come into direct contact with the oil.

Chapter 3

1 Limestone is alkaline so is likely to increase the pH of the soil (make it less acidic).

2 At pH 8.0, the following nutrients are less available:

- boron (B)
- iron (Fe)
- copper (Cu)
- zinc (Zn)
- and, most importantly, phosphorus (P) (because it is needed in larger quantities).

3 Reduction in yield. Leaves are discoloured. Older leaves drop off plants prematurely. Plants more prone to pest/disease, crops do not store so well in storage.

4

	Subsistence	Commercial
Arable	C	A D
Pastoral	E	B
Mixed	F	

5 Reasons could include:

- maximising the yield from the crop plants
- reducing costs by using resources as efficiently as possible
- improvements to crop quality/reduction is pest and disease problems
- efficient use of the grower's time.

6 Speeding up of the breeding programme, which may take many years if only trial and error is used. The opportunity to introduce a new characteristic that is not naturally found within that organism.

7 Use a different insecticide that has a chemical formula different from the original one. Use biological control to reduce the problem without the need for chemicals. Select different varieties in the next season that are more pest resistant.

8 Use a range of insecticides on a rota basis to reduce the risk of resistance to any particular one. Use crop rotation to reduce pest numbers. Only spray when absolutely necessary, not routinely.

9

	Too little irrigation	Too much irrigation
Nutrient availability	Lack of uptake due to insufficient water availability	Leaching of nutrients through the soil so unavailable to crops
Root growth	Stunted growth due to lack of water for essential processes	Risk of root death due to lack of oxygen in the soil (air spaces filled with water)

10 There may already be sufficient nutrients in the soil but the plant is unable to access them due to drought. Pest or disease attack might impact on the plant's ability to use the nutrients. The addition of too much fertiliser may damage the plant (damage the roots). The fertiliser added might not contain the nutrient that is in short supply (and an abundance of others).

11 Terracing

Contour ploughing

12 Advantages:

- reduces wind speed
- might provide useful shade for a crop
- might provide a habitat that supports natural predators
- its roots might help stabilise a soil and prevent it blowing away.

Disadvantages:

- might shade the crop and reduce growth
- will compete for water
- makes it more difficult to cultivate fields
- might provide a habitat that supports pests or diseases.

13 Use of (permeable) netting or mesh.

Chapter 4

1 Liquid water is found on the surface of the Earth in oceans, lakes and rivers. It is also found inside plants. Water turns from a liquid to a gas, water vapour, in a process called evaporation. The water vapour then condenses to form clouds. Liquid water falls from clouds to the Earth in the process of precipitation. Some of the water is prevented from reaching the ground by plants in the process of interception. Water that reaches the ground may enter it in a process called infiltration. The rest enters rivers by run-off.

2 Because it is salty. Consumption of salt water leads to an increased loss of water to rid the body of the salt.

3 3% of all water is fresh. So 0.3% of 3% is surface water. That is 0.03 × 3 = 0.09%. Lakes form 87% of this. That is 0.87 × 0.09 = 0.0783%. Thus less than 0.1% of all water on Earth is in lakes.

4 The process of desalination, however carried out, consumes a lot of energy, which is abundant in oil-rich countries.

5 Glacial water is unlikely to be important as it exists in regions that are very cold, so it would cost a lot of energy to melt it in order for it to be used. Groundwater requires the drilling or digging of wells, which requires funding and technology. Large numbers of humans are without either the funds or technology to pursue either of these water sources and so rely on surface water.

6

	Advantages	Disadvantages
Environmental	Flood control Creation of habitat for wetland species	People have to be moved The life cycles of fish and other aquatic organisms may be disrupted
Economic	The generation of electricity in hydroelectric power plants Irrigation Tourism and leisure Provides access by boat to otherwise inaccessible areas	Very expensive to set up
Social	Flood control The provision of water	People have to be moved People downstream of the dam may be affected in terms of water supply and the enrichment of soil, which floods bring

7 Very simply, all dams over time accumulate silt behind them (in the reservoirs), and when this reaches the height of the water in the reservoir, many of the dam's functions become impossible. For example, if no water flows through the turbines, no electricity can be generated and a reservoir that no longer exists cannot store water or provide a route for boat travel.

8 Both typhoid and cholera can be transmitted through contaminated water. This is because they are both caused by bacteria that enter the water. On the other hand, the organism that causes malaria does not live in water. It lives in the body of female mosquitoes, which transmit it to humans.

9 Potable water is water that can be drunk safely. Sewage treatment is not normally designed to produce potable water. However, in more advanced sewage treatment plants a tertiary level of treatment disinfects the water with chlorine. This makes it potable.

10 This is because some countries produce large amounts of the gases that cause acid rain in industrial processes. Other countries, hundreds of miles away, may produce only small amounts of these gases. Because the gases enter the atmosphere, winds can blow them from a producer to a non-producer. Scandinavian pine forests were badly damaged by acid rain gases from northern Europe.

11 Rain is formed by a process of evaporation of water from surfaces of water bodies. Any contamination by pathogens in that water will be left behind in the water body, and will not be carried in the water vapour. Rain falling on a roof should be relatively pure. Rain that is collected in a pond or lake is much more likely to be contaminated with pathogens.

12 Malaria can be treated using certain drugs. Because a vector carries it, mosquito vector eradication would also be suitable.

Both cholera and typhoid are caused by bacteria, which can be carried in human faeces. The best way to control these diseases is improved sanitation. Good sanitation is designed to separate human faeces from the water that humans drink. A clean water supply will be free of these bacteria; in the absence of improved sanitation, this can be achieved through chlorination.

Chapter 5

1 Both types rely on the movement of seawater to move a turbine, which then generates electricity. In the case of tides, this movement is generated by the gravity of the Sun and Moon, which cause the water to rise and fall twice a day. Wave energy relies on the perpetual movement of the waves caused by wind. Waves are more variable than tidal, which is also more predictable.

2 The coast constantly experiences waves. These can be converted into electricity all the time as the turbine in the Islay LIMPET turns the same way whether the wave is coming into the tube or leaving it.

3 Sewage pollution makes water unsafe to drink because of the pathogenic bacteria in sewage. These can cause diseases such as typhoid and cholera. Seawater is fairly unlikely to carry such bacteria, although it is possible especially near the coast and river mouths. The main reason that seawater is unsafe to drink is because of its high level of salt. The salt cannot be excreted by humans without using more water than is gained by drinking seawater. So, drinking seawater will cause dehydration.

4 They are near coasts so it is much easier to fish there. The water is quite shallow, so there is a good supply of sunlight for photosynthesis. The sea receives minerals from the seabed, so in the open ocean the shallow, lit area is too far above the seabed, in most situations, to receive the minerals.

5 The normal ocean current system in this part of the world acts to bring minerals to the surface. These minerals encourage the growth of phytoplankton, which are food for fish. When the current system is reversed due to El Niño, this upwelling of minerals stops and phytoplankton numbers fall, thus starving the fish.

6 **a** Cold current, dashed lines; warm current, solid lines.

b Both A and B are affected by a north-flowing cold current that serves to stir up minerals from the seabed. These enter shallow waters, where there is plenty of light, and, by the time the currents reach the tropics, it is warm. Water is, of course, abundant, as is dissolved carbon dioxide, so all the requirements for good growth of phytoplankton are present: water, carbon dioxide and light for photosynthesis, and minerals for the manufacture of proteins and other chemicals. Abundant phytoplankton leads to a high population of the fish that feed on them, and the fish that eat the fish that eat the phytoplankton, along the food chain.

7 **a** The trend is upwards and, despite El Niños in 1957–58 and 1965–66, this is not affected because the catch is still relatively low. There was a small decline in 1965–66.

b The dramatic fall in 1972–73 was probably caused mainly by the El Niño, but over-fishing is now becoming important so, despite no more El Niños until 1982, the decline continued through these years.

c Once the serious El Niños of 1986–88 were over, the fishery began to pick up, possibly due to measures designed to stop over-fishing, so stocks are recovering.

8 Culturing of marine fish is very difficult because the fish need different foods at each life stage, and this is difficult to supply for carnivorous fish, which are the ones we like to eat. Farmed fish easily succumb to diseases and parasites. Marine fish farms have negative effects on their surroundings.

9 Environment: it could reduce over-fishing and, most especially, the taking of bycatch. Fishers: it is much less risky in terms of danger at sea, and financially as the yield is more predictable. Consumers: The fish may be much less costly than the expensively caught wild fish. There are some suggestions that farmed fish are healthier.

10 Each tick mark on the pie is 10%, so there are 60% over-fished and about 6% depleted, which is a total of 66%, which is definitely unsustainable.

11

Reason for over-fishing	Possible solution
Large destructive nets	Control of net types
Large diamond-meshed nets	Inclusion of square-mesh panels
Large boats	Licensing, restricting
Boats that can stay out at sea for weeks	Licensing, patrols
Satellite location of shoals	Limiting by law
Human population growth	Any measure to reduce this

12 The large-scale fishery operation would never have to call in at a port, so it is much harder to monitor the catch being taken compared with the small-scale operation, where inspections can easily be carried out.

Chapter 6

1

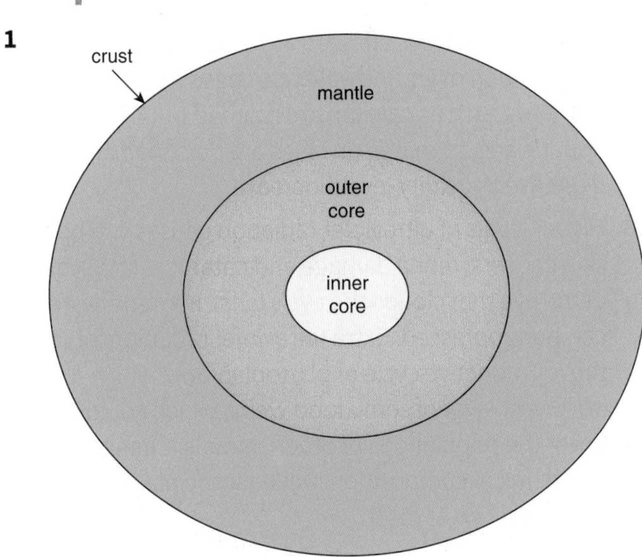

2 The oceanic crust is younger; heavier; made up of mainly basalt; thinner; it can sink and is renewed and destroyed.

3 A slab or piece of lithosphere (crust and upper mantle) that moves.

4 Answer will vary depending on where you live.

5 Edge or margin of tectonic plates/where plates meet, move apart or move together.

6 Convection currents in the magma of the mantle.

7 **a** destructive

b destructive

c conservative

d constructive

e destructive

8 **a** Friction is created and pressure is released when the oceanic plate is subducted. This takes place in the Benioff zone. At a collision zone earthquakes occur as the two plates move towards each other.

b Pressure builds up as the two plates lock together. When the plates slip the pressure is released in the form of seismic waves.

9 **a** At 700 km down the subducted oceanic plate has disintegrated and the magma rises to the surface, where it erupts through a crack or weakness to form a composite or acidic volcano.

b Two plates move away from each other due to convection currents, creating a gap or weakness. Magma rises and erupts through the gap. The basaltic lava may build up and appear above the sea surface as a shield volcano.

10 Himalayas = Eurasian and Indian plates

Andes = Nazca and South American plate

Rockies = Pacific and North American plate

11 An earthquake is when the ground shakes or moves in sudden jerks. Earthquakes result from a build-up and sudden release of tension, usually along a fault line.

12 The focus is where the earthquake begins underground, and the point on the Earth's surface, directly above, is called the epicentre.

13 The Richter scale on a seismograph.

14 A hole or crack (fissure) in the crust through which magma erupts. It can build up to form a cone-shaped mountain.

15 Liquefaction, as this is the only earthquake hazard.

16 Lava is magma that erupts at the surface of the Earth.

17 Found between 5° and 20° north and south of the equator.

18 Ocean temperatures of over 27° (one condition) and water depth over 60 m (second condition) so that there is an increase in evaporation and release of energy. Little wind shear (third condition) to allow vertical development of the storm.

19 Sky becomes cloudy, wind speed increases, rain with sunny intervals. Wind speed continues to increase to over 119 km h^{-1}. Large cumulonimbus clouds and very heavy rain. In the eye of the storm the sky is clear, winds are light and there is little rain. Temperatures are warm. After the eye has passed cumulonimbus clouds form again, with the return of heavy rain and strong wind. Wind speed and rainfall decreases. Sunny intervals.

20 The energy source (warm ocean) has been removed.

21

Flash response	Slow response
Urban	Forest
Ploughing downslope	Rural
Wet soil	Dry soil
Impermeable rock	Light rainfall
Heavy rainfall	Permeable rock
Rapid snowmelt	Ploughing across the slope

22 Answers will vary.

Chapter 7

1 gases, gravity, nitrogen, 78.09%, oxygen, argon, carbon dioxide, 0.03%, ozone, stratosphere

2 Used by plants in photosynthesis and plants support other life; a greenhouse gas; raw material for carbonaceous skeletons.

3 Troposphere

4 Troposphere: temperature decreases with height (6.4 °C km^{-1}) as warming effect of the Earth's surface through conduction and convection diminishes with height.

Stratosphere: temperature increases with height as ozone absorbs incoming ultraviolet radiation.

Mesosphere: temperatures decrease with height as there is no water vapour, dust or ozone to absorb the incoming short-wave radiation.

Thermosphere: temperatures increase as atomic oxygen absorbs ultraviolet radiation.

5 Any two of carbon dioxide, methane, CFCs, nitrous oxides.

6 The Earth receives incoming short-wave radiation from the Sun. About half of this radiation is absorbed by the Earth's surface, around 20% is absorbed by the atmosphere, and 30% is reflected by clouds and the Earth's surface back into space. As the Earth's surface warms, outgoing long-wave or infrared radiation is released back into the atmosphere. Greenhouse gases absorb some of this radiation and deflect it back to the Earth's surface. These greenhouses gases act like a blanket trapping the radiation.

7 CFCs stay in the atmosphere longer than methane (1000 years compared with 12 years) so their impact continues into the future

8 When the atmosphere contains gases and substances in harmful amounts.

9 1B, 2D, 3A, 4C

10 CFCs

11 Smog (smoke and fog) occurs where the burning of fossils fuels in industry, homes and vehicles provides additional particles that act as condensation nuclei for fog to form around.

The enhanced greenhouse effect is where more heat is being retained and there is a warming of the Earth's temperature because of an increase in concentration of greenhouse gases.

12 People: breathing difficulties; acidification of groundwater makes water undrinkable and can cause diarrhoea and stomach upsets; aluminium leached from the soil into the groundwater has been linked with pre-senile dementia; limestone buildings are chemically weathered; crop yields decline.

Environment: trees affected as foliage dies; acidification of groundwater damages tree roots; nutrients such as calcium are leached out of the soil; aquatic and animal life in lakes are poisoned and decrease as acidity levels increase.

13 Higher levels of ultraviolet radiation causes sun burn, skin cancers, retina damage and cataracts (a disease of the eye that clouds the eye's lens). Immune system can be suppressed. Extra ultraviolet radiation inhibits the reproductive cycle of phytoplankton, which make up lowest layer of some food webs, which could lower the populations of other animals. Changes in biochemical composition makes some plant leaves less attractive as food.

14 Impacts will depend on the country discussed but there could be a rise in sea-level, leading to possible forced migration, more erosion and the need for more money to be spent on sea defences. The change in climate could be considered and how it could affect the economy or people's lives.

Chapter 8

1 Similarities: they both show slow early growth but then fast growth in the middle time period.

Differences: there is a plateau in the small mammal population, but none in the human population. This is because the small mammal population size is limited by the natural carrying capacity whereas the human population size, so far, is not limited due to constant technological advances in agriculture.

2 The livestock are cattle and possibly other animals kept by people. These animals need to feed on plants. The plants are described as consisting of sparse grassland, suggesting there will not be enough food for all the livestock and that their presence may damage the land even further.

3 On an island it is likely there will be no natural predators of the herbivore. Other natural checks to population growth, such as disease, may also be absent. The population will thus grow until it is limited by food. Since the food of herbivores is plants, it is likely that this large population will damage these. They may be restricted in growth and fail to reproduce at a rate that replaces losses to the herbivores.

4 **a** There could be a disease or wars during this time. The Black Death occurred in the 14th century.

b 6400 ÷ 1000 = 6.4 times bigger

c There has been increasingly better medical care, leading to higher survival of both young and old. There has also been a better food supply leading to longer life. Finally there has been better sanitation, leading to higher survival of both young and old due to a reduction water-borne diseases. A fear of old age has led couples to have a large family, so their children can look after them in the future.

5 Any two from each side of the table.

Push	Pull
Drought/famine	Good supplies of food whatever the weather
Poverty	Well-paid jobs
Poor links with outside world	Good roads
Poor services	Hospitals, schools, water, electricity
Work on the land only, subsistence	Factory/shop/office work for a wage
Desertification	No comparable pull factors
Sea-level rise	No comparable pull factors
Seasonal weather events such as monsoons, cyclones, etc.	No comparable pull factors

6 If birth rate is greater than death rate then we would expect growth, but if emigration + death rate is greater than immigration + birth rate the population will decline.

7 The size is the number of individuals in a named area. This area may be a country, a town or any other defined region. Density expresses the size on a per unit area basis. The area is not merely named but its size is known.

8 **a** $\frac{325\,127\,634}{33{,}77} = 9\,627\,706\ \text{km}^2$

b Vatican City

9 Because the most dense does not have a very large population but a very small area. (It is Monaco with 37 620 people at a density of 18 812 km^{-3}. This is because the area of the country is only 2 km^2.)

10 The dependent members are those such as children and the elderly and disabled. These people do not produce and are supported by those who do, the independent members.

11

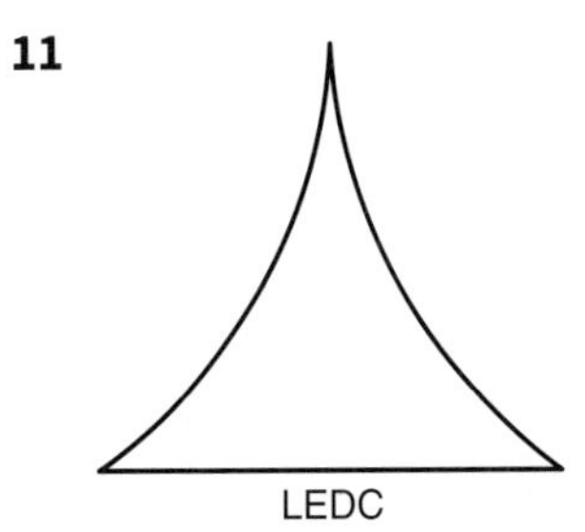

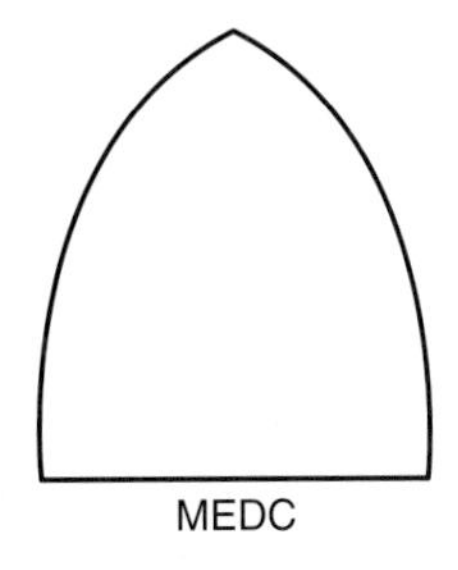

12 Because both the birth and death rates of boys are different from that of girls. The populations of the two sexes are thus different from the start of life.

13 **a**

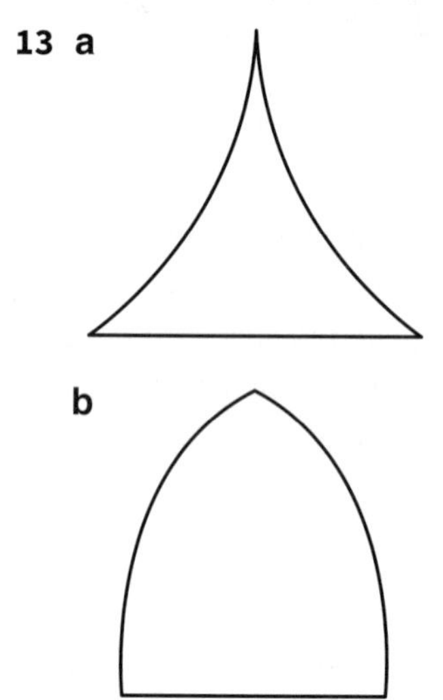

b

Chapter 9

1 It might be that grazers in the field will not allow it to live there. Plants in the field may compete for light and stop it growing there. It could be due to soil water content, which may be much less as the area becomes more open. Soil pH is likely to be higher in the field due the lower amount of fallen leaves, which, when they rot, produce an acid.

2 An ecosystem contains a number of species of animals and plants each of which has a population, lives in a particular habitat and occupies a niche. They all live together in a community.

3 **a** In the woodland ecosystem shown, all the energy for life comes from the Sun. The energy is in the form of light and is trapped by plant leaves in a process called photosynthesis. This produces the gas oxygen and uses the gas carbon dioxide. The food that is made in this process is then converted into everything that the plant needs. Organisms like plants that make food are called producers. Also in the woodland are pictures of some consumers, they are:

squirrels, birds, insects, deer, mice, foxes, rabbits.

Some of the consumers are predators, such as the foxes and some birds. Both the animals and the plants use the food they either eat or make to supply energy for their lives. This energy is released in a process called respiration. This process also releases the gas taken in by plants.

b All the living things in the picture live in a particular habitat:

the mice live in the grassland

the birds live in the trees

bacteria live in the soil.

Some abiotic (physical) factors are shown in the picture. These are:

(Sun)light, water (as rain), carbon dioxide in the air, rocks

One food chain in the picture is grass → rabbits → foxes,

another is leaves → insects →birds.

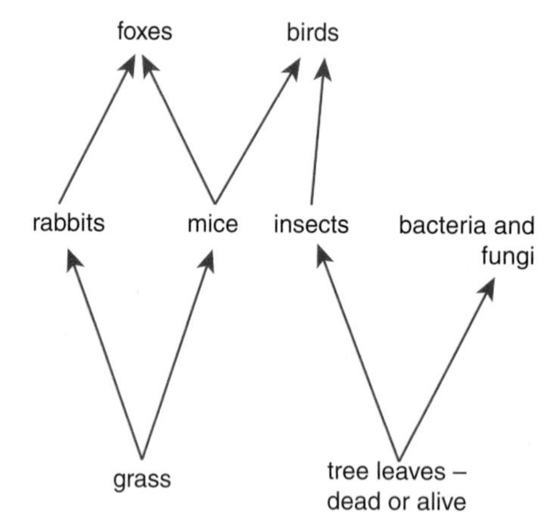

The one animal not shown on this web is the squirrel.

There are five populations of animals in this woodland, deer, rabbits, foxes, squirrels and mice. In addition there will be many populations of insects and birds of different species. All the animals in the woodland live in a community.

c **i** Fox, ground-living medium-sized predator

Birds, tree-living small predators

ii Mice and rabbits for grass

iii Fox

iv Trees pollinated by insects

4 The atmosphere

5 Sugars, proteins

6 Both processes involve the breakdown of organic material, which releases energy and produces water and carbon dioxide. Both need oxygen. Decay is always the breakdown of organic matter in dead plants and animals and is carried out mainly by bacteria and fungi. Respiration happens both in bacteria and fungi during decay but also inside the bodies of all living things.

7 a

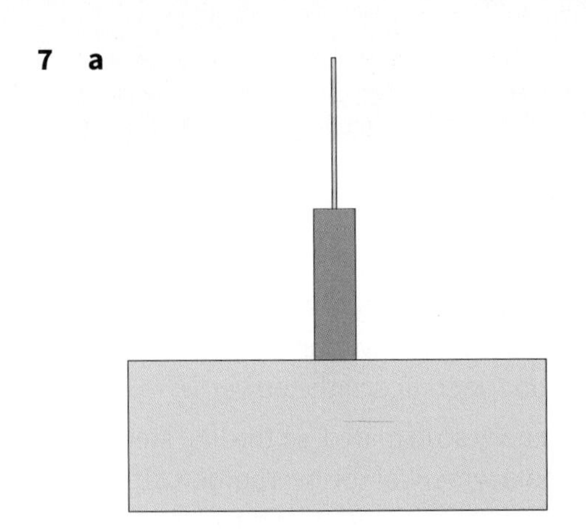

b i $3000 \div 40\,000 = 0.075 \times 100 = 7.5\%$

ii $450 \div 3000 = 0.15 \times 100 = 15\%$

8 b iv

c ii

d i

9 Modern crop plants lack variety and we may need some of the genes in wild plants in the future, for example in the event of severe climate change. Some of the genetic diversity may lead to the production of chemicals that may have uses for humans, for example in medicines or as pesticides.

10 Decrease in incidence of the water-borne diseases. Reduced habitat for aquatic plants and animals. Increased food production if the land is used for agriculture.

11 a It is likely to decrease it (a little) as the mature forest is carbon neutral but the fast-growing palm trees are a carbon sink.

b The biodiversity is likely to decline as the mature forest will have many species of trees, other plants and associated animals. The oil palm planation will have only the oil palm trees and a very few other plants and associated animals.

12 a

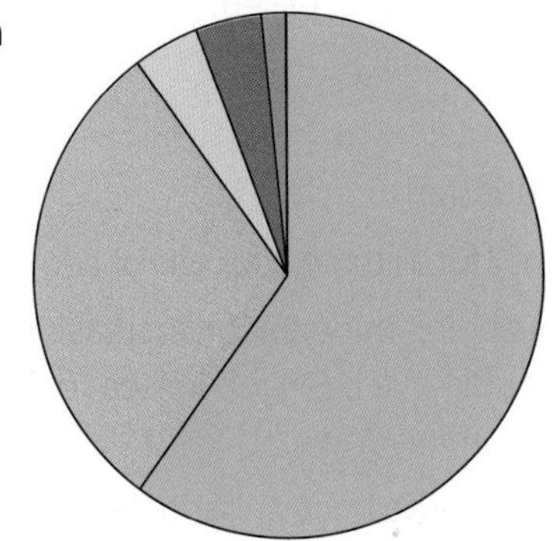

b 30% of $14\,285\ km^2 = 0.3 \times 14\,285\ km^2 = 4285.5\ km^2$

13 Meets: Staying in local accommodation helps local people. The whales are likely to be looked after (conserved) as they form the resource from which money can be made. Whales mainly live in natural areas, only a very few are kept in captivity.

Does not meet: The travel involved, both to the area and on the boat trip, will probably involve the burning of fossil fuels, which has negative effects on the environment.

14

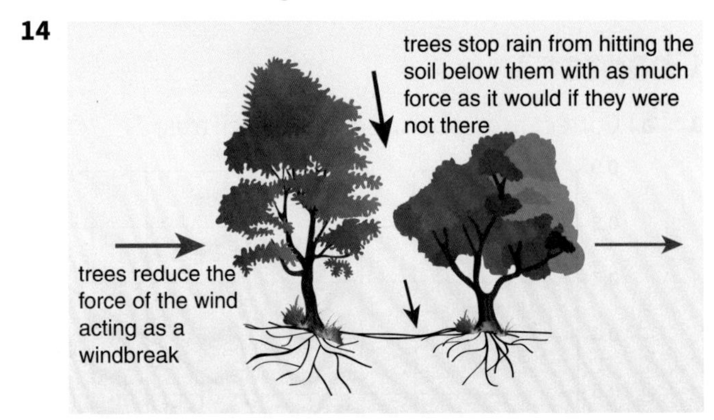

15
- Trees enrich the soil
- They provide food for animals and people
- They provide firewood for people
- They protect the soil from erosion
- The animals provide the farmer with food, including milk
- The animals enrich the soil

16 In an extractive reserve local people are given some of the responsibility of managing the land and have the right to remove products from it. In the core area of a biosphere reserve no extracting of products is allowed, only monitoring and maybe some research.

17 Animals do not produce a naturally hardy stage like the seeds produced by many plants. So, animals must be bred generation after generation in order to keep them alive in captivity but plants can be preserved as seeds for many years.

Answers to End-of-chapter questions

All exam-style questions and sample answers have been written by the authors. In examinations, the way marks are awarded may be different.

Chapter 1

1 a Correct axes labels. [2, one for each axis]

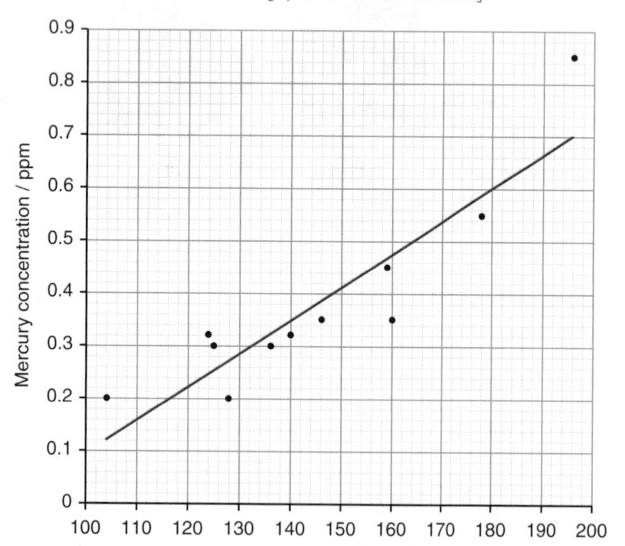

b As the fish get longer the concentration of mercury gets higher. [1] This is probably because longer fish are older fish. [1] This in turn means that they will have eaten more over their lifespan. [1] If what they ate was contaminated with mercury this could have accumulated in their bodies over those years. [1] Smaller younger fish would have accumulated less. [1]

c No more than about 130 mm long. [1]

d It could be concluded that the mine is unlikely to be the source. [1] As far as 100 km from the lake mercury levels in the river are undetectable. [1] It is likely that the mercury comes from the air, as the only other possible source. [1]

2 a Ore [1]

b 1 tonne of aluminium is gained from 5 tonnes of bauxite. [1] This would leave 4 tonnes of waste. [1] 25 tonnes would produce 5 × 4 tonnes = 20 tonnes. [1]

c 1 tonne from 5 tonnes of ore, so 25 tonnes would need 25 × 5 tonnes of ore = 125 tonnes. [1]

d Pollution by caustic soda, which would raise pH in any water courses it entered. [1] This material is hot so that would also cause problems in the environment. [1] To provide the electric current for the smelting, electricity is needed and its generation may cause environmental issues, depending on the source of the power. [1]

e The ore is usually strip mined, so the first step would be replacement of the overburden. [1] The addition of fertilisers [1] and then the planting of suitable vegetation would follow this. [1]

3 a Sedimentary [1]

b A deep shaft is drilled down into the hill above the coal seam. [1] This allows workers and machinery to be lowered to where the coal seam is located. [1] The coal is then dug out from the seam with machinery and transported to the surface through the same or a different shaft. [1]

c Coal, between 290 and 250 million years. [1]

Oil, about 205 million years. [1]

d [2, one for each box]

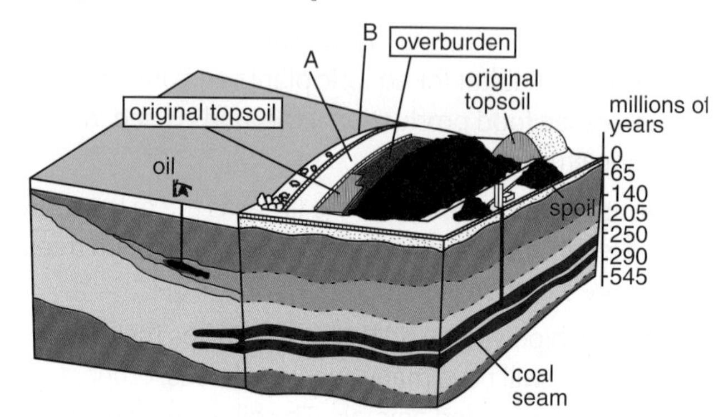

e The spoil heap is covered in the overburden [1] and then the original topsoil. [1] After this fresh soil (A) is added [1], which may be fertilised. [1] Finally, plants (B) are placed in the soil. [1]

4 a 1980, discovery

1993, peak production

2010, exhaustion [2 for all three, 1 for one or two correct]

b The mineral was being mined at an increasing rate [1] and there would have been job losses [1] and plans to close the mine down. [1]

c In the world outside the mine substitutes for the mineral could have been found. [1] In addition, products made from the mineral may have been recycled, so reducing demand for freshly mined supplies. [1]

Chapter 2

1 Uranium lasts a long time, so although non-renewable it will last hundreds of years. [1] It does not produce carbon dioxide in power generation. [1] It is a reliable source of energy once installed (unlike wind/solar) and not reliant on new supplies arriving (like fossil fuels). [1]

2 Advantages: less space in land fill, reduces the amount of methane (a greenhouse gas that is produced by composting). [1]

Disadvantages: toxic fumes in the atmosphere may affect health, adds to carbon dioxide in atmosphere, impacting climate change. [1]

3 Any four from:

- Risk of toxins from fracking entering the water table.
- The mixture of chemicals used are toxic and may affect local residents.
- Fracking uses a lot of water, which may reduce availability for other purposes.
- Noise pollution, so fracking in an area will affect the local community.
- Natural areas will be destroyed when new drills are developed.
- Fracturing of lower levels of rock may be a cause of additional earth tremors.
- Loss of land for other employment opportunities (tourism, farming, etc.) [4]

4 Any three from:

- Not all countries may have agreed.
- Not all ship captains are honest and may not abide by the rules.
- Difficult to police large oceans.
- Difficult to identify who has produced any pollution found. [3]

5 Any three from:

- Oil will affect the food web and access to light.
- Toxic effects of the oil on the reef.
- Reef is also affected by detergent chemicals used to clean up/disperse the oil.
- Machines in the area might cause physical damage to the reef. [3]

6 **a** Bar graph [1]

b

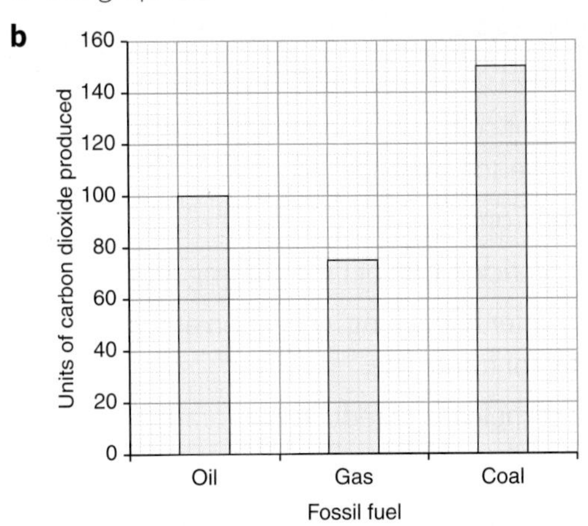

c The table only shows the carbon dioxide that is produced. [1] You also need to consider other pollutants such as sulfur dioxide and nitrogen oxides [1] which contribute to acid rain. [1]

Chapter 3

1 **a** Mineral particles [1]

Organic content [1]

Soil water [1]

Air [1]

b A drought will have no impact on the amount of mineral particles or organic content in the soil. The use of water by plants and evaporation will reduce the proportion in the soil, increasing the amount of air present. [1]

2 Changing the pH will affect the ability of the plant's roots to take up the nutrients it needs. The change may increase or decrease their availability. [1]

3 Any three from:

- Introduction of new high-yielding varieties, such as rice cultivar IR8.
- Improvements to irrigation.
- Development and use of pesticides.
- Improved farming education and knowledge.
- Increased mechanisation. [3]

4 Any two from:

- Less build-up of pests and diseases as a different crop is occupying the same soil space the following year.

- Use of different types of crops means that a nutrients are less likely to be wasted.
- Inclusion of legumes adds nitrogen to the soil.
- Different cultural techniques for different crops improve soil structure. [2]

5 Any three from:

- Use of trickle-drip or clay-pot irrigation.
- Rainwater harvesting, collection and storage of water for future use.
- Use of mulches to reduce evaporation from the soil.
- Use of more drought-resistance crops.
- Only apply when weather/soil conditions demand it. [3]

6 Any two from:

- Excess nutrients might harm the crop (root death, toxicity).
- Risk of nutrients leaching into water supplies (resulting in eutrophication).
- Fertilisers in water supply might be harmful to humans (blue baby syndrome).
- Excess fertilisers also waste money for the farmer. [2]

7 Ability to grow a second crop might mean more food/income. [1] If a crop is a legume it might help provide nutrients for the main crop. [1] The risk of complete crop failure is spread if two crops are grown. [1]

Chapter 4

1 The Earth has about 1.4 billion km^3 [1] of water. The majority of this (about 97%) is in the oceans. [1] The rest is called fresh water [1] and is found in rocks, where it is called groundwater [1], frozen in the poles [1] and glaciers [1] and as surface water [1] in rivers, lakes and swamps.

2 Supply of water [1]

HEP [1]

Flood control [1]

Water supply [1]

3 Both typhoid and cholera are water-related diseases and both are caused by bacteria [1]. Malaria, however, although water related is caused by *Plasmodium* [1]. Both cholera and typhoid have symptoms of diarrhoea [1] and vomiting [1] but typhoid also causes a skin rash and abdominal pain. [1]

Some diseases can be prevented by vaccination but of malaria, cholera and typhoid only cholera [1] and typhoid [1] have vaccines available. Of the three water-related diseases, malaria [1] causes the most deaths worldwide.

4 Primary treatment involves processes that remove large particles and silt. [1] Secondary treatment involves the removal of organic matter [1] and some of the bacteria in the sewage. [1]

5 The decomposition of organic matter [1] from dead algae or sewage [1] is carried out by bacteria, [1] which use up large amounts of oxygen. [1]

6 **a** At D the effluent is untreated and will contain a large amount of organic matter. [1] The effluent will also contain high numbers of bacteria from humans. [1] At E the effluent is treated and so will contain much less organic matter and fewer bacteria.

b This is because the sewage treatment plant will have removed most of the organic matter from D [1] by filtering and settlement [1] and the action of aerobic bacteria. [1] The number of bacteria from humans will have decreased because of competition with the bacteria in the sewage works [1] together with unsuitable environmental conditions. [1]

c Sulfur dioxide [1] and an oxide of nitrogen. [1]

d The factory has a tall chimney so the gases do not enter the atmosphere until they are high up. [1] Air movements (wind) will carry these gases away from the factory and lead to acid rain in the distant forest. [1]

e The run-off from the field contains minerals such as phosphate and nitrate from fertilisers. [1] These minerals lead to rapid growth of algae in the estuary. [1] When these algae die they are decomposed by oxygen using bacteria. [1] The oxygen level in the water will then fall. [1] Living organisms in the estuary that require oxygen will decline. [1] In addition living organisms higher up the food chain will suffer from a lack of food. [1] This is called eutrophication. [1]

Chapter 5

1 a Axes right way round [1], axes labelled correctly with units [1], all points plotted correctly [2].

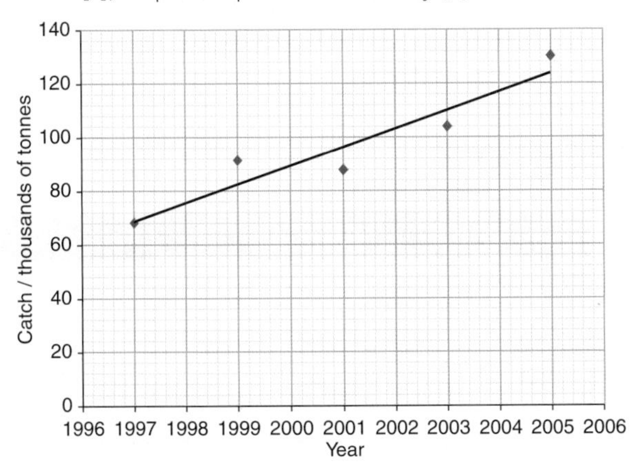

b If assume a straight line of best fit, as shown on Figure 5.22: 90 000 tonnes in 2000. An acceptable line of best fit [1], correct answer based on that line [1].

c 2005 is 131 – 68 for 1997 = 63 tonnes [1], so this an increase of 63 ÷ 68 × 100 = 92.6% [1]

d This may be due to an increased fishing effort [1], more people fishing [1] or improvement in methods. [1] It could be a combination of any or all of these factors.

2 a Sunlight, water, carbon dioxide [1]

b Minerals [1]

c The currents moving up from the seabed carry the products of the decay of organisms, which have fallen to the bottom of the sea after death. [1] These products include many minerals. [1]

3 a Mangroves provide an important habitat for other organisms [1] so their clearance will cause a loss of this habitat [1] and therefore genetic depletion. [1] They also protect the coast so this would cause problems if large areas were cleared for ponds. [1]

b As long as the creation of pools is not clearing big areas of mangroves things may be OK. [1] Sites that do not support populations of important mangroves might be sought. [1] The ponds could be used for a while and then allowed to recolonise while they are cleared in new areas. [1]

4

Food type	Feed Conversion Ratio	
Salmon	1.2	[2]
Beef	8.7	[2]
Pork	5.9	
Chicken	1.9	[2]

b Agree in that the salmon (which is a marine fish) shows the best food conversion ratio [1]. This means you can get more protein from it for a unit mass of food than any of the, non-marine, foods listed [1]. However, salmon is only one kind of marine fish so the conclusion is limited it to that [1].

c World fish catch has levelled off at under 100 million tonnes 20 years ago [1]. It would seem to be unlikely that it will grow again, and indeed it may fall in the future [1]. Farming of fish may provide a substitute for this lack of growth [1].

Chapter 6

1 The Earth is made up of three [1] layers. The outer layer is called the crust [1] and is divided into the oceanic crust [1] and the continental crust. [1] The top layer floats on the mantle, [1] which is semi-molten. Molten rock is called magma. [1] Convection currents [1] are formed in this layer by very high temperatures. The core is the third layer and extends from 2900 km to 6370 km down.

2 a Destructive [1]

b Destructive [1]

c Constructive [1]

d Constructive, destructive, conservative [1]

e Constructive [1]

f Destructive [1]

g Constructive [1]

3 a Thick covering of ash [1]; ash covering buildings, cars, crops [1]; death of livestock, crops, possibly people [1]; lack of food [1]; collapse of roofs [1]; weight of ash brings down power lines [1]; lack of drinking water [1]; transport disruption [1]; breathing problems [1]; ash can block out sunlight [1].

b Not possible [1]: unpredictable eruptions [1], cannot predict where deposits will land [1], cannot stop it happening. [1]

Possible [1]: spray water on lava [1], roof adaptation [1], diversion channels [1], protecting people by hazard mapping [1], warnings [1], education [1] , evacuation [1], training emergency services. [1]

4 Impact of storm surges [1], high winds [1], heavy rainfall causing flooding [1]. Other impacts could be spread of disease [1], loss of crops and livestock leading to famine [1], landslides destroying buildings. [1]

5 a Drought is when there is a lack of rain over a long period of time. [1]

b Droughts can occur anywhere in the world. [1]

c Droughts in the Sahel region of Africa occur when the ITCZ is prevented from moving northwards. [1]

d Drought is associated with high pressure systems. [1]

e El Niño brings droughts to Australia and floods to South America. [1]

6 Short-term problems: contaminated water leading to diseases [1]; crops and livestock destroyed leading to starvation if a poor country [1]; disruption to transport routes. [1]

Long-term problems: homelessness, so people may move away from the area [1]; cost of rebuilding [1]; losses to the economy as businesses may be forced to close down [1]; in richer countries very expensive to have insurance cover. [1]

7 For statement [1]: Higher population density can lead to rapid spread of disease and food shortages. [1] More people living in temporary accommodation. [1] Urban areas are more at risk from earthquakes because of higher population densities, so greater building densities and more deaths through collapsed buildings. [1] More potential for fires as gas pipes fracture. [1]

Against statement [1]: Buildings in urban areas may be better protected from earthquakes and more able to survive tropical storms. [1] Emergency services are greater in number and hospitals more accessible. [1] Rural areas can become isolated and aid slow to arrive, leading to famine and lack of medicines. [1] However, rural areas may suffer more in drought as farmers lose their livelihood. [1]

8 a 1.30 am [1] 7 pm [1] 7.3 [1] 7.8 [1] 34 [1] 661 [1] 1500 [1] 30 000 [1]

b The place in the Earth's crust where the earthquake starts is the Focus [1]

The place on Earth's surface above the focus is the epicentre [1]

c Japan – the plates move parallel (sideways) past each other causing friction. [1] The plates get locked together and pressure builds up. [1]

Ecuador – plates move towards each other because of convection currents in the mantle which causes forced movement of rock against rock. [1] The oceanic plate is forced down under the continental plate, which is known as subduction, and pressure and friction trigger earthquakes in the Benioff zone. [1]

d Predicted aftershocks would be a reason for people to refuse to return to their homes. [1]

e Any two items from the following list, with a suitable explanation, one mark for each: tents for shelter, clothing, food, medicine, clean water, chemical toilets, sniffer dogs

Chapter 7

1

Gas	Formula	Abundance
Nitrogen [1]	N_2	78.09%
Oxygen	O_2 [1]	20.95% [1]
Argon	Ar [1]	0.93% [1]
Water vapour [1]	H_2O	0.2–4% [1]
Carbon dioxide	CO_2	0.03% [1]
Methane [1]	CH_4	Trace
Ozone	O_3 [1]	0.00006%

2 Temperature line [1], temperature inversion label. [1]

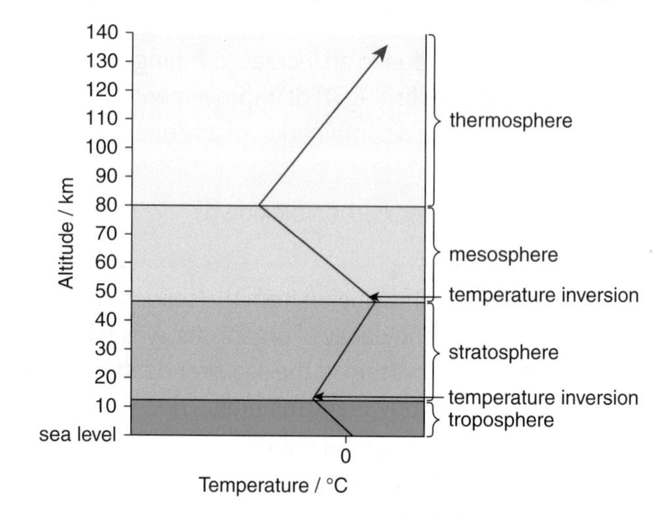

3 a Vehicle emissions [1], factories and industries releasing gases and chemicals [1], power stations burning fossil fuels. [1]

b Acid rain and weathering of limestone buildings [1], smog, puts tourists off [1], poor visibility [1], delays for transport, e.g. planes [1], breathing difficulties and other health problems [1], dirt on washing. [1]

c Chemical sprays [1], methane from cattle [1], burning vegetation [1], emissions from vehicles. [1]

4

	Enhanced green-house effect	Ozone depletion
Type of radiation involved	Long-wave (infrared) radiation [1]	Short-wave (ultraviolet) radiation [1]
Atmospheric layer that absorbs the radiation	Troposphere [1]	Stratosphere [1]
Direction of travel of radiation when absorbed	From the Earth [1]	Towards the Earth [1]
Example of a pollutant gas	Carbon dioxide [1]	CFCs [1]
Action of pollutant gas	Traps outgoing radiation and so causes an increase in temperature [1]	Creates chlorine, which reacts destructively with oxygen [1]
International agreement to combat problem	Paris Climate Conference [1]	Montreal Protocol [1]

5 Answers could discuss rising sea levels [1], loss of homes [1], forced migration [1], financial costs of defending coasts from erosion [1], rising temperatures leading to changes in agriculture [1], more droughts and less water resources [1], changing habitats and loss of biodiversity. [1]

6 Some LEDCs may want to develop industry and therefore do not want to reduce harmful emissions. [1] LEDCs may not have the money to implement strategies to reduce pollution. [1] Some governments believe that some strategies will not be popular with voters or industry and may harm economic growth. [1] A lack of monitoring. [1]

Chapter 8

1 This is because more boys than girls are born [1] and men die younger. [1]

2 Density is the number of people in a known area [1] expressed as the number area^{-1} (such as km^3). [1] Distribution tells us where people live. [1]

3 This is because, although Russia has 142 098 141 people its area is vast at 17.1 km^2 [1], giving a density of only $\frac{142\,098\,141}{17.1}$ = 8.32 people km^{-2} [1]

4 Because Tuvalu has a very small area of only $\frac{9916}{381.39}$ = 30 km^2 [1] housing its 9916 people. [1]

5 **a** The percentage of babies and children up to four years old decreases from 11.5% of the overall population in 2006 to 7.9% in 2026. [1] The largest increase is in the age range from about 30 upwards, for example people aged 40–44 increase from 5.8% in 2006 to 7.3% in 2026. [1] However, the rate of increase slows above 70 years old with an increase from 2.6% to 3.7%. [1] So, the population is beginning to age. [1]

b They could transfer funding from care for the young, such as nursery and normal schools, to care for the elderly. [1] They are also likely to need to increase provision of various forms of health care for the ageing population. [1] This may mean both dealing with illness but also improving preventative medicine. [1]

Chapter 9

1 If agree: It is true that biofuel comes from plants that have only just taken the carbon they contain from the atmosphere. When the next crop is grown the following year, the carbon emitted when the biofuel is burned will be taken in again by this next crop. [1] So, within 2 years carbon in will equal carbon out. [1]

If disagree: While all the above is true, the land used for growing these crops could be used for growing food, [1] which is in short supply in large areas of the world. [1]

2 All ecosystems (except those in the deep sea) rely on organic chemicals, mainly sugars, for their continuation. [1] These substances are made in photosynthesis using light form the Sun [1] that is trapped by chlorophyll. [1]

3 **a** Between 150 and 20 years ago there was a huge reduction in area of wetland. No wetland was found in the south 20 years ago. The biggest loss was in the east. [1] Between 20 years ago and today there has been a slight increase. [1] One area has re-appeared in the south [1] and the western area has nearly doubled in size. [1]

b To conserve the wetland that remains some kind of nature reserve could be established. [1] This would attract money for the preservation of the area, possibly compensating landowners for not draining their land. [1] To extend the wetlands it is likely that the government or some private (maybe charity-funded) organisation would need to buy land that has been previously drained. [1] They would then need to remove the drainage infrastructure and do whatever else was necessary to bring wetland back.

4 The fact that they eat the same food suggests that they may compete [1] for it when together. [1] Species A is clearly more adapted to living in colder water than B. [1] So, when they are together B outcompetes A in the warmer water regions and is the only one when found there. [1]

5 **a** Second tropic level or primary consumers. [1]

b That living things are very different in size, [1] so 15 trees are not equivalent to 15 sapsuckers. [1] This means that few trees can support thousands of sap suckers. [1]

c energy in 15 trees

mass of 15 trees = 15 000 kg [1]

so energy in 15 trees = 15 000 000 × 5 kJ = 75 000 000 kJ [1]

energy in sapsuckers

mass of sapsuckers = 8 500 000 × 0.01 g = 85 000 g = 85 kg [1]

energy in sapsuckers = 8 × 85 000 kJ = 680 000 kJ [1]

energy in insect eating birds

mass of insect eating birds = 350 × 5 g = 1750 g = 1.75 kg [1]

energy in insect eating birds = 1750 × 10 kJ = 17500 kJ [1]

energy in predatory birds

mass of predatory birds = 3 × 100 = 300 g = 0.3 kg [1]

energy in predatory birds = 300 × 10 kJ = 3000 kJ [1]

Correct figure [2]

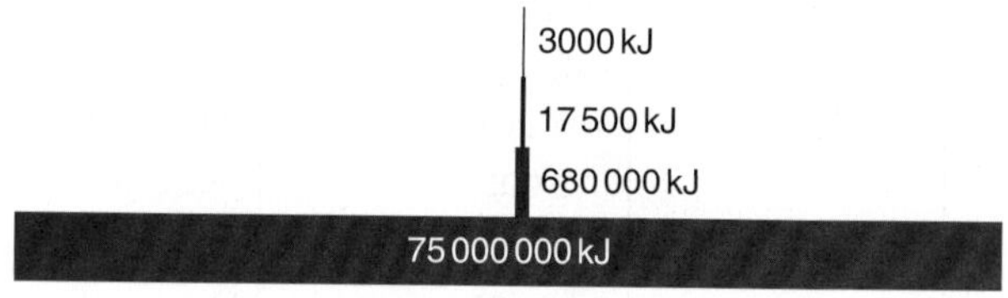

3000 kJ

17 500 kJ

680 000 kJ

75 000 000 kJ

Answers to Case study questions

All questions and sample answers have been written by the authors.

Chapter 1

The Antamina Mine in Peru

1 The ore is valuable and in demand so even though transport costs will be high the mine should still be profitable.

2 Rainfall and melting snow will dissolve some minerals. Sediments and dissolved minerals will move down the mountainsides and collect in the valleys. This water will be toxic to many organisms and will flow away from the mine.

3 **a** Further deposits have been found and the productive life of the mine has been extended by many years.

b It is too difficult to cover bare rock on steep slopes. The exposed rock will weather over time and may release less harmful substances. The location is so remote that the visual scar on the landscape will not be seen.

Chapter 2

Biofuels: the future of fuels or a misguided technology?

1 Bioethenol will mean the country is not dependent on supplies from other countries, reducing risk if there is political conflict, global price rises, a shortage of global supply. It may also be a crop with a value if exported.

2 It's a renewable source of energy. Fairly low technology. Different crops are suited to different regions. Absorbs carbon dioxide.

3 Bioethanol crops might be better suited to their land. The crop might be more profitable than food crops.

A house that needs no energy. Is it possible?

1 The house will only use 10% of the standard house's energy (1.5 dm^3 m^{-2}, rather than 150 dm^3).

2 So few houses have been built in this style because:

- it is new technology
- not many people have the skills to build them yet
- they are very expensive to build
- the savings made do not outweigh the costs of building.

3 There will always be some energy loss, and the use of solar panels, etc., is only effective in certain weather conditions.

Chapter 3

The impact of wind erosion

1
- Unexpected drought over a number of years.
- Soil particles were light (less water) so more easily blown about.
- Large areas ploughed up, few windbreaks.
- Cultivating the soil broke it up into smaller sized components.
- Deep-rooted grasses no longer there to hold the soil.

2 Farmers had bought the land and wanted to grow crops to make a profit from their investment. No central control as to what was grown (and how)

3
- Starvation
- Need for large quantities of people to relocate
- Loss of jobs
- Impact on local ecosystem: limited topsoil, few plants, and associated impact on food web.

4 It prevented the land from being used for arable production and allowed it to return to grassland.

Flower power

1 **a** This is a (large-scale) commercial arable farm: the bulbs are being sold for profit rather than food (commercial) and there are no animals involved in the production (arable).

b (From Figure 3.18) There is a lack of windbreaks to slow the wind speed down. The area is very flat. (From the text) There is a large amount of organic matter that is easily blown away when dry.

2 • The wind might cause the chemicals to be blown into other areas (drift).
- Ran will cause them to run-off into the water courses (drainage channels).
- Pesticides might affect other animals not intended to come into contact with the pesticides as it moves in the drainage water.
- Excess nutrients in the water can cause ecological damage through eutrophication.

3 For:
- The way the country is governed does not tell farmers what to do, it would remove some of their freedom
- The farmer aims to make as much money as possible, growing bulbs is more profitable.
- Selling good abroad (exporting) is good for the economy of the country, these are valuable goods that are demanded around the world.

Against:
- (Worldwide) food is in short supply, using the best land would increase yields.
- Control of what people grow would mean there was less waste (as products would not be left unsold).
- The supply of food is too important to be left to chance and 'market forces', governments should take responsibility for feeding the world population.

Chapter 4

A multipurpose dam on the Ramganga River at Kalagarh, India

1 A large project such as this requires a major amount of planning and maybe an environmental impact survey will be carried out. Major investment and funding will need to be acquired both within the country and internationally, maybe grants from several organisations will be needed and the building might have to be phased as funding becomes available. Workers will need to be recruited, building materials and equipment will need to be brought in and agreements will need to be worked out with local people, especially any landowners who will need to be relocated and compensated.

2 a A dam must remain intact or else a huge amount of water can be sent very suddenly down the valley causing the loss of lives, property and habitats. An earthquake could cause the dam wall to break and so the area must be monitored for this, and if there is to be a problem then action will need to be taken to strengthen the wall or release some water in a controlled fashion. Evacuation of people living downstream of the dam might need to happen.

b Sedimentation behind the dam will cause the water flow to slow down and this will lead to a decrease in the production of electricity and so economically the dam is less efficient.

3 a Local people can benefit from the production of jobs in the building and maintenance of the dam. They might also be provided with electricity that they did not have before, or their supply might reduce in cost. They have access to the stored water for irrigation or domestic use. If the dam encourages tourists they will benefit financially. Also they themselves might be able to use the reservoir for recreation. On the other hand it appears that the gates are opened in a fashion to suit the dam authority and not the local people. This means that the supply of water is intermittent and they are not provided with it necessarily at the best times. Fish populations have been negatively affected and so the local people will have less food from fish. Also farmers have seen a decrease in the fertility of their soils.

b The country will benefit from the revenue acquired by the selling of electricity and this may not be to the local people. They also gain funding internationally from foreign investments. However, the dam will have cost a lot of money and it may not pay this investment back to the government completely.

The improvement in infrastructure allows other businesses to thrive in the country. Lower unemployment saves the country money. Tourists will bring in extra income to the country as a whole.

Improved drinking water will save money for health care.

Chapter 5

The Newfoundland cod fishery

1 The area is on shallow water where a warm current meets a cold one. All this combines to provide conditions highly suitable for the growth of phytoplankton. That is plenty of light and carbon dioxide, together with minerals forced upwards from the seabed by the currents.

2 a The catch shows a slow but fairly consistent rise from 1850 until about 1958. Between these dates catches rose by about 150 000 tonnes, from 100 000 to 250 000. At this point the catch rose steeply to 800 000 tonnes by 1967. It then fell away just as rapidly to more or less zero in the early 1990s.

b Peak is 800 000 tonnes and in 1976 it is 120 000 tonnes, so the fall is 800 000 – 120 000 = 680 000. So percentage fall is 680 000 ÷ 800 000 × 100 = 85%.

c 1941

3 There is a small region of the Grand Banks area called Smith Sound. In recent years scientists have found that cod stocks here have done well there. They think it might be possible that these fish will migrate and lead to a recovery of cod over the whole of the region.

Questionnaire

a Are you or were you involved in fishing in the Grand Banks?

Yes/No

b If yes, for how many years?

1 >1 >10 >20

c How long do you think it might be before cod fishing can restart in the Grand Banks?

never now next year in the next ten years sometime but a long way off

Chapter 6

Hurricane Patricia: the impact of a tropical cyclone

1 a Between 5° and 20° North so sufficient Coriolis force to provide spin, and warm ocean temperatures above 27 °C to produce high rates of evaporation. Formed in October because ocean temperatures are at their highest then in the Northern Hemisphere.

b On 20 October it started off in the eastern Pacific and moved westwards. On 22 October it started to veer north-west, and on 23 October north-east.

c Jalisco

2 a Regular storm warnings, storm shelters were opened, people were evacuated, electricity was shut off and the army, navy and police were deployed.

b Risk of loss of life and injury, damage to buildings by strong winds and storm surge, no electricity, water supply contaminated by sewage and salt water so fear of disease.

3 a Transport: airports closed, highway 200 blocked, roads washed away. Infrastructure: electricity shut down, power poles and transmission towers blown down. Water supply contaminated.

b Tourists were evacuated so loss of earnings in the resorts. Tourist industry may have been damaged as people are scared to visit. 24 000 hectares of crops destroyed so a loss of income and jobs. Banana crop destroyed so impact on export earnings. Large cost (69 million US$) of rebuilding.

c Landfall was in a rural area with a low population density. It was a compact storm so did not cover such a large area of Mexico. It rapidly lost strength as it passed over the Sierra Madre mountains and very little impact from a storm surge as the coast is mountainous.

Chapter 7

Acid rain in China

1 Two clusters below pH 4.5 on the coast and in the south-east. The pH levels of 4.5 to 5.6 are also found on the coast and in the south-east. The reason for this is the concentration of population in cities such as Shanghai and along the coast leading to high vehicle ownership, industries and power stations. The west and north of China have lower levels of above 5.6 because of lower population densities.

2 a Acid rain results from burning fossil fuels in factories and power stations, which releases sulfur dioxide and nitrogen oxides into the atmosphere. Vehicle emissions add further nitrogen oxides. This is dry deposition. If these gases mix with rain droplets in the atmosphere, weak solutions of nitric and sulfuric acids are created that can then

be moved by winds. These solutions will eventually fall to Earth as acid rain and can occur at some distance from the source. This is wet deposition.

b Yes, because acid rain can be carried by winds long distances from the source, across international borders.

3 Use more renewable energy: burn less fossil fuels and reduce amount of acid rain gases. Encourage cleaner traffic and less of it: less vehicle emissions. Flue gas desulfurisation: reducing amounts of acid rain gases.

Chapter 8

The one-child policy in China

1 **a** About 20 000 000

b 1.7 billion

2 The realisation that a lot of people were becoming dependent and fewer independents were available to look after them. The disproportion between the numbers of men and women, in the sense of too many men. It is difficult to make the policy work in rural areas.

3 Due to the very powerful totalitarian government that was in a position to control virtually all aspects of national life.

Chapter 9

Mayan Biosphere Reserve, Guatemala

1 **a** The local people will gain an income in many ways from the tourists attracted to the area. They will be able to guide, transport and accommodate tourists as well as sell local produce and products.

b The world at large will benefit by having a very biodiverse area, which may contain many as yet unknown beneficial organisms, conserved.

2 As long as the take from hunting remains below the sustainable level the birds can be taken and conserved at the same time. This is because living things are not a finite resource, like gas or oil, but reproduce. Careful setting of quotas and closed seasons should allow hunting without exterminating the birds.

3 This would need sampling techniques. The exact requirements would determine which. If a study was needed into the effect, for example, of a road or train line on plant or sessile animal populations, quadrats with transects may be the best way to do it. If you wanted to see how some form of development in part of the forest had affected animals, random sampling in that area, using nets and pit-fall traps, would be best.

Scarlet Macaw

1 In 1990, the peak was 230 birds. In 1994, the peak was 195 birds. Over 4 years 35 birds were lost, which is $35 \div 4$ birds y^{-1} = 8.75 birds y^{-1}

2 Before management began in 1994, macaw numbers were down to about 220 (we do not know when the one value for numbers in Figure 9.27 was taken). During management, numbers rose to nearly 230 by 1997 and by 2000 had reached around 263. Numbers did then fall to about 227 in 2003 but this is still above pre-management levels.

3 Likely because this species is iconic and much sought after by birdwatchers, a very common group of ecotourists. Tourism is hugely important in Costa Rica so anything that attracts them is worth keeping in the wild.

Answers to Extended case study questions

All questions and sample answers have been written by the authors.

Chapter 1

1 Even though ore was left in the mine, the cost of extracting it would have been greater than its worth.

2 1 000 000 000 extracted

1 331 372.7 tonnes of metal obtained (= sum of copper 1 299 978 tonnes, molybdenum 31 000 tonnes, gold 31.7 tonnes, silver 336 tonnes and rhenium 27 tonnes)

So mass of waste = 1 000 000 000 – 1331 372.7 = 998 668 627.3 tonnes

Percentage waste = 998 668 627.3 ÷ 1 000 000 000 × 100 = 99.87%

3 a

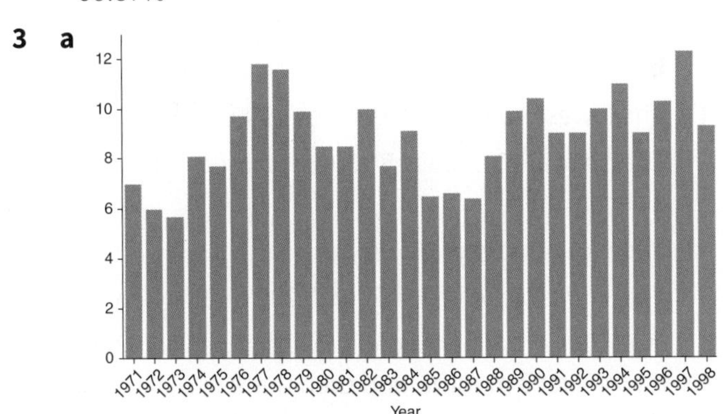

b i The trend is mainly upwards, with a rise from just over 6 mg kg^{-1} wet mass to nearly 12 mg kg^{-1} wet mass, which is almost double.

ii The mining of copper at the Island Copper Mine on Vancouver Island has so far (in just 7 years of operation) led to a doubling in the level of copper in the commercially important Dungeness crab. This is both a commercial and environmental disaster. Commercial for those who depend on the crab for their livelihood and environmental for everyone else. It is a clear example of bioaccumulation as the crab is a top predator in the delicate marine food web of which it is a part. If this trend continues it is likely to wipe out this source of income and be a harbinger of major problems in Rupert Sound.

iii The conclusions reached in the 1978 report have, thankfully, been proved wrong. After an initial doubling of copper load in just 7 years, the levels fell for the next 10 (with some minor deviations along the way). More recent trends have been slightly upwards but the evidence of over 20 years of monitoring suggests that the concerns expressed in 1978 are unlikely to be well founded.

c *Metacarcinus magister* is a top predator and as such will show evidence of higher levels of copper very early on in the mining process.

Chapter 2

1
- Poor route planning (avoiding the ice but too close to the reef).
- Inexperience of the driver.
- Single-hulled vessel.
- Lack of information about the hazards in the area (possible).

2
- Direct toxic effect from contact.
- Swallowing oil.
- Eating prey covered in oil.
- Bio-accumulation (build-up of poisons over time).
- Lack of oxygen to breathe in the water.

3 Lack of employment as tourism affected. Fish stocks (and associated industries) also lost.

4 Any three from:
- Better sonar/radar to look for obstructions.
- More staff on duty.
- Better trained staff.
- Emergency equipment kept in port to deal with spill more quickly.
- Use of double-hulled ships.

5 We still need oil in large quantities and there could be shortages if we do not exploit it here. Drilling has already occurred so stopping now would not be reversible. Lessons have been learnt from the *Exxon Valdez* and good systems are now in place. There is little other employment in the area. Stopping the oil industry will have major economic effect for the region.

Chapter 3

1

	Commercial farming
	Arable
Intensive	

2 Sugar cane provided them with an additional food to consume. Plants were close together, which ensured there was a large supply.

3 **a** Cane toads are found in the north-east of Australia, spreading from the coast.

b Approximately 35% of Australia may be affected.

c Some parts of the country will have unsuitable climatic conditions (e.g. too cold, too dry).

4 Lack of predators, able to out-compete native animals for food and space. Have a toxic liquid on their skin. Mobile.

5 How effective the toads were at controlling the target beetles. What other animals the toad would eat. Environmental impact study: impact on native wildlife.

6
- Pesticides may affect a wide range of wildlife.
- Long-term effects of pesticides are not known.
- Biological controls have a narrow range.
- No unwanted chemicals on foods, etc.
- They are naturally occurring animals.
- If the biological control has a narrow prey range, they will also reduce in numbers as the pest does.

7 The virus is a natural organism and can be transmitted from toad to toad without the need for each one to be captured for treatment. The virus will only effect toads and not other animals.

However: there is a risk of the virus affecting other animals we are not yet aware of, and the death caused by the virus might be cruel (because it takes the animal a long time to die).

8 Solutions could include:
- new types of pesticide
- genetically modified sugar cane that is pest resistant
- use of traps to capture the beetles.

Chapter 4

1 **a** Haiti did not have any incidence of cholera for nearly a century so it seems reasonable to suggest that the cholera bacteria was brought in from somewhere. A group of aid workers had entered Haiti from Nepal. The strain of bacteria was identified to be similar to a Nepalese one. The aid workers had their camp on the Artibonite River and the camp toilets leaked into the river. The cholera bacteria are carried in faecal material, which would have been in the sewage from the toilets.

b The map shows that there is an area in South America where there has been an outbreak of cholera. There is a land route up through South America and across Central America into North America. From here there is a relatively short stretch of water across to Haiti. Cholera bacteria could have been carried up along this route by animals or human carriers.

2 The installation of latrines will ensure that faecal material from humans, which might contain the cholera bacteria, will be removed and so not be allowed to infect drinking water. Thorough cooking of food will kill off bacteria that might have infected the food after being in contact with water (maybe from washing). This will then mean that cholera bacteria will not infect humans. Hand washing will remove bacteria that might have got onto the skin after using latrines, and so reduce the chance of cross-infection that way.

3 **a** 15 November, 100–15 300

b 7 November, 500

4 The lowest number in 2014 was 1000.

The peak in 2012 was 15 200 (or whatever the answer given in 3a).

The reduction was 14 200.

The % was therefore 14 200/15 200 × 100 = 93% (93.42).

5 In 2015 the number of cholera cases was constant for the first 3 months, and then there was a gradual decline until July, when there was a slight increase.

6 The peak in cholera cases in 2012 coincided with a peak in rainfall. This can be explained by the mixing of sewage with drinking water due to flooding causing sewage to over-flow out of sewers and ditches.

7 There is evidence for and against the statement that Haiti has managed to control cholera.

For:
- The peak in 2012 of 15 300 has been reduced to a low of 1000 in 2014.
- Reduced by 93%.
- Even the peak in 2014 of 7500 is lower than that in 2015, at 15 300.
- The total for 2014 was 27 388 and this was already a reduction of 90% of the peak of 2011.
- Haiti has taken the action of using more latrines, and providing education about cooking food and washing hands.

Against:

- There appears to have been an increase in August 2105.
- There are still fluctuations in the rainy season.
- Haiti has not tackled its sanitation problems, it says that in 2014 inadequate sanitation still existed and partly caused the rise in late 2014, and so the likelihood of cholera spreading is still possible.

Chapter 5

1 **a** Norway is 33%, Chile 31% and the rest of Europe 19%, which is 83%, so the rest have 17% of the market.

b Around 1985, as before this date salmon were not being farmed.

2 The wild ones are likely to expend much more energy in searching for food and avoiding predators in the wild environment.

3

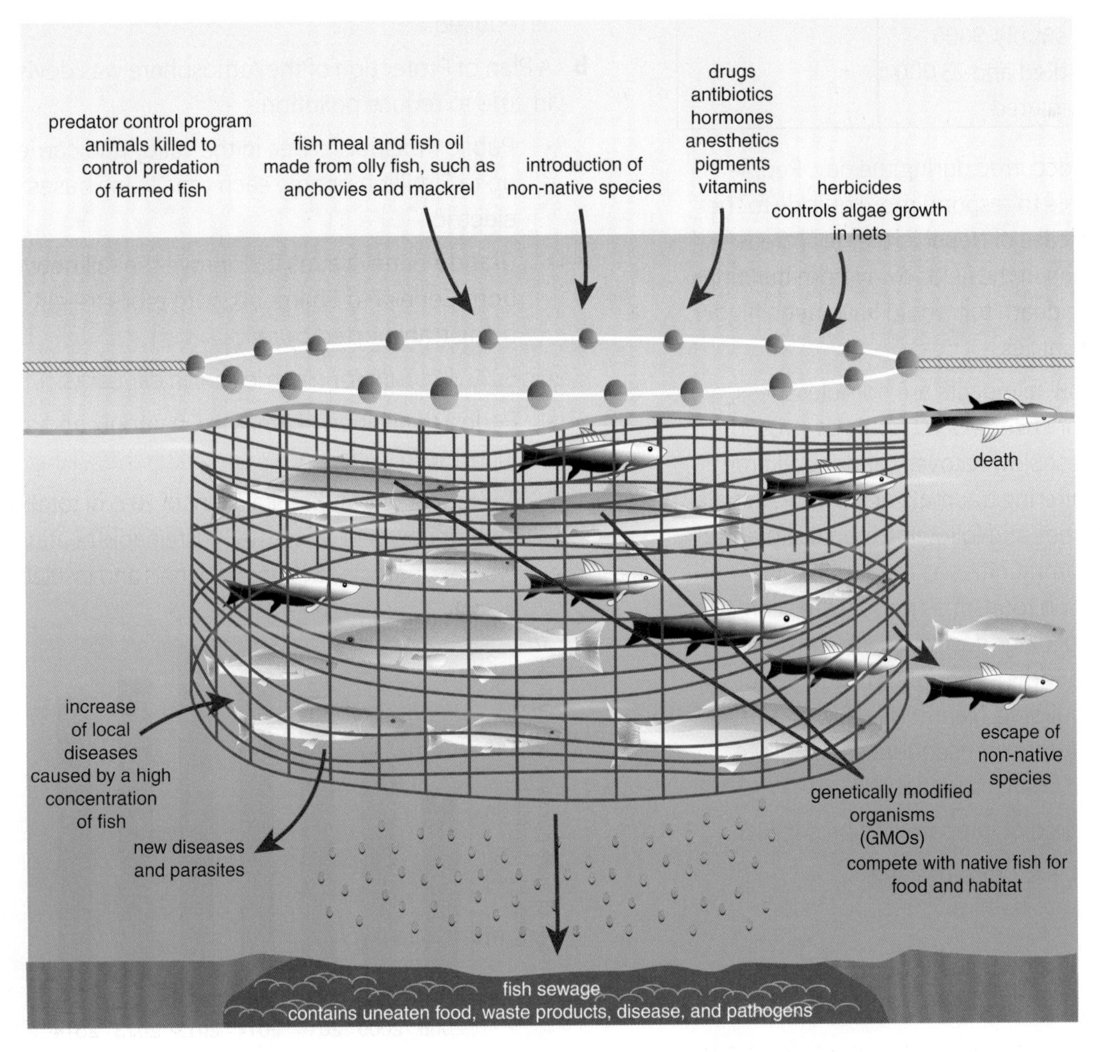

Chapter 6

1 At Nepal the Indian plate is colliding with the Eurasian plate. It is a destructive plate boundary. New Zealand has many earthquakes because the Pacific plate meets the Indo-Australian plate. At Christchurch these plates slide past each other.

2 Nepal is on a collision zone between the Indian and Eurasian plates. Earthquakes occur when friction builds up and is released. Christchurch is on a conservative plate boundary where the two plates slide past each other. Earthquakes occur when the two plates lock together and then suddenly slip.

3

	Nepal	Christchurch
Date of earthquake	Saturday 26 April 2015	Tuesday 22 February 2011
Time	11.56 a.m.	12.51 p.m.
Magnitude on Richter scale	7.8	6.3
Depth of focus	11 km	5 km
Distance of nearest city from epicentre	Kathmandu 80 km	Christchurch 10 km
Short-term impacts	Avalanches, blocked roads, buildings destroyed, infrastructure destroyed, airport shut down. Food, medicine and water in short supply. 9000 died and 23 000 injured	185 died. Buildings collapsed in the city centre. Suburban residents were evacuated. No electricity or water for 7 days

4 Both earthquakes occurred during the day. People were awake and able to respond more quickly to the earthquake. In the case of Nepal in the rural areas people were working in the fields away from buildings that collapsed. The death toll would have been higher at night in both countries.

5 In Nepal the long-term impacts are homelessness, and lack of schooling for children as schools destroyed. Dealing with injuries. Slow recovery and rebuilding process. People suffering trauma. Lack of food initially as no storage facilities and following crop not planted. Isolation of rural communities as road rebuilding takes time. Impact on tourism as people are scared to visit and historic buildings destroyed. In Christchurch impacts are on economy as people worried about visiting. Cost of rebuilding. Mental issues with survivors. Less long-term consequences as able to rebuild quicker and finances available.

6 Suggestions from predict, prepare and protect list.

7 Refer to Figure 6.14, e.g. cross-bracing.

Chapter 7

1 **a** Nitrogen dioxide, particulates and benzo(*a*)pyrene.

b

Source	Nitrogen dioxides	Particles PM10	Benzo(*a*) pyrene
Transport	85%	23%	12%
Domestic	9%	56%	21%
Industry	6%	21%	67%

c Nitrogen dioxide: transport
Particle PM10: domestic
Benzo(*a*)pyrene: industry

2 **a** Temperature inversion

b 2000 m

c The steep sides of the valley trap the pollution if there is high pressure. In winter, more domestic fires are used for heating.

3 **a** People become ill and take time off work, health care costs, tourists stop visiting the valley and so income is reduced.

b A Plan of Protection of the Atmosphere was devised in 2010 to reduce pollution.

- Public transport is free in the valley and carries up to 3 million people each year. Many buses are electric.
- Grande Geneva aims to improve the rail network from Geneva to Chamonix, with more freight being transported by rail.
- 50% discount for electric cars in car parks.
- Pedestrianisation of areas in Chamonix and an increase in cycle lanes.
- Tax reductions and a local grant of 20% of total costs for homeowners who install sustainable heating systems, particle filters, solar panels and insulation.

c

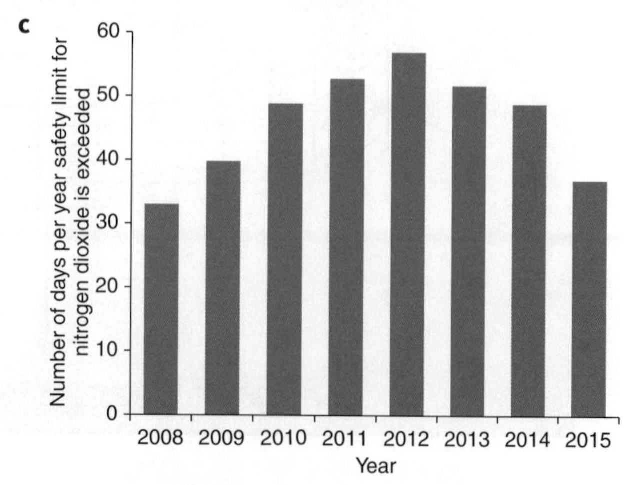

d 2012 had the most days (57) when nitrogen dioxide levels exceeded safe limits. Since then the number of days have decreased so the strategies could be said to be effective.

Chapter 8

1

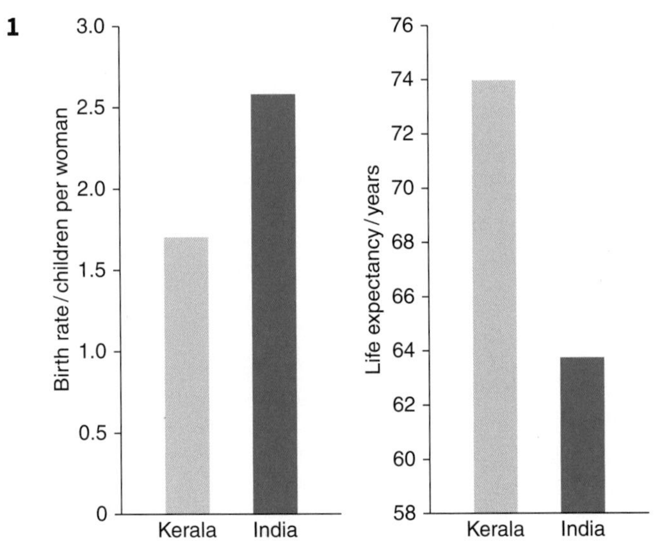

2

Literacy rate / %
100
80
60
40
20
0
Women
Men
India
Kerala

3 Women gain more status and thus have more control within their family. This in turn allows them to have a say in the number of children in the family. Specific education about birth control again gives women some control over the number of children. Educated women are more likely to get jobs and have less time for child rearing.

4 The period over which a woman can bear children is limited. In most cases it would end at about 50. A later marriage therefore reduces the number of years over which a woman can have children, which leads to fewer children.

5 **a** In Kerala, the fall in birth rate was 5.6 – 1.7 = 3.9.

This is $= \frac{3.9}{5.6} \times 100 = 69.6\%$

In India in general the fall in birth rate was

5.6 – 2.6 = 3.0 This is $= \frac{3.0}{5.6} \times 100 = 53.6\%$

b The case study states that 'it is thought that each year of female education reduces birth rates by 10%'. So, a fall of nearly 70% in Kerala would take 7 years and of nearly 54% in India would be just over 5 years.

6 The number of children has gone down. For example, up to age 9 there were about 7.6 million in 1991 but only 4.8 million in 2021. The number of older people has grown. Over 60s was 3.4 million in 1991 but 7.3 million in 2021. (Many other comparisons could be made.)

7 The population of Kerala is beginning to age and this brings its own problems. Hospitals may have enough places but they may be of the wrong kind, the emphasis shifting from care of young pregnant women and children to that of older people. Previous investment in schools and teachers will now become redundant as the population of young people falls.

Chapter 9

1 Plants will colonise it after it has been left and these will die and decompose. This will add mineral nutrients to the soil. These will, over time, build up to sufficient levels to grow crops again.

2 **a** $5 \times 1.25 = 6.25$ g

b $5 \times 0.75 = 3.75$ g

3 The soil on the island is manly red (laterite) due to high iron levels. Deforestation and subsequent soil erosion is washing this red soil into the rivers, which finally deposit it in the sea around the coasts. This loss of soil has worrying possible consequences for the environment, agriculture and the people. Gradually, the land will become useless for the growth of even the hardiest of plants, as it may end up as bare rock. This may be reversed but only over thousands of years.

4 In 18 years the pattern would be:

- 2 years of crop growth at 900 kg ha^{-1} $year^{-1}$ = 1800 kg
- then 4 years of no crop
- then 2 more years as above = 1800 kg
- then 4 more years no crop

- this is 12 years, so this can happen one more time, giving a further 1800 kg.
- so the total in 18 years would be $3 \times 1800 = 54\ \text{kg ha}^{-1}$.

5 The huge size and poor road infrastructure of the island, much of it being very isolated. Also, the fact that most of the people rely on the land for their survival and it is hard to stop them using it when it is basically means life or death to them.

6 They may use animals as food. The animals may attract ecotourists so there could be a loss of potential income if they are lost. Some of the animals may be important in the functioning of the ecosystems on which the people rely.

Answers to Practical activity questions

All questions and sample answers have been written by the authors.

Chapter 2

How well do materials reduce heat loss?

1 Adding an insulation layer slows down heat loss (meaning less energy is needed to replace this heat).

2 Jar B shows that heat loss is reduced most by a thick insulation layer. It also shows that the effect is not simply because the jar is no longer transparent.

3 The jar would stay hotter longer by using extra insulation (a warmer outside temperature will also have an impact).

Chapter 6

Interpreting storm hydrographs

1 Hydrograph A = 3 h. Hydrograph B = 12 h.

2 Hydrograph A has a shorter lag time; higher peak discharge; more rapid response to the storm; discharge falls quicker after peak

3 Hydrograph A = urban drainage basin. Hydrograph B = rural, wooded drainage basin.

4 Hydrograph A because there is a short lag time so the water in the form of overland flow reaches the river very quickly.

Finding out whether there is a relationship between two sets of data

1 Pakistan 2005

2 Japan 2011

3 No correlation between magnitude of an earthquake and the number of deaths. Supporting data from two contrasting earthquakes.

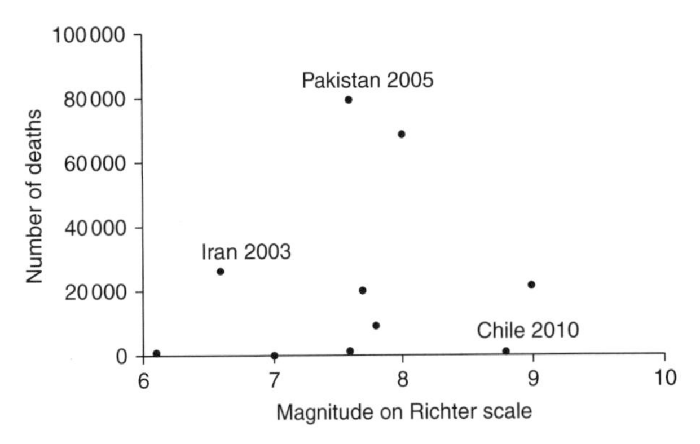

Axes need to be labelled.

4 Ideas such as variation in population and building density; level of development; location of epicentre; time of earthquake; level of preparation; danger of aftershocks; long-term effects such as lack of shelter, water and spread of disease.

Chapter 7

Testing the effect of different levels of acidity on the germination of seeds

1 To compare results against a 'baseline' and to see if the effects were due to changes in pH level.

2 Temperature, number of seeds, age of seeds, size of Petri dish, light.

3 Average length of root (mm).

4 Increase pH range, increase sample size, more time for growth.

Glossary

Abiotic: non-living components of the environment that may affect living things

Acidic volcano: a volcano that is made up of just lava, it is steeped sided as the lava does not flow easily, and it builds up into a convex cone-shape

Adit: the entrance to a horizontal (drift) mine

Aerosols: sprays containing fine particles and/or droplets that become suspended in the atmosphere

Age pyramid: a diagram that shows the proportion of the population that is male and/or female in different age groups (usually 5 year intervals)

Algae: plant-like, photosynthetic organisms that lack true stems, roots and leaves

Algal bloom: the rapid growth of algae in water, caused particularly by a surge of nutrients

Antecedent soil moisture: the amount of moisture present in the soil before a rainfall event

Antinatalist policy: a national or regional policy that aims to discourage couples from having children

Aquifer: water stored in porous rocks under the ground

Arable farming: the production of crops from land

Artesian aquifer: an aquifer in which the water is under pressure

Asthenosphere: the layer of the Earth below the lithosphere, it is hotter and weaker than the lithosphere above and is capable of plastic flow (deformation of material that remains rigid)

Basalt: A fine-grained extrusive igneous rock formed by the cooling of lava at constructive plate margins

Basic volcano: a broad volcano built up from the repeated eruption of basalt

Benioff zone: a zone of earthquake foci in the upper part of a subducting oceanic plate at a destructive plate boundary

Bioaccumulation: the build-up of a substance in the body of a living thing

Bioethanol: the creation of ethanol from fermentation

Biogas: the creation of methane from the breakdown of organic materials in an anaerobic digester

Biomagnification: the process in which the concentration of a substance in living things becomes higher at progressively higher levels in a food chain or web

Bioremediation: a process in which living things are used to remove toxic chemicals from a natural site

Biotic: living components of the environment that may affect other living things

Birth rate: the total number of live births over time

Boiler: a vessel used to heat water to convert it into steam

Brackish water: water that is salty but not as salty as seawater

Bund: an embankment constructed around the edge of an area to reduce the loss of a liquid (such as water)

Burner: a receptacle used to hold fuel as it is burned

Bycatch: animals caught by fishers that are not the intended target of their fishing effort

Carbon sink: a vegetated area where the intake of carbon dioxide from the atmosphere in photosynthesis exceeds its output from respiration, so the net flow of carbon is from the atmosphere into plants

Carbon store: a mature vegetated area where the intake of carbon dioxide from the atmosphere by photosynthesis equals its output from respiration, so the mature plants store carbon

Carnivore: another name for secondary and tertiary consumers

Carrying capacity: the maximum size of a population that an environment can support in terms of food, water and other resources

Chlorination: adding chlorine-based substances to water

Chlorophyll: the green pigment in plants that traps light energy

Cistern: a vessel in which water, usually potable, is stored, forming a type of covered reservoir

Climax community: the stable community characteristics of an area that persist as long as the climate does not change

Cod end: the closed end of a fishing net

Collision zone: a destructive plate boundary between two continental plates, resulting in fold mountains

Community: a group of populations of different species that live together in an area and interact with each other

Composite volcano: a volcano built up by alternating layers of lava and ash, conical in shape

Condensation: the process in which water vapour turns in to liquid water, the opposite of evaporation

Conservation: the protection and management of natural areas

Contour ploughing: a technique where the furrows caused by ploughing follow the contours of the land

Contraception: a range of methods used to prevent pregnancy

Convection currents: transfer heat from place to place, denser colder fluid sinks into warmer areas, heat from the Earth's core causes convection currents in the mantle

Critically endangered: a species that is at extremely high risk of becoming extinct in the wild

Death rate: the total number of deaths over time

Decomposers: organisms within an ecosystem that derive their food from the bodies of dead organisms

Deep mining: a type of sub-surface mining

Density: the number of people living in a population in a defined area

Dependent variable: the variable that is measured in an experiment

Dependent: those people in the population who are not economically active (working) and so rely on the those who are working for their needs

Depletion: a reduction or loss

Desalination: the removal of salt from water

Desertification: the process by which fertile land becomes desert

Dieback: the death of a tree or shrub that starts at the tip of its leaves or roots and spreads towards the centre of the plant, caused by unfavourable environmental conditions or disease

Discharge: the volume of water passing a measuring point or gauging station in a given time, measured in cubic metres per second (cumecs)

Disease: a pathogen (fungus, bacterium or virus) that attacks a plant

Distillation: the purification of a liquid by boiling a solution so that the liquid evaporates and can be collected when it condenses at a lower temperature

Distribution: where populations of people either do or do not live

Double-hulled: a ship design that uses a second layer, allowing the cargo to remain safe if the external layer is damaged

Drift mine: is a mine in which the entry is more or less horizontal

Economic exclusion zone: the zone around a country's coastline that is under the control of that country

Economic water scarcity: a situation in which there is enough water available but the money does not exist to extract and/or treat enough of it for human needs

Ecosystem: all the living things (biotic components) together with all the non-living things (abiotic components) in an area

Ecotourism: tourism in which the participants travel to see the natural world, ideally in a sustainable way

Effluent: a discharge of liquid waste

El Niño Southern Oscillation (ENSO): the change in the prevailing winds that leads to a change in the pattern of currents in the oceans of the south Pacific

Electromagnetic induction: a process used for generating electricity that uses the movement of a metal coil and a magnet

Endangered: a species that is at high risk of extinction in the wild

Endemic: a species found in only one area, often a country

Environmental impact assessment: a process by which the probable effects on the environment of a development are assessed and measured

Epicentre: the point on the Earth's surface directly above the focus of an earthquake

Erosion: the movement of rock and soil fragments to different locations

Euphotic zone: the top 200 m or so of seawater through which light can penetrate and in which photosynthesis can happen

Eutrophication: a sequence events starting with enrichment of water by mineral nutrients or organic matter that leads to a reduction in oxygen levels in the water and the death of fish and other animals

Evaporation: the process in which liquid water turns into vapour, the opposite of condensation

Exponential growth: when the growth rate of a population increases rapidly over time

Extensive production: farming that is spread over a wide area and uses fewer resources per metre of land

Extinction: the process by which a species or other named group ceases to exist on the Earth or in a named area

Family planning: methods used by a couple to decide when and how many children to have, may be practised by couples and encouraged by governments

Famine: a lack of access to food, often over a large area

Focus: the location under the Earth's surface where an earthquake originates

Fold mountains: mountains created where two or more tectonic plates are pushed together, compressing the rocks and folding them upwards

Food chain: a diagram showing the relationship between a single producer and primary, secondary and tertiary consumers

Food web: a diagram showing the relationship between all (or most) of the producers, primary, secondary and tertiary consumers in an ecosystem

Fossil fuel: a carbon-based fuel, formed over many millions of years from the decay of living matter

Fracking: the common term for hydraulic fracking, the process of obtaining oil or gas from shale rock by the breaking open to rocks using water, sand and chemicals

Fungicide: a chemical used to control fungal diseases

Gene: a sequence of DNA that is responsible for a characteristic of a living organism

Generator: a machine that converts mechanical energy (such as movement) into electrical energy

Genetically modified organism (GMO): An organism whose genetic material has been altered by genetic engineering

Geochemical: the chemical properties of rocks

Geophysical: the physical properties of rocks

Granite: A coarse-grained intrusive igneous rock comprising the minerals quartz, feldspar and mica, it is formed at destructive plate margins

Greenhouse gas: a gas that stops energy in the form of heat from being lost from the atmosphere

Greenhouse: a building made of glass or similar transparent material that is used manage the environment for plant growth

Groundwater: water in the soil, and in rocks under the surface of the ground

Groundwater flow: the process by which infiltrated water flows through rocks

Growing blueprint: the growing requirements of a crop throughout its life, which a grower can use to maximise the yield

Habitat: the place within an ecosystem where an organism lives

Herbicide: a chemical used to control weeds

Herbivore: another name for primary consumer

Hydroponics: growing plants without soil, with the nutrients the plant needs dissolved in water, this technique is often used in conjunction with a growing blueprint

Igneous rock: rock made during a volcanic process

Impermeable: does not allow water to pass through

Independent: those people in the population who are economically active (working)

Independent variable: the variable that is deliberately changed in an experiment

Inert gas: a gas that rarely reacts with other elements because it is stable, now referred to as noble gases

Infiltration capacity: the maximum rate that water enters soil

Infiltration: the process by which water seeps into the ground

Insecticide: a chemical that kills insects

Intensive production: farming that aims to maximise the yield from an area using a large amount of resources

Inter tropical convergence zone (ITCZ): a low pressure belt that lies around the equator, where the north-east and south-east trade winds meet, it receives high precipitation because of intense heating from the Sun

Interception: the process by which precipitation is stopped from reaching the ground surface by the presence of trees and other plants

Interception: the process by which vegetation prevents rainfall from reaching the surface directly, the intercepted rainfall is temporarily held as interception storage and then either falls directly to the ground or is evaporated back to the atmosphere

Intercropping: the technique of growing other crops between the rows of a main crop, maximising the use of nutrients and water

Island arc: a chain of volcanoes, generally with an arc shape, that run parallel to an oceanic trench at a destructive (oceanic–oceanic) plate boundary

Lag phase: the period of time in population growth when an organism is adapting to its new environment and growth is slow

Lag time: the time difference between peak rainfall and peak discharge

Lahars: mudflows of volcanic material, caused when ash mixes with heavy rain or water from melting snow

Leaching: the movement of a soluble chemical or mineral away from soil, usually caused by the action rainwater

Least concern: a species that is widespread and abundant

Legumes: plants that contain nitrogen-fixing bacteria in their roots to produce a source of nitrates

Limiting factor: of all the factors that might affect a process, the one that is in shortest supply

Liquefaction: the process where loose sediments with a high water content behave like a liquid when shaken by an earthquake

Lithosphere: The outer and rigid layer of the Earth, comprising the crust and the upper part of the mantle

Loam: a soil that is mixture of sand, silt and clay, combining the best properties of each

Log growth: when the growth rate of a population increases rapidly over time

Long-wave radiation: outgoing or terrestrial radiation, as the Earth produces very little visible light or ultraviolet radiation, all radiation from the Earth is infrared

Magma: molten rock below the surface of the Earth

Malnutrition: not having enough of the correct nutrients to eat, causing ill health

Mesopause: the upper limit of the mesosphere, temperatures remain constant in this boundary layer

Metamorphic rock: a rock formed from existing rocks by a combination of heat and pressure

Migration: the movement of people into (immigration) or out of (emigration) a region, country or other area

Mineral: a naturally occurring inorganic substance with a specific chemical composition

Mixed farming: farming that practises both rearing livestock and growing crops

Mulch: a natural or artificial layer on the soil surface used to reduce water evaporation and weed growth

Natural disaster: When a natural hazard causes damage and the people affected are unable to cope

Natural hazard: a naturally occurring event that will have a negative impact on people

Near threatened: a species that is likely to become endangered in the near future

Niche: the role of a species within the ecosystem

Noble gas: a gas that rarely reacts with other elements because it is stable, previously referred to as inert gases

Non-renewable: an item or resource that exists in a finite amount that cannot be replaced

Ocean trench: a depression of the ocean floor that runs parallel to a destructive plate boundary

Open-cast mining: a type of surface mining

Open-cut mining: a type of surface mining

Open-pit mining: a type of surface mining

Ore: a rock with enough of an important element to make it worth mining

Organic: derived from living organisms

Osmosis: the process by which water molecules pass through a semi-permeable membrane from a weaker solution to a more concentrated solution to reduce the difference, it is an essential process in plants for water uptake from the roots

Overburden: the rock and or soil overlying an economically viable mineral deposit

Overfishing: when the number of fish that is caught is greater than the rate at which the fish reproduce, leading to a fall in fish numbers in an area

Parasite: an organism that lives in or on another organism, it gains nutrition from that organism but gives the other organism no benefits

Particulate matter (PM): a mixture of very small particles and liquid droplets suspended in the air

Pastoral farming: farming that focuses on breeding and rearing livestock

Pathogen: a collective name to describe disease-causing organisms (bacteria, fungi and viruses)

Percolation: the vertical movement of water from the soil into the underlying rock

Pest: an animal that attacks or feeds on a plant

Pesticide: a chemical used to control pests, but also, less accurately, used as a collective term to describe pest- and disease-killing chemicals

Photochemical smog: air pollution in the atmosphere accompanied by high levels of ozone and nitrogen oxides from vehicles and caused by the action of sunlight on the pollutants

Photosynthesis: the process by which plants or plant-like organisms make food in the form of carbohydrate from carbon dioxide and water using energy from sunlight

Physical water scarcity: a situation in which there is simply not enough water for human needs

Phytoplankton: small organisms in the sea that can make their own food and upon which almost all other sea creatures depend for their food

Plate boundary: Where two or more plates meet, the three main types of plate boundary are constructive, destructive and conservative

Plate tectonics: A theory developed in the 1960s that helps explain the formation of some of the important features on the Earth's surface and how the continents move

Polar vortex: a circulation of strong upper level winds that surround Antarctica and keep cold air locked in above the continent

Pollen grain: the structure in plants that contains the male sex cell, it is carried to the female organ by pollination

Pooter: a device for retrieving small animal from nets, pitfall traps, etc.

Population pyramid: a diagram that shows the proportion of the population that is male and female in different age groups (usually 5 year intervals)

Population: all the organisms of one species living in a defined area

Potable water: water that is safe to drink

Precipitation: the process in which liquid water (as rain) or ice particles (as snow or hail) fall to Earth due to gravity

Prevailing wind: the direction from which the wind nearly always blows in a particular area

Primary consumers: organisms within an ecosystem that derive their food from producers

Primary pollutant: a pollutant that is emitted directly from the source

Producers: organisms within an ecosystem that can carry out photosynthesis

Pronatalist policy: a national or regional policy that aims to encourage couples to have children

Proppant: a material, such as sand, used to keep cracks in the shale rocks open to allow gas or oil extraction

Prospecting: a process of searching for minerals

Pull factors: factors that encourage people to move into an area

Push factors: factors that encourage people to move away from an area

Pyramid of numbers: a diagram that represents the numbers of organisms at each feeding (trophic) level in an ecosystem by a horizontal bar whose length is proportional to the numbers at that level

Pyroclastic material: very hot gases, ash and volcanic bombs, pyroclastic flows can reach speeds of over 100 km h^{-1} at temperatures of 200 to 700 °C

Quadrat: a frame of known area used to sample organisms that do not move, such as plants

Quota: the legal limit on the amount of fish that can be caught

Rainwater harvesting: the collection of rainwater, for example from the roofs of buildings, and storage in a tank or reservoir for later use

Random sampling: a sampling method in which the sampling device is placed using random number tables or the roll of dice

Rate of natural increase: the birth rate minus the death rate

Remote sensing: a process in which information is gathered about the Earth's surface from above

Renewable: an item or resource that will not be used up or can be replaced

Reservoir: an artificial lake where water can be stored

Resistance: the ability of a living organism to survive when exposed to a toxic chemical (such as a pesticide or herbicide)

Respiration: the process by which living things release energy from food to carry out the processes of life, such as movement

Reverse osmosis: the purification of water by pumping it at high pressure through a fine membrane

Richter scale: a measure of the magnitude of an earthquake, taken with a seismograph and with a scale of one to ten, ten being the most powerful, it is a logarithmic scale which means that if an earthquake measures two on the scale it is ten times more powerful than an earthquake that measures one

Ridge push: a gravitational force that causes an oceanic plate to move away from the crest of a mid-ocean ridge and into a subduction zone, it works together with slab pull

Rift valley: an area where a continent is being stretched and the central block moves downwards

Risk: The probability of a natural hazard occurring and the losses or damage that might result from that natural hazard

Rock cycle: a representation of the changes between the three rock types and the processes causing them

Rock: a combination of one or more minerals

Run-off: the process by which water runs over the ground into rivers

Sanitation: the conditions necessary for health, such as providing clean drinking water and the safe disposal of sewage

Sea-floor spreading: the process by which oceans are formed at constructive plate boundaries, new oceanic crust is formed as two oceanic plates move apart

Secondary consumers: organisms within an ecosystem that derive their food from primary consumers

Secondary pollutant: a pollutant that forms through chemical reactions with primary pollutants

Sedimentary rock: a rock formed from material derived from the weathering of other rocks or the accumulation of dead plants and animals

Service reservoir: a reservoir in which potable water is stored

Sewage: waste matter that is carried away in sewers or drains from domestic (or industrial) establishments

Shaft mining: a type of sub-surface mining

Shield volcano: a broad volcano built up from the repeated eruption of basalt

Short-wave radiation: incoming or short-wave solar radiation, visible light and ultraviolet radiation are commonly called shortwave radiation

Sial: Another name for the continental crust, which is rich in silicate and aluminium minerals

Sima: Another name for the oceanic crust, which is rich in silicate and magnesium minerals

Slab pull: the force at a destructive plate boundary, where the oceanic plate sinks beneath the adjacent plate, as a result of its own weight, the descending plate is pulled by gravity through the asthenosphere

Solar power: harnessing energy from sunlight

Stationary phase: when the growth of a population has slowed to zero

Strato volcano: a volcano built up by alternating layers of lava and ash, conical in shape

Stratopause: the upper limit of the stratosphere, temperatures remain constant in this boundary layer

Strike rate: the frequency with which attempts to find a desired mineral are successful

Strip mining: A type of surface mining

Subduction zone: a zone where the oceanic plate is deflected (subducted) down into the mantle, at the surface the subduction zone coincides with ocean trenches

Sub-surface mining: a type of mining used when the deposit is covered by a deep layer(s) of unwanted rock

Supervolcano: a volcano that erupts at least 1000 km^3 of material

Supply and demand: the relationship between how much of a commodity is available and how much is needed or wanted by consumers of the product

Surface currents: movement of the surface water of the sea in a constant direction

Surface mining: a type of mining used when the mineral is either exposed on the surface or overlain by only small amounts of overburden

Surface run-off ground into rivers: the process by which water runs over the ground into rivers

Surface water: water in lakes, rivers and swamps

Systematic sampling: a sampling method in which the sampling device is placed along a line or some other pre-determined pattern, the most common pattern being the line of a transect

Tectonic plate: A piece of lithosphere that moves slowly on the asthenosphere, seven major, eight minor and numerous micro plates have been identified

Temperature inversion: when temperatures increase with altitude

Terracing: the artificial development of flat areas (for growing crops) in a sloping terrain

Tertiary consumers: organisms within an ecosystem that derive their food from secondary consumers

Thermopause: the upper limit of the thermosphere, temperatures remain constant in this boundary layer

Through flow: the process by which infiltrated water flows through the soil

Transect: a sampling method in which sampling devices are laid out along a line already placed across an area

Transpiration: the movement of water up plants and its subsequent loss as water vapour from their leaves

Trophic level: a feeding level within a food chain or web

Tropopause: the upper limit of the troposphere

Tsunami: a large wave created by ocean floor displacement or landslides

Turbine: a machine, often containing fins, that is made to revolve by the use of gas, steam or air

Upwelling: areas where minerals at the ocean floor are brought to the surface by currents

Vector: an organism that carries a disease-producing organism, such as the mosquito which carries the malarial parasite

Volatile organic compounds (VOCS): chemicals that easily enter the atmosphere as gases, mainly from evaporation

Vulnerability: The characteristics and circumstances of people in a community that make them susceptible to the impacts of a natural hazard

Vulnerable: a species that is at high risk of becoming endangered in the wild.

Water tower: a type of reservoir where potable water is stored for immediate use

Weathering: the processes that cause rock to be broken down into smaller particles

Weed: a plant growing in an inappropriate place

Well: a hole bored or dug into rock to reach the water stored there

Windbreak: a permeable barrier, made of either living vegetation or artificial material, used to reduce the impact of the wind on an area

Acknowledgements

The authors and publishers acknowledge the following sources of copyright material and are grateful for the permissions granted. While every effort has been made, it has not always been possible to identify the sources of all the material used, or to trace all copyright holders. If any omissions are brought to our notice, we will be happy to include the appropriate acknowledgements on reprinting.

Cover image: jose1983 / Getty Images; Fig 0.1: Luciana Calvin/Getty Images; Fig 0.2: Picture by Tambako the Jaguar/Getty Images; Fig 0.3: Istvan Kadar Photography/ Getty Images; Fig 0.4: Mark Boulton/Alamy Stock Photo; Chap 1 Rocks and minerals and their exploitation: Fairfax Media/Getty Images; Fig 1.0: VanderWolf-Images/Getty Images; Fig 1.2: Alexey Bragin/Getty Images; Fig 1.3: Andrew Cribb/Getty Images; Fig 1.4: Unidentified/Getty Images; Fig 1.5: Taylor S. Kennedy/Getty Images; Fig 1.6: Gary Ombler/Getty Images; Fig 1.7: VvoeVale/Getty Images; Fig 1.8: Gary Ombler/Getty Images; Fig 1.16: rechitansorin/ Getty Images; Fig 1.18: BlackAperture/Getty Images; Fig 1.19: zeitgeist_images/Getty Images; Fig 1.24:GunterMarx/ WC/Alamy Stock Photo; Chap 2 Energy and the environment: Joe Raedle/Getty Images; Fig 2.0: Arctic-Images/Getty Images; Fig 2.6: Brazil Photos/Getty Images; Fig 2.7: sdlgzps/Getty Images; Fig 2.10: Photofusion/ Getty Images; Fig 2.12: lindwa/Getty Images; Fig 2.16: NICOLAS ASFOURI/Getty Images; Chap 3 Agriculture and the environment: Comstock/Getty Images; Fig 3.0: FREDERIC J. BROWN/Staff/Getty Images; Fig 3.7: BruesWu/ Getty Images; Fig 3.11: Chris Nowitzki / EyeEm / Getty Images; Fig 3.16: Charles Phelps Cushing / ClassicStock/ Getty Images; Fig 3.20: ullstein bild/Getty Images; Fig 3.21: Geography Photos/Getty Images; Fig 3.22: Ian Waldie/ Getty Images; Chap 4 Water and its management; Jie Zhao/Getty Images; Fig 4.0: Ashley Cooper/Getty Images; Fig 4.5: Bloomberg/Getty Images; Fig 4.6: Google Maps 2016; Fig 4.11: Thomas Lohnes/Getty Images; Fig 4.18 (bottom): Tommy E Trenchard / Alamy Stock Photo; Chap 5 Oceans and fisheries: Portra Images / Getty Images; Fig 5.0: Clicks/Getty Images; Fig 5.1: Brazil Photos / Getty Images; Fig 5.3: "Image copyright: B.S. Halpern (T. Hengl; D. Groll) / Wikimedia Commons / CC BY-SA 3.0"; Fig 5.17: Dorling Kindersley / Getty Images; Chap 6 managing natural hazards: Arctic-Images/Getty Images; Fig 6.0: Ignacio Palacios/Getty Images; Fig 6.5: Steve Fleming/Getty Images; Fig 6.7: Guenter Guni/Getty Images; Fig 6.9 (top): Harvepino/Getty Images; Fig 6.11 (top): LatitudeStock / Emma Durnford / Getty Images; Fig 6.14: Photograph by Alastair McLean/Te Ara; Fig 6.16: Chris McGrath/Getty Images; Chap 7 The atmosphere and human activities: VCG/Getty Images; Fig 7.0: Larry Busacca / Getty Images; Fig 7.3: DuKai photographer/Getty Images; Fig 7.6: China Photos/Getty Images; Fig 7.9: Ginny Battson/Getty Images; Chap 8 Human population: Bloomberg/Getty Images; Fig 8.0: TED ALJIBE/Getty Images; Chap 9 Natural ecosystems and human activity: Alex Dissanayake/Getty Images; Fig 9.0: Aunt_Spray/Getty Images; Figs 9.23: Gary Skinner/GJSSEC; Fig 9.24: AlanJeffery/Getty Images; Fig 9.28: Cambridge IGCSE Environmental Management 0680 Paper 1 Q6 June 2007; Fig 31a, Fig 31b: Gary Skinner/ GJSSEC; Fig 9.31c: NASA - digital copyright Science Faction/Getty Images.

Index